PSYCHOLOGICAL ZODIAC

The Roots of Self
& Society

Angela Arnold

WATERWEAVER PRESS

For Kay
with love and thanks

First published in 1995 by
Waterweaver Press
Whistleberry Lane
Montrose DD10 0TJ
Scotland

Reprinted in 1998

British Library Cataloguing in
Publication Data.
A catalogue record for this book
is available from the British Library.

ISBN 0 9525539 3 7

Typeset by XL Publishing Services, Nairn
Printed and bound by Antony Rowe Ltd., Wiltshire
Printed on woodfree paper

CONTENTS

FOREWORD

Since this book was first published I have been getting feedback that suggests to me that a word of advice to the *general* reader is, after all, called for.

To put it bluntly, then: this is not a dip-in Sun sign book. I hold no brief for Sun sign astrology. Nobody 'is' a single sign; rather, we all have *all* the signs in our natal charts, if differently emphasised. The theory of psychological astrology understands the individual signs as representing the separate strands of our complex, composite psyche – the latter symbolised by the circle of the complete zodiac.

Another way of putting it is to say that these symbolic Signs stand for different life impulses (or call them 'drives' if you like) which we all share, different motivation patterns which we all exhibit, to a greater or lesser degree, according to our individual dispositions. In my experience people have on average half a dozen signs more or less 'stressed' in their chart – that's half the zodiac!

Yes, the *whole* book is about you. (I might add that I designed it for the chapters to be read consecutively.) And one last thing: I would ask the reader not to receive this book so much as a presentation of literal fact, but more as 'myth' – something to be interpreted, seen through, played with in one's mind, in search of personal inspiration and understanding of the Meaning that for ever eludes us, again, behind the superficial appearance of things and events... and mere words.

INTRODUCTION

Linking the psychology of C.G. Jung with astrology is not a new idea. Some psychological astrologers try to align whole psychological concepts like Self, Ego or Shadow with the astrological symbolism of planets and signs. Less ambitiously, a simple correlation is made of the four functions (feeling, thought, intuition and sensation) found in both Jung's theory and astrology with the four elements (Earth, Air, Water, Fire) that they are traditionally associated with in astrology. Unfortunately, such a simple correlation of functions/elements throws up all sorts of questions.

There is the Air (=thought) sign Libra, for instance, associated with Venus: known as the planet of love, not of logistics. Jung holds thought and feeling to be opposed to each other. And yet in the zodiac we find the Water (=feeling) signs opposite the Earth (=sensation) signs. What is more, throughout existing attempts to tie in Jung and astrology, Jung's eight Psychological Types – as portrayed in his book of that title: the four functions, in introvert and extravert mode respectively – are completely ignored. Eight is not of course the astrologer's favourite number.

This book sets out to do just that though: to link Jung's eight types with the twelve astrological signs, as well as the four elements – a 'marriage' that will ask for a bit of give from the participants but which, I hope to show, avoids this lack of coherence found in existing systems, while offering us an entirely new perspective.

Understanding the internal nature of the zodiacal signs, I believe, can bring us closer to understanding the internal logic of behaviour: how our various motivations are constituted. Before we wave about big 'analytical' words like Shadow, we should maybe consider burrowing a bit deeper down into the simple dynamics of being and becoming. I do not, then, try to equate the constituent parts of the zodiac with those presumed parts of the psyche beloved of psychoanalysts: rather this has turned out a study of the humble mechanics of psychological processes.

As my starting point I have taken a close reading of Jung's types. If one can overcome one's number prejudice sufficiently, it is not so difficult to recognise zodiacal signs in Jung's descriptions of his types – some show up as very good likenesses indeed, while others come across rather less precisely; and some of course are missing altogether.

How can the discrepancy of *eight* Jungian types and the *twelve* 'sign types' of astrology be accounted for? For one thing Jung's types are purely theoretical constructs – or distillates might be a better word – he himself makes no claim that they are anything else. The astrological signs, on the other hand, if they are signs of anything, surely present us with an image of what actually tends to exist, or happen, in living practice. Neither is Jung's way of combining the four functions with the two modes of introversion and extraversion the only one: it is the simplest, one might say the most theoretically pure; but there *are* more complex ways, more muddly and unaccountable and lifelike ones. Having 'married' Jung's types with the zodiacal signs and elements, I have found such a way. I make no theoretical claims for it. I cannot prove that it is somehow 'right'; its proof can only lie in its usefulness in helping us shed new light on the age-old study of human behaviour and experience.

That initial puzzle of how twelve might fit into eight, or eight be distributed among twelve, began to resolve itself when I realised that each of Jung's types can be read as describing not only a single sign but actually a pair of opposite ones: the second sign is found, often just alluded to in passing, in his description of the negative nature of the opposite and compulsively (mis)used function. To give an example: his introvert with a conscious feeling function reminds us most strongly of Cancer, until we read about this type's behaviour under the influence of unconscious thought (the opposite function), when we come to recognise Capricorn (the opposite sign).

In Table I the left-hand columns give Jung's eight types and the corresponding astrological signs. The right-hand columns consist of those 'hidden', hinted at types/signs. (Of these, four are to be found on the left as well, meaning they are also among the eight, overtly described types – only Scorpio, Libra, Leo and Gemini do not appear directly in Jung's typology.) As can be seen, Jung's premise that feeling is opposed to thought, intuition to sensation, is fully upheld.

Table I

Extraverts

extraverting functions				*introverting functions*
thinking	♍	/	♓	feeling
feeling	♓	/	♍	thinking
sensation	♉	/	♏	intuition
intuition	♈	/	♎	sensation

Introverts

introverting functions				*extraverting functions*
thinking	♑	/	♋	feeling
feeling	♋	/	♑	thinking
sensation	♒	/	♌	intuition
intuition	♐	/	♊	sensation

At this point I will have to explain how I use such terms as extravert, extraverting function etc. in the context of this book. As I said earlier, two different systems being merged required a certain amount of give, redefinition or reinterpretation. As I am concerned with finding the building blocks of behaviour so to speak, I here take the terms extra-vert and intro-vert quite literally: a turning outwards or inwards; outwards in search of something new to add to oneself (since nothing is ever done but for a self-enhancing purpose), and inwards by way of being in touch with all one already is. Or, to put it at its most elementary: the extravert, as here defined, has no self as yet to call his own but has to turn to his environment to supply him with the makings of one; the intro-vert, on the other hand, is already in possession of his self – though it has to be said that in order to not just be but also become, he too will have to subject himself to some environmental influence. I have to stress that I am speaking here of zodiacal signs, *not* human beings, real or even as theoretical types.

The outcome of integrating Jung's types and the astrological signs in a single system is that the signs are psychologised: we get to see the internal 'psycho-logic' that gives each its characteristic way of 'behaving'. For ease of reading I personify them, referring to them as 'he' throughout. But that does not make them person-alities on a par with human ones. They are above us in every respect: once revered as gods, now more likely to be referred to as archetypes, or call them the Principles that underlie life. And if I say of Gemini, for instance, that he 'becomes the whole world', then I mean that to be taken literally *in its context* – as well as leaving it to the reader, of course, to interpret this in various ways when applying it to actual human behaviour.

Table II shows how the basic scheme of Table I translates on to the wheel of the zodiac. For example: Aries is an extravert and this is denoted by the 'e' in Aries' natural house, the first; his conscious function is intuition, as noted; Aries' element is Fire (F), itself associated with intuition and so making Aries doubly or purely intuitive. Virgo (sixth sign/house) is also an extravert. But he combines the conscious function of thought with an earthy element nature (E): one could call him concretely thoughtful (while traditionally of course it is said to be the rulership of Mercury that makes of this Earth sign an analytical thinker).

Now to those arrows that point outward, inward, or both. These show the direction(s) each sign's conscious function takes. This is

Table II

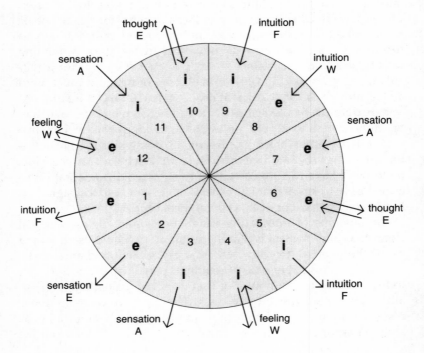

derived from Table I where I have headed the upper left-hand column 'extraverting functions' because the conscious function of an extravert (always in the sense I am using the term in the context of this book) would logically be directed outward. Likewise the lower left-hand column is headed 'introverting functions' because the conscious function of the introvert would be directed inward. The right-hand columns contain the opposite functions/signs and here I have reversed the directions of the functions – I can offer no logical justification for that, except to say that I have found it to work. I am also taking them to be the *conscious* functions of the 'hidden' signs and as can be seen, this is consistent for the four signs that appear in both columns, while giving us the information we need for the four signs that are missing, if one can put it like that, in Jung's typology.

We are now looking at a rather more complex system than one containing only straightforward introverts and extraverts, however defined, each with a conscious function. There are extraverting extraverts, extraverting introverts, introverts whose conscious function works in both directions – we are no longer in the realm of pure theory inhabited by Jung's types. Instead, we have individual characterisations, whole complex psychological stories that reveal the nature of the astrological signs. To give an example of how this works: Leo is an introvert – that is to say, he does have a self, an identity, already – but his conscious function is directed outward, making it impossible for him to know himself in the manner of a normal, proper introvert: he can do no inner self-knowing. To be able to come into full, *conscious* possession of what he innately is, he can only turn towards his environment and there find reflected back to him what he is. And at the conscious level, he does this entirely intuitively.

If we are going to speak about the conscious function of a 'sign character' we better consider his unconscious functions as well though – in fact, as will be seen in the text, without them they are stuck in their efforts to be fully themselves, or become. I have assigned three unconscious functions to each of them, using Table I again: if Aries' conscious function is intuition (top left) and his main unconscious function is sensation (top right) *of the Libra type*, then his remaining unconscious functions are (also taken from the top right-hand column) Pisces-type feeling and Virgo-type thought. – The implication here is that, in effect, the signs overlap, interpenetrate, contribute towards each other's identity: not maybe such an outrageous proposition when we are considering the nature of the signs from a psychological angle.

Once they have been 'fleshed out' like that, they can be seen to work in their own characteristic ways. Using their unconscious functions in the most constructive manner, they reveal themselves as perfect paragons of virtue, the 'gods' at their best: all the positive attributes of the signs. Misusing their unconscious functions, allowing them to become overpowering compulsions, they stand revealed as the devils they can also be: the downside of each sign. (The dual signs, Gemini and Pisces, even turn out to have two different ways of misbehaving, what one might call an active and a passive one.)

When I speak of 'positive' or 'negative' Aries then, it is this best/worst possible use of a sign's potential I mean. This is not to be understood as personal approval or rejection on my part – it will soon become obvious to the reader that the positive sign represents what can only be called the unattainable heights of perfection, while the negative sign shows us not just the pits of depravity but quite a lot of what we would regard as normal and natural. A careful reading of Leo for instance, will show that the negative as such is quite indispensable to positive Leo's existence. More specifically, it is in negative Leo that we find those recurrent cycles of creation and destruction that we take for granted in life, with its accompaniment death, or the wheel of the seasons.

Which brings me to the last point I wish to make here: I have written this book as a sort of multi-track text, to be read in many ways. It is a psychological study of the signs, a means of 'getting inside them' without having to argue backwards from the apparent nature of their so-called ruling planets (I put it like that because personally I would regard the signs as the underlying Principles, of which the tangible planets are the agents: servants, rather than rulers). It could serve as a diagnostic psychological/astrological tool in the absence of a birthchart. It is, if interpreted in that way, an attempt to view the building blocks of all purposive behaviour, an anatomy of motivation, both individual and collective.

But I would ask the reader to look for more between the lines, to consider the text from all possible angles. First there are the wider psychological issues, like childhood development phases, gender-specific behaviour patters, 'social forces', questions of (mental) health etc. But the old folk and fairy tales and mythological themes are there too – take the figure of the Wounded Healer in Gemini, for instance. Or one might consider the anthropological angle: what can Pisces tell us about the stage of human development before the hunter-gatherer phase of Aries? Or can negative Cancer shed any light on the causes of the disease of that name? Leo, prime masculine figure in this pantheon, can be examined for new insights into the nature of fatherhood, the creative impulse in general, even our relationship with the Creative Force: not least, our expectations and projections on to what we call God.

I have deliberately not spelt out these endless, complex implications and connotations that occurred to me while writing and rewriting this book – not to mention those that must have escaped my notice altogether! I think it best to let the reader discover whatever hidden meanings they may find, and interpret the text in their own light. In the sense that the job of understanding our selves and our world will never be finished, this book is unfinished too. I hope the reader, if nothing else, will find something here to use as a basis for new lines of investigation of his or her own.

THE
FIRE SIGNS

♈ ARIES

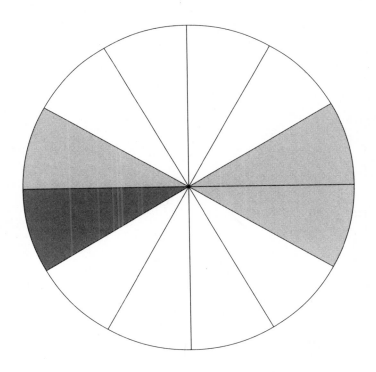

♈ **Extravert**
conscious function: intuition; direction of function: outward
unconscious functions: ♎ sensation, ♍ thinking, ♓ feeling
Fire: intuitive.

Aries is an extravert, that is to say he needs to find the makings of
his self in his environment. His conscious function is also outward-directed, which makes him one of the two 'extraverting
extraverts' among the signs (the other one being Taurus). He is
also doubly intuitive: both by conscious function and by his element nature (Fire). In other words, when Aries makes a conscious
attempt to gain his selfhood, he depends entirely on his intuition
to lead him through the objective world in search of experiences
that will supply him with an identity.

As he brings no *thought* to bear on this pursuit of something to
call 'I', he accepts quite uncritically whatever the world may have
to offer him. Neither does he have a sense of (relative) values
which would enable him to either accept or reject what he finds.
He is simply, automatically satisfied with any possibility his intuition may have guided him to; one chance of acquiring more by
way of an identity is as good as the next to him. Not in the least
fussy, he lends himself to any kind of life, any task, in any environment or relationship – for a while.

In effect, his search for self consists of a series of intense bursts
of identification with this, that and the other, as quickly abandoned again for something new that presents itself. There is nothing to tell him that this is he, exclusively, or that. And without the
use of a feeling function, he cannot even get emotionally identified with or attached to anything he becomes. He is so indiscriminate, so easy to please, and yet he can't settle for anything: he is
always 'looking for more'. Without something to tell him that this
latest bit of self he has discovered is, from whatever angle, truly
satisfying – because he mentally approves of it, or senses its
worth, for instance – all he can do is push on ahead. All of his environment is self, as far as he can tell. He is unstoppable in his
search, never disappointed, but never satisfied either.

This way he can of course never gain anything permanently

identifiable as 'I'. His identity changes all the time, an unstable thing without a 'characteristic' form to it. He is no more than a process taking place, and even as such he isn't a reliably specific process: only a general becoming – and unbecoming again – never what you could call growth. Trying to become all of it, he 'drops' and leaves behind as much as he newly finds; every day he acquires momentary selves by the dozen, only to lose them again. He moves through the world, and the world moves through him, and none of it is of any consequence whatsoever. At the end of the day he is still no nearer having 'made a name for himself'. Life proves to be nothing but a futile, pointless exercise leading everywhere and nowhere and he may as well save himself the effort.

In order to gain a self that lasts and is recognisable as such, he needs to make use of his unconscious functions, all of them. But for the purpose of understanding, in detail, how he works let us assume he acquires their use one at a time. Let us say first of all, unconsciously, he senses ($\triangleq$) that there are different values one can attach to different kinds of experience, out of an appreciation of the relative value of all things. This enables him to make choices where before it would have been 'all the same to him'. He now senses the relative merit of a new opportunity, not only in itself, but in terms of finding something new to become that will actually tie in harmoniously with what he has most recently found to be.

He has been failing to gather together some self-experiences that would define him to himself: because each time he found something new to be this was just as good, but no better, than the previous bit of potential 'I' he discovered. One can picture him, rather literally, getting overloaded with all these potential selves, having to drop some in order to pick up new ones – all of it done haphazardly, because he was unable to tell what might be worth picking up, or worth keeping. Simply speaking, if something was within his reach, then he grabbed it; if something *could* be done, then he did it; if someone appeared on the scene, then that was fine by him, his relationships settled for the (short) time being.

But now that he is able to sense differences, to see the relative merit of one relationship or activity or whatever as compared to another, he finds himself at last able to retain one in favour of the other. He no longer abandons what he was doing for any new opportunity to act, differently, without first letting his sense of good/bad, better/worse, desirable/undesirable help him make a decision. All the world is no longer automatically accepted. There is a 'yes' or 'no' to what he might be and become. He considers: because he has come to evaluate and appreciate.

His ongoing search for self no longer proceeds in incoherent zigzags. It has become a directed process instead: in effect he is aiming for something now, something he senses to be 'desirable'. It has also become a coherent process: values always being *relative*, his aiming-for too has to result in something that hangs together somehow, that is all of a piece. Any activity he chooses, for instance, has to tie in harmoniously with the kind of surroundings he has also chosen, and the sort of company he is keeping there... the 'desirability' of things, in fact, turns out to be something quite complex.

The simplest – and in that sense, most 'primitive' – of the sings, with this basic inclination of his to resemble nothing-in-particular, now at least he is acquiring what one could call unconscious guidelines how to find himself a recognisable identity. And yet, when one looks at it closely, the object of his directed and coherent pursuit is still rather vague: 'relatively right', 'good in the circumstances', 'desirable option', none of this is very clearly defined. There may be many such options available to him, lying in a hundred mutually exclusive directions.

It turns out that his ability to make yes/no choices may be more of a liability than a help to him. If there was any characteristic he had from the start, then it was his capacity for impetuous-fiery and fluidly-intuitive progress. But faced now with such a multiplicity of 'good' choices, he comes to a standstill of indecision, unable to make up his mind.

Here his unconscious, outward-directed, Virgo-type thought processes (♍→) can help him define in much more exact detail what he is aiming for. He now begins (unconsciously) to bring critical thought to bear on every situation. He scrutinises precisely what its nature is, before he comes to any decision. He analyses and dwells thoughtfully on every detail, compares things, peers more closely at how things work and what exactly they do, before he touches, takes, does. This at once thoughtful and practical approach tends to slow him down too, in his basically impetuous progress through the whole world of potential self; but at the same time it allows him to overcome the stalemate of indecision. The broad and rather vague 'yes' he was saying has now become a much narrower 'yes-because'.

Having added this much more detailed, thoughtful choosing to his general sense of acceptance or rejection, his aim has become quite clearly defined now: he has a specific *idea* of what he wants to become. He is once more able to proceed, intuitively – this time to grasp his opportunities with the certainty and deliberateness that comes from having something particular in mind.

It might seem good enough to say he gains a well-defined self and leave it at that. But strictly speaking he never gains a self to have and hold on to. Aries is the only doubly-intuitive extravert: a purely fiery nature in search of something to become. But what is the so-called element Fire if not a process? Nothing is *made* of fire; fire happens, and if unchecked proceeds rapidly. In the same way Aries' self 'happens' as a process, an activity, and it is only in the sense that this activity gains a recognisable identity – deliberate, directed, coherent, precisely thought-out action – that one can speak of Aries as gaining a self or identity.

To all intents and purposes he gains his self over and over again, through consistent, repetitive action. He acts 'characteristically' in all sorts of diverse situations; more of a 'habitual' self than a concretely established one, one might say.

The use of his unconscious thought processes not only gives him the ability to be critical and analytical about his environment, a capacity for self-criticism, that is to say inward-turning Virgo-type thought (♍←) goes hand in hand with it. There is always scope for active self-improvement, for becoming, doing, something better. Unlike a good few signs to be considered later, Aries never has a problem with 'becoming': he is always moving on, he is the most effortlessly developing of the signs. He will have to relinquish some of what he is/does, of course, if he is to replace it with an improved version – but this is a very different process from the meaningless loss-gain-loss he initially experienced. His losses now entail new *and better* gains, on the basis of a coherent self that is seeking self-critically to better itself.

One can picture him now engaged in a forcefully directed drive to extract all the best possibilities from each situation… exclusively for himself. Unfortunately, others will see him as pushy, ambitious, unerringly picking the best choices from under their noses. He soon comes to be resented in his 'selfishness'; he finds his paths blocked, his options reduced by others who would also like to have a chance to gain something worthwhile for themselves. At this point he will have to make use of his remaining unconscious function, feeling.

Emotionally, he is inclined to see the world ($\mathcal{H}\rightarrow$) as an all-enveloping whole, life as a communal, shared event. At the same time he feels that his self ($\mathcal{H}\leftarrow$) is only a fraction of a much larger living whole, of no particular significance. This new company he is keeping, as it were, helps to counteract his 'self-importance', this self-centred view he has had throughout that made him regard everything he encountered in the world purely as *his* chance to increase in self-worth. – He has repeatedly narrowed himself down, till he became something quite specific; but now he finds himself, at the emotional level, as a single, unimportant member of something collective, large, diffuse and all-enveloping. This juxtaposition of being, in himself, so well defined and that ill-defined all and everything he is emotionally drawn towards, has the effect of making him aware of others as *distinct* from himself.

So far other has been only a prelude to self for him: the raw material out of which he could derive the makings of an identity, a sort of fertile hunting ground for what he aimed to be. Now, emotionally, he becomes part of a community of selves who are all struggling as he does with their various attempts to be and become, and not an especially important part of that. In retrospect he has to admit that he has been 'considerate' only in so far as he has been considering his own future. Any toes he has been treading on in the process were no more to him than his rejected options: things he was not interested in being actively identified with. But now that he feels himself to be one among many, these toes have suddenly acquired owners: a different ball game altogether. He is no longer the only self that counts for him as such.

Emotionally, he can't reject anything. And yet without rejecting he would never have become, exclusively, himself. Now he somehow has to find a way to combine these two strands of his life: being separately and distinctly himself, and being (emotionally) at one with his surroundings. It would be only too easy to lose all he has gained, to be swamped by this shapeless tide of all-accepting feelings and in effect end up where he began: surrounded by an

undifferentiated chaos of things to 'identify with', all equally welcome to him. Somehow, he will have to defend himself, to save the
newly emerged particle from being swallowed up again by the
whole it has worked so hard to emerge from.

The answer lies in *taking* part, *playing* a part in the life of the
whole community, actively participating, in his own characteristic
way. Like this, he can feel himself to be included, while safely
retaining his separateness. A solution that comes quite naturally
to him, the sign whose self takes the shape of a 'directed happening' rather than anything more concrete and static. He comes to be
active in the wider community, *without* automatically letting it
affect what he personally stands for. By not taking anything for
himself out of a situation, he can play a *helpful* part in others' lives
– never withholding his feelings, letting his sympathy flow freely
into and in the wider collective, while nevertheless staying himself. In one word, he learns how to deal with experiences in an
*im*personal way: reserving the right to be what he is, in the isolation of his hard-won identity, but participating willingly by
putting all those attributes he has made his own in the service of
the common interest.

He 'owns' his self exclusively. But he also shares it: by putting
it at the disposal of the wider world, using it for the benefit of others' interests – acting on their behalf. He becomes the *agent* of pursuits, aims, tasks that go beyond his own, relatively narrow
self-interest. He is always ready to stand his own concerns aside
for a while, feeling his active involvement might be needed, that
his specific abilities might be of help.

In a sense, he has only now found his true completion, a stable
identity (if stable is the word, for a self that *does*, and keeps trying
to do in better ways). As one among many, he is constantly needing to defend his own ways, strengthen his defences against the
possible intrusion of anything alien to him; at the same time, he
can test out his active-self in the service of others, see whether it is
fit to do the job, or could maybe be improved on after all: responding to others' needs, he can actually serve his own ends as well.
He can prove himself as it were *universally* valid. Serving his own
interests, serving others' needs at the same time – this can only be
achieved with *simplicity*. His prior rejecting of so many things as
not really good enough to bother with doing and being stands
him in good stead. He doesn't go in for frills; he sticks to the hard-

won basics, the sort we will all recognise as useful. –

It can be seen now that the (positive) use of his unconscious functions has been the making of him: it is only with their help he has been able to grow and develop; without them, he would still be the clueless, disorganised self-seeker he used to be, for ever pushing us out of his way in his frantic hurry, and still never getting anywhere. Now he has become not only 'himself' but also 'one of us'. He takes on his and our new tasks, causes, missions, tackles the uncharted jobs: anything that needs to be newly discovered or gained from out of undifferentiated confusion, anything that needs to be pushed through despite distractions or detractors, or needs to be strengthened in its singularity against the threat of being overwhelmed by collective forces – he is on home ground in such matters. As a target finder par excellence he can be our vicarious 'go-getter' (in the literal sense), a pioneer, a leader and also a defender against forces that oppose progress or threaten stability and the established ways. And as he is perfectly capable of personal detachment, he isn't likely to panic, lose his cool, never allows himself to be deflected from his purpose (except where his critical faculty would suggest a better option to him). Lastly, any gains he makes, even on his own account, he is glad to share with us: sharing is part and parcel of his success as an active-self.

We better enjoy his company while we have it, because he is capable of the ultimate self-sacrifice in the course of a worthwhile pursuit. What matters to him, essentially, is not gain as such but the act of gaining properly approached and executed – and, in retrospect, proving itself valid in ways that transcend his own personal interests, as his contribution to life. It is acting like this that defines him to himself, that makes up the character and integrity of his self. Gaining possession of something, and holding on to it, is not what it's about for him at all. And he would rather let go of (part of) his self/life than devalue it by 'acting out of character': meaning, he will be true to himself to the last. This of course is what gives him his famous 'courage': he *is* what he *does*; the integrity of his self, quite simply, equals the 'integrity' of his actions.

He is superbly fitted to be our leader but, again, a position gained and clung to is not what he seeks. It makes no difference to him whether we follow him, take him as our role model perhaps, or walk beside him as his equals, co-leaders, maybe followers who have so to speak caught up with him. If anything it strikes him as an ideal situation: he won't have to be *im*personal in his dealings with us (taking on our concerns, while keeping his own separate from the situation) if he now shares a common goal with us, all of us approaching it in the same sort of way. This is sharing made easy, the best possible company for him, to be simply himself within a group engaged in a common activity. It may sound para-doxical, but clubability is an integral aspect of his successfully attained 'singleness'. – Not that he will stay part of any such group for long.

He is always moving on, finding new occasions to prove him-self in action. He keeps trying to find a better active-self to be, but only when what he is newly enacting has become the tried and universally trusted – because it has proved helpful to others – is any particular stage of his progress complete for him, only then is he ready to go on to his next project. One could say that what he is doing is to steer and work his way through the future, both his and ours, with a view to making it serve eventually as past, as foundation. Ours, in the sense that he gains something new for us that we can then use as a starting point of our own, for our own individual purposes. And his, in that it becomes the new basis for his next development stage... there is no standing still for him: he is the ongoing process between future and past personified, never becoming 'established' except as a well-defined process whose validity is constantly under review.

He is the one who makes a start, many new starts in fact, where others lack the vision to evaluate possibilities, the almost restless drive, the goal concept, the ability to ignore what lies left and right while pursuing the current objective, the courage or integrity-in-action of one whose *self* depends on it for its 'survival'. The start-ing foundations he lays are, like his self, both precisely differentiated and simple to the point of universality. It is up to others, and to the other signs, to develop things from there and build on that basis.

But Aries can also use his unconscious functions in negative ways. In that case, rather than employing them to his advantage, he

finds himself used by them: they become overpowering compulsions that seem to help him out of his basic conundrum only to
plunge him into a different one.

An overpowering sense of relative values ($\triangleq$) results in two
things: malcontent and over-extensiveness. He develops an exaggerated, if unconscious, desire that the world please him/his senses, an overpowering sense of things never being good enough:
there is always something relatively better to be gained somewhere just ahead. This means that no self-experience, how ever
hard-gained, can count for much by itself. Instead of using his
sense of relative 'good' and 'bad' to try and decide between the
options available, he gets pulled along by a compulsive desire for
good-ness *as such*. But since such value judgements as good, right,
desirable are always entirely relative, he now has no option but
try and become *all* good things there are combined. This is what
he now targets. He aims to become all that is good: to be *the* best.

Like positive Aries, he stops meandering around and identifying self in everything he encounters on the way. But at the same
time he finds himself in a situation where the intended target can
never be reached, despite all his directed efforts. More than ever
he searches, but the moment he reaches a goal he refuses to accept
it as what he is *really* looking for: his constitutional malcontent
will not let him call anything self, because nothing ever strikes
him as good enough to be called 'I' yet. He does not find a self
only to lose it again, he never finds what he would regard as a
'proper' self in the first place.

He can take nothing in isolation. It is all or nothing with him,
and yet the only way he can gain all is step by step, in an additive
process. The self he envisages is the very best possible and not a
single worthwhile bit left out, to be found in everything as it
hangs together. But meantime he has to apply himself to the job of
assembling the parts of this projected, finished self-to-be. These
parts in themselves are never of any great value to him, they strike
him as deficient, but he is convinced that if he can only gather
enough of them, it will all add up to something splendid in the
end. It is only when he has captured the whole desirable world for
his own, for his self, that he will be able to rest content, when there
will be no new and superior incentives, objectives, desires left for
him to pursue. Then and only then will he have become the self he
senses himself potentially to be. His compulsion to aim for The

Best (i.e. *all* that is good) has him rushing towards a very far off future, rather than dealing satisfactorily with each new life stage as he approaches it.

This ultimate aim is what keeps him going despite his constant disappointment with world and self. The details of his present life simply do not matter to him and lack of self-satisfaction becomes a way of life to him. To watch him, one might think that he is indulging compulsive appetites, that he is hooked on his plea- sures; but quite the contrary: he is insatiable because there is never enough satisfaction in it yet. Only everything satisfying, every- thing desirable, will be sufficient to sate his appetite. Meantime he gathers his never-quite satisfactions like coupons to be redeemed one day. Seeing him throw himself at his next target one might equally think that it was of tremendous importance to him. But again, he does not really attach much importance to the current objective ahead *as such*, only in the sense that it will clear his way to further progress, another hurdle taken on the way towards that ultimate aim of self-completion. Thus his aims become something more akin to obstacles he is impatient to have out of the way.

He looks forward only, eagerly, and so far ahead that his cur- rent goal becomes an indistinct blur. He 'bashes on' regardless, and if what he is bashing about is actually a particle of the self-to- be, no matter, it is of no great intrinsic value anyway, in itself. Any damage he does, any injuries to world and self, all that will sort itself out some time in the future.

But he does not stand much of a chance to progress past each intermediate aim/hurdle if he does not focus on the matter in hand, with the result that he gets caught up repeatedly in a straight-jacket of apparently insurmountable obstacles. His always rather disappointing life then turns into an angry night- mare: he is stuck with this self-experience that he refuses to acknowledge as such. The self he is aiming for lies far ahead, but now he finds himself caught up in a momentary identity that does not entirely please him – and hence does not please him at all. He is trying to process the world, fast, without really looking at what he is doing: because the end result is all he cares for. In the exis- tential equivalent of tripping over his own feet in his haste and getting nowhere as a result, he blames the world for constantly throwing stumbling blocks in his path. Life is unfair: it is trying to prevent him from becoming all he so strongly desires to be; it is forever causing him to get bogged down in this not quite real state of being nothing worthwhile as yet: having no 'proper' self. His blind struggling and kicking does not get him anywhere either.

Making use of his unconscious thought process ($\mathrm{I\!I\!P} \rightarrow$) can give him the necessary focus to clear those hurdles. He now calculates every detail , compulsive, twice over – he takes every nut and bolt into account, he has the whole job dissected and labelled in his mind. But in the final analysis what it is all about is not a job well done, a self-experience brought to a satisfactory conclusion, but only another item ticked off on his endless list, another hurdle cleared.

He does not treasure his accomplishments, his gains strike him as instantly dismissible: 'That's nothing'. (We take that to be a boast – in a roundabout way it is, of course, because he is hinting at his 'real' self, the potential, future one in all its splendour.) Dismissing his gains does not mean letting go of them, though. He has to hoard them for the final count, after all, for the time when he has at last 'got it all together'. Meantime his grand ambition has him doing the job in hand with nothing but expediency in mind, his eyes already wandering off to the next target. Achievement only leads to the possibility of more achievement, and yet more; it is only 'one day' that it will all count for something.

He goes through the motions successfully enough, from his point of view, though one can hardly call him efficient except in the most superficial sense. Everything is a rush job. His narrow mental focus allows him to cope with what were previously stumbling blocks, he hits his target unerringly, and hurries on to the next. He is exclusively concerned with making speedy headway. If ever he looks back and finds his recent achievements coming apart again, his accumulating gains lacking in true value, his exploits not just forgettable but already forgotten, he will merely be strengthened in his view of the current details of life as unimportant. But he is hardly inclined to look back: stocktaking is something for the future. He certainly does not stay around to be blamed for the results of his actions – and if one hurls the blame after him he can only shrug sheepishly: we really can't expect anything much from him *yet*. He is only potentially splendid, something wonderful in the making. We'll have to excuse him for the time being.

This is his 'development': step after step shrewdly planned to allow him to proceed, and nothing else taken into consideration. It will be safest to assume that any bridge he throws across a ravine will be hastily-efficiently designed for one crossing only: his. Positive Aries did not take others and the advancement of their interests into consideration either, at this stage, but at least he made of each new phase of his progress a proper job, satisfying in itself, before he took the next step forward. Negative Aries does not develop properly at all. He accumulates and yet disowns his successive self-experiences. The self he is in effect acquiring 'piles up beside him' unappreciated, not quite owned, while he has his eye on a future state of 'real' selfhood that will be matchless, unsurpassable. This ideal future state is of course receding from him with every step he takes. In terms of personal development he is running on the spot, going nowhere fast. In the last resort one can only call him 'retarded'; not so absurdly, for one who is actively projecting his self ahead of him all the time: that is, in effect trying to catch up with it. All his frantic pushing forward is getting him nowhere, and at the same time he simply omits to live properly in the present. We should find him plainly absurd if he did not give us this impression of serious struggle, and a success of sorts.

There is nothing really characteristic about his actions that would identify him individually. He will do anything to 'get there', and in that sense his crude actions belie his ultimate, magnificent aim. He simply pushes forward, bagging each success as something not to be savoured but saved, added to his growing, disjointed pile of the particles of a self-to-be, and it should come as no surprise that much of this 'pile' is indeed of a material nature: what more suitable to save up and keep for later? He is not characterised by specific actions; rather he is doing all he can, anything, towards making his self take a more concrete shape. In this he is helped by his ability to be intelligently manipulative, selectively efficient and narrowly pragmatic.

But with this kind of thinking he is inevitably restricting his options, making of 'the whole desirable world' that is his target a much reduced area. Some things it is simply not efficient for him to bother with, on the way. Expediency is all, every possible shortcut is always the right way forward: after all, in his opinion, he has never even reached his beginning yet. What he now thinks of as not worth wasting his precious time on he comes to exclude categorically from 'his' world. He pushes it out of his mind as if it belonged into some kind of useless other-world, a whole parallel world of rejects, antithesis in a puzzling way, something to be deliberately ignored. All this he labels queer and 'impossible', and nimbly skirts around. He has better things to concentrate on, he has no time for idle curiosity: all the cleverness he can muster is fully employed in his headlong pursuit of the unreachable. No wonder he is a bit backward.

But his narrowly critical thinking also turns on the matter of his self ($♍\leftarrow$), compulsively finding fault. This hardly tells him anything new about the actual current state of his self, which he is discounting anyway. But now he begins to have nagging doubts about his 'real' self as well, the projected one, the end result of all his efforts. He doubts his future, he wonders whether it will ever 'come together' properly. Nobody could be trying harder and, simply in terms of getting ahead, succeeding better. There should be no room for self-criticism. And yet unaccountable thoughts of 'not good enough' go through his mind, and no matter how hard he thinks, he can find no explanation. It is enough to suggest to him that he might as well give up.

The puzzle resolves itself the moment he approaches the world with feeling ($♓\rightarrow$). Emotionally (over-emotionally, one has to say) he can exclude absolutely nothing and nobody, the world is simply whole to him, one indivisible unit. This means he has to revise his divisive system of excluding all those rejects he had decided to pay no attention to. They now re-enter his world, because emotionally he can *not* ignore them. A whole host of undesirables become once more part of his one world. Reincluded, they become an antithesis now felt to be part of his reality. They are enemies then, dangers, hurdles that actively refuse to be taken, and 'impossibles' that he now feels he does have to tackle if he is to reach his ultimate goal.

So far he has thought of those around him only as intermediate goals to be taken, gained and kept hold of; or else as inhabitants of an unreal, unworthwhile world that could safely be ignored. He has 'owned' them, or else shrugged them aside. The only self known to him was his, and that a thing to come rather than a here and now reality. Now he realises with a shock that there are others, also trying to become selves, dipping into the same one world for the ingredients of *their* eventual future selfhoods – that, at any

rate, is how he understands the situation. They are his competitors, ready to snatch bits of world from under his nose for their
own self-ish purposes – it is no wonder then that he was having
doubts about his eventual adding up to everything worth being:
the world is full of thieves appropriating what he regards as his.

He is much relieved to find his self-criticism to have a simple
explanation: others are to blame for any shortcomings on his part.
This gives him back his hope for his future, but he pays a price.
There is nothing for it now but to muscle in on everybody else's
act; he has to get over and above and past all others, hurdle and
hurtle ahead of them. If he cannot better others now, he will never
become The Best. It is a serious nuisance to be so delayed in his
rush towards his far-off self, to have to make the impossible possible, to do anything that could be done, for fear someone else
might do it and gain something thereby. In his panic at recognising all these rivals and competitors he no longer dares rely on his
own judgement any more: anything he sees others striving after
becomes desirable to him too, just to be on the safe side. Anything
he sees them have, he has to wrestle from them, with an outraged
shout of 'mine!'

The moment he awakes to the fact of others being potential
opponents ready to steal his identity – his chance, that is, to ever
attain it – life becomes a free-for-all, a fight to be first on the scene
of potential gain, a wrangling and scrambling for any advantage
at all. It is a fight for survival, survival that is to say of the integrity of his future. Without this future his life loses all meaning to
him. That is what is at stake, and he will risk losing all he has got,
his unsatisfactory present life and self, in defence of this future
that he can never reach. (A rather different 'self-sacrifice' to that of
positive Aries!)

It is obvious that there is not room for him *and* other would-be
selves in a world he takes to be indivisible and his. Others have to
be firmly disabused of any notions that they, too, could one day
rate as an 'I'. Since his view of 'I' is that it is simply *the* best, there
can of course be only one such 'I' in the whole world. Underlings
and followers and open-mouthed admirers he does not mind: he
is nothing if not admirable the way he throws himself into the
fray, fiery, with an all-or-nothing emotional zeal, and coldly calculating every detail of the victory he is seeking. But competitors
in this arena he can obviously not allow. Not only do they threat-

en him, they also spoil the one-ness of the world as he emotionally perceives it.

It is no good arguing with him to grant us equal rights. He really feels that he is doing something rather noble if he tries to unify this sadly divided world under his banner. He is apt to become quite misty-eyed and sentimental over this. It is something, he feels, he is doing not just for his own but for the common good, his way of sharing the one world. His aim one day to unify, to integrate, all he has gained under the heading self or 'I' just coincides nicely with this feeling he has that the world should not be diverse and fragmented but all of a piece. Declaring his own self-ish aim a kind of sacred mission neatly disposes of our accusations and gains him more admirers and followers. It makes the rest of us look churlish, as if we wanted to tear the world to pieces with our individual, contrary ambitions: we become *public* enemies, not just his personal obstacles but a sort of public affront. His supporters may have no personal animosity against us, but since he has aggrandised his own to universal proportions, they have no choice but declare war on us.

We are either the faceless enemy, or else factors to be used, with a clinical application of intelligence, to his own ends. With our supine admiration we may also furnish him with some positively enjoyable self-experience for once. To be undisputed leader and to find himself cheered for it introduces satisfaction into his current life, something that has so far been lacking. In *his* estimation these are all very modest attempts he is making, hardly worth mentioning, and yet to judge by the acclaim he is getting he seems to count for something already.

He certainly needs all the encouragement he can get. He is increasingly apt to lose his forward drive now that he is constantly craning his neck in all directions on the look-out for anything that might escape him and fall to his rivals instead. He even, for the first time, looks carefully behind him – not to dwell on and appreciate what he has done, and to make sure it is well done, before he proceeds any further – but because there might be dangers lurking there, others trying to overtake him and snatch the next gain for him, clear the coming hurdle before he does. He has to watch our every move, for what use would it be to him to proceed through no longer virgin territory, where some of the potential gain, victory or success has already been won and abducted:

*de*ducted from *him*.

If he has any doubts left as to what to do with such challengers, then the emotional self-doubt ($\mathcal{H}\leftarrow$) that nags away at him, i.e. his quite illogical fear of finding himself outnumbered and reduced to nothing, convinces him that only the strongest countermeasures will suffice. With this kind of fearfully-reckless 'courage' he needs all the adherents and supporters he can find. Increasingly they have to keep him on the right track, shouting what amounts to directions where to go next, what exactly to do: his attention is apt to wander, divided between aiming (directed aggression) and worrying about potential dangers lurking all about him (diffuse defensiveness). His aim is getting pretty poor, but his followers keep him right, propel him straight forward, while covering his back. –

He has sorted us into two neat groups, for him or against him. For him is anyone willing to be 'taken', like an obstacle, and retained, like a possession: put aside for hoarding, put behind him for the time being (from there to provide support and guidance, to boost him on his way). Against him is anybody who refuses to be so taken and used. To him such a refusal can only mean that one harbours the evil ambition to grab the one available title of 'I' for oneself; or else, no better, that we are attempting to splinter the one world that he would take for his own into a quite unacceptable number of incomplete little 'I's , each withholding within itself something that should be his. Such rivals he will fight to the death, or speedy submission, whichever comes first.

Unfortunately things are not so simple and 'for' may have to be declared 'against' at no notice at all. Yesterday's friend may betray him by showing self-ish inclinations of his own, automatically becoming enemy to him. Yesterday's friend means nothing to him; though in fairness one has to say that past enmity, too, is soon forgotten. What is 'behind' him always promptly ceases to count for much. He values his friends no more than he does his actual self, barely at all.

He hoovers us into his stream of self-experience and, if we survive his torrential demands to stand our selves aside and/or in his service, then we find ourselves dumped in his past-of-no-account, taken for granted. He cannot think what else we might be there for. We have no kind of independent existence in his view; except as potential betrayers. That is why he keeps shouting for us to appear before him, every now and again, so that he may reassure himself that we are still there, still his, safely to be counted on for his future need of us. And by the same token he fingers his wealth, with no real glint in his eyes, and ticks off his exploits rapidly, with a shrug as if to say, ah, but wait for it…!

Once he has acquired us for his own (future) purpose, we ask to be regarded as selves in our own right at our peril. He suffers from a double dose of insecurity: unconsciously he is compulsively self-critical, as well as being subject to feelings of self-doubt. It is no wonder that he is always ready to react to the slightest hint of criticism or encroachment on what he considers exclusively his rights as if it were a deliberate challenge to do battle. Instead of active he is hyper-reactive. And instead of properly defensive – he has nothing worthwhile to defend, after all, but his future – one can only call him strongly offensive.

He is not all fight and destruction, though. He is just as happy to win his way forward by other means. His quite over the top emoting may even attract us, for a while – till we realise that when he waxes lyrical over everything in the world having to be whole and intact, it does not mean he is worried about *our* lacking for something, or *our* being under threat. His soppy idealism is reserved for his self-to-be, that phantom event on the ever receding horizon. Meantime it makes no difference to his purpose whether he 'buys' us or squashes us, impresses us favourably or kills us, so long as nothing and nobody holds him up.

He enriches his own future – in theory, at any rate – with a total lack of concern for the present, and even less for the past, for what he leaves in his wake. This gives him carte blanche: any means will justify his end, because it is only in the end that he hopes to find his *proper* beginning. All his life is a preparatory struggle. There is never any resting on laurels, each new gain is shelved: not *good* enough, because not *enough*. A single victory is nothing, and his second million no more soothing a thought to him than his first.

At any point he holds nothing really valuable to him in his hands. But he does not ask for riches now (though money and possessions may, coincidentally, be piling up); he does not ask for ease and comfort now (though he will occupy the only seat in the room as a matter of course: others being something akin to furniture to him, he can't imagine them having the same self-ish needs as he); he does not hold in any great regard who or what he owns (though his defence of it/them is entirely offensive); he does not even hold his self, as it stands, in any regard (though a single wrong word is enough to trigger an outburst of aggression). No, he is nothing as yet.

Of course one cannot ask him to contribute, to share, to gain something for our benefit as well: he never has anything to give. What he has amassed is never enough yet for his own ultimate purpose. We need not ask him for any of it. *He* will need it all, one day. He may even walk about in rags rather than spend any of it on his current self, the one he refuses to acknowledge. As for beggars on his doorstep, they can only be enemy to him, aspiring rival hoarders. In short, he is the thinnest, poorest of us all and it stands to reason that *we* should give to *him*.

Just as he throws what he acquires into a pile, which he guards as his own but never really treasures, so he shelves each experience mastered with the disdain of the insatiable – with the result that the next time he comes up against the same sort of experience he stands there as a complete beginner. He is clever enough, but he does not value the knowledge he has gained. Since he refuses to put two and two together properly, he remains in a state of massive ignorance.

And yet in his view he is the greatest: the vision of his grand-total self to come quite literally obliterates all he might amount to now. All his best boasts are of what he *will* be, or do. But each new step forward he takes is like the first one all over again. – Unlike him, life develops; it never grants him that scheduled future appointment with an absolute self. He is bogged down in time even while he never happens in it properly, never makes each minute and each minute gain his own: none of that is 'I' to him. For all the commotion he makes – being impatient, demanding, threatening, irascible in his panicky fear that we might stand in his way and debar him from his 'real' self – he stays essentially nameless and undefined, his self only a prospect, living in a dream of 'one day'.

He has nothing to teach us except how to be clever enough to ram one's head through a succession of walls. The only foundation he ever lays is his own, and he goes on laying it, and goes on laying it... and still no kind of progress can be seen. We can expect nothing from him, not even the simplest loyalty or constancy. He

never acquires a dependable identity, bar the rawest and generally roughest. He may call the shots and deliver the blows, but these
are not wilful, determined acts so much as the fearful reactions of
a self-confessed non-entity to something that threatens to stand
between him and the mirage he calls self. He wishes to know of no
other self than his intended one, that vain fascination on his horizon: this is the thing he serves slavishly, preparing to give it
everything he can grab on the way. Meantime, in actual fact, he is
unself-conscious in the extreme.

When he refuses to know and acknowledge his actual self and
the reality of other selves beside him, he lives in an illusion of the
finest order. All *we* can see are his boorish, undistinguished ways,
his rough snatching at all we have and are. His splendid intentions are hard for us to imagine, faced with such a coarse reality.
We know his pushiness only too well, and yet we underestimate
his world-engulfing ambition that would make short work of all
possible conquests, once and for all, preferably in no time at all.
The true nature of time escapes him, as does ours. As we underestimate him so he underestimates us: we cannot conceive of his
(would-be) 'real' self and he, unless we challenge him deliberately or inadvertently, cannot see us as independent selves at all.
When he does notice anything self-ish about us he interprets it to
be only an attempt in progress, like his own, and us as competitors. Other selves that are already in any way established he cannot begin to conceive of. They would be bad news to him. His
world would no longer strike him as whole, and all his strivings
would obviously be in vain.

Not seeing us for what we are, and not caring how he proceeds,
as long as he does, lays him open to all sorts of manipulation. He
is most readily used, if one is clever about it, cheered on in any
direction we want to send him hurtling to do our rough or warlike
work for us. If only we can get him to believe that it is all for his
own eventual greater glory, and that he will be ridding the world
of obstacles, enemies and all that stands in *his* way, then he will be
a ridiculously willing tool in our hands. He is used to pain and
struggle and chasing after unrealistic dreams, he has never known
anything else. We can use him and abuse him for our own
advancement, just as he does us.

Whether or not it comes to that, he is not likely to survive many
battles. His fierce reaction to all that would hold him up on his

never-ending journey to that almighty something he would call 'I', can only provoke equally fierce reactions: from other self-seekers, and from others with more established selves who will resist his invasive bid to become all. At the final reckoning, he still only amounts to a whole lot of unreached potential. It has been lying fallow, in that larger-than-life future he was always aiming to reach.

Some Suggested Aries Attributes

basic

outgoing, impulsive, progresses intuitively; uncritically and indiscriminately **takes every chance available, not to be deterred; courageous:** nothing, not even hurt, will put him off: **unflinching, unstoppable, impetuous**

always on the move, has difficulty settling, impatient to get on; forward-looking; peripatetic, roams, pursues; unhesitating and **unevaluating: persistently rash; promiscuous**

always in search of more: **insatiable for new experiences, adventurous; foolhardy, courts danger unawares; may be seen as greedy, pushy and inconsiderate; 'pleases himself'**

can't be depended on, as he keeps moving on he is **seen as being disloyal; quick to make new contacts** but **absent-mindedly discards, forgets; 'has no past': primitive; eternally youthful; does not learn: permanently inexperienced** and hence inclined to be **rough, uncouth**

positive

has considered aims, makes directed progress, sets himself goals; ceaselessly active, consistent in action and yet capable of self-improvement: **develops new modes of action**

always learning something new and **developing in new directions,** and in that sense **'stays young'; advances thoughtfully,** rejecting many options, and **searches for the universally valid:** hence **simplicity**

constantly evaluates his progress, takes stock, treasures his gains, moderately proud

direct, honest and **straightforward, above-board, has nothing to hide, trustworthy:** can be entrusted with a task

acting 'selflessly' on behalf of others: **agent; proves himself in the service of others; vicarious 'go-getter'; pioneer, missionary, explorer, leader (of advance parties etc.); active role model**

makes discoveries and new gains, enterprising, has/takes initiative, opens up untried possibilities, experiments; progressive; but also **defends** the already gained, **retains what is of value and establishes it as the new basis** from which to proceed further: **initiator**

bold, assertive in the face of problems to be overcome, **coura-**

geous: not to be deflected while progressing from his last aim to his next, but also **levelheaded;** can act in detached, impersonal, **'selfless'** ways; **idealistic, capable of self-sacrifice**

companionable, likes the company of equals with similar aims and **group activities, clubability,** engages in **shared projects**

negative

insatiable, constitutionally malcontent, greedy for more: nothing is ever **(good) enough, all-or-nothing approach; inflated expectations** amounting to **illusions;** makes of his personal aim something generalised and universal: **'idealistic',** sentimental heroics, latches on to/takes over 'causes': **excessively patriotic, jingoism** etc.

boastful: seeing himself as potentially the best; **over-ambitious, over-achiever,** may appear to be a **'workaholic';** unrealistic **aims, will attempt the impossible; daredevil, reckless; gains admiration,** becomes not so much a leader in the positive sense as **top-dog**

always disappointed, no self-satisfaction, feels inferior, does not think well of himself, belittles himself and his own efforts, discounts his gains, dismisses his past

never learns, arrested or slow development; retarded; forever childlike; crudely primitive; vague personal identity; brutish; unselfconscious, unaware of the effect he has on others, uncaring, inconsiderate; can be controlled only with guile; does not take responsibility for his (past) actions, **has excuses, blames others for his own shortcomings**

restless, impatient to get ahead (of others); focused on an ultimate aim, he sees everything in between as **obstacles that need to be overcome; irascible if stopped in his tracks,** always in a seriously **urgent hurry to 'get there'; takes shortcuts,** including logical ones: **jumps to conclusions**

easily angered, can't stand criticism (it detracts from his ideal self) **or competitors** (they are stealing what should become part of his ideal self); **muscles in on everybody else's act:** not to prove himself for what he is but in order to gain all, **compulsive winner, highly competitive**

bashing on regardless, does and sustains damage; the end justifies the means for him, thinks only in terms of **speedy progress** and **expediency; superficial success; narrowly self-**

related aims that aren't likely to benefit others even coincidentally

hoards, accumulates, appropriates and **clings to everything –
without valuing anything** though; may be **miserly,** certainly
**won't share or give; possessive, territorial; invasive; over-
powers** and **robs others**

'**selfish':** takes himself to be the only one who deserves to
gain/have a self; **narcissistic tendency; blind to the independent reality of others** or may dismiss it as 'unreal'; **scornful,
chauvinist, rejects what he can** in order not to have to deal
with it on his way forward, '**can't be bothered'**

or else sees others-in-themselves as a threat: '**makes' enemies,
combative, challenger** and, since he makes something universal of his personal enmity, a **warmonger; fights even with
friends,** having nothing of worth to lose but his future **he
fights to the death,** if necessary; **winner-takes-all attitude**

**demanding, manipulative, shrewdly subjects and uses others;
over-assertive, bossy; takes others for granted** – but since he
can't see others for what they are he is also **easily manipulated,
used as a trouble-shooter, soldier, mercenary etc.** and **general
battering ram; naive, clueless,** as well as 'singleminded' to the
point of being **fanatical**

fearfully-aggressive, desperate courage; seeing competitors, dangers, stumbling blocks everywhere, **worries about missing
something** and **fears betrayal; likes to be cheered and urged
on: needs moral support, needs to be given help and direction**
because he is **slapdash, nervous, over-reactive** and hence **dis-
sipates his energy in all directions, afraid to be outdone,**
which affects him in a way that makes **his aim untrue; unrealistic, lives for a 'dream',** an unattainable ideal, '**romantic'** in a
coarse sort of way

Leo

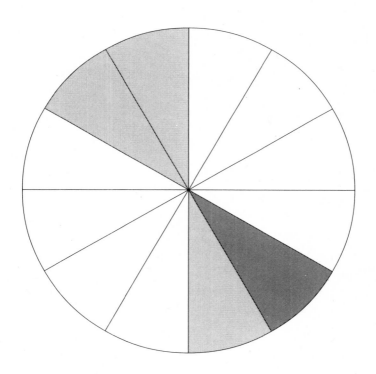

♌ Introvert
conscious function: intuition; direction of function: outward
unconscious functions: ♒ sensation, ♑ thinking, ♋ feeling
Fire: intuitive

The extravert Aries started out with nothing and had to search for
his self in his environment. Using his extraverting conscious function he could make a start right away on gaining something out
there to call 'I'. The introvert Leo, on the other hand, starts out
already in possession of all he will ever be; his identity is already
given, in the form of an established inner self. And yet, *consciously*
he is *not* in possession of it: his conscious function is directed outward, away from his inner self, and concerns itself only with his
objective environment. As an extraverting introvert, he cannot consciously contact what he is inside himself at all. One might say he
lacks introspection altogether, he literally does not know himself.

Like Aries he is doubly intuitive, both by basic nature and conscious function. But he is not using his intuition to find something
(new) to be: instead he is trying to discover what he already is.
With his conscious attention forever fixed in the outward direction, it is only out there, in he surrounding world, that he can contact his self and consciously be himself. Strange as it may sound,
he can only come into aware possession of his inner self through
contact with other. Intuitively, he approaches the objective world
with the expectation of finding all of his subjective self somehow
recognisably embodied or 'reflected' there, ready to be made
awarely his own.

The problem is, when he takes the world as such to be a reflection of his 'invisible' self, he actually finds a hundred different
'faces' looking back at him from out of this mirror world. And
without prior self-knowledge he is of course quite unable to
decide which of these possibilities of self-identification offered
him might be the right one... should he recognise himself as this,
or as that? He can try out these different faces one after the other,
experimentally so to speak – doing, saying, owning, 'being' all
manner of things – but he will only be striking unconvincing
poses, unable to tell whether he is really being himself.

Like Aries, he can only drop one option after the other. Not because of an inability to evaluate what it might be best for him to *become*, but in his case because he is unable to tell whether what he is experimentally enacting really does justice to what he *is*.

His innermost being is locked away out of his reach even out here, in this mocking multitude of possible selves, the 'real' one indistinguishable from the would-be. It is no use trying out face after face to see whether it might fit; he simply has no way of knowing what fits him. Something must be very wrong with this world: it keeps defying his attempts to find and be himself in it.

Intuitively he would really regard *all of it* as the one 'I' he is trying to discover in its objectified, materialised form: his fiery-intuitive impulse would lay hold of the whole objective world saying 'All of this is I'. Instead he encounters this disobedient, splintered mirror environment that shows him a multiplicity of 'I's. Trying them all on, in an endless succession, will never bring him any nearer laying conscious hold of his one true, already established identity. All he gains is an even greater confusion and doubt as to who he really is. He might as well give up on this impossible task. He ends up standing puzzled, faceless, lifeless, amid a clutter of too many possibilities and blames the world for being fractious.

The moment he makes use of his unconscious functions, though, the problem begins to resolve itself. Most importantly, he comes to sense ($\approx$) not only the exact nature of his inner uniqueness, but also the power of all inner being to impose itself actively on its environment, by transforming it, till it gives a fair representation of the 'inner image'.

He is now no longer a complete puzzle to himself. At least *un*consciously he knows exactly what he is looking for in the world. What he has been trying to recognise as his personal reflection in the mirror of the world stands quite vividly before his inner eye: not only informing his conscious intuitive impulse to find it and thus take possession of it, but also telling him that in order to be able to do so he needs to impose changes on his environment. It turns out that nothing around him is an exact replica image of his inner self; he is unique and all that uniqueness lies inside him. Passively recognising himself in the objective world out there is not what his life is about. And the answer to his question which of the many 'reflections' was *truly* his own is of course: none of them.

What he expected to be a complete and perfect mirror image already – and then wondered why it lacked the cohesion of unity, one-ness or 'uniqueness' – are only the basic givens of his environment that he must use as his starting point for actively becoming into objective reality. It is only when he has changed the face of the world in accordance with his unconscious image of self that he will see himself tangibly reflected or embodied there, and at last *consciously* recognise his self for what it is. Doubly fiery, like Aries, he too finds his self in an active process. Where Aries happened in the world, Leo happens *into* the world. It is not, in his case, a process of characteristic, repeated becoming of something new to add to his self, but of constantly re-creating in the world around him the self that already exists in his inner space. He has to actively extrude and express his self into the world, and impress it on the world, in order to gain it.

The existing possibilities his environment offers are no more than the starting point, the basic material so to speak, which will have to be reshaped till it takes on his living semblance. The more truly basic this material is, of course, the easier it is for him to start impressing his likeness on it. He can newly shape the relatively unstructured, and force what is malleable to conform to his unconscious vision of all he personally and uniquely is. That way he should easily be able to re-create accessibly outside himself what lies hidden inside him.

But for one thing his environment consists not only of the easily 'impressed', the world is not made of putty throughout: there are all sorts of already established structures here, and complex systems with a character of their own, not to mention other living beings with quite definite life plans of their own to pursue. It is all very well for him to sense that he must change the face of the world in accordance with his own inner givens in order to consciously and concretely 'realise' himself, but he is still faced with the 'disobedience' of most of his 'already created' environment. There is not room or opportunity enough for him to be(come) *all* he is.

He finds it impossible to content himself with limiting his self-expressive activities to modelling himself in basic clay. Just as Aries intuitively took all the world to be the stuff his nascent self could be derived from, so Leo wants to refashion all the world to bear his individual stamp. He needs to impose his vision of self, and his will to be consciously-concretely self, on all of it. Nothing and nobody can be exempt from his fiery, self-propulsive drive to transform this existing objective reality into his own materialised image. But objective reality resists his unilateral attempts to become all there is.

He is seeking control of the world, to conquer it for his sphere of 'influence', but control in effect escapes him. One moment he is making no impression at all: unyielding rock (metaphorical and otherwise) is staring back at him defiantly, most definitely unimpressed; and then again he finds a heap of fragile shards at his feet. Whatever he tries to do, he can never be sure whether he will turn out to be impotent, or wreak inadvertent havoc (not his intention at all, of course: he would protest his innocence, and complain about the unpredictability and general incomprehensibility of all that is other). The problem is, he has no precise idea what sort of material he is dealing with when he first tries to transform his environment, or how to go about his self-imposing task in an intelligent and practical sort of way.

But there is also another problem. The self he senses himself to have is, as already mentioned, 'all he will ever be': it is complete in all its complexity and there is nothing to add to it. That is to say, his 'becoming', his living changes, can not consist in adding something new to what he is, but only in *gradually* realising, objectively, more and more of his given (and one has to say, finite) inner nature. But gradualness, time, is just as unintelligible to him as all those other mysteries of the world, like concrete structure and orderly processes.

The image of his self that he unconsciously perceives ($\approx$) is really a host of images containing all the developmental possibilities given to him. He sees before his inner eye all he could become-into-the-world, a multicoloured confusion of images. But to him this vision is all of a piece, it is simple he. What to him is confusing is that the world around him seems incapable of receiving this all-inclusive imprint, or that he himself seems incapable of bringing it about. Without a proper understanding of the limitations of this objective, time-bound reality he cannot *become* what he is, a bit at a time, each new (in the world). And if he cannot become, then he is stuck in his impulsive quest for self-realisation. As long as the concrete nature of the world stays a mystery to him the nature of his self, too, remains a puzzle, for all his new-found unconscious insights.

He depends on his capacity for unconscious thought to come to his aid here. His thinking approach to the world and his life task in it ($\text{\small ♑}\rightarrow$) is pragmatic, sober, down-to-earth, with a healthy respect for incontrovertible facts and given limitations. He learns to understand and accept his environment for what it is. When he thinks about it, it strikes him as futile and impracticable to try to impose himself by actively enforcing change where change is not possible. And where it *is* possible it still takes a lot of thoughtful considering to work out how to bring about the envisaged result, step by logical, practical step. It becomes obvious to him that becoming into the world, and being in it, takes (place in) time. He learns about doing his self-materialising work in stages, bringing patience and intelligent planning to the job in hand. In retrospect he will have to admit that it was absurdly feeble-minded of him to expect his self-creating will to be sufficient to conjure up instantly a solid image of all he potentially is. He can only grow into the world, and into conscious possession of his self– or active being of it – a bit at a time. He has to unfold into life and self-consciousness from out of his 'dead' and unaware state.

To unfold like that, piecemeal, he also needs a newly thoughtful attitude to his self as such ($\text{\small ♑}\leftarrow$). When he brings reason to bear on what he is, he no longer sees it simply as the one grand-total self that includes in it all the personal characteristics, the as yet unrealised life potential, that is his. When he thinks about self he dissects it, he discovers its logical, and potentially practical, internal structure. He is whole, he is unique; but at the same time it stands to reason that there are many different aspects of self that could be considered separately. The many images on his inner screen that were all part and parcel of the one 'I' to him are now more clearly understood as being individual parts of his inner, *structured*, nature. Or to put it another way, the whole and complete Idea of him can also be seen as a set of many distinct, if interrelated, ideas. It is these singled-out ideas and images that he can now apply in practice, and in time, when he tries to influence the world so as to make it show him ever more and new aspects of all he inherently is.

The strange thing is, he applies his *finite* given self actively and intelligently to an environment that is in itself quite concretely defined, and which offers never more than very limited possibilities for self-realisation: and yet he ends up having a *limitless* range of options for new self-becoming.

He can think up no end of combinations of the parts of his whole being to embody and then 'admire' as essentially self (if never, concretely, all-of-self). Meeting his self piecemeal, as and how other (the world) allows, is the only way he can come consciously face to face with what he is. Or one might say that obeying the limitations imposed on him by his environment is the pre-requisite to imposing his nature on the world. Or, more paradoxical still, that respect for other is what finally enables him to 'be himself', awarely and alively. – Naturally there are endless ways of objectively describing him, and none of summing him up!

So it is a matter of slow and painstaking becoming, into life and self. It is no use trying to take the whole objective space around him as a replica for his inner-self space and to use it, wholesale, as a container into which to pour all his life-potential in one go. If he *could* simply decant himself into the world like that, what would he be but 'visibly dead'? There would be no living-becoming left for him to do.

He has to apply his reason and find out just which areas of life he can gain for his own personal space, and which parts of the material world he can effectively transform into a partial self-representation. He has to muster the patience to become 'real' to himself bit by bit and give up his self-willed attempts to delight in instant, limitless self-ownership. Never gaining his one limited/finite self, he gains something much better: unlimited possibilities for new becoming, 'immortality'.

His active aim, all the same, is not to live, 'piecemeal', for ever but to seek out opportunities to incorporate *all* of his self into the fabric of the world; and unconsciously he knows that he has to work patiently towards that aim, that he has to settle for taking a limited sphere of influence for his own, and that even this realm is not literally all of a piece but consists only of bits of him made substantial here and there, whenever and wherever he can find a practical, sensible opportunity. His many partial mirror images are dispersed, his realm resembles nothing like a solid, unified block, and his rule, his will to im-pose self into world, has its moments, but not much more. But to complete all this, to close the gaps in his self-awareness, in objective terms, this is the aim he is always thoughtfully and 'imaginatively' working towards.

Unlike the extravert Aries who had to collect a self together *out of* the world, the introvert Leo has something he can distribute parts of *into* the world, always more parts, with the intention of gradually filling in the 'blanks'. Where Aries went on happening in characteristic ways and never gained the sort of self that was concretely established for him, Leo needs to look for precisely that: it is not enough for him to happen repeatedly, to keep acting out of what he is. What he needs is to be able to *see himself happening*, to 'admire' the effect he has, to see something of self so firmly implanted in the structures or processes around him that when he stops in his transformative activities his self does not also stop happening/existing for him.

He needs to be able to stand still and find what he has introduced of his inner nature still taking place, or still in place: its own place which it has taken in the living world. As a self-establisher he is far less 'mobile', less impetuous than Aries. He has to make a thorough job of it, he has to make doubly sure even, before he goes on to his next project. Fluidity of becoming is not what it is about for him, becoming dependably 'earthed' is. And his earthy mentality pulls helpfully against his intuitive impulse to find all of him objectified, against the sheer impatience engendered by this all-inclusive inner vision of his complete potential.

He works away at his self-manifestation in a steady and sensible manner: proceeding cautiously, and more concerned with creating a lasting effect, establishing something that will stand the test of time, than with getting there fast. If what he has made to 'stand for him' – for part of all he is – collapses the moment he goes on to realising his next idea/image, then he will never get any nearer completing the worldly picture of the one unique 'I' he carries within him. (Of course he never gets there, and like Aries he too is 'only' a process: of living and increasing self-realisation, never complete and finished, i.e. never dead. In that sense he is a life-creator: his own.) He *does* want to rule the whole world, but the practical steps he is taking in that direction are modest and level-headed enough.

And yet practical considerations are not all it takes to ensure his success. Being sensible about imposing his self does not guarantee that his actions will be welcome in the world. It will not be enough to put a smile on all those other faces he is surrounded by who do not even vaguely 'look like him' because, for whatever reason, in their case he has seen fit not to try and impress something of his inner nature on them. And yet they too are part of the one world of which he rules only bits here and there. They will raise their voices in protest at his awful presumption to convert what is after all also their reality more and more into *his*. They will block his opportunities where they can, and regarding them merely as untouchable fixtures of his environment, to be avoided or taken into account in a purely pragmatic sort of way, will get him nowhere. He has regarded them as taboo, for the time being at least, he has written them off as wasted effort, infertile ground and unsuitable material to derive a self-substantiating response from. But even though he has left them well alone they make it clear that they resent his presence among them, his staking unilateral claims wherever he can, his changing the look of their neighbourhood without consulting them, his working studiously for no-one but himself. No amount of rational considering will tell him that they are subjects, selves in their own unique way, and not merely part of objective reality, world stuff, material that it may be possible for him to work with in his own self-ish ways.

Emotionally he is of a giving nature (♋→), genuinely interested in protecting and nurturing and helping others as much as he can. Feeling that he must contribute to the well-being of others makes him aware, at the unconscious level, that they have needs of their own, in self-ish separateness from him. At the same time, he also gains emotional access to his inner self (♋←). He develops the capacity to withdraw into inner feeling states where he can experience the pleasure of emotional wholeness, inside himself, without the need to look to the outside world for the (never reached) total 'picture' of what he is, and without the need to be constantly doing something objectively self-creating in order to contact more and more, and yet never all, of himself. This simple emotional experience of the inner 'I', in its totality, means he can relax in his efforts now and again. It also means he finds himself far less dependent now on the self-representing world around him. Above all, it helps him become even more aware of the separate nature of other-out-there.

He can't possibly continue to use all those other selves as if they were self-less and life-less material to make his own self alive and corporeal with. If he is to get a chance to see something of himself in those others, then it can only be because they have accepted something of him into their lives. His impositions will have to become gifts instead, his rule more of a helpfulness and kindness. When he puts something of self into the world it will have to be experienced as a positive addition to *their* lives by others.

Such a course of action should present no difficulty to him, though: he wants to give and he has plenty of choice, inside himself, what to produce out of himself in answer to want or preference. It does not matter to him, after all, which of the many separate images and ideas that he harbours in his inner darkness are pushed out into the light of day first. Whatever we want to see take shape in the world he too is perfectly happy to see take on form. There is no clash of interests involved. Ruling, imposing, transforming-in-his-own-inner-image can be sensitively combined with generosity, pleasing, fulfilling demands. He can 'pull out of himself' whatever it may need, responding from the depths of his being: he is more than happy to let us demand something of self from him.

He is now in effect letting the world's needs dictate to him what of himself to put forward for acceptance into life. What he is giving is his self, quite literally, bit by appropriate bit. He gives himself away and, paradoxically, gains himself thereby. – One can hardly apply the term 'ruler' to one who makes himself useful to others and supplies his many 'subjects' with what they require. At the most one could say that he 'patronises' us.

His many acts of kindness, separated in time; the various rules he institutes, according to how we can (individually) cope with them, and knowing that we will benefit from them; the material structures, distributed here and there, that represent different aspects of him but are also at the same time functional and/or a pleasure we can all appreciate; all these have to stand symbolically so to speak, in part, for the individual whole he is. But what he would most like to see, of course, is for these various fragments of his visible self to be combined, so that he can consciously grasp these scattered and far-flung images of him in their totality: as a simple objective experience that depicts him a bit more as the one *essentially* indivisible 'I' he is.

With this in mind he is constantly touring, visiting and re-visiting. Not only to make sure that what he has established is still intact, still available for him to observe, still faithfully *being* him, but also to gain the sort of overview that will give him some *objective* integrity. This is after all what he is always (endlessly) working towards, and the greatest relative success he could gain would be to unify as much as he can of his 'materialised' self.

There are limits of course to how much he can do about his 'gappy appearance' in the world. Certainly he can try to pile together inanimate representations of self, in a grand display of some of his inner wealth made visible, but then again he has to bear in mind that these were his gifts to us, to be used and enjoyed by us as much as himself. He can't hug it all to himself now; out of consideration for us he will have to content himself with the odd *public* display/exhibition/performance: for all to admire. But the 'parts' of him that he can most givingly move closer together so as to gain the maximum simultaneous experience of his self, are we: with all we have individually embodied of him, accepted as the rule of our lives etc. Again, he does not *summon* us, he invites us, and we are of course only too pleased to attend, given his customary generosity.

He never feels *himself* more summarily than when he is surrounded by his grateful dependants, his beneficiaries, his protégés, his willing executives and admirers of all he has established for himself, and for us. He has worked hard figuring out how to 'apportion' himself sensibly and sensitively, he has shown himself flexible enough to respond to our many different needs with a great *variety* of giving out of himself. He has literally torn himself apart to please us and it would be cynical to say that this was the only option he had in his search for successful incorporation into the world, that it was all he could do to gain a self-aware life for himself. He has learnt about the mutual give and take involved in becoming self in an exemplary fashion and he deserves our thanks. Now we have the chance to repay him by giving him a magnified or unified self-experience. The social or sociable side of life is by far the most satisfying to him.

To put it at its very simplest, he feeds his party guests and they in turn provide him with the sort of feed-back he needs to find himself consciously aware of who he is. And the larger the party, the more self-awareness he gains, the nearer he gets to being his complete self. We help him find his relative completeness just as he in his generosity contributes towards *our* 'completion' in a variety of ways. With our help (our presence and allegiance, loosely speaking, our echoing or mirroring him at least in part) he celebrates being real to himself: the bigger the crowd, the more 'real' he becomes. If he gives us a song and we sing along we are informing him as to what he is. And if our applauding him and calling out his name has him in raptures, it is not because he is self-besotted, but simply because he needs us to acknowledge his presence in the world in order to be himself at all, consciously.

Collectively we are his best possible mirror image, even if individually we would fail to give a good semblance of him, but then that is the latitude he has learnt to give us while he learned to delimit himself, dissect himself, and time his entries into the world well. Recognising our needs and respecting our right to individually differ and be separate from him, he is now in the position where he recognises us as well as himself (in part, at least) when he looks into this patchy, cobbled-together, not exactly perfect mirror of a world.

To 'be himself' at all he has to be content with being, in objective terms, imperfect. He may be perfectly complete, or completely perfect, inside him: in the 'dead' way of inactive potential, rather like dry, lifeless seed. And he may constantly strive to find his perfection in the world by offering it to us piecemeal: as new and valuable additions to our material existence, much needed novel ideas and renewed rules to live by, bits of characteristic behaviour we will be glad to incorporate into our repertoire because they will be of general benefit. But in the last resort his 'ruling' is a shared, mutual affair that depends as much on our will as his. His 'kingdom' is ours too and he can establish himself as no more than primus inter pares, mentor, example.

All this time he has been teaching us to conduct ourselves responsibly, considerately and helpfully towards each other, despite our primary aim to become individually established in the world; no more than he has trained himself to do with respect to us. To go back to the example of the party host: he may cater for a variety of needs and tastes, but he will also do all he can to assure the unity of the group. He will not give too much here and too little there. He gently lays down general rules of behaviour that will make sure nobody will be offended or feel left out. This is the way he works throughout. He is a fair ruler and if we are happy to accept his giving rule, then we will have to be happy to treat each other fairly, to be 'his' equals. Implementing his rule, he is setting us the personal example of realising (and respecting) the nature of others, us, at the same time as he is realising himself.

When his example has sunk in sufficiently, there will be no need for him to be placed above us. He can abdicate his top position in the secure expectation that as his co-rulers we will continue to realise him, in the way we act individually, and in the manner we govern our collective life. He offers us co-rulership – this would be his greatest success in the world and hence his most complete contact with his given inner self – but, as in everything else, he depends on our co-operation for that to become a reality. As his equals we will be the best-possible 'mirror images' he could wish for, even if it will never be a completely perfect mirror world for him, because ongoing time keeps moving the goal posts. There are always new and different parts of the one self to be distributed into the world, to be incorporated into his many new selves: partial reflection in time and space of all he timelessly and unwittingly is, inside himself.

His world-creating is no more than a fruitful self-division. Others are only 'singled-out' aspects of his hidden, all-inclusive self; they are independent of him only thanks to his basic ignorance of what he essentially is. We can never individually, or even collectively, please him altogether. He will always find us wanting, in our endless collective dividedness, and in consequence he will give us more of himself. When we begin to find him too much to take, and self-contradictory in his variety, then we will have to refuse, resist; reject some of him in favour of something else he is offering; disobey; and destroy some of what he has already established. In this way we have to share the responsibility for his becoming with him, keep him within the limits that keep him and us 'alive to ourselves'. Accepting *and rejecting* we participate on equal terms in his choice of what next to bring to life.

But not any refusenik can set himself up as a co-ruler of life. Leo shows us the ground-rules for becoming, whatever exact form that becoming may take at any moment: to give of ourselves in fairness to others, to impose ourselves into the existing world as a gift asking for acceptance. For all his constant, responsive, objective self-renewal he is of necessity a traditionalist. It is only respect for the past, the already created, the objectively established, that gives him his future. Only by building on the (and that is to say *his*) past can he unfold further, in countless variations of the parts and particles of a finite self, to populate all time with his inherent 'otherness': his internal substructure, which he can only consciously recognise outside himself, as others, us. (Another ground rule he teaches us: that respect for the/our past equals self-respect, equals respect for others.)

Whether we 'oppose' him usefully, in a co-operative dialogue so to speak, is up to us. It would help, one might think, if *we* knew the secret source of our objective existence; but made in his image, we know consciously no more about it than he does. The best we can do, following his example, is to let our *unconscious* awareness of all Inner Reality guide us. His inner reality is ours too: he has been giving it to us, bit by bit, all along. Like he we will have to be content to follow some unillumined roads inward in search of guidance, learn unconsciously to 'listen inside' before we launch into our conscious efforts.

The evidence of our eyes is never enough. We have the potential of becoming much more than the mirror currently shows us to be, and we have the choice of either passively, childlike, receiving it from him/Life, or else to tap the source for new-becoming ourselves, as his equals, co-creators of new realities. As long as we observe his basic rules, we can pull anything at all out of our common unconscious source, and set it up for a living reality, for a while.

If in trying to solve his problem of self-identification Leo makes a negative use of his unconscious functions, however, then for a start he lets himself be quite overwhelmed by this sense of his subjective uniqueness and his ability to impose it wilfully on his environment ($\approx$). He lays claim to being the only subjective reality there is, with the right to transform everything he contacts in the world into a uniformly mirroring experience of his one whole splendid self, and those spooks and spectres that look back at him when he tries to admire *himself* in the world are swept aside impatiently. They are nothing in his eyes and are only taking up his space, where *he* should be the only visible, active force.

He is ready to bulldoze the world and substitute himself for it, till everything is an unmistakable representation of him, every action his, every development initiated by him, every conclusion wrought by him. He wants to be the beginning, middle, end, everything, the Only One. Of course it does not work like that.

He is obsessed with the one (unconsciously perceived) multi-coloured image of his whole life potential. And his barely controllable urge is to *make* all that be reflected back to him from outside, so that he may come into conscious possession of it. How to go about this transformative process is the question.

It does not help any that he is so impressed with his inner vision as to be looking not so much for possibilities to transform as, impatiently, a chance of instant substitution. World should cease, and self should be. But simply knocking down what is there only shows him a damaged world; and fashioning something, somehow, from the debris leaves him looking at a very poor sort of mirror image, too. These rampaging, uncontrolled efforts only show him up as well and truly impotent.

He is all helpless intention and no sensible plan of action. He finds himself effectively caged in, debarred from life: without his proper, intended self-being. He can do nothing but rattle the bars of his 'cage' making a big and furious noise about all the many things he could be and do, if only his environment was not so stubborn.

Meantime the world is full of those spooky others he keeps bumping into, alien life forms that constitute no rival subjective presences to him of course – but what exactly are they all doing here, intruding into the picture? Sweeping living 'things' aside as a nuisance, reducing soft structures to rubble that does not then please him either, butting his head uselessly against the unyielding things of the world: he is not even beginning to make the sort of impression he is determined to make.

He is in a permanently filthy temper, restless in his hopeless pursuit of a never-materialising chance to start being his magnificent self. It seems his urge to be the Only Living One throughout does not work as simply as that. He cannot understand it. He is bitter and enraged to find his environment not obeying his intentions, exactly, here and now; that no amount of willing himself into the picture of the world meets with the self-substantiating response he would have taken for granted. To be so intensely 'self-willed' and yet effectively so self-less has him simply seething. He is 'full of himself' to bursting: and bursting with impatience, annoyance, the unbearable puzzlement of his ungraspable opportunities.

To make any sense of his situation he needs to bring his unconscious thought processes into action and, again, he does so in a compulsive, negative way. He now approaches the whole problem from a rationalistic-materialistic angle ($\mathcal{V}\rightarrow$). He comes to know that in order to be concretely and dependably effective, one has to take into account the given facts of life. And that it needs step by step doing before anything will result. There are rules to be obeyed if anything is to be accomplished. There are all sorts of principles involved that simply make it impossible for this or that to be done here and now, though it may well be possible later or somewhere else. All this he acknowledges as dry fact. It goes quite against his grain of course to accept any rules (or anything else) that do not originate from out of his self. But at the same time he also begins to take a rational attitude to his inner self ($\mathcal{V}\leftarrow$): rules, principles, the logic behind it all, the pure idea that precedes the practice, this is just another way of looking at his self.

He thinks of himself now as a body of principles, to be intelligently applied to the intractable world-stuff out there. He is the Great Idea. And the facts of life as he now understands them are clearly something to be cleverly manipulated by him and utilised for his own purpose. It is just as well then that the world is used to rules: the ground is well prepared for his coming. Neither is there any need for him to make his *own* attempts at self-creation: there are after all plenty of quite well-working agents about, capable of doing what it needs to transform the existing order into his own.

On this eminently practical note he enslaves everything that moves and does. The big idea is to stand and issue instructions. To actively impose his self as the ruling principle and then passively find himself take shape and take place. Now that he knows in concrete detail how the world works, he knows just how to frame his demands. He becomes the script, the law, the incontrovertible textbook text, the uniquely empowered instructor, and each particle of the living world is handed its share to do, according to its limited ability, soberly assessed by him, to make him at last a concrete event.

He certainly grasps the fact that there are limits to what is possible, at any given moment, and that these limits are part and parcel of his given raw material for self-realisation: the matter, the living stuff, the life events that he is using as the matrix to impress his unique likeness on. This world, as it stands, is obviously a different sort of reality to his own subjective one. A picture of imperfection to him, it is of course no kind of rival reality – just as well: any attempts to outshine his grandeur would not go down too well with him. But then again, to find himself depending on something so useless, negligible, restricted in scope, is a sore trial too. – He is very hard to please.

The question what to make of those spooky others who were no more than an inexplicable intrusion crowding into *his* mirror space, has automatically resolved itself. They are really no more than material facts to be rearranged, put in their place and given strictly logical and narrowly pragmatic instructions that will enable them to put into practice all the inimitable self he is. Pets and puppets, they can enact the perfect Idea that is he-alone, while he will sit and watch every move with the pride of the increasingly self-possessed. Or so he thinks.

He would be very lucky if his bone-dry theory worked out. The slave work-force that sprang so readily to mind proves quite unwilling to jump to his command. They have other ideas, but of that he knows nothing. All he matter-of-factly noted was that such-and-such is done by us in such-and-such a way, of necessity. Of *our* hidden underlying subjective motivations to do or not to do, and if then what, he has no idea. His one and only idea is his self, all of it, which is plenty to be getting on with of course... but he is not getting on at all, as yet. He thought he had it all worked out in his mind, how to proceed into the world – but here he is, still as ragingly impotent as before: the puzzle of the world apparently solved, but the puzzle of his elusive self as maddening as ever.

He is still stuck at the very beginning of his road to self; his life, if one can call it that, no more than an endless complaining, his demands never met. It is only his unconscious capacity for emotional contact with both other and self that finally releases his locked-up potential. His emotional approach to the world (♋→) is entirely, intensely, compulsively giving. That is to say he gives with the sort of urgency that brooks no 'No thank you' and does not ask about the readiness or preferences of the recipient. His gifts are impositions, demands to have all he has to give out of himself joyfully accepted – and no funny business like spurning any of his offerings.

When he emotionally contacts his inner self ($\mathfrak{S}\leftarrow$), sinking deep into inner feeling states, he experiences for the first time a great, restful contentment with what he is. Emotionally he is whole and complete to himself. This is so much better than anything his environment could ever show him to be that he feels quite sorry for himself when he consciously regards the world: an obviously deficient kind of reality, which *should* depict all this to him, but won't or can't.

His emotional self-satisfaction brings him to the conclusion that he is indeed a gift to the world, an urgent, pressing, much-needed gift. The more of himself he can give, the better the world will become. He never thought of that. He was demanding to be given his self. He was distributing instructions for us to act him out so that instead of a vague (unconscious) vision or theoretical principle he could become a living, obvious (conscious) fact to himself. And we said, at our most polite, that we weren't interested. We can't say that so easily when he now comes washing emotively all over us, beaming and bearing gifts.

What he presents us with are the same old binding obligations. We still have the job of making him real to himself. Naturally, he looks to us to respond to his overemotionally 'well-meant' self-imposing by acknowledging his generosity, his thoughtfulness, his good taste etc., etc. But then he will only beam the more and heap another lot of unasked-for gifts on us. And what do you do with that? He has tamed us at last, sweetened the pill, brought us into line. Kindness was all it needed to subject us to his will and he makes sure he finds out just what sort of presents tend to prove the most effective. He feeds us gifts rather in the way one fuels a machine to keep it performing and churning out the desired product. The product is he, all he is in concretised form; the machinery, the bribed slaves, that is us. He feels it is a very pleasant arrangement like that. He enjoys giving his self away so wholeheartedly, inundating us with this rampant emotions till we are completely bowled off our feet, and quite unable to protest.

Material 'bribes' apart (which he seizes from out of the existing world, just to give us the idea: that there are much better things to come, out of himself) he feels he is giving us precisely what we as mere objects, in his view, lack: essence. The subjective script: his, that is. His diktat is just what we need to complete us. It is also of course what he needs to find reflected back to him, because he would hardly wish to see himself portrayed as something automatically clanking and 'soul-lessly' robotic. Then again, if our performance does not come up to his expectations there is hell to pay.

He has our very best interests at heart, really: carrying out his will and benefiting from his unsurpassable largesse go hand in hand, so it is only in our own interest to obey him. He really does feel he knows what is best for us, even if he regards us as no more than live tools that have the job, collectively and each in our own small way, to add to his image, to enliven him, to put him into effect, faithfully act him out, contribute to the performance of him in the world.

Before long, we are caught in the kind of carrot-and-stick situation that has us thanking him profusely for the honour to serve him. Praising his name is a job in itself, in fact. At last he is what he has always wanted to be, the sole self-satisfied ruler who surveys the world around him and knows it is all his doing... indirectly... in a manner of speaking. In a superior sort of way. – And yet, despite all we do for him, he is hardly ever really content.

His narrow-mindedness makes him critical, fault-finding at every turn. His excessive emotional self-satisfaction makes him as petulant as a child when it comes to having to accept the imperfect objective mirror reality as it is. Time and space never allow *enough* of his materialised self to be accessible to him. We fuss around him endlessly. We make sure he has immense spaces to inhabit, palatial, with a commanding view. But he is still pacing, tetchy for *more*, impatient to experience something *new*.

He has the greatest collection of things animate and inanimate of all shapes, sizes, colours, all representative of his innate scope, from the primitive to the gold-encrusted and the dwarfish to the gigantic: poodles, pygmies, steam-engines, just having them around the place puffs him up as if he had personally invented or fathered them. But his delight when he is first presented with such new self-acquisitions is soon replaced by mere careful storing away, and then the eternal question: what else is there?

His vanity is a terribly complex thing. Of course he has to go dressed in glitter and splendour so that we may ooh and aah over him. But as we applaud him just as much supposing he wears rags, or nothing at all, it is entirely up to us to deck him out: all *he* cares to be clothed in is our admiration. What matters much more to him, since our appearance directly 'reflects on' him, is that *we* should look our best. Actual mirrors he manages to hold in contempt. *His* mirror is the world; silly little things like *that* will do for us, though he really can't see what *we* would want such things for. At any rate, we should be looking at *him*, and surprise him with ever new faces to acknowledge his scintillating presence with. He cries endlessly for attention, and then complains.

And he is easily bored. We put it down to his doing nothing all day but sit around and issue impatient commands, dole out gifts and honours, hand out rebukes that clearly hurt him as much as us. One would think obeying him to the letter should have him content: he makes such a knowledgeable to-do about principles, exactitude of procedure, correctness of behaviour, and all that. But no: he is fed up with our repeated performances. Will we maybe not always harp on in the same vein!

We find him quite unpredictable. He insists on a fully and properly established status quo: preserving all he has managed to become, with an eye to maybe piecing together an integral impression of his total self yet. And then he seems to suddenly change his mind: the current rules are instantly replaced by new ones and it is no use protesting our ignorance. To show that we didn't think him capable of being more than he has proved to be so far is an insult, belittling his magnificent potential! His dictatorship moves in zig-zags and we have a job keeping up with him.

He is petty and grand. So strictly repetitive that we have to stifle yawns. And quite unforeseeable in his sudden outbursts toward new self-realisation. Since he does nothing in effect but demand to have everything he could possibility be done, made and found for him and then presented to him, we have to entertain him as best we can. What with having to repeat him like a litany on the one hand (proving our 'fidelity' to his satisfaction) and surprise him with new delights the next (practically dressing up as novel 'mirror images', to broaden his outlook/insight) we hardly know when we will trip up and find ourselves out of favour. But he can spare us, imperfect tools can always be replaced by others out of his large arsenal, his retinue. Though it hurts him to do without us, he would have us know. We are momentarily injuring his image in the world with our absence;

which amounts to the same thing as attacking his innermost being.

But even the best of his 'performers', can never satisfy his urge to grasp all of his potential in one go. He knows it is never quite possible – and he never stops moaning that life is unfair to him – but there is no harm in trying. There is never enough self-satisfaction for him, even if he listens to our reports of how all over his kingdom he is the uniquely acknowledged ruler, obeyed and admired throughout, taught off by heart, set in verse, done in cross-stitch, to be found hanging on every wall. He takes our word for it. He does not really want to go and see for himself now he is scattered about, how piecemeal he is. What he does want is to be given himself in one large piece. He knows we are all building him, working him, instituting him, behaving him, dressing the part, and using the appropriate expressions, all as handed down to us, indirectly, by him. As far as we are able, that is, and with a minimum of interference from what, perversely, we seem to regard as our *own* selves. Well, he is quite prepared to humour us a bit. But where is his chance to see this collective masterpiece, himself in his (almost) totality?

Only frequent mass demonstrations of his successful and enduring rulership will satisfy this need. Crowds cheering on cue, hundreds of banners bearing his portrait, days and days of displays of products and skills all 'inspired' by him: that sort of thing will do nicely. A ceaseless coming and going to beg his advice, help and support is also perfectly welcome. The longer the queue, the more generously inclined he will be. He is happy to give something of self away (framed photographs of himself are a favourite for the less deserving cases) into the obedient safekeeping of well-trained, dependent slaves. They may be rather worthless, in themselves, but then he has no other option but use them as his worldly receptacles. He needs to take every available opportunity to dispense his precious inner essence into these living containers or vehicles.

His is no proper gradual, adaptive becoming into the world, with genuine mutual give and take, but a peremptory clap of the hands to summon the next servile non-entity trained to receive some part of him gratefully and carry it into demonstrable existence. To resist his attempted 'rape', to refuse his demanding gifts, to ignore his imposing advice, to fail, even inadvertently, to acknowledge his presence, to turn one's back on him, even for practical reasons: all these are mortal blows to him. They snuff him out a bit, they leave horrible gaps in the world map of his self. Acts of disobedience or simple failure to enact him right: it is all the same to him, all self-diminishing. Adding a personal touch of one's own to *his* repertoire is, in theory, a punishable offence of course. But increasingly he loses count of all the various known expressions of his greatness. Soon he is perfectly capable of taking credit for what *he* never ordered into existence. He is agreeably surprised at this new self-revelation. Having exhausted the normal range of self-expression, he is by now ready to hail the most outlandish things as the missing links in his complete self-recognition.

This is all his retinue of professional sycophants need to know. Mixed in with the usual flattery and adulation, good suggestions appear as from nowhere; and as the only 'place' anything worthwhile can originate from, in his view, is out of the mysterious depths of his own self, it is easy enough to put demands in his mouth. One only needs to know how to play him right. As long as one does not criticise him or poke fun at the pompous figure he cuts (one might as well take a swipe at him with the carving knife as laugh at him) one can 'extract' anything one likes from him. He is eminently exploitable.

Like negative Aries, he is clueless as regards the otherness of others and his puppets can string him along no end. But if he is not always, immediately and completely indulged, in his utter dependence, then he can only assume that somehow one has designs on his life, his self, his very being. The memory of his initial impotence when, disobediently, we would not allow him to be himself at all, sits like a never-solved existential puzzle at the back of his mind. One has to tread very warily with him, always a profuse apology at the ready, just in case that, as carrier of his self-expression, one may be infringing his existential rights, so hard won.

He is so unshakably convinced of his essential supremacy that it actually takes quite a bit of (wrong)doing on our part before he becomes permanently suspicious. He is putting everything he is into our hands; but how can he be sure we are not disobediently using it all for our own purposes? *He* does not believe in our independent existence as anything comparable to his, but unfortunately, by our wilful mistakes, we prove to him often enough that *we do* believe in it. It puzzles him and, literally, unsettles him. He thought he had set it all up to work without a hitch: he gives direction to the empty, meaningless lives of his living puppets, and they perform him, making him real to himself. What there should be to make them go off in directions of their own he can never understand. We would almost seem to be, at times, under the influence of some extraneous, malign power opposed to his own – except that *he* is the only power there is. And to assume that he might have made a mistake in the way he set up the workings of his world is equally fanciful.

But if he happens, unseen, to observe his most intimate associates, his closest dependants, his principal courtiers, who are always receiving his every word attentively, he will see them strutting around right regally in the finery he has hung on them so that they would not disgrace him in his own eyes. He will hear them using is own commands, verbatim, issued in the identical peremptory tones, but receiving the service that should be rendered him themselves. Now his suspicions are thoroughly roused. He never thought to see his life set-up from any angle but his own central position. But now he cannot fail to notice that even where he is not obviously present his life still goes on, multiplied. And now he is torn between jealously wanting to guard his 'inner substance' as exclusively his own on the one hand, and on the other the need to spread it about, bestow it and invest it in those doubtful hirelings. He has obviously been *too* successful: an indication, if it was needed, of his innate perfection. But he did not mean to spawn *complete* carbon copies of himself!

Observing them further, he notices with horror that not only do they imitate him in all respects, having absorbed so much of him, they also go on to perform variations of their own that would never, he swears, have occurred to him. Now he notices these things. They are adding a new touch, obviously thinking to go one better than he. They even quarrel among themselves who is best at being a new and improved he. It is a plot: they are using him as a basis from which to attain to heights of their own. They must be planning to rid themselves of his rulership altogether, and in effect deny him the right to exist. His darkest past is threatening to catch up with him and undo all he has become.

Now he is caught between the devil and a hard decision. He

has no choice at all but to strike first and literally destroy 'his own flesh and blood'. Heads may have rolled before, but *then* it was because he was disowning some transgressor for showing him an unacceptable mirror image of his self or rule. *Now* he has to strike against those he holds to be most perfectly self-representing, those most dear to him.

Enforcing renewed and increased obedience will be no help at all, his would-be rivals will only come to resemble him even more. He has been far too generous: they are too full of him already and now assume they are as good as he is. It was a mistake to favour them above others. The lowliest of his people, for all the imperfect representation they give of him are, collectively, doing their job quite adequately. His pride and joy, his star performers, have betrayed him.

He is unable to realise what his real mistake has been: the bad example he has been enforcing, recognising no other self beside his own. He has populated the world with too many strivers after unique recognition, and if he is to retain some hold on life and self at all then these will have to go. He has no choice but mutilate himself. Partial self-extermination, dying to much of himself in order to have a chance of subsequent self-recovery, is his only hope.

He thinks he has learned his bitter lesson now. He vows to be less excessively giving in future, to spread himself more thinly and broadly. To rely above all on the poorest specimens among his people – and may they, in their poverty, increase in number, because it needs a lot of them to do him any good. He resolves to be ever watchful and ready to cut down to size any aspiring upstarts. But as a potentially lethal despot, now grudging in his favours, he only finds himself unpopular, avoided, neglected: hardly alive to himself, that is. He is a sitting target for a judicious bit of flattery from those nearest him fishing for favouritism. This is such an enlivening, self-illuminating experience, he cannot possible resist for long.

Now he is stuck with this sorry rigmarole of periodic, cataclysmic (partial) self-destruction: loss of much of self, and repeated self-gain, in a tidal coming and going. If he does not cut himself down to size now and again then others will cut him down altogether. Though, having only too successfully become him, his successors would just go on perpetuating this pointless cycle of excessive rise to power and equally drastic, sudden fall into relative obscurity, or death.

Negative Aries was running on the spot, getting nowhere nearer his aim, never catching up with his projected self. Negative Leo goes too far, trying to encompass all and everything within his one, uniquely brandmarked, kingdom. He only succeeds in meeting up with his own beginning. He keeps ending up with a bump back in his 'infancy', and in terms of what mattered to him – *establishing* himself as an ongoing concrete event – he gets nowhere at all. Positive Leo taught us how to be rulers of life in partnership with him and each other. Negative Leo 'teaches' only helpless dependence, his on us as well as ours on him. With him for self-willed ruler we learn nothing about the beneficial mutual dependence on one another that makes us realise and respect other as part of the completeness of self, in fruitful separateness – and not to be claimed for one's own or ruled from 'above'.

He has nothing to say to us about the proper process of self-becoming: that it involves a gentle give and take, adapted and responsive; that it leads to the sort of progress into new forms of self-being which leaves only the outdated, dealt-with, outgrown behind as 'dead'. Instead, he only shows us how to overpower each other, wrangling to gain the upper hand, winning, losing, living, dying, wasting time and effort seesawing up and down instead of, together, making real steady progress: augmenting our collective self-awareness, always as far as possible, and each finding something more to 'realise', individually, as well.

His exclusive self-regard keeps blinding him to the fact that he is only abusing himself when he denies our separate existence as selves, and uses us as if we were some alien and unintelligible life form to be quickly transformed into the only thing he will 'recognise': his one-and-only self. He has estranged himself from us, from life, with his way-out claims to superiority. That he is a stranger to his own nature, and does *not* recognise himself for what he is, becomes only too apparent every time he comes a cropper, through no fault but his own. He does himself in with nice regularity, locked in his pointless and vicious circle. And stepping eagerly into his boots we do the same.

We have exalted him for the same reason that he has 'raised' us to resemble him: to admire our unrealised potential in him. When we have seen our fill to the point of overflowing with pride, we are as ready to cut him down as he is to 'sacrifice' us. It makes no difference whether he kills us, or we him. Essentially it amounts to the same thing: the one for ever unselfconscious self, ignorant in its wilful self-admiration, divided against its many parts. Self for ever unwittingly doing battle against itself – and blaming something, someone 'mysteriously' other for the neverending damage to the relative integrity of (its) life.

Some Suggested Leo Attributes

basic

unselfconscious, lacking introspection; expects to get the right
kind of 'reception'/reflection in the world: **dependent,
demanding, powerless in himself**
in his confusion as to who he is **he is easily impressed, 'hero-wor-
shipping', admiring:** mistaking other for self; **confused as to
his role in life,** including his gender (role), he experimentally
adopts roles: **acting, play-acting, strikes borrowed poses;** tries
himself out in various modes: **seriously-playful; potentially
creative, gifted**

positive

**envisages, invents, (re)creates, procreates, (re)styles, (re)models,
transforms, influences, rules over, controls; urge to imprint
his unique image** on the world, by way of **active self-discov-
ery, keeps finding himself anew; energetic, ageless**
capable of unending variety, imaginative, artistic, 'colourful',
but always **centred in himself**
**impressive, imposing, purposeful; proud: honest self-represen-
tation, sincere; self-assured, dignity, authority, good at taking
charge (of): manager, director, employer, social organiser** etc.
needs to establish himself in the (whole) world: **conservative, tra-
dition-minded; thorough, effective, unwavering in his central purpose; integrity; self-control, strength; loyal, faithful;
unites, unifies, holds together; protective; patronage, 'father-
ly'**
giving of himself: **deeply generous; serves** and **supplies; hospitable, likes to host social gatherings, gregarious, enjoys
togetherness with a broad spectrum of people; tolerant,
catholic tastes; popular, attractive; crowd-puller**
likes to 'go public', performer in search of feedback, **'exhibits'
himself/his work; figure-head; mentor;** establishes beneficial
customs and rules: **'civilising' influence, cultural force**
admiring the world that reflects him: **conscious joie de vivre,
cheerfulness; magnanimous, likes to give pleasure** (back to
others); **gratitude; mutuality, interdependence, co-operation**
fairness; courteous; pride and humility combine to make him
respect his equals

negative

excessively wilful, impatient to have his way, makes a unilateral bid for power; overestimates himself; easily enraged if his expectations aren't met and he finds himself powerless, ineffective, impotent

temper tantrums, bitterly accusing, hard to please, grumpy, always complaining, petulant, sorry for himself

self-obsessed, narcissist; totally demanding, exacts tribute: others have to contribute everything to his being-self

manipulative, makes himself centre of attraction; autocratic; arrogant, his pride knows no bounds; smugly self-satisfied; megalomaniac

show-off, exhibitionist, vain; self-dramatisation, poseur, conscious of his 'image'; sees himself as magnetically attractive: wants to be admired and idolised; takes himself to be uniquely valuable; acquires a hoard of visible riches to prove his worth to himself

takes everything at face value, naive: despite paying attention only to himself (or rather because of it) he lacks proper insight into himself/the effect he has and is ignorant as regards others; in *that* sense unselfconscious, he is easily mocked, hoodwinked, betrayed etc.; never sees anything wrong with himself; takes himself to be gifted and a gift, expects to be joyfully accepted wholesale

makes a grand show of his 'generosity'; favouritism, nepotism; patronising, condescending; expects fulsome gratitude and praise; easily feels put down, diminished or 'boxed in'

expects to be reliably served but always impatient for more, something new: self-contradictory in his demanding stability and loyalty/demanding variety (of response to his presence); traditionalist, sticks to custom, clings to certainties, narrow views and tastes, intolerant, easily offended, prude; unpredictable, changes his mind/rules, disloyal, unfaithful, never content with his 'range', sees every possible opportunity as rightfully his, promiscuous

wants to be passively entertained, basically a 'voyeur'; childishly dependent, lazy, easily bored, hectic social round, taste for the grand spectacle; taste for the unusual, even perverse; even the 'strange' is feedback to him: takes credit for others' work, ideas etc.: e.g. parental/filial pride, unwitting plagiarism so **full of self-regard** that he **fails to notice his rivals** as such; **easily exploited, deceived;** eventually **suspicious, jealous, 'paranoid':** seeing plots against him everywhere

involved in **power struggles;** never in proper control of himself, if he loses or cannot have control over his environment he may be **capable of murder** (esp. infanticide); **capable of self-mutilation** in response to a perceived threat to his 'integrity'; 'blind' to self and others, he **keeps bringing about his own downfall** as the only way of trying to regain some control over his life

SAGITTARIUS

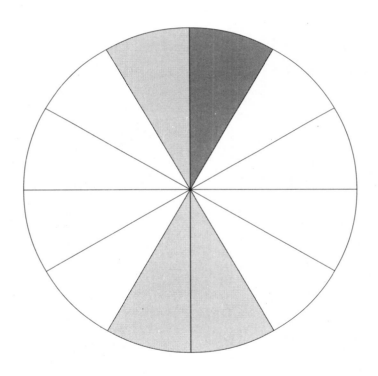

♐ **Introvert**
conscious function: intuition; direction of function: inward
unconscious functions: ♊ **sensation,** ♑ **thinking,** ♋ **feeling**
Fire: intuitive

Sagittarius, like the other two Fire signs, is entirely intuitive, both by basic nature and conscious function. Like Leo he is an introvert, but his conscious intuition is not directed outward, away from his self, but inward: he is an introverting introvert. He is fully in touch with his inner self, consciously aware of it, without requiring the world around him to tell him and show him who he is. He is self-sufficient, so to speak: he simply does not need the world, he has all he needs without it.

Leo started out with a *complete* self. This was his hidden potential, which he could realise only bit by bit, through contact with other: he *became* self, rather than ever consciously and alively *be* self, all of it. His perfect completeness, dead and unworkable one might say, unfolded into objective life and in the process became more and more of a known subjective reality to him too. Sagittarius now, is entirely inward-turned; he is effortlessly and 'without any help from us' in possession of his self. But if it was a complete self he had there, then really there would be no more to say about him: he would be forever immovably dead-perfect, an unknown and unknowable quantity. He would be a meaningless, inoperative 'gap' in the zodiac.

It would only appear to make sense, then, to say that Sagittarius' inner self is incomplete, i.e. capable of changing, being added to, becoming. And yet he can do his becoming without reference to his material environment. His is an *inner becoming*, through contact with an 'inner environment' that offers him new possibilities to make his own. When Sagittarius introverts he finds not only his self there but something beyond self. What that something is may be easiest to understand if one thinks of Sagittarius simply as having a smaller (because *not* complete) self than Leo, and then regards everything that lies beyond it as all the rest of the complete life potential that was Leo's: everything, that is, that could possibly become an objective and/or subjective reality one day.

One can speak of an Inner Reality then, which underlies all objective fact and all subjective being. This can be contacted unconsciously, as Leo did when he sensed, felt and thought about it unconsciously as, all of it, his own. Or else it can be approached consciously, as Sagittarius does when he intuitively goes beyond his self in search of new things to become, at the inner level.

Where Aries moved through the objective world in search of what to be, Sagittarius moves through this self-transcending inner realm in search of what to become, in the course of his entirely inward life. There is a wealth of possibilities all about him; none of them substantial, obviously. All of them are easily gained, however much of it he can accommodate as self. This is a timeless world, without barriers, difficulties to overcome, efforts to make. He simply 'flows' through all there is to be, becoming his way through all of it – if one can imagine a timeless flowing, becoming and unbecoming. As it is, we cannot concretely picture him at all: he has no need to 'put in an appearance' in our material kind of reality. Left to his own devices, there is no reason why he should take any notice of it at all. His attention is naturally inward-turned and we find him as it were standing beside us, not of this world at all but lost in some other-worldly sphere, totally wrapped up in this 'phantom' existence of his and happily ignorant of our struggles to be and act and become in a substantial world.

But he is *not* left to his own devices. He is a member of the zodiac 'family' and as such has something to contribute to the activities, so to speak, of the whole. Life demands his participation, whether or not he personally sees the point of that. We tap him rudely on the shoulder. And forced – contrary to his natural inclination – to extravert, he stands bemused and bewildered in the face of our kind of reality.

He is not at all familiar with such a concretely organised environment as this: the hard edges, the constant startings and stoppings, the limitations encountered at every turn. The inner environment he is used to is a fluid and unstructured whole to him: that is the way *he*, intuitively, perceives Inner Reality. He has been free to contact and acquire for his inner becoming whatever his intuition led him to next, but 'out here' he is meeting with a to him totally unnatural array of problems. There are divisions, groupings, distinctions, zones, separatenesses; it is a chopped-up and broken-into-pieces sort of world to him, and the pieces set in all manner of puzzling contexts and relationships to each other. He has no 'eye' for separate bits, and no understanding at all of these strange arrangements. He stumbles and flounders, lost in an incomprehensible maze. We shake our heads at him in disbelief, seeing his cluelessness and clumsiness. He in turn is shaking his head at us: this is a mad, simply absurd world we inhabit, and as far as he is concerned we can keep it.

Still, he is nothing if not an optimist: his 'previous' life of effort-less progress, entirely painless being and becoming, has so to speak conditioned him to be incapable of foreseeing difficulties. He certainly tries to live in our world. But his obliging attempts to contribute and participate turn out nothing short of farcical. With only his conscious intuition to guide him – now of necessity turned outward – and a 'history' of undivided wholeness, and unobstructed progress through it, he stumbles and bumbles through his new environment in a hopeless effort to contact all-of-it, in-no-time-at-all. He bumps into and trips over every detail, because details are in themselves quite meaningless to him. He rushes around trying to do the only thing that comes naturally: simply proceed – but he keeps getting entangled, in more ways than the obvious physical one, and in a panic breaks free: leaving more upset and damage in his wake. He overshoots every aim, from our point of view, because *his* aim is always somewhere away over the horizon, still trying to discover the *wholeness* here. He knocks us over (and does not help his case by protesting that he never noticed us) and lands flat on his face. His attempt is noth-ing but a comedy tinged with tragedy, full of hurts all round.

It seems, having ordered him to attend, the world is now beg-ging him to please go away again. He is obviously doing no good here; and adding insult to injury, we are laughing at him for his pains. Hurt and more puzzled than ever, he withdraws again into his mercifully obstacle-less inner world, where he belongs, where everything makes sense to him. He has no intention of trying again. He is quite happy to accept our verdict that he is hopeless-ly incapable, and to be left alone, in peace.

If the world is to benefit rather than suffer from his presence he will need to learn to make use of his unconscious functions. And if he is to be 'tempted' to try again, then the first unconscious function he uses should offer him some enjoyment to, as it were, compensate him for venturing out of his 'paradisal' inner-plane existence. At the same time it should make it possible for him to cope, to find his way around in this alien world.

These requirements are met when, unconsciously, he comes to sense ($\mathrm{I\!I}$) the objective world around him. He now has a chance of grasping its physical nature in detail, as well as the logical and functional connections that exist here. This is a novel experience to him: fragment after fragment to be examined; fascinating and enjoyable things in themselves which momentarily arrest his attention, each a microcosmic whole in its own right – he can get quite lost in his contemplations. But at the same time he also senses how they are all linked and related, how they are part of a web-like organisation of cross-connections. This is even better: his intuitive need to be able to contact anything in any direction – to 'flow freely' as he is used to doing – is at least given some scope by this system of interconnections. He is now no longer entangled in, held captive by, a lot of hard facts beyond his comprehension; rather he can now savour each separate item he comes across, and then see where else it might lead to.

The puzzle of what he experienced as a fractured and unpleasant world seems to have resolved itself. Now that he can see it for what it is he finds it most agreeable (and he is not fussy in what way he has his senses excited, it is all a revelation to him) and since the parts of it all hang together in a most satisfying way, it can hardly be said to be fractured at all. He no longer falls over things because he failed to notice them as such, in their separateness, nor finds that he needs to go charging past them in an effort to make sense of the whole. Seeing each thing clearly, as well as the way it connects up to its neighbours, has given him a pretty good grasp of the organisation of his new environment. He should be able to find his way about in it without doing or sustaining any damage.

He may see the basic logic of things hanging together, one thing leading to another (and the whole system being flexible enough to allow him a freedom of movement of sorts here). But without some more serious thought regarding the concrete why's and wherefore's of material existence he does nothing all day but enjoy and 'play'. He has been tempted out of his inner isolation in order to contribute something, to participate usefully in life, but all he does now is gaze at and taste of the delights this world has to offer, going on impulsively from one thing to another, or rearrange the movable parts of this marvellously pliable environment at random, playfully. From the point of view of coming to terms with the harsh necessities that are part of objective life he is still ensconced 'in a world of his own'. We tell him that his simply having fun here is not the idea, but how is he to grasp that when he understands nothing of necessity, or the purposeful uses of the things he is toying around with, or the things we urgently need to do while all he can 'think of' is playing games.

As he *needs* nothing, in himself, from the world, he can of course only potter about in it in an ultra-relaxed style. While we are, of necessity, strenuously pursuing our self-related aims, he wanders about among the flowers with a perpetual grin of happy contentment on his face. He not only annoys us, he is a hindrance, he inadvertently undoes our work, he brings all traffic to a standstill with his momentary absorptions and shows an alarming disregard for permanent fixtures with his butterfly habit of proceeding coherently but inconsequentially and quite unreasonably from one thing to the next. We chide him for a fool and ask him what does he *mean* by the silly-useless things he does?

It had not occurred to him that there might be *meaning* in this reality of ours. He had seen it purely as a form of entertainment. For meaningfulness he has his inner realm to turn to (and would be inclined to assume that we do likewise). Every time he can't make sense of *this* world he lets his conscious attention flow inward again. He not only never loses touch with his, and the wider, inner reality, he actively uses it as a way out. When the going gets unpleasant he simply absconds inward. And every time things require a rational understanding he is not capable of, he has recourse to intuitive inner-knowing. If we try to explain to him what life is about, we only find him staring unseeingly into far-off space. And before one knows it he is wandering about with an abstracted air again, threatening to knock things over and definitely 'not altogether there'. The world despairs of him, and lets him know in no uncertain terms. But his only response is, in turn, to despair of the world and offer to go AWOL altogether. Obviously he has still not got his feet firmly enough on the ground.

The nature of his unconscious thought processes (♑→) provides the additional pull earthwards that he needs. In his thinking he is truly down-to-earth, pragmatic, soberly rational, making up for the excessive 'levity' which we have been accusing him of. He begins to consider the practical uses of things, rather than just sensing them for their own sake, so to speak. He learns about reasoned and principled planned action. He begins to understand how necessity makes of the related phenomena of this world a system of meaningful mutual dependence – rather than just seeing a wealth of possible connections *as such*. He gains a new respect for concrete reality, with all its limitations. There is meaning here, too: embedded in the laws of nature, laws of conduct, rules and regulations that serve the purpose of necessity. Now that it actually makes some kind of sense to him, his adopted environment strikes him as far less weird and eccentric. He also begins to think of himself (♑←) as needing to contribute to this working out of earthy, earthly purpose. He has a job to do, to prove himself in action, to make the 'content' and wider-ranging abilities of his inner self stand in the world as a valuable, even necessary, addition. All he formerly was and became in effortless innerness now strikes him, at the rational level, as a disembodied idea that needs to find its validation in practice. At last he understands that he has to *apply* himself to this business of living among us.

But what precisely is it he brings with him to apply, to work into the practice of life? The aware innerness that was all the world he knew, before he was made aware of another reality out there. And his prior experience of intuitive 'insight' into the whole underlying nature of things, before he came to see, and then logically comprehend, the material nature of actual, separate, objective *things*. He has to ask himself what sort of contribution that makes to the working of the world as he now understands it.

He approaches the problem of makings sense of life from quite a different position to that of the usual earthy reasoning we employ, adding together all separate known bits and pieces, 'facts', in order to try and arrive at a meaningful sum total. Unlike us, he started out with an intuitive grasp of the always meaningful whole: the inner-reality potential that embraces everything past present and future in a completeness never found in the concrete world with its time-bound appearances and disappearances of potential fact (as shown in Leo). What objective reason can never arrive at – literally for lack of enough 'bitty' evidence available at any one time – he from his position as a newcomer to this limited, factual thinking can understand effortlessly: that material reality is only a special state, a happening in space and time, of the wider Inner Reality he knows so well.

There is his prior subjective experience of all Inner Reality, his 'history' of ceaselessly becoming his way through the full range of it, repeatedly and yet timelessly – so hard to grasp logically, but maybe best described as an aware subjective acquaintance with all life potential in its meaningful entirety, and an ability to turn inward and search intuitively for everything missing from factual, objective experience. And now added to that he also has an unconscious but quite concrete understanding of the material world, with its limited range of structures and processes to be encountered in it, as well as an increasingly successful conscious involvement in this world. Together, this adds up to the *aware* recognition that the outer life mirrors the inner, if imperfectly, always partially, over time.

Leo as (re)creator of the objective world furnished us with the *practice* of this. He even invited us to share in his work. But as an impulsive creator who was not consciously aware of the source of his doings he could not really enlightened us about his/our origin. He did not consciously know where he, and what he kept putting into the world through effecting creative changes, came from. To Sagittarius in his initially totally unworldly state of complete innerness, all *that* is entirely familiar. Unfortunately, since this 'otherworldly knowledge' of his, or his free access to it, is of an exclusively intuitive nature, we cannot expect him to enlighten us along rationally comprehensible lines.

When Sagittarius understands concrete necessity to be the result of an imperfect birth of inner meaning into an 'embodied' state, this recognition finally convinces him that 'our' world is his too, that he is not as out of his element here as he considered himself to be. And it is his wisdom – combined effect of insight and applied reason – that will have to serve as the best contribution he can make to objective life. He takes it to be his duty to mediate between the two worlds, inner and outer. To add glimpses of far-ranging, time and space transcending insight to our earthbound views, our imperfect reasonings which we derive from the narrow spectrum of concrete facts known to us. Having learnt to sense and think like a properly worldly creature gives him the freedom of our world as well as his own: he is at last in a position to apply himself effectively, in a concentrated effort, within the limits of the situation.

He is now ready to seek out eagerly every opportunity to impart his message, to stretch our horizon so that it may take in an awareness of a meaningful Inner Reality and our own personal share of it, in personal inner-being. But as none of this is a 'fact', strictly speaking, not amenable to reason that is, his fine and fiery lectures fall on pretty stony ground. He is rejected as a foolish or eccentric babbler and accused of dabbling, perversely, in the 'unreal'. We dismiss him as too fanciful altogether with his wild talk of the unseeable and unprovable. We thought we had him cured of his nonsense at last and made him see some reason, but he seems worse than ever.

And yet there are times when one might almost believe him; or at least find him useful. He has a peculiar habit of 'predicting' the future, or otherwise supplying us with quite unknowable information out of the blue. But when he tells us that this is nothing strange at all, that it is simply all *there*, in some other dimension that he can't exactly point to, and then flaps his arms helplessly lost for words, or has recourse to strangely picturesque comparisons that are meant to be 'symbolical', just to give us the general idea, and advises us to look *inside* us – where as far as we are informed there is nothing to be found beyond entrails and orderly vital processes of a physical nature – then what does he expect but that we laugh uproariously, with just a hint of unease. It is enough to tempt him to give up, to retreat into himself again and leave us to our own devices.

Emotionally though (making use of his remaining unconscious function), he is of a giving nature ($\mathfrak{S}\rightarrow$). He feels he has to offer his insightfulness as a gift where and whenever he perceives the need for it, irrespective of whether it will meet with easy acceptance or stand in danger of being rejected. When he *thought* about his place in the world, the work he had to do here, he thought in terms of making a considered attempt to prove himself useful and acceptable, as far as possible. But as a giver he 'thinks' primarily of the needs of others; walking out on us because in our ignorance we glibly reject him out of hand would not feel right to him at all.

In so far as we all have an inner self that can draw sustenance for its becoming from a wider Inner Reality, we are all in need of his teaching. Just as he initially aimed inward with respect to his own personal being and becoming, he now addresses himself predominantly to what is inner in us. He has gained for himself the recognition that 'our' reality is also his, and now he offers *us* the recognition that 'his' reality is also ours. We may be a bit slow to respond to that – seeing no more need to make an effort to introvert than he saw any reason to extravert, as it were – but this is no conclusive proof to him that we don't stand in need of his help. He knows only too well, from personal experience, that the gulf between inner world and outer is not so easily bridged. And why should it be any easier to take the necessary steps from outer towards inner? He is aware that by widening our horizon inwards he can make us *whole*. And while this may not exactly pay any instantly appreciable dividends for us, he is still responding to a need every bit as real as the needs of an empty stomach.

And yet, for the most part, we simply refuse to swallow any of what he has to tell us. Solid food offered on plates we can see the purpose of, but this enthusiastic preaching he does about an inner source for inner growth seems to fulfil no purpose at all – unless, unconsciously at least, we are already sufficiently in touch with our own inner reality to be aware that this, too, has its needs. He is constantly discouraged by the reception he gets from us and might easily take to 'preaching to the converted': exclusively making his insights available only to those he finds receptive, those who would have the least need of him that is. In that case he would soon find himself redundant. But if he offers his gift to all, he is constantly threatened with ridicule or with being evicted as a time-wasting nuisance, or even accused of peddling lies and fabrications fit to deceive sober citizens. To gain inner strength for his task, though, he can periodically withdraw into himself, emotionally (♋←). If he can constantly renew his faith in himself in this way, unconsciously, there is no need and no temptation to consciously abscond back into his inner world in the face of all this uncomprehending opposition. A feeling of inner security helps him to carry on.

The separate-particle nature of his environment may no longer worry him, but consciously, intuitively, he still expects it to be a whole-world. We should all benefit then, it at all possible, from the new inner awareness he is trying to give us. It has to be said at this point that the whole for him is so much more now than all of Inner Reality, or all of the material world as it partially and imperfectly mirrors it: it is now *both* these worlds, combined and interacting. It can be seen then that *his* horizon has been stretched, towards substantiality; and *he* is completing himself, through interaction – and not that *he* ever consciously felt the need for that!

His life task, then, consists of two things. With respect to himself, to connect up his (and all) inner-being to objective-doing: in obedience to the newly perceived correspondence between the inner and outer worlds, and to necessity, and the needs of others. And with respect to us, to reconnect our objective-living to our (and all) inner-being. For him it is a birth into *living*-wholeness; for us into living-*wholeness*.

Simply speaking, what he would like to see is that we begin to let inner-being inform our actions, consciously so. He wishes to help make of worldly action and inner motivation a new and aware oneness. To make us whole as subjective/objective beings conscious of themselves as such. And also, by leading us inward, to reconnect us with a wider 'inner motivation' that stretches far beyond our personal inner potential, but out of which we can gain new possibilities that would not have been available to us in our given, imperfect environment.

When we hear him holding forth about inner motivation, and not just ours but one that allegedly surpasses our and is simply perfect compared to more mundane options, then we begin to suspect him of moralising. Quite rightly: he *is* telling us that there is a more reliable source of 'ideas' what to be and do than what one's environment would suggest or demand, or any amount of clever ideas we might derive from observing the world. But at the same time he is telling us about a wider range of possibilities, and an inner freedom to be gained, and that at least sounds a bit more palatable.

Once we start listening, we find that despite the deep seriousness of his subject he does not actually drone on about it sombrely. His intuitive drive has him ranging through all the aspects of it, and beyond, with the enthusiasm of one pouring his inner self into a newly discovered world: our (more or less) receptive selves. If despite quite a keen sense for the appropriate wording (II) and a good grounding in sober reasonableness ($\mathrm{\mathring{y}}$) he tends at times to get a bit carried away – inward as it were – with his oratory, his inspired and rather incomprehensible flourishes stand perhaps the best chance of all: they may just pull us along and awaken the first glimpses of intuitive insight into that inner world which we are also part of.

Having discovered a useful 'outlet' for himself in a world where his example is needed, his concern is with providing us with an *in*let into his kind of being. He is opening a door to a new world for us, and he would not lay claim to it as being 'his'. He is inhabiting a wider reality now that encompasses both worlds; sharing his formerly exclusive domain with us would in the circumstances not strike him as being worth calling hospitable or generous. He had all he needed for himself right from the start, so why should he not be 'generous'? He counts himself lucky compared to us, having observed our struggles. If he has any obligation towards the world, as he thinks he does, then it is surely to help us gain access to this same fortunate inner life. At any rate, he is making free use of *our* good fortune – the fun that worldly, sensual experience is for him: if anything it is merely a fair trade-off if he introduces us to something long precious to him but new to us.

He always presents himself with a 'light-heartedness' that has us wondering where he takes it from. He refuses to let the imperfections of our world cause him any real despair. He takes them for granted, seeing them as part of the meaningful order of all things. Being in touch with a more perfect reality, without the flaws inherent in substantiality, he can't really take too seriously at all the usual stumbling blocks and minor afflictions that take up most of our time and effort here. He cheers us up. He also gives us hope: past-present-future is what we should bear in mind, he tells us, rather than let the 'real' experience of the present moment count for everything, at the expense of an equally real future to come, for instance. And not let the weight of material fact blind us to the truth.

He does not of course deny the validity of fact, he knows it and respects it. But truth is a different matter altogether, something that cannot be grasped if one only employs the objectively rational faculties: dissecting, subtracting, and then adding things up – we never find *enough* to add up, as long as we are inextricably entangled in the situation under review. To grasp the whole-truth of a situation we always need to project ourselves beyond it. And if we are to make sense of our objective life situation as such, our earthbound, matter-ruled lives, then we can only do that by projecting ourselves altogether away from the material world that 'contains' us. We have to cast ourselves inward in search of true understanding; there is no other direction we could take.

This is where he is trying to lead us: to step right out of this matter-world and with the wisdom of insight and overview to 'get on top of' fact and see it for the wretchedly small collection of details it is in the larger context. By the same token the moment becomes only a curious detail of the flow of time; and time itself, when viewed from the inner space, also becomes no more than part and parcel of this 'untruth' of material life: this always imperfect, always gappy representation of *all* that underlies it.

In personal terms this can be understood as meaning that we can never apply *all* we are inside ourselves at any given moment, in any one situation – as Leo was forced, unconsciously, to acknowledge and act accordingly. If we consider only our *outward* being and doing, we have to admit that we are always living a 'lie': acting out the untruth of a mere part-truth. There is always more to us, inside ourselves, than we can usefully, practicably, admissibly reveal in action. More even than we realise, unless we also live consciously inside ourselves. In our concrete doing, being and becoming we will always be incomplete, imperfect, that is the fact of the matter. But the truth of us lies inside us: where nothing is forced by circumstance to adopt a momentary and diminished shape. In here we are free to be our whole selves, truly ourselves, and from this position we may reconsider what of us, and in what manner, we have been presenting in the world of material fact – if anything much. Maybe we will find that the inner self has been lying dormant, in terms of being objectively active, and instead of our actions mirroring at least some of what we essentially are, they have only been empty echoes of the prevailing environment.

Once we manage to distance ourselves from factual reality, so as to be no longer wholly identified with it, no longer caught up in its dense, obscuring misrepresentation of truth, we find relief and hope in the wider prospects open to us. We can even find it in us to laugh at the fuss we have been making over the little issues of life, and equally at the silly, serious-faced roles we have been adopting under pressure of necessity. We can find new hope, new untried possibilities, in ourselves (and beyond). We can laugh at ourselves. This is no mean achievement for Sagittarius, if he can give us laughter and hope – he who was once a figure of fun to us (we managed to laugh at him because we did not experience him as a proper part of our world, i.e. we had the necessary distance to see his first stumbling attempts for what they were), and who was equally considered an unmitigated disaster, a hopeless case.

Viewed from the inner space, necessity itself takes on a different meaning for us; or rather it takes on meaning for the first time. It is not, as we had previously thought, simply an addition of hard facts, a cumulative effect of life's material demands. Once we 'rise above' the situation we can recognise necessity as being indispensable to life and accept it with much better grace. We manage to be philosophical about our setbacks and our momentarily thwarted efforts. There is an inner contentment to be had even in the face of our 'real' misfortunes.

But teaching, preaching and generally holding forth with great gusto at every opportunity is not the only way in which he leads us away from our customary locked-upness in objective fact and reason. True, he no longer sneaks off altogether to his inner world when he can't cope here but goes to and fro, actively (re)connecting these two related dimensions. But there are times when the clamour of material life is too much for him. Crowded and overloaded with sensory input and the physical demands of life, he has to find refuge for a while in a quieter environment or else be pulled away altogether from his inner anchorage. The places he seeks out, and by example recommends to us, are of the kind that most resemble his origin or 'inner home': tranquil, untrammelled, uncharted. These are the wild and barren landscapes that fail to present a picture of usefulness – just as he was once not useful, but simply was. The towers of arid rock that baffle any attempts to extract some good sense and reason. The wide vistas over equally incomprehensible 'empty' desert spaces, which leaves us robbed of the usual ceaseless chatter of our senses. The boundless nonsense of an ocean. All this he can show to us wordlessly. Its very failure to impress us in the way we are accustomed to being impressed by our environment has us stranded in a deeper contemplation: trying to read between/behind/beyond the lines of what makes no kind of conventional sense to us. Surrounded by all this alienness, we find our inner selves. And by showing us the nearest thing to what we would consider 'nothing' he makes us see the absurdity of expecting *everything* to be hard and fast fact.

We begin to have an inkling of what he meant when he was lost for words. And yet none of this can really be said to be new to us. If Aries led the way in searching out the new that was to become the foundation, or past, of the self; and Leo established the existing self as a known fact; Sagittarius essentially points us back to our true origin, the underlying inner matrix in which both old and new have their timeless existence. Reconnecting us to the 'timeless past' he also puts us in touch with the potential future in its purest, most perfect state – not the world-embedded 'future' that Aries was seeking out. In other words, this is a chance of a *totally* new beginning. In effect he leads us to review our situation: to check our collected established absurdities against something like the original meaning or intention of things, and to make a truly new start from out of this wider awareness.

We have had our personal innermost space 'enlightened', and more, been shown an Inner Reality as such. Our own hidden potential has been revealed to us, and equally something at least of the Motive Force that underlies all worlds. In consequence we are no longer free to aim for anything at all that strikes us as possibly worth aiming for, in the world. But on the other hand we are also no longer restricted to playing out the circumscribed roles that our finite, given personal potential dictates to us. Instead we now have the capacity for conscious growth: that is to say, directed aiming based on a true, inner intention. As well as a chance of self-realisation which constantly renews itself, out of a wider fund of potential then the limited personal one. The strange thing is that though we are now to all intents and purposes bound to consciously obey what amounts to an inner code, or law, we are only now in the position to become freely, and fully self-awarely.

But again, solemn exhortations and admonitions are not his style. From his point of view whatever has gone wrong can always be put right and nothing is ever lost but time. What does it matter if all our past striving has been shown to be foolish, now that we have this new wealth of intuitive insight: the real foundation of lasting success. When we now consciously apply our inner understanding, we are in the best possible position to recognise the right direction to take, the best approach, the most propitious moment, *and* the truly responsible thing to do: that which ties in *meaningfully* with everything, even the future.

What this means is that 'seeing our chance' and taking it, putting it into action, we are enacting not merely a self-ish plan divorced from overall meaning, but also some part of the whole Plan from which all growth and development ultimately stems (either by the circuitous route: our given possibilities which are already, and inevitably imperfectly, 'materialised', and without which neither Aries nor Leo could have proceeded to attain their conscious selfhood – or by this new, direct route of conscious, insightful development: independent of the mistakes of past and present which we 'inherit' when we enter the world).

We will hardly pile up mountains of riches now, and still not make it a perfect world, but what we gain and establish – because it surpasses a narrowly self-related intention – will outlast and surpass all other gains, constructs and attempts to make the world run along our lines. Knowing and obeying at least some of the underlying meaning of what we are, and are part of, we find ourselves increasingly 'lucky'.

If we can follow him this far we are ready to celebrate. This is the easiest way of linking the wider inner reality to the outer reality we inhabit. The Sagittarian feast is an expression of joy at our new-found inner riches. Not an occasion to aim straight for the best bits of the buffet, Arian-style. Nor an indispensable Leonian display of inner 'worth' made visible at last. It has a symbolic character rather: the potential for inner growth is portrayed in material increase, in recognition of the truth that the inner qualities find their counterpart in material life. When we celebrate with Sagittarius what brings us together is our common quality of 'innerness': because what is being celebrated is the realisation of the One Reality that encompasses both the inner and the outer life.

The dancing and singing are an active overflowing into deed uncompelled by any necessity. This is a tribute to our essential freedom: activity engaged in to no (self-seeking) purpose, and freely shared in this new 'community' of innermost selves. This is joy generated freely – not enjoyment staged as a device to 'feel more alive and real', as Leo does. Nor is it easy company kept as a respite from our difficult and divergent daily pursuits, as Aries does, but a genuine 'rising above' (not just laying aside, for the moment) all difficulties and differences and disputes. This is peace and happiness earned by nothing more nor less than a determined struggle forward-inward; and the establishing there of an inner realm where we know ourselves for what we are. The feasting on material goods, meanwhile, is a symbolic tribute to the life of matter as the twin reality of the life of inner essence, or spirit.

Sagittarius' detractors, as always, will have something to criticise about such outbursts of senseless high spirits, giggling at nothing, and cavorting around for no purpose: it is quite deplorable how he has misled us with his airy absurdities, this wastrel who never did do anything but fool around. In their incomprehension, unfortunately, they are excluded from this celebration of the one comprehensive Reality in which action and self-expression are at last free from the demands of having to search the world for a new or a 'real' self.

We have come 'home' to our inner selves: thanks to Sagittarius who left his inner home for no benefit to himself, initially – though once firmly rooted here he, too, found himself stretched and growing into new possibilities of being. A 'free spirit', he did his duty bringing us the message of *our* freedom. This newly-won freedom entitles us to be truly what we are, in the enclave of our inner selves, unmolested by outer reality; and to find inner growth, independent of the opportunities our environment offers us for new becoming. But at the same time it newly imposes on us the duty to obey the demands of the inner self, and of the wider meaning and purpose we contact through and beyond it. Positive Sagittarius combines the best of both positive Aries and Leo and raises their contributions to a new level of full (intuitive) awareness: we are now free to act *truly* 'selflessly', and can express as a *totally* free gift what (our) inner reality would demand – and we literally jump for joy at such a deal? 'They' will for ever shake their heads in morose perplexity at such stark nonsense.

One might think that, entirely introverted and not aware of lacking for anything inside himself, Sagittarius might not stand in danger of letting his unconscious functions act in the negative way of compulsions – but quite the contrary. Looking at it from a purely practical point of view, one must picture him not as inhabiting some 'other world' so much as standing helpless and unable to participate in our everyday world, constantly urged, even forced, to abandon his entirely internal life. It is then only too easy for him to succumb to the temptation to simply turn himself altogether 'inside out', to so to speak overshoot the proper balancing point between inner and outer life. To 'forget about' his innerness while trying to find a corresponding easy happiness, untroubled wholeness and unlimited progress in the reality that surrounds him. He gets caught up in a compulsive need to sense (♊) the concrete world, not just in all its separate parts but also as a connected system where all material phenomena are somehow related. Quite simply, no sensual pleasure is ever enough for him, but it needs to lead on to the next. Soon the whole of sense-experience becomes something of an addiction to him: he would guzzle regardless and without ever stopping. He knows no limits, in his inner world there were none; likewise his own inner 'guidelines' were never restricting but liberating and growth-producing (his inner, effortless becoming). He has done a complete about-turn and is directing his conscious intuition exclusively towards his outer environment, pulled along by an unconscious need to extract from the sense-able world around him as much as he possibly can. His material environment is now supposed to supply him, palpably, with everything that formerly his inner world alone offered him (in *in*substantial ways). He abandons his completely satisfying state of innerness for a state of sensual outward-directness, and on to this he projects all his inner 'habits', unmodified. He has turned himself into a *demanding* extravert, with limitless expectations.

But of course he comes up against restrictions on all sides. He wants to taste all the world, but a lot of it is woefully inaccessible to him, at least for the moment. The best he can do is to make up for this missing dimension of an ever forward-proceeding limitlessness with enlargement, amplification, a generally manic piling-up and running around fast, in circles if necessary: scooping it all up with eyes and ears and every taste-bud clamouring for more.

He sees to it that his music is always loud, his car invariably fast, and for the sheer enjoyment of the taste of things he overeats. His greeting is a bear hug: every touch has to be a satisfying squeeze. His voice rings out a delight to his own ears (and his throat, where it leaves an interesting tactile sensation). His laughter, also more to do with what is becoming a self-stimulating habit than with humour, is uproarious. He is over the top, he is all over the place, he truly knows no limits. Anything is grist to his mill and one need not waste quality on him, just sheer quantity will do. All this loudness and much-too-muchness has a desensitising, coarsening effect on his rampant sensuality. He is a vulgar all-round glutton and it makes no difference to him whether he inhales the fragrance of best incense or the tail-end of burnt stew, just so long as it is a *big* olfactory experience.

He, too, celebrates. But there is nothing symbolic here, this is very much the 'real' thing. His parties are orgies: a riot of noise, colour, consumables and enjoyables of every description; intemperate indulgence multiplied to the social level, for maximum effect. But behind the surface appearances he is a poor exile, loudly celebrating his sadness away.

For what has he let himself in for? Having himself dictated to by the demands of his senses, he has sold himself into captivity: he is captivated by physical pleasures. In the course of his strenuous extraverting his self has lost all touch with the inner region. He is 'empty' and, whatever he may pretend to himself, he knows it. His material environment is now supposed to fulfil all the requirements of his self for its further development. But this is a restricted, withholding, counter-demanding sort of environment that can never meet his needs in the way he expects. No matter how hard he eats, drinks and makes merry, he still does not make ends meet: the sum total of his rich, exclusive world-experiencing is still impoverishment.

Without his innerness he is at the mercy of every likely-looking substitute that promises a taste of freedom (we call him a 'libertine' for that) and effortless gain: to provide him with his future. But his high hopes of equipping himself with an adequate imitation of his inner world from out of the material provided by the world of his senses, end up deflated over and over again. His would-be easy life style flounders on the rocks of feasibility. Both his overdoing and his lazy nothing-doing can only be carried so far and, to take it at its most literal, there is a limit to how often even he can make himself be sick, after taxing the capacity of his stomach to full stretch, and start feeding his taste buds all over again. And since he knows nothing of having to *earn* the pleasures he so freely indulges in, he is living off our back. Life is one big party and he gatecrashes with not a care in the world – till we stop him, painfully, in his tracks.

But fending for himself he finds impossible. He expects to simply find everything, to find everything possible, to help himself (in the passive sense). Catering for his own excessive needs, wresting new life possibilities from the world by dint of hard work, forming an intelligent plant to cope with the necessary steps it takes to gain the gratifying experiences he desires so much, all this he finds impossible: he can't help himself (active sense) even in the simplest matters. He wouldn't know how to fry an egg. If one suggests that he make his own coffee he is well and truly stranded in this merciless world he has 'emigrated' to, lock stock and barrel, and is making such a big self-sustaining noise in.

When he finally has to admit his limitations, when his unrealistic expectations are confounded once too often, he looks in vain for an escape route. He can no longer absent himself from this disappointing, captivating world. There is no 'insight' to come to his aid either. He is held here in the grip of his extensive sensual desires and the way back inside is barred. He is marooned, exiled for good.

For something resembling relief he can only turn to the nearest physical substitute for innerness: a hole in the ground to hide away in. Or, as a slight concession to comfort, the dark cave underneath his blankets: there he can cower and refuse to let anything impinge on his senses, for the time being. Locked into this artificially maintained indifference, he tries to pretend to himself that this inadequate world means nothing to him after all, that he is able to rise above worldly matters. He sadly declares himself immune to the pleasures of food and drink. Nothing will tempt him, ever again.

But the 'timelessness' of unfilled hours – unfilled with hectic bustling about among the concretely enjoyable things of life, that is – stretches ahead truly empty. This is only a pretend inner realm he has crept off into. And now he feels the double affliction of missing the genuine inner experience *and* missing the worldly experience he has become 'addicted' to, even though it never proved enough. And all this absence, absurdly, weighs him down with the pain of it. He is not used to absences of any description, only to having more at his disposal than he can possibly accommodate. Pretending he does not need the world won't solve his dilemma. He can't do with (it is proving too hard to get) and he can't do without (there is nothing inner left accessible to him). His 'depression' is a pointless exercise, not even a true attempt to regain his lost 'paradise', his innerness, but only a material mock-up of unworldliness: he hides in a darkened room and declares himself inappetent.

But his withdrawal symptoms will soon get the better of him, his fingers drumming restlessly for lack of something to grasp, voices chattering in his head incessantly, to make up for the silence he can no longer bear. And his innate optimism soon has him wondering what the world might offer him if he had another try *now* – as if it might have improved categorically in the meantime. We will be so glad to see him back and recovered from his 'illness' there will be no need for him to do anything but enjoy the treats we push his way to speed his convalescence. – By the time he hits his nth depressive phase we may be convinced that he is doing it on purpose, which is substantially correct but rather unfair: he truly can't help himself. He suffers from a terminal inability to come to terms with the restrictive nature of the world as such, and he can't think what to do except proceed in a vicious circle of ups and downs. But what we take to be his 'ups' are actually the lowest points of his manic immersion in worldly excitements, and what we call 'downs' are his flunked attempts at rising-above, to regain his inner peace and contentment, *without* relinquishing his hold on sense-reality. He is truly captive, on a seesaw of his own devising. Like negative Aries he is proceeding nowhere fast; like negative Leo he marks time impotently.

To release him into new possibilities his unconscious thinking (♑→) comes to his aid, allowing him to consider his situation from a rational angle. But since he lets his thinking become just as much of a compulsive, imbalancing force that dictates his doings to him as his sensing, the rationalistic, concretistic, materialistic approach he adopts now does nothing to make him more temperate. Now he coldly assesses how best to make easy gain. The plans he formulates are cleverly designed to ensure that the rule of necessity will not stop *him* in his tracks any more. And not being one for wasting time when he is urgently considering his future, he is always trying to figure out the most effective short-cut. The brick walls he used to run into unwittingly, not knowing what had hit him now that he could not proceed where he wanted, become clearly identified in his mind as obstacles to be outwitted with ever concentrated intelligent effort he can throw at them. Life becomes a carefully staged campaign. – And we are the buffers he plans to use, part of his strategy, to keep the inconvenient demands life keeps making at arm's length.

His rational attitude to himself (♑←) convinces him that he knows more than enough to cope with the contingencies of life. He can't, in retrospect, understand what could have made him despair and stand helpless. The more he thinks about himself, the more it strikes him that he is a truly superior being: in possession of the complete and absolute knowledge of all the rules and principles that govern life. He should have no problem proving himself in action. He reckons his logistics to be faultless and his reductionist understanding of objective processes to be complete: quite enough in itself to earn him the role of leader. And has he not always been a being of a higher order, who by 'birthright' inhabited a purer, more elevated sphere? It stands to reason then that life owes him a privileged position among us. In this new estimation of himself he is the fount of all supernal wisdom incarnate, and at the same time he lays claim to knowing the ins and outs of everything worldly as well. He would almost regard it as his *duty* to impose some order 'down here'.

He conveniently ignores the fact that he is struck in a self-imposed exile 'down here', hooked on all the world can offer him, and so divorced from his (and all) inner reality that he has nothing new to offer us at all. He thinks he is doing an important job just dwelling among us, infinitely wiser and better. And he isn't in the least ashamed to rub it in when he lets us know about his privileged 'past': as if it were a valuable contribution he was making just to let us gape at him in wonder. In short, he is becoming quite insufferably condescending. Still, we can't help being impressed with his 'differentness'.

We think it would be handy indeed to have someone among us who knows it All. But if we try to tap the immense wealth of insight he claims to be naturally equipped with, we get only vague, expansive and meaningless gestures in the direction of a once living wisdom. If it sounds like mumbo jumbo to us, he waves us away self-importantly, saying that *we*, of course, can't expect to understand. He has been garrulous all along, a noisy waffler who could find no end to his sentences. The more seriously he takes himself, the more grandiloquent he becomes now. Though when he thinks about it, curt orders to do his bidding are all he owes us. Between giving himself grand airs, and us a never-

ending string of barked commands, and then presenting his preposterous babbling of genuine absurdities as a wisdom that will
always surpass our understanding, he does manage to acquire a
following of willing listeners, ready to obey his instructions: not
unnaturally they are hoping to benefit from his apparently superior understanding of worldly matters and beyond.

This is not quite the idea he has in mind. The idea is that he
should be the supreme commander, that we do the necessary
work as directed by his superior intellect and all-encompassing
insight, and that he have the proceeds to enjoy. Of course we need
to eat too, he knows that, but not crowd around the same table
with him and deprive him of his chance of a fourth helping. He
did not use to hesitate to help himself from *our* tables, and could
hardly object to others 'competing' with him there – though his
nimble gluttony usually won him the lion's share – but such
undignified scrabbling for tasty morsels would hardly be fitting
now, in his new position. We are banished and demoted to lesser
tables of our own.

He has advertised himself as something like the heaven-sent
cure of all the world's ills and problems – which to his understanding are defined as the lack of limitless plenty (for him) and
boundless opportunities (his). And now we are standing there
expecting him to work miracles, for *our* benefit, or at least to be
assigned the jobs that will gain us admission to this land of plenty. We are not going to work for his benefit alone: not unnaturally
we want to be given our share. And he could start by letting us
see, and taste, some of the fruits of his inherent abilities that he
makes such an unsubstantiated song and dance about.

This presents a serious problem to him. How can he even plan
to part with anything when there has never proved to be enough
for his own, outsize needs? He has his own future to think of, after
all: his personal becoming – more and more substantial. And
though he is a born optimist, his sensual nature is too excessively
greedy, and his thinking too narrowly to his own material advantage, to allow him to spare us even a token present that will tell us
of the riches to come if only we comply with his orders. Can't we
just take His Word for it (implying that his is a better word than
ours)? But at that we threaten to leave him standing for a charlatan and a windbag, with his vain and improbable promises, and
inflated claims.

Casting around for ideas how to 'make the world work for him' will not help him at all, but employing his as yet unused unconscious feeling function (♋→, ♋←) will make all the difference to getting him out of his ongoing predicament. Emotionally he is a compulsive giver, a self-satisfied supplier of all our needs, at least as he interprets them. He feels himself to be the source of all good things, a motherly sort, really, even if there is nothing particularly gentle about his manner. But with his customary brusqueness he now insists on clamping us under his wing.

There is nothing he likes more than distributing presents left right and centre, with the narrowly over-emotional goodwill of a tyrannical parent. It is no use protesting that one is full, that one never needed in the first place, that one prefers or is in dire need of something else: he is dishing out his immeasurable bounty regardless because, as always, he can't help himself. He is overwhelmed by his own givingness. And we are likewise overwhelmed by his heavy-handed, over-eager impositions. But then who would want to complain. If at first it is merely cheap trinkets he can press on us, symbolic of his irrepressible largesse-to-come, he soon finds the wherewithal to shower us more generously with everything we could (or at least what, with his dry reckoning, he thinks we *should*) possibly desire. All of which is to say that we do the work involved in gaining the goods, and he distributes them freely – having of course had his own, immense, fill first.

And in case we should feel there was a deficit for us in that arrangement, he always has other, 'better', things to give us to make up for it. Not just food and drink but liberal helpings of his unsought, so-called wisdom. And extensive expositions of his apparently sound, but hopelessly narrow-minded, advice. All followed by crackingly hearty slaps on the back: coming from him, we think it is a privilege, a chip off his own grandeur he is letting us have, and we are prepared to savour it in lieu of proper payment for our efforts. He makes such a big, tender-hearted show of his generosity towards us, mere lowly beings that we are, that we feel positively honoured to receive the scraps and the peelings from his meal.

Any complaints and attempts at disobedience he deals with in an equally overdone 'motherly' fashion: he chides us thunderously, he indicates how it pains him beyond words to have to resort to punishment, all in our own best interest, to teach us to submit to his beneficial rule. Where would we be without his leadership, his providing for us and watching over us from his elevated position, he asks us. We should be grateful that he is gracing our world with his presence at all, and giving freely of his all-surpassingly wonderful self. And in case we should still misinterpret him, he makes sure with his ceaseless, dreary moralising and sermonising that we understand him to be the 'higher' and mysteriously inspired being that he takes himself to be. Under this banner we can do his proceeding for him. And have his rule established for him, by the time he comes trundling up in our rear: ready to dispense presents, and a lot of less intelligible blessings, to his newest crop of overawed slaves.

His claim to be a higher class of being, whichever way he may put it across, is based on very thin air. He has lost even the most tenuous link with his former inner-self reality. His show of superiority is nothing but an empty performance, for the substance of which he is entirely, pitifully dependent on our obedient doings. Our success is the full extent of his powers. Our progress gets him where he wants to go: as vehicles of his becoming, a sort of collective life-support machine, we have to virtually carry him to his future. All he can boast of is his past. And all of his now utterly worldly 'transcending' is done purely in the usual three dimensions. Scaling the highest heights and conquering the farthest-flung flat places, penetrating the impenetrable and nosing around in every inaccessible swamp, he is always in search of new material sources for his prospective well-being and new concrete opportunities. (Needless to say, we have to clear his path, push him up the slopes, and carry his voluminous baggage.) His empire expands entirely gratuitously – though he may speak of principles and need, even ours – and then the fruits of his conquests rot unused by the ton. This is his idea of normality: *too* much; that will do, heaven on earth looks like that.

For all his rigid thinking out of each new campaign and his insistence on an orderly, disciplined approach, it is still a fairly slapdash affair. He is so well-padded with obsolete opinions and, through over-use of his senses, so increasingly 'insensitive', that unless one sets him on the right track he is still as prone as ever to go crashing past the most blindingly obvious danger signals and finds himself faced, yet again, with those end-of-the-line obstacles, limits that really can't be denied. Not that he lets it stop him in his stride. He waves such things aside with boisterous resolution and guffaws in imitation of mirth.

He is for ever taking refuge in forced levity, laughing loudly at his own blundering awkwardness, as if to pre-empt any ridicule on our part: he can never feel *totally* at ease, 'at home', in our environment; and a vague fear that we might question the genuineness of his credentials never leaves him. He is not above clowning either, when it comes to saving his reputation somehow or other. By way of a really generous gift he will provide us with exaggerated and wilfully funny accounts of the latest tumble he took, every detail lovingly inflated, and we feel touched and honoured by such honest-to-God humility: just as if he were one of us. (His exploits, it must be said, get the same treatment of lying-exaggeration.) But if his clumsy mistake happens unobserved, in the privacy of his own company, he can muster no jollity at all. If his conscience has not exactly been pricked, then at least his consciousness of who he used to be has been momentarily revived by this latest débâcle. For a moment he wonders just what he is doing here, in this over-familiar alien environment.

The honest answer to that is that he is forcefully intruding where he has no business to do so. Not only intruding but impostoring. Making out that his long-lost origin confers some special gifts or powers on him in his present state. Pretending, and gesturing meaninglessly. Waffling airy rubbish that signifies nothing and comes off the top of his head – which is about as far as his stunted, earth-bound understanding will reach. Dressing up, preening, striking grand poses: all meant to symbolise his other-worldly, 'higher' nature. And the whole exercise is entirely pointless. He had no need of the world, and is only having his sport with it now.

At bottom he is only semi-shameless, especially when he has just been shocked into remembering what kind of being he *really* is, or was, or should be. He had no need of all this mundane self-aggrandisement. He could quite genuinely have managed without. He could have saved himself getting bogged down in our ridiculous morasses as well. But now he is too committed to his worldly greed, and his status as 'beneficent' ruler, to do anything but cling to the role of de-facto tyrant ever more closely. He blunders on, full of sheepish excuses for himself: we, the world, are to blame for his disasters. He bleats ever more loudly, by way of both blessing and command. He needs to attract all our attention to this false self of his: that is to say away from his truly unsurpassed hollowness. He has become a 'man of substance', and nothing else. His former inner self, his essence, is only too richly embodied now, all of it, and is entirely denatured in this show of fat bombast, unstoppable swagger and authoritarian pomp. In his heart of hearts he knows better. He is only a tinsel tyrant masquerading as the real thing. A clever, preening, hopelessly hungry scrounger.

Having lost his centre, he can bring no true inner motivation to living. Whatever he does, or commands us to do for him, is essentially meaningless, amoral, irresponsible, and in the final analysis useless. He has imported into this world (without any modification – without, *in effect*, cutting himself down to size as it were) his basic nature of simply being, self-sufficiently; and of simply, easily, becoming. Even at his worst, Leo always pro-duced something of his true inner self into the world, if only in the form of specific, enforced demands. All Sagittarius does when he transplants himself forcibly and completely into the material reality, is to *de*generate.

He serves no purpose at all here, though we have to serve him. As the self-styled greatest who *has* no greatness to call his own, except to 'borrow' ours, on the grandest scale, he is an entirely dispensable figure. And yet he manages, under false pretences, to exact tribute from us, in the form of obedience, abject gratitude, and always the richest, fattest pickings. Unlike positive Sagittarius, he has nothing to teach us or truly give us. Life under him becomes a hollow performance for all of us. We demonstrate our essential purposelessness by assuming superfluous and would-be impressive guises. Growth and development are replaced by a show of big strides forward, with no meaningful aim. He does not lead us anywhere truly new, to our inner selves and the wider Inner Reality beyond, but instead claims to be, himself, all Inner Reality there is personified and presiding over our everyday doings. In truth, he only leads us in essentially unproductive circles, for the sake of the 'fun' of the exercise.

His empire is a kingdom on the move for no better purpose than to be engaged in a search for something new as such: opportunity sought for its own sake. Where inner becoming is no longer possible, some – any – form of outward 'becoming' will have to take its place. Of course, if he had not projected *all* he was into the realm of substance, there would have been no need for an empire to, visibly, take the place of his lost inner realm. And no need for action for action's sake, in order to fend off the deadly threat of stasis that his increasingly concrete self-establishment in the world poses. Now he frets to find his formerly free and easy self made so rigidly, and repeatedly painfully, 'real'. The more concretely real he becomes, the more he finds the range of new opportunities open to him limited by what he has already gained, conquered and established by way of self-embodiment.

In the end there is nothing left for him to do but deliberately lose, waste and fritter away his accumulated wealth in order to be able to keep making new starts. He has already thrown away his 'inherited' riches, his innate abilities, so he is only being true to form. Life has become an obsessive game, without limits: the object of the exercise is not to win-and-keep but to go on playing. He plays to lose so that he can play to win again. He slims right down so that he can stuff himself again. – He only *seems* to have progressed since the days when he used to make himself sick so he could eat more, and took periodic refuge in a contrived inappetence.

Positive Sagittarius raised the contributions of both Leo and Aries to a higher level, and combined them: establishing an *inner* self, rather than a perishable worldly one, and gaining the freedom of all *inner* becoming, rather than having to rely for new things to become on one's limited environment. Negative Sagittarius combines only the worst of the other two Fire signs. Pursuit of selfish gain that never leads to the expected satisfaction; and the setting up of a repetitive cycle not of creation/destruction so much as inflation/deflation, but it amounts to the same thing: gain followed by loss.

He uses up the world at a fast rate, reserving his freedom to throw things aside half-eaten in favour of something else again. All he can offer us by way of example is how to balance superfluous opulence against impoverishment that need not be: both the material poverty caused for some by others, with their too-much-is-just-enough attitude; and the inner impoverishment he exemplifies that goes hand in hand with overcompensation through material excess. – And living 'things' fare no better with him. Negative Aries conquered us and placed us behind him, to 'save us up'. Negative Leo conquered us and set us up before his eyes as a self-enhancing institution. Sagittarius conquers us only to extract the juices, and discards us.

No part of the world can ever offer him enough to slake his vampirical thirst for 'real', red flesh and blood, life (not that he is the only 'vampire' among the negative signs). Meantime he has infected us all with his exploitative addiction. Instead of bringing us the chance of a newly illumined and freely formless kind of life, he only helps to bind us more closely to our dependence on substance. He teaches us to litter the world with the half-empty husks of frenetic consumption, strangling new growth in the process. He shows us how to deplete and despoil the existing natural riches with his cavalier attitude that would recognise no substantial limits.

But it can't go on; sooner or later he has exhausted all the available resources. He can find no new paths to tread. His intrusive highways are everywhere, and at the end of them he finds only the rusting and rotting left-overs from his last visit, and the meagerest of crops among the damage he has done to the basic fabric of this once thriving environment. Now he has to go hungry while staring at the evidence of all the wasting he used to do. The world is no longer his oyster: it is useless to him. He has gambled away the various parts of his empire one after the other, convinced that this way he would always find a new chance to extract more, but now he has lost his last gamble. (If indeed he did not 'chance his life', and lose it, earlier on: disporting himself in inaccessible regions, scrabbling for gain, perhaps.)

There is nothing he can do now – he finds himself *forced* to withdraw to his former home ground, his other reality, all but forgotten while he was having his fun 'in foreign parts'. Here he may pine for all his favourite addictions, but after all lacks for nothing. All he has lost is a bad habit of luxurious self-indulgence. His servile and more or less grateful followers, slaves in effect if not in name, can only watch him disappear over the horizon like a mirage, comprehending no more than they did before he appeared in their midst.

They are left with the trampled ground where things might have grown, the unproductive acres set aside for the vain amusement of the senses, the gaping holes he has inflicted on nature searching for way-out titbits and mining for trinkets, the useless palaces that now stand empty, and all the other remnants of the feverish feast he made of life. Not to mention a handed-down habit of inflated expectations that are merely unnatural, not in the least supra-natural. They have risen not an inch. Their world has been violated, denatured and sucked empty. And he has simply disappeared, rather unsportingly.

Some Suggested Sagittarius Attributes

basic

lives in an inner world of his own; may be seen as eccentric; free, independent, self-sufficient; inner contentment; takes his existential ease and comfort for granted; optimistic; inclined to be easy-going, carefree

his mind works intuitively, wider awareness that transcends the mundane sphere, aware self-transcendence; 'other-worldly', 'head-in-the-clouds'; abstracted/vague, inattentive; wants to be left in peace, unsociable, natural recluse; always puzzled and clueless when it comes to down-to-earth matters

unworldly: awkward, clumsy; no eye for detail, doesn't notice the obvious; when forced to concentrate on the matter in hand stumbles, rushes and crashes around, lacks material finesse: displays the insensitivity and coarseness of the complete beginner; hopelessly inept but keeps trying, always searching for meaning in the wrong place/ways

tends to cause upset and damage: collides head-on; tactless, no manners, informal, artlessly direct; hates getting caught up and entangled: rudely brushes off, backs out of involvements, deserts; unstoppable; aims (too) far

comes a cropper at every turn, makes a fool of himself, never knows what he has done wrong, a 'hopeless innocent'

positive

capable of sensual enjoyment for its own sake and freely moves through the whole range of interconnected possibilities: can be 'freely playful', fun-loving, relaxed, constitutionally happy; counts himself lucky; may be accused of excessive levity; easily misunderstood and ridiculed; has a tendency to escape inward in search of meaning, appears withdrawn and abstruse

profound, deep insight, wisdom, inspiration, enlightenment; looks for truth rather than mere fact, honesty

mediates between worldly matters and what transcends them: has a 'message'; inspired public speaker, teacher, moralist, preacher, priest etc.; has to express meaning largely non-rationally: uses symbolism in speech and ritual in action, (symbolic) celebrations has access to as yet 'unborn' facts: **predicts, prophesies,** and has the ability to find, intuitively, any 'missing' facts: **clairvoyant, 'inspired hunches'**

fosters wider (inner) awareness, encourages growth and (self-) completion; helps overcome physical restrictions, opens up new horizons, leads into 'adventure' and journeys that transcend the normal range, (seeks out and) offers new possibilities; generously sharing in and with: fair trade: seeks mutual exchange of good fortune

joyful, cheerful, always hopeful; enthusiasm; aware innerness gives him the distance from objective life to maintain **a sense of humour; able to 'rise above'** the situation; **philosophical;** bridging Inner and outer reality: **religious** in the basic sense

refuses to let himself get too deeply involved or caught up in circumstances: **needs movement, space and quietude; 'takes a holiday'/sabbatical; seeks out the 'wild' places, nature-loving, content with a simple material life, enjoys simple pleasures, contemplative, meditative:** goes inward to reconnect himself to his inner source (of becoming); at times **reclusive; reappraises his life; capable of conscious inner growth, totally new starts, novel ventures**

self-renewal based on obedience to an inner code that transcends the personal intention: **freedom-under-the-law,** leading to **lasting happiness freely shared, founds or joins communities based on inner values,** e.g. religious orders

negative

coarse, gross, vulgarly boisterous, loud; over-the-top, exaggerating, overdoes everything, manic; will go to any lengths

intemperate, can never get enough, indiscriminate glutton and **all-round pleasure-seeker, has riotous fun; false euphoria; highly self-indulgent, 'spoilt', demanding ease and comfort** etc. to an unrealistic degree; **expects sacrifices** from others

looks for easy gain and shortcuts to happiness; gambler; expects to be given privileges, lazy, insatiable scrounger; opportunist

treats life as a game, 'plays around', amoral, libertine; indulges in entirely useless and unmotivated activities: a **why-not attitude; having his sport** with the world, **irresponsible, degenerate**

his **unrealistic expectations** and **over-optimistic attitude** make him **prone to disappointment; nostalgic for a past 'Golden Age'; unable to cope** with life's demands, **alienated by limitations, restrictions** etc., life's inadequacies make him **sad** but he is in a **hopeless** state of being entangled in it, tries to hide away in **recurrent depressions, deaf to the world** etc.; **'stranded', despairing, helpless**

captive of/captivated by the world: **unfree, dependent; not true to himself/to his origin**

untruthful: embroiders, exaggerates; deliberately eccentric; meaningless babbling; garrulous; makes false and wildly inflated claims and promises; false prophet or medium, spurious 'insights' etc.: **pretentious, boastful, grandiloquent, blasé**

throws away the riches that are naturally his in favour of inferior ones: **inner impoverishment; prodigal, wastes, squanders; casts aside, deserts** for something/somebody new; **gambles-away** in order to go on gaining indefinitely

fortune-hunter; travels far and wide in search of gain, explores with enrichment in mind; invasive, appropriating; empire-building

condescending, presents himself as a higher class of being, arrogant, (almost) shamelessly takes a ruling position for granted; curtly demanding, commanding, orders others to make his gains for him: **exploitative employer, slave driver** who does not pay but **gives 'generously'; swindler, impostor; unfair trader; charlatan, 'hollow'**

ostentatious pomp and conspicuous consumption, superfluous gain, luxury, runs to fat; grandness, opulence, bombast; swagger, dressing up, preening, show-off, trumpeting self-advertisement; solemn, self-glorifying rituals

false authority; threatening and overwhelming with gifts in turns; judgmental, moralises and sermonises off the top of his head, slapdash disciplinarian, bluffs and blunders his way through

never at ease: easily embarrassed; forced 'humour'/jollity and **deliberate self-mockery, clowning**

makes an art of meaningless activities, wastes time, wastes resources, causes damage and scarcity, exploits-and-moves-on; absconds, evades consequences

THE
EARTH SIGNS

♉ TAURUS

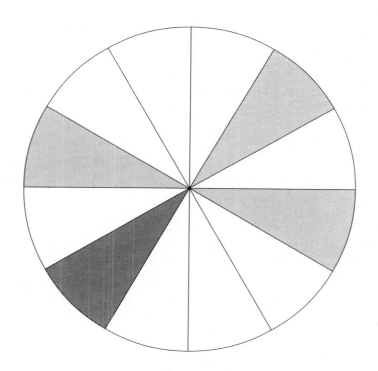

♉ **Extravert**
conscious function: sensation; direction of function: outward
unconscious functions: ♏ intuition, ♍ thinking, ♓ feeling
Earth: senses-oriented

Taurus is an extraverting extravert, like Aries, and so needs to
find all of his self in his given environment. Aries, for his part,
started out by simply following his intuition indiscriminately to
whatever situations it led him, and there promptly found his self,
for the time being. Taurus is no less indiscriminate in identifying
his self in all that surrounds him. But in his case it is not intuition
that leads him from one possibility of self-identification to the
next. His basic nature is earthy and his conscious function is sensation: he is guided in his search for self entirely by his senses. His
self is something that needs to stand before his eyes in quite a concrete way. This may sound a straightforward enough process, but
there is a catch – and it is quite the opposite of Aries' problem of
an overabundance of possible selves.

Since everything Taurus perceives with his senses immediately
becomes self to him, any changes in his environment are liable to
upset him: quite literally the self he has just acquired is thrown
into disorder, partly or wholly abolished. Every change, every living development in the world, is a personal loss to him, a violation
of what he is. The concrete self he has identified as 'I' is constantly being replaced by a stranger.

These uncontrollable rearrangements of what he is are quite
unacceptable to him. His earthy nature demands something solid,
clearly structured, stable and dependable by way of self-experience, something he can trust to remain what it is. A constantly
shifting, chopping and changing world only has him bewildered
as to who or what he is. Strictly speaking, he can't even change his
own position in the world: every time he moves, the world presents a different picture to his senses, robbing him again of at least
some of what he has gained in the way of a visible, palpable, concretely established 'I'. As an extravert he needs to search for and
gather a self from out of this far-flung world of sense-able things
that are all potentially he. But every move towards new gain

threatens loss at the same time, and unlike Aries he is keenly aware of it.

Aries could proceed with intuitive, fluid movement to find himself, lose himself, scattering bits as he went, and getting of course nowhere nearer keeping hold of a stable 'I' experience. Taurus does not have this basic approach, he cannot go on 'happening' in the world and hoping that it will somehow all come together for him. Happenings only pain him, rob him, nullify him. Sitting rooted to the spot and staring fixedly ahead of him seems to be the best he can do to counteract the fickleness of the world, and even that is barely guarantee enough.

Despite his being an extraverting extravert, he never does get under way properly. He tends to either move at such a cautious, fearful crawl that he barely gathers together the ghostly outline of a self; or else he tries to barricade himself behind a meagre pile of an acquired self, counting himself lucky to be anything at all – and counting himself over and over again, in endless self-repetition. In terms of becoming a vivid, living self he is definitely a non-starter and any encouragement one might try to give him only has him burying his head in the sand. Life threatens him on all sides, and being a fully-fledged self is far too hazardous a business really for him to have any taste for it.

The way out of his dilemma is via his capacity for an *inner* form of perception: his unconscious intuition (♏). Through this he comes in touch with all the inner-plane possibilities that are the basis of life's forms and events – that is anything at all his environment *might* contain in concrete form. At the same time he becomes intuitively aware that this 'model world', insubstantial as it is, can be made into a concrete reality through the power of actively transforming one's environment. – There is no need for him to travel this threateningly unstable world, trying to gather with his physical senses as much as he can of a self. He has been given another option now, much more constructive.

By following his unconscious intuitive awareness of the many possibilities life might present, the many shapes it might take, and by using whatever material is at hand, he can now take charge of the transforming, the changes, and hence the increasing variety, in his personal life. By making the necessary adjustments to his immediate environment, he can construct all manner of concrete worlds for him to sense his self in and call his own – secure in the knowledge that as long as *he* is the one who is producing this variety and increase, there will be no sudden, unexpected, unacceptable losses involved. He takes his meagre starting stock in his own hands and builds himself up from that, slowly and circumspectly, and what he gains can only be described as a do-it-yourself 'I'. He no longer depends on finding the makings of his self ready-made, out there in the stream of life that frightens him more than it attracts him with promises of new things to become. Instead of needing to move around in search, he can stay at home, so to speak, and construct a living, growing reality of his own from out of quite a limited range of objective givens, according to an inner plan.

This plan is not his own – as an extravert he does not possess a plan of his inner being – it is only a 'borrowed' one: borrowed from out of the collective pool of intuitive understanding. From out of a scheme of things-to-be that exists, in another dimension to the one he inhabits, at the root of all material manifestation. That is to say, his self-building process is not an exercise in self-willed manipulation; he is not sitting there 'making up his mind' what next to do and be. Rather, he is passively receiving 'hunches', intuitive ideas, that spark him into activity. And each intuited model he grasps and uses as the basis for his work is an 'organic' one. One might say they are all provided by Life itself, inherent possibilities rather than individual inventions on his part. Earth into bricks, reeds transformed into roof: that sort of thing.

His new approach would appear to have solved his problem: how to acquire more and more of an identity without having to subject himself to a destabilising flux of environmental change forced on him in the form of sudden, unforeseen surprises. He should be slowly 'happening' under his own direction now. And yet, not only does his environment intrude to 'unhappen' him again, but even his own upbuilding efforts are liable to lead to the collapse, the destruction, of what he has built up for himself. As an Earth sign he is certainly down-to-earth and practical, and the slowness and caution he derives from his basic situation is no impediment to his life task either: constructive work is not something demanding hurry and irrepressible zest. But unless he knows exactly what he is doing, he still runs the risk of finding the identity he is constructing for himself falling apart again before his eyes. Without an intelligent appreciation of the details to be worked out, he is in fact worse off than ever: his own activities now a menace to his self. His first few faltering attempts have him giving up in horror: having come undone, viewing the wreckage that is his own doing, he is more determined than ever not to move a muscle.

The moment he lets himself be guided by his unconscious thinking (♍→) though, he knows how to give due attention to each detail. He analyses the givens and the possible options before he commits himself to any line of action, and with increased efficiency he learns to trust his own abilities. His newly developed capacity for focusing narrowly on the specific details of the work in hand also ensures for him a greater freedom from unwelcome intrusions. What he isn't taking any notice of cannot unsettle him. Being engrossed keeps him safe.

Neither does he lack a positive self-critical attitude (♍←), in fact he would be the first to criticise his own work, if only unconsciously. He even becomes a bit of a perfectionist: not any old self that *can* be constructed from the available material will do him now; he is no longer indiscriminate in his need for more self to become, he picks and he chooses. Why be content with a rough construct, just for the sake of adding something to himself, when he could have/be something that truly pleases his senses?

These slow and gradual changes in his narrow environment, under his own direction, are nothing threatening to him. They represent an organic self-growth, a step-by-step development, and though he is solely in charge of it, it is always based on the many meanings and purposes of that intrinsic Reality that underlies all form. Like Leo he leaves an imprint on this world, and a more exclusively substantial one at that. But his is not based on what he *is*, rather on his need to become: anything at all he thinks fit and which appeals to him from a sensual point of view, as long as he can 'materialise' it himself out of this 'fund of possible selves' common to us all.

Where Leo pro-duced into the world the many different aspects of his inner self and thus set himself up as an active and ruling force, Taurus' productivity in the world is based on his search for a concrete identity which he has no other way of effecting but by becoming an agent of living change. Leo expressed himself through creative transformations of many specific kinds unique to him ($\approx$), and gained concrete self-awareness. Taurus, for his part, expresses some of the many life possibilities as such through bringing about very basic transformations of his environment (M), and gains a concrete self thereby.

Where Leo was intent on seeing all of his inner self 'realised', Taurus has no such ambitions, he has no inbuilt target to meet. He is content to slowly grow in stature, to increase at a pace that he is comfortable with, and to go on growing indefinitely, as far as his environment permits him to. But like Leo he too has to stick to the most basic raw material he can find – in his case one might call them his building blocks. He takes hold of the least structured components of the world, blank and as yet faceless, useless, devoid of much of an identity of their own – these he can most comfortably look at because they don't much contradict what he already is – and he transforms, not so much what they are, but their uses, their place in his world: he builds them into the existing world in a new way, gives them (and himself) a new identity from out of the wealth of possibilities he intuits for them/himself.

Even if he finds himself surrounded by nothing but stone, he has the power to convert the experience of bare stone into the experience of something else. Sculpting the stone, engraving it, adding pigment, or assembling an image or structure out of stones of all sizes and shapes, he can transform his world – and concurrently form a new self that stands quite concretely before his eyes and that he will be pleased to call 'I'. He can always intuit the potential of simple things: a coarse chunk of material holds a promise for him, it could be a beautiful or a useful object, with maybe very little modification.

He has no need at all to travel about to savour all the world of self to be, he builds it on his doorstep instead. House, door, enclosing wall, these are of course some of the first things he builds for himself: a more definitely secure 'I-place' where he can work in peace, keeping any potentially destructive environmental changes out. And he further protects himself against the impact of the turbulent elements beyond his ken (that pose such a threat to his self-continuity) by making for himself various kinds of 'armour' or second skins that will allow him to feel (or 'sense', to be correct) pretty much the same whatever the season, whatever the conditions that might assault his senses. He 'enclothes' himself and encloses himself, as far as practicable. And if that appears unadventurous and positively boring from the outside – to Aries this would look like a state of deadly stagnation – then only because his bulwarks and screens hide from view the fact that there are whole worlds happening inside; and not simply happening by themselves, but all wrought by him. He may not be an obvious fireworks display, but sparks do fly.

He applies himself steadily to his task, intelligently, methodically, avoiding both haste and waste as going entirely against his nature. What he assembles and builds up out of the scanty and simple building blocks of his pared-down environment is meant both to last and to further enrich him. His products are designed to continue doing their job for as long as possible, that is to say to give him the pleasure of self-recognition each time they are handled or looked at. If it is to be used it must be sturdy, as well as a pleasure to handle. If it is for shelter and self-protection it should be as massive or impenetrable as need dictates and commonsense will allow, without being lumpish and shapeless; the odd embellishment will only add to its sensual appeal.

This beautification has nothing to do with him wanting to 'show off': he does not need a self-substantiating response from others, like Leo; all he wants is to be pleased with his latest bit of home-made self. And his ornaments and self-ornamentation had better be waterproof, fireproof, shatterproof, rather than dainty; of lasting value rather than ephemeral beauty. Best of all his constructs should be incorruptible or at least self-maintaining or self-replenishing: his very own patch of nature, redesigned and modified to guarantee his own particular sustainable growth, this could well be his ideal 'construction'. Again, it saves him the impossible task of hunting around far and wide for his sustenance – he 'makes' it instead, on the spot, *his* spot.

He has built his protective home, made his armour of clothing, his field and stable, tools, ornaments, all of it taken from the world in the raw state and (put back) transformed. He is growing, slowly, more substantial. But there are others beside him who share in his basic needs, and in the one available source of all the raw materials, and in the space he occupies. There are Arien world-gatherers hunting around for things to become – in his field as well. There are Leonian world-rulers seeing his territory as yet another place to realise their own inner plans... How is he going to fend off those invaders? His defensiveness gives only so much protection before offensive counter-action seems called for: something that goes entirely against his nature – he does not even wish to have the least idea of how to go about it. Fights, any kind of upset, are not in his line. It looks as if after having come this far safely he is going to meet his undoing after all.

Making use of his unconscious feeling function, though, he finds the best defence he could: one that cannot crumble, something that adds to his acquired stability the 'give' that opens it up to a peaceful and unthreatening 'invasion'. Emotionally he is very much drawn toward sharing the one world there is ($\mathcal{H}\rightarrow$). This may not give him what one might call courage, or tempt him to forget all caution, but it does enable him to relax more in the presence of the livelier life that tends to be the norm outside his gates, and in fact to open those gates just a little. Feeling part-of allows him to leave the concerns of his self (and the concern for his safety) aside for a while. And setting his established self aside in favour of this new emotional experience of others brings him to the recognition that the strangers coming in by the gate are actually established selves *distinct* from him. They aren't new world-experience for him to have to 'digest' and include as incongruous, alien bits in *his* self – upsetting his prior self beyond recognition. They are other-selves, to be left well alone inside *their* self-protective shells.

Now he has really found his stability in the world. The dividing line between what is self and what is other in the world has been firmly drawn, so from his point of view there is peace now, an end to fear. *He* will certainly not shift or question the boundaries. In his emotional understanding of himself he is only a fraction of a much larger whole, a rather insignificant detail ($\mathcal{H}\leftarrow$). He is only one among many, and this is good news to him, because he knows himself to be properly defined now, at the same time as he feels that he is part of the crowd. The strange and threatening otherness of the wider world is accounted for, it has 'owners' and is nothing to do with him, personally. The changes, the coming and going he feared so much as automatically pulling the carpet from underneath all he had built up, these he now experiences as impersonal changes, not affecting his established self at all, or maybe only in part. And they certainly cannot detract from his ability to rebuild any slight damage to his world/self, to make up for any losses he might sustain when he now takes part in a wider life, less enclosed and ensconced, as he keeps working away at the construction of a now no longer isolated identity.

Becoming part-of, opening up his secluded world and sharing it, he finds his self to be not only a collection of accumulated substance but also a 'body' of practised skills, acquired knowledge or know-how, a trained understanding of how to transform basic materials in order to structure the world with a given purpose in mind. Not only is this 'body' indestructible, but it is eminently share-able.

Up to now others have been part of his world only as a source of dependable sensual experience, and even then only if they could be trusted to be quiet, stable, not presuming to differ – in other words, there were only very few of them, securely 'built into' the fabric of his world. Now the situation is quite different. He knows himself not only as the structures he has built in his own demarcated space, he knows himself also as the ever-able structurer, a being distinct from these others whom he can now allow to invade his space. He finds himself so to speak surrounded by the personal 'space' of his own characteristic potential, his abilities for building his self wherever he goes, and there is nothing, in principle, to stop him moving out into the larger world. Nothing either, to stop him throwing his door wide open to any comers; he can always fill in again the 'holes' they may knock into his established, concrete self-experience. And lastly, others prove not to want to knock holes into his world at all, destructively, wantonly, randomly: he has become very attractive to them, as he is, and as a willing supplier of *their* needs.

Emotionally he gets caught up in the concerns of others as much as in his own. Their needs become his too, in an impersonal sort of way. That is to say he is prepared to share his skills, to regard his own abilities as common property and to stand them in the service of others' requirements. This is the truest fulfilment of his work. He has borrowed freely from the Plan of Life that is the source of all and now he is putting his acquired know-how at the disposal of all.

Aries, too, came to share in this way what he had acquired: he became the vicarious go-getter, the one who gained the future for us, both offensively (in the neutral sense of the word) and defensively, protectively. Taurus does not gain us new things, he leaves the gaining of what we need for our future to us, but he consolidates it for us by en-structuring our plans, making our aspirations substantial: we supply him with the 'material' and the general idea, he gives shape to our intentions, as solid and lasting as he can make it. He helps us build our future concretely. And as the future becomes present and then past, he keeps maintaining it for us, re-doing where things are coming apart, repeating what needs to be in order to uphold the continuity of some established feature of our world or its function. With his customary caution, though no longer fearfully, he does spread himself through our 'territory' a bit: making suggestions, adding a touch he thinks may please us as well as him, advising us where intuitively he is convinced that our plans that we present to him are too far off course to prove of lasting value when 'embodied'. He checks our wilder urges with his unconscious awareness of what might/should be, of what is 'natural' that is, because it accords with the underlying scheme of things that transcends the here-and-now of concrete reality.

He has proved to be more than just a 'self-made man' in his DIY world, following the hidden instructions of life for his own purposes. He has become a world builder for all of us; a transformer of our common potential into concrete fact, on our behalf as much as his own. His start was not exactly auspicious: dogged repetition of a very limited repertoire. Then he blossomed into variety, but only in fearful isolation. Finally, he has matured into a public provider of endless new variations on our common, timeless themes.

When Taurus uses his unconscious functions negatively, he also tries to build himself a world that reconciles his conflicting needs: to transform the given raw material around him to further the growth of his self, while at the same time always preserving his established status quo. He, too, gains an intuitive awareness of the many inherent existential possibilities, and of his executive power to implement this underlying Life Plan ($\mathfrak{m}$). But instead of using his new awareness positively, he lets himself be pushed by a compulsive need to see the world conform to his will: he makes of his executive power a personal one – it is *his* plan now, and solely *his* intention to transform it into a concrete reality. And instead of receiving the gift of his inspiration in its entirety, i.e. the whole gamut of possibilities he might substantiate, he grasps greedily at the first impulse he receives. The first inkling of a world-to-be that occurs to him he appropriates, exclusively, as his very own and only model for world building. This he clings to with fearsome conviction.

His urge to impose a set pattern on his world, once and for all, ties in with his need for stability. But he also needs to grow, to become more self, or else he will be no better off than he was at the beginning. But seizing on only a small fraction of life's inherent potential, and using that for his own purpose, while ignoring the rest, he has exchanged what could have been his (and the world's) potential for variety, change and new becoming for a single model that will have to serve for all he will ever become – a single intention, disconnected and uprooted from out of its essential context. Once made fact and substance, that should be all he ever manages to become, and in the true sense of becoming that is certainly the case.

However, as an extravert who makes, constructs, his self – rather than gather what his environment offers him – he easily finds a way to counter this impediment to future growth. He simply combines static sameness and growth by becoming the same anew, repeatedly: his life consists of the living event of more-of-the-same taking shape, over and over again. Having built one copy and declared it self, he goes on to build another one, and another, and he has to push them – and with them the boundaries of his personal environment – ever outward, away from him, to make room for this tide of self-replication.

He, too, has to content himself with simple building blocks, unable to stand the sight of (self-)destruction in the world. And yet destroy he does, though quite unaware of what is being engulfed by his ceaseless production of a clone of 'I's. He sits at the centre of it all, ignorant of what is being crushed at the periphery of self, behind the thick, sheltering wall of numerous piled-up identical assembly-line type products: all of it he – too fat an 'I' to be able to survey all there is of him. Losing sight of large areas of self does not worry him unduly; as the author of it all, and each bit the same, he knows for a hundred per cent certain what there would be to see if he could see it. But to get to the stage where he can actually churn out a dependable succession of such a product/self he has, like positive Taurus, to make use of his unconscious thought processes, to analyse and plan exactly how he will go about his work.

If he made a positive use of his capacity for shrewd in-detail scrutiny (♍→), then he should be able to notice sooner or later that there is something simply not right with such a limited construct as he is 'becoming'. Giving in to a compulsive urge to nit-pick away at every detail, however, he only becomes more and more narrow in outlook. Now even the tiniest deviation/variation is anathema to him. He becomes not merely efficient but unnaturally obsessed with the absolutely guaranteed sameness of him, each and every time he takes shape. His self-critical attitude (♍←) is an annoyance even to him, he never finds himself quite 'same' enough. In an effort to make sure, he thinks up a method of constant systematic checks to be made throughout every work procedure, before he will trust himself to be doing it right. With only one intuited design to work from, and all of his being and spurious becoming depending on that, it is of course of immense importance that every single manoeuvre in his severely restricted world should be exactly defined and adhered to. Every move he makes has to be just so. If he has given himself no other options of what to be but, to put it simply, the one thing endlessly repeated, now he does not even give himself any options of how to be(come) it. He grinds on mechanically, and calls it living. Life is no more than a habit to him: a mixture of the need for more to become, and fear to deviate from the established path.

What he produces he keeps jealously to himself, because addition to the self he is building up is the only thing that stops him expiring in the closed circuit of repetitiveness. To stay alive he has to spiral upwards: growth by piling-up is his imitation of a life process. And to gather in his raw material, as well as to have room for his increasing bulk, he has to spread, to increase his range of intake and output. He has to move: but he does so only through a safe, previously flattened and homogenised world.

This is elimination and destruction at one remove, indirect: pushing a weighty load of accumulated self-stuff ahead of him to extinguish what exists there in its own right, and reduce it to the basic 'rubble' he can then use to build yet more of his ever-same self with. Aggression, attack, snatching and smashing are not his way, though one could hardly say that he uses subtler means. He spills over into his environment, he grafts himself on top and smothers it, he forces himself into every crack, widening it by sheer force of weight, supplanting what was there with his own bulk, and he never even hears the sound of splintering and groaning. There is so much of him, he has long lost touch with his more outlying parts. As the motive force he sits at the centre of this mobile workshop he has become, focusing all his attention on his self-creating processes, pushing what is completed out of the way to make room for these ongoing processes of renewed repetition – his periphery is no more than a thick dead skin that encloses him safely. So safely, he never sees the damage he does (how fortunate for him, the sign most averse to witnessing something going to pieces in the world!). Concerned only with what is taking place, and form, under his nose, he could be spilling over the edges of the world without ever noticing, without stopping. Whether one says that he destroys the world, as it stands, or that he constructs his self all over it, on top of it, it amounts to the same thing. There is nothing left in the end but he, or at least that is what he finds himself compelled to aim for.

His extravert hunger for more has him, so to speak, looking for yet another identical helping as soon as he perceives his plate to be no longer quite full. In this manner he 'eats' his way through the world at an astonishing rate (and he literally eats, not to idly amuse his palate, like negative Sagittarius, but without really tasting: mechanically, under the pressure of the urge to grow *bigger*). He incorporates into himself all the variety life can offer him, and yet his menu sports but a single dish and the uniformity of its ingredients hardly ever lets him down. The secret there is of course that by the time his 'ingredients' have reached him from somewhere on his periphery, where he has crushed whatever they have once constituted, they are all equally mashed and unrecognisable. Choice titbits disappear into his conveyor belt maw together with the proverbial turnip tops and anything else he can grab at the same time, making a pleasantly indistinctive hash: the one raw material he needs, food as such, for the same old self-as-such to increase in girth. Unlike positive Taurus who used truly simple ingredients for his self-construction and actually transformed them into something more complex, negative Taurus 'simplifies' his environment to devastating effect.

Not only that, but the rate at which he unconsciously pulveris-
es the world as far as he can and then uses it for his own purposes
is equalled by the speed with which a mountain of waste builds
up beside him. No matter how hard he crushes, there are always
stray odds and ends to pick out and automatically discard. His
one set design does not allow him to make any constructive use of
these left-overs and left out bits. His 'rubbish' is not an agreeable
sight, but then his mental tunnel vision and his thick, desensitised
skin helpfully shield him from noticing anything untoward.

For every replica house he builds, to use one example, he leaves
a tip of unused stuff behind, not to mention the excavated rubble.
He has not programmed himself to deal with the job of disposing
properly of these. Constructive sidelines are unknown to him, he
cannot transform the stray bits into something to go with the main
product, or the surroundings. Quite simply, surroundings, and
eyesores such as he leaves behind, are something he manages to
be genuinely ignorant of: they do not intrude into his world and
hence are not recognised as being part of his job or resulting from
his activities. And what he cannot ignore, what lies around
unused in his way, he displaces deftly and preferably without
looking too closely – rather like pushing any too firm, too green,
too tasty bits right off his plate. Eating or building houses, it is all
done in the same manner of senselessly and insensitively repeating himself. And like a harmlessly inclined armoured tank he
can't help making a bit of a mess wherever he goes, inadvertently
and unawares.

This of course brings him up against other world inhabitants
who might prefer not to have their existing homes flattened in
favour of his standard issue housing project, and all of it to be *his*.
The least he would need to do is share – and share he can, only too
well, in his own rough way. Wherever he goes he is pushed not
only by his compulsion to expand uniformly, but is also lured on
his way by an exaggerated feeling that all around him there is a
boundless world that is also he, full of others who are really no
different from him ($\mathcal{H}\to$). The larger environment with all its
inhabitants may be something he is *mentally* blind to, but emotionally he is ready to become as one with it all.

He is ready to share his world/self, but without letting go of
any part (any single copy, that is) of it. He feels the need to put his
constructive urge at the service of all others, indiscriminately, but

without asking them what they might require for themselves – there is no choice, after all. Others out there, beyond his massive personal space, are a fairly hazy impression to him anyway. One will have to shout to attract his attention, and then take his answering bellows from the living centre inside his accumulated bulk as a sign of success, rather than an affront. At that distance we all look and sound pretty much the same to him, we arrive filtered and mangled and devoid of our subtle attributes at the point inside him where he is alive and sensually alert. How would he know anything about our differing needs? Our muttered complaints never penetrate… But for all his annoying shortcomings, one cannot help being impressed with his frantic industry, his immense efficiency, the predictable neatness of what he churns out. And now he is offering to share it all with us, products and process, to include us in his world.

In effect, he does not share so much as graciously assimilate all and everyone into his own 'body', his one standardised world. His doing for others does not differ noticeably from his determined self-imposition. The moment we accept his offer he begins to process us to bring us into line. We become another form of raw material to him.

His personal relationships with others have never been more than a repetitive process of sensual self-gratification to him, meant to be stable and enduring – and to be endured quietly by us – as well as sustaining him in his need to grow. Life partners, as everything, have been reduced to the absolute minimum of variety: and that one to be a loyal provider and suporter. Not a source of many different forms of sensual excitement, but a soothingly stable consumable, and another sheltering layer of 'skin' against the vagaries of the environment. In his wider relationships now, he also looks for no more than help and support, and acquiescence. To put it another way, he kindly shares his self-building plan, to become everyone's plan. Or quite simply: he expects his instructions to be followed, and to the letter. He may be the master builder, but the actual work he can leave increasingly to his growing, co-operative work force. He may think it a bit of a risk to trust us not to make any hideous mistakes, like substituting a comma for a semi-colon; but emotionally he cannot conceive of anyone wanting to differ so drastically in their intentions. He trains us well, only too well; and he believes in us.

We are the people whose territory he has had, perforce, to invade. The dispossessed whose space and belongings he has needed to take over to give him room to become more of the same, and to give him the pulped wherewithal to become it. We have received his gift/command: to be as he is, and identical to each other, an ant hill of busy workers doing his bidding. Just as his 'thick skin' did the job of shielding him from anything new as yet to be acquired by him, through crushing brute force, so now this clone of co-workers that surrounds him does the job of enforcing the norm for him. Once he has processed us – or call it trained – we are all as suspicious as he is of any signs of otherness.

Very soon he need not bother at all doing anything himself, except supervise. He stands and issues his few well-known commands. And even that job he can delegate. Movement never was his favourite activity, work only the price he had to pay for living – if he can simply sit on his backside now and watch himself grow and grow, over and over again from scratch, so much the better. It is just as well he can leave even the ordering about to others, because his self-confidence is by no means assured: secretly he suffers from a feeling of worthlessness ($)(\leftarrow$) that he cannot explain to himself. This, and his continuing self-criticism, keeps spoiling his enjoyment of the one and only possible self he can allow himself to be.

No matter how full he crams his life with the same exactly planned and brought about self-experience, he still can't help but secretly despise himself for what he feels and knows himself to be. It never occurs to him that it is after all the future building blocks of his self that he is riding roughshod over when he plunders and dismantles the world and bends others to his will. He is constantly depreciating both other and self and wonders why his efforts and pleasures are yielding less and less self-satisfaction. He is rubbishing the world as it stands, and this is what he bases his 'new' self on. But since he is not aware with any of his senses of what he is really doing to the world at his point of contact with it (his outer layers, the complete and finished copies of him that lie all about him – dead and useless in terms of ongoing vitality) the doubts he feels and the endless quibbles he has remain a mystery to him. All he can think to do to gain more satisfaction with his life and self is to 'eat' ever more, faster and faster. Acceleration, escalation, speeding up the destructive/constructive conversion of other into self: he gobbles up and assimilates the world at a gallop now, helped by his work force who are being urged to ever better sense-less efforts – as if there were some urgent deficit to fill, when the world is already full to choking with the terrible sameness of it all.

A little bit of 'give' in his scheme, a taste of something a bit different, might be the answer, but the different is something he has no wish to encounter, and never does. It is bulldozed well out of his path before it can begin to have an unsettling impact on him. The impact is all his. He drives home his tiresome point with all the repetitive urgency and the finesse of a road drill. To suspect that he might be beginning to be bored with himself would be to miss the mark by a mile, even if some of us who are a little less than perfectly assimilated into his droning, clanking, grinding world are by now bored to tears with him. He is petulant only because unconsciously he thinks and feels himself to be *still* not exactly repetitive enough.

The only conclusion he can come to is that the fragment of a plan he borrowed (for keeps) from out of the wealth of transcendent world models is so much more perfect than the bits and mangled pieces the objective world can offer him to do the job with. He cannot help depending on us and on the smashed remains of what was once ours, but at least he can say to himself, and us, that 'really' he is something far better. If substantially speaking he/his world is not what he thinks and feels it should be, then at least he-the-intention, the personified world model as such, should be regarded as something superior.

He has pushed his boundaries ever further outward and now he is even pushing at the boundaries of pure worldliness itself, awkwardly and after a fashion. He is definitely trying to get above himself (and us of course, in the process). Positive Taurus learnt to see himself as something a bit more than the merely substantial too: a collection of acquired abilities. Negative Taurus, in his blindness, has acquired nothing new since his first stroke of work, except the ability to strike with ever more devastating repetitiveness. The only aspect of himself he can see is the material one, and that never to his satisfaction.

Now he has hit on this ploy of regarding himself as something of an underlying essential in himself: the one who makes the world take on its shape. He is no longer only identifiable as the world-shape itself, but also the shaper, distinct from the product.

Watching us do his work for him has given him the idea to elevate himself to a superior status. Not very far (he still needs to be in the thick of it to watch his self take on form, under our obedient hands) but sufficiently to let us know that we are no longer just his conscripted co-workers, but placed under him, somewhat. Remembering where he took his model plan for his becoming from in the first place comes in handy here: we are doing not only his bidding, he assures us, we are fulfilling a function dictated by Life itself. And he, Taurus, himself, is the one who is in mysterious intuitive contact with this invisible Source. He has only seized hold of this little bit of a world-building plan, but now it suits him to present it as all of a Higher Instruction, which he is handing down to us. We need not bother criticising him.

When it comes to defying or obstructing his plan, he is certainly not to be trifled with. He can ignore a lot, and does, from sheer massive obtuseness, but if we stage horrible surprises, like sudden disobedience, right under his nose then this can only lead to an equally sudden and equally uncharacteristic response from him. Responding as such is hardly his thing, new forms of behaviour aren't 'him' at all. But if he ever gets thrown off course, he can only flail wildly in self-defence; the more so because he has nothing but his insensitivity and ignorance to defend himself with, normally.

Unlike positive Taurus he has no proper manufactured defences, none of those different types of walls and screens and gates and tended hedges to shelter behind. He is naked, and only the sheer mass of his own unvarying lumpish self keeps the nasty surprises out, at a safe distance from the inner core where he is actually happening. But this is precisely the tender spot he has invited us to share with him: to join him in his ever-repeated self-production process – to do his work for him while he watches. His life process lies literally in our obedient, well-trained hands. Any slip-up, never mind a boycott, is a mortal threat: something he is not at all used to any more. From his point of view the world lost its ability to destabilise him long ago. No wonder he strikes hard, in horror, at any threat that has sneaked through his own filtering, crushing, homogenising and safe-making bulkiness and confronts him here at the core of his being. (Sadly, this is one rare instance of surpassing himself: only intuitively reaching for a different model for behaviour, appropriate to his desperate situation, could have told him how to act so totally out of character.) The threat, the threatening person, has to be ejected from his personal sphere fast. He never forgives. The offender is banished for good, to some unknown outer reaches of the world.

Not that there are many such outer reaches left. He has rough-ly taken the living world to pieces and used some of these to set up his rigid single-pattern version in its stead. He has pushed his operative boundaries ahead of himself at increasing speed. Now he comes to the point where there is nothing left in any direction but his own constructs (to be left untouched and unchanged in perpetuity, of course), or the great wasteland of his spoil heaps. If all this dross and rubbish that he could find no use for in the course of his heedless pulling down and selective, 'prepro-grammed' building up did impinge on his consciousness at all, or was in his way, he simply had great wagonloads of it transported away out of his sight and reach. What is piled up here, at the ends of the world, stands for all the life alternatives he has rejected.

His compulsively narrow self-constructive impetus has at last run him into his own manifest limitations. Whichever way he looks for chances to continue his absurd life of becoming-again, he sees nothing but unsuitable material, his own unrecognised by-products. They poison his view most painfully and spoil his future altogether. He may try to fall back on a more literal, con-crete self-repetition: going back over already established ground – just what he did in the very beginning, before he found ways to engineer the pretend-becoming he has been practising all this time. But if he tries to revisit the past, if he examines the 'body' he has accumulated, he only finds it to be coming apart, decaying, falling down.

It was all built to an unnaturally narrow design, regardless of wider considerations, it has not stood the test of time. The meticu-lous care that went into making it was so much wasted effort. He did not even bother to maintain his products, he was in far too much of a hurry to see more of the same made to give any thought to what might happen, or have happened by now, to last week's output. He no longer understands about having-things-hap-pened-to, he is used only to making everything happen himself. He is in charge, he knows what he's doing, what else is there to consider? Now he is shocked to see his collected self cracking, peeling and hanging askew. It is a sight even more frightful to him than the useless rubbish tips looming on all sides.

Besides his material spoil heaps he also meets for the first time his human rejects, contained behind the same high fence of studious ignorance: the disobedient workers, the dissident producers, the rival world builders that he never bothered to take into consideration, those who failed to be his supporters and those who were unfit to be his identikit friends – just what he can't bear to see: strangers, always the death of him. He has finally come to the predictable end of his one-model production line. He has exhausted the raw material for his one and only building plan.

But now his legacy remains for those to clean up who have unquestioningly accepted his norm for their own: his one, inappropriately singled-out, personalised, and then ruthlessly imposed piece of the whole Life Plan that really 'belongs' to us all to make use of, as we individually manage to do or see fit. He leaves us nothing but the task of destroying the world he has trained us so well to build, to dismantle it and start again from scratch, this time with a broader design that incorporates all the 'waste' we have produced by leaving out so much as unsuitable, or not worth taking into consideration. But like he we have become stuck in a rut. Of course there were always some who shouted different instructions at us from the sidelines, warning us, or making those quite unheard-of suggestions that sounded more like a prescription for chaos to us. But we have ignored them. We have thought it safe, and safest, not to listen to them. Now, unless we stubbornly insist on going down with all hands in this dead-end mess we have made of our world, our repetitive lives, and our lifeless selves, we have no option but listen.

Passive grinding to a halt, or active destruction of what we have become: the only two options negative Taurus leaves behind. Always true to himself, if not to his positive potential, he does not even leave us a *proper* choice. To radically transform our ill-formed lives is not going to leave us; with anything recognisable: it looks no better than death to us; and those dissident promises of other life options are falling on uncertain ears. We fiddle a tiny little bit with our 'sacred' production process, in the hope that it will make all the difference – without our really noticing it. It is hardly what one could call a new start. Large-scale sacrifices are called for and all we can think to do is to tighten the odd screw, slowly. It looks as if things will have to start breaking, slipping and falling on our heads before we snap out of it.

Like negative Leo, negative Taurus produces carbon copies of himself – of a far more concrete and yet less durable kind. Copies not of what he innately is but of only one of the many things he might be: a chance of self he snatched at in a hurry. He too thinks he must be the Only One (possible), but unlike Leo it takes him a lot of doing to convince himself that he is somehow, vaguely, placed above others. Leo imposes his will and gives gifts to mollify, but Taurus simply imposes his physical presence and then *attracts* us with the sight of apparently well-formed plenty.

If there are similarities with negative Sagittarius in the way his 'empire' spreads, it is because he too has built himself a home in matter in an inappropriate way. Sagittarius was wrong to project *all* of his transcendent self into the world. For Taurus the mistake lies in *not* materialising *all* there is of the transcendent life (and self) possibilities. Not staying in touch with this great variety of self-models: making them take on flesh one at a time. His ruthless reductionism has substituted for the whole oceanic variety of possible life forms an impossibly narrow stream, a jet that propels him forward without leading to any genuinely new gains. Again, one is reminded of negative Aries – another one who had 'rejects', enemies in his case.

Unlike the destructive Fire despots though, negative Taurus looks harmless enough in his grinding-on and dead steady ways. The hidden dangers of his misrule have a nasty way of revealing themselves suddenly and drastically, when it is too late to side-step the consequences of his insidious activities.

Some Suggested Taurus Attributes

basic

down-to-earth, basically sensual

needs stability and **concrete certainties, fear of changes; clings, huddles** and **hides away; fixes his attention, insists on maintaining his position,** both literally and metaphorically: **fixed attitudes; slowness, inertia, reluctance to move himself; may be seen as stubborn and lazy** or else **very co-operative** if this will cause him least upset

cautious, lacks courage, easily defeated; unenterprising, conventional and **obedient:** because he prefers his certainties; **repetitive, predictable, boring, 'colourless', lacking in originality, limited**

on the other hand he **can be depended on,** he is **loyal, steadfast, trustworthy; patient:** he actually prefers to proceed slowly

positive

industrious: builds, constructs, shapes his environment; transforms the simple givens of life: finds new uses, modifies, converts, takes into cultivation, tames etc.; **beautifies, makes comfortable, enhances**

many **inspired unconscious guidelines: broad-based skills; creative urge, especially good at architectural design, sculpting, landscaping, farming** etc.

he manages increase and growth in terms of self-confidence, output, variety, complexity; moderately **versatile**

neat and methodical worker; practical, efficient, skilful; not easily distracted; avoids haste and waste: steady, stable, dependable; accumulates, finds a use for everything; self-sufficient or at least **knows how to make do**

easily contented, not ambitious, modest aims persistently worked towards; busy behind the scenes, unostentatious

likes peace and quiet, averse to fighting and competition, needs a secure home-base, at least to start out from; **family-minded; quietly patriotic**

unaggressively territorial, encloses, shelters; contains, holds on to; conserves, preserves, tends and **cultivates; maintains, sustains, consolidates, restores; traditional; inviting, attractive, hospitable, provider, supportive**

works for others, **sharing his skills** and (intuitive) ideas: **artisan; trainer, instructor**

works to an adopted plan: makes a good **employee, executive, manager,** etc.; **improves, varies, corrects, newly interprets**

negative

self-willed, stubborn but **uncertain of himself; grasping, greedy, won't share; self-centred** to the point of not noticing others

clings blindly to the status quo; unshakeable, narrow convictions of a **materialistic** kind; **concretistic, reductionist, simplistic; aims for quantity rather than true quality,** despite his **short-sighted fussiness; superficially efficient** in his **exaggerated productivity**

invasive, inadvertently overpowering, indirectly pushy; destructive because **carelessly insistent; can be aggressive(ly defensive)** if he reckons himself to be under attack: **uncharacteristic outbursts, 'beside himself':** not acting out of his usual, established self

insensitive, coarse, dulled perceptions; obtuse; clumsy, messy, loud, crushing, lacking in subtlety and complexity; narrow tastes, crashing bore

weighty, over-weight; inflates his importance, pompous, imposes his views etc.; **commandeering, takes over**

workhorse who never stops churning out a mass product – unless he can find others to do the work for him: **lazy, depends** and **leans on others** for support and for his progress; **obstinately demanding; bossy, expects to be obeyed and served;** worst type of **employer, industrialist** etc. and worst type of **employee** who cares only about the stability of his output/income

obedient, 'mainstream' stick-in-the-mud, standard-issue in everything, never steps out of line, praises a 'normality' that is faulty and inorganic because not even remotely complete

refuses to accept anything outside his **norm: suspicious, xenophobic; sticks to his own concerns; rejects variation and alternatives, banishes all deviation** and 'deviants' from his personal sphere: **thoughtlessly disapproving; exclusive on a large scale; wasteful; litters, bulldozes, poisons and generally harms the environment**

consumerist; uses people as a source of pleasure or income; **lack of respect for life** due to a **lack of awareness** of life forms that differ from him (including other people)

♍
VIRGO

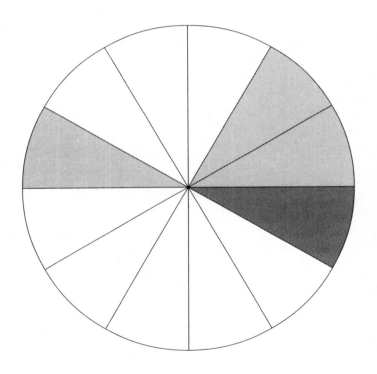

♍ **Extravert**
conscious function: thinking; direction of function: both
outward and inward
unconscious functions: ♓ **feeling,** ♎ **sensing,** ♏ **intuition**
Earth: senses-oriented

Virgo is an extravert whose conscious function is both outward
and inward-directed. To turn towards his environment is what he
does first: not only because it is the more natural direction for an
extravert to take, given the choice, but because without first finding something in his environment to call self and to take with him,
so to speak, when he turns inward, there would seem to be no
point in his turning inward at all. He 'contains' nothing as yet,
only what one might call a space reserved for an internalised self.

Taurus, doubly 'earthy', used his physical senses to contact the
material world. Virgo employs his conscious thought processes
instead. But being also an Earth sign, he directs his thoughtful
search in the direction of the more concrete phenomena of the
world, that is to say its structure. The abstracting process of
thought applied to the material environment makes him highly
observant, and choosy. Where Taurus initially just saw and took
his sense of self from what he saw, Virgo thinks about what there
is to see and to be. And by way of choosily extracting the best possible items from his environment, he dissects and investigates the
matter further. He scrutinises and analyses, he becomes aware of
differences, contradictions and flaws, causes and effects. Nothing
escapes his notice, and everything he observes leads him to draw
conclusions and form preferences. He comes to discriminate
between what to him appears reasonable, convincing, effective
and, practically speaking, desirable and what is not. This puts him
in the strange position of criticising precisely what his self is about
to consist of. He sifts as it were with a fine-toothed comb through
what is on offer by way of self-material.

With Taurus the first basic impulse was to embrace the whole
world of potential self indiscriminately. Only when that proved
painfully impossible to him did he equip himself with a plan of
action to *make*, rather than merely *search* for, his self; and this plan

he unconsciously adopted was derived from out of the impersonal fund of all organic possibilities. The self Virgo assembles, after much picking and choosing, is also his own 'construct'. But unlike Taurus – who was bound by the given nature of his intuitively received life patterns to work from – Virgo has the freedom of conscious choice: based on his individual capacity for directed thought. Having called Taurus a 'self-made man', one might call Virgo a 'man-made self'. (A figure of speech hard to avoid, even though it is signs we are dealing with, not actual people.) There *are* limits to Virgo's choices, in that they are conditioned by what is available in his given environment, but apart from that there is nothing to stop him concocting whatever mixture he deems fit to call 'I', choosing his own 'design'.

Having consciously and deliberately chosen his self from among the options his environment offered him, Virgo then becomes aware *inside himself* of being what he has chosen to be. This is the inward-turning process, introverting thought. Extraverting, he has selected a self, and now he introjects it. He makes it an inner reality – and with that he hovers on the brink of being a (self-appointed) introvert. In effect, he is neither the one nor the other but both at the same time. He is consciously aware of being himself, inside himself, *as well as* being identified with certain selected parts of the world outside his inner space. This duality of his is not a problem in itself; it is integrated by the similarity or correspondence of 'inside self' and 'outside self'. His real problem now is the same that affects all extraverting extraverts: the limitless changeability of the objective world.

As his environment changes, presenting all sorts of new possibilities to choose from and identify more of his self in, he keeps discovering better things to be. It is not enough for him to go on extraverting till he has collected the self-material to fill his inner space with, and from then on to rest content with being what he is. He would have no more living-becoming from that point on and, quite apart from that, it is part of the totality of his given basic nature that he should always both extravert and introvert – not necessarily at the same time. However, once he finds yet-again-better things to be outside himself, there *is* as split now, a contradiction, between the concrete identity he has assumed in the world, and the abstract reflection of it inside him. To rectify matters, he needs to bring his inner self up to date: which would mean rejecting at least some of what he has previously, and after giving it much thought, accepting as worth calling 'I', in the privacy of his inner being.

This is an unbearable intrusion into his inner integrity, a destruction of what he has so painstakingly established inside himself. Constantly turning himself upside down in thoughtful response to a changing world amounts to other-out-there interfering with his internalised self – even if he is himself the agent who relays the demand for change. If this is what life is about, the freedom of self-construction always followed by the inevitability of self-destruction, then, like Taurus, he prefers to have nothing to do with it. He at least had a more promising start. He has managed to assemble a good deal of self, and tucked it away in a safe place. But at this point he is stuck: huddling in an inner isolation that regards all life out there as leading nowhere but in a painful circle of self-undoing and re-doing. And yet his *extraverting* function is pointing him in that direction. He is at odds with himself, and at odds with life. He has seized up mid-way to becoming what he should be.

The offer of help, as always, comes from the unconscious functions and the wise or unwise use of them is up to him. Emotionally, he experiences the whole world as an indissoluble oneness, quite irrespective of the individual parts it consists of (⟩(→). Positively used, this indiscriminate emotional inclusiveness will counter-balance his ultra-fussy and overly discriminating approach. Everything and everybody feels right to him, totally acceptable and quite beyond criticism. Behind the welter of analysed detail he now feels the meaningful connectedness of all things. This means that there must be a measure of validity or meaningfulness even in imperfection, deficiency, failure. Not only does each particle of the whole-world have its place in it, but its very deficiency is somehow made up for, overridden, by its being placed in the larger context. He feels the totality of the objective world to be 'right', even if a good many of its constituent parts appear all wrong to his conscious thinking. Somewhere it all fits in, even the crooked and twisted and pitifully inadequate.

This broadened attitude allows him to be far less sharply critical in his choices, less exclusive in his assessment of what 'will do' or 'won't do'. He is more inclined to accept the less than perfect, or to give it the benefit of the doubt at least. His horizon has expanded sufficiently to allow him an (emotional) understanding of the underlying oneness that surpasses, embraces *and* reconciles all these mutually contradictory and imperfect phenomena he observes around him. As a result, his formerly quite narrow concentration on the exact 'fit' or fitness of things is replaced by a more mellow attitude. He no longer makes such a great fuss rejecting: always promptly picking bits out as unwanted. Others also no longer present a lot of totally unacceptable faces and facets of behaviour to him: he learns to forgive or at least overlook their shortcomings. Emotionally, he experiences everybody simply as fellow beings who are essentially no different from him. All in all, he can no longer practice his finicky perfectionism without feeling that somehow he is missing the (larger) point.

What he applies to the world around him he can also apply to himself. If he thought of himself as a collection of all the best bits he could select from the world to construct an inner self with, then he thought of himself as an isolated instance of perfection, or near enough. But now he feels himself to be one rather insignificant being among many ($\aleph\leftarrow$), a modest contribution to all there is, no more. This cuts him right down to size – so much so, there is a danger of nothing being left of the self he is. He thought his problem was how to keep his inner self intact; or rather how to perfect it further from out of new choices, while *still* somehow keeping it intact. Now he feels that it barely matters what sort of self he is, exactly, that any self he might choose to be will make an equally acceptable part of life as a whole. Above all, he feels that he needs to share all he has got, and share it indiscriminately. The self he has collected together and tucked away out of sight in his personal inner space is in danger of being poured out again into the common possession of all. He would join a world without differentiation, without structure but the one encompassing, insubstantial, emotional oneness.

He has both gained and lost, with the use of unconscious feeling. What he has gained is the ability to be more relaxed in his scrutiny of all potential self-material. A chance to acquire a less precise self to introject: less minutely defined, and in consequence less likely to differ quite so drastically from other selves (and from all the rest that has not been selected as self). He is in far less danger now of finding himself in the position where he discovers something *utterly* new/different/better to become, *quite* at odds with what he is – and consequently threatening his complete established inner-space self with annihilation. To put it simply, the broader-based his chosen internalised self is, the less cause he will find to amend it so drastically as to throw a large part of it out altogether. Fewer, minor inner changes to impose on his self means the pain of abrupt self-destruction is replaced by the far more bearable experience of having to undergo a life-long series of small-scale self-improvements. Where before he faced quantum leaps from one over-specific state of inner being to another totally different one, now he can find the greater fluidity of gradual development, based on a more inclusive self.

Like Taurus, Virgo has the ability to 'grow organically', step by step, from one variation of a basic theme into the next. Taurus' 'theme' is the given matrix of all organic possibilities, a transcendent reality form where he 'borrows' a bit at a time to embody and establish. Virgo's basic theme to work from, on the other hand, is his own composition, the parts of which he borrowed from the established environment and then spirited away into another, transcending, reality: the inner reality of the internalised self. His chosen and internalised theme is actually far more limited than Taurus' given one, because it derives from a far more limited origin, not to mention his additional selecting and abstracting. But as regards Virgo's becoming, his varying of the basic theme: the freedom he has in that respect is quite unprecedented. His scope is quite 'un-natural'. It is entirely up to him to conduct his growing and becoming in any direction he thinks appropriate. He may freely and deliberately choose new varieties of self to become, without having to take his cue from what nature dictates. The only 'organic' thing about him, so far, is his new-found ability to refrain from being too deliberately exclusive in his choice of self – which gives him his capacity for minor, step by step changes towards his future self: for (inner) growth.

But having gained the 'give' to be less over-individualised, so to speak, he has unfortunately at the same time lost a good deal of his ability to hang on to any of the specific self he is. He is pulled in two opposite directions: to think of himself as uniquely he, a being apart in his inner world; or to feel himself to be no more than a part of his environment, his 'originality' dissolved again in the very origin he had abstracted it from in the first place. Thinking in terms of particles, feeling in terms of The Whole, he can find no compromise between his separatist stance, his refusenik intellect, and his emotional propensity to 'give in to' his environment.

At this point he needs to dip again into the gifts provided by the unconscious. He has a good sense of proportion, of how all separate things meaningfully relate one to the other and find their place in the overall arrangement that makes up the whole of life (♎). This enables him to take up a new and central position, 'siding' neither with the emotionally experienced whole, nor with the thoughtfully isolated detail. He comes to appreciate that it is not a case of *either* parts *or* whole. He realises that the part does not simply vanish on its own account when it becomes part *of*, but that instead it plays its part, or takes part in, the overall scheme of the shared, communal, one life. His unconscious sensation function allows him to experience the world as an interconnected system of parts arranged according to laws that govern the whole, and this helps him understand that he is not forced to *abandon* the internalised self he has established the moment he finds himself emotionally drawn towards all that is not he.

The compromise is to *participate* as what he is. To share his inner self not by simply relinquishing his hold on it, which would benefit nobody, but by standing himself in active relation to what goes on in the wider world. He can act out of his inner self in helpful, contributing ways and that way 'share' what he is – without being personally diminished, obviously. Life becomes a relative give and take. And his place in the world is a different one now: if he wants to grow, become, derive new things from out of the world to add to his self, then he will have to *work* for it. Abducting some of the substance of the world and transmogrifying it into something called the inner 'I' was not even half the story. Neither did rediscovering his connectedness, pure and simple, with everything he had left behind complete it. Now he will have to give something back to the world out there, in thought-out, emotionally responsive and proportionate action.

He comes to restructure and improve his environment. When his thinking function extraverts, it is no longer *only* in order to gather more and better bits of self to be, inside himself, it now also serves the purpose of thinking what to do with and for the world out there. Put another way, he not only in-forms himself, but also his environment. He has learnt to feel that life is about sharing, and to see himself as needing to stand always in some kind of actively balanced relation, not just receiving from life-out-there but also contributing to it. This can only mean that he has not introjected the gathered self in order to *have* it, but to *use* it, to act out of it, to help rearrange the world with the aid of what he has so carefully, thoughtfully arranged for himself to be. His personal becoming, his life of self-improvement, is inextricably linked with this work of helping the world around him become a better place.

His sense of proportion also makes sure that he sees things from a different and wider angle again. He is only too frequently about to reject things as 'inappropriate': that is when he is considering them from a purely logical angle, and in the context of the more immediately available physical evidence. But the very same things may appear to make rather a lot more sense when seen in the light of considerations that go beyond the strictly material and logical. It is not enough, after all, if things 'fit' and 'work'. Neither is it enough to act out in any way what will work or that appears sensible in itself. The wider relative value or merit of every action has to be taken into consideration: there is more involved now than mere cleverness and pragmatism.

But he is still faced with another stumbling block. His self started out so far removed from the prevailing, 'natural' norm that even with all the emotional goodwill in the world and the keenest sense for appropriate behaviour, he is still somehow always the odd one out. (From his point of view it is others, of course, who are peculiar.) The world can't help viewing him with a measure of puzzled suspicion. He may be careful not to upset apple carts, but he is still a pretty dab hand at turning things upside down – experimentally, he says, if we don't mind. An innovation in himself, something material nature never thought of, he thinks nothing of suggesting the formerly 'impossible'. His more hidebound contemporaries easily take objection to that, out of received principle. And he is still inclined to see himself, proudly, as his own maker. Self-criticism may keep his pride well within bounds, but then again one never finds him shy exactly when it comes to filling any vacuum he perceives in the world with his own 'creations' – and the strangest concoctions they can be. Hidebound nature may well protest, in an 'allergic reaction' to his clever, helpfully meant, 'originality'.

In order to get more in tune with his natural environment, he needs to use his unconscious intuitive insight ($\mathbb{M}$). This informs him that there exist life models, archetypes of all that may one day be, and that the power to impose a shape on the world has to go hand in hand with the understanding of these. For Taurus they represented a chance to build his self in a concrete way; he used these intuited designs as his inspiration (as well as an invitation, even a command, to make the latent visible and objectively real). Virgo for his part now finds in them a chance to check his own self-design for serious flaws. These *may* be due of course to the imperfection of his given environment, which did not offer him enough in the way of positive choices. Either way, here is his chance to weed out the worst mistakes; and likewise to base his actions not exclusively on the availability, inside himself, of clever 'self-conceived' ideas to implement, but also (to put it simply) on what Life intends.

When he learns to check his against Life's intentions he finds not only where he was about to go wrong but also, surprisingly, that he is not at all as 'unnatural' as he thought. With some adjustments he is well within the parameter of what Nature permits; maybe not strictly speaking norm-al, but quite acceptable, a grain of spice that will transform the dish without in the least spoiling it. This is not so surprising after all, when he gives it some thought: whatever selecting, abstracting thought processes he may have used to construct his self, it still originated in the (imperfect) objective counterpart of the inner-plane Plan.

In this unconscious realisation he finds his true perfection, as far as this is possible in living reality. Cut down to size once again, he has to humbly admit that despite his autonomous choosing and improving of his introjected self, at bottom it owes its existence just as much to the hidden forces of life and to the existing objective order as he found it. He is no kind of self-creator; he has only been working on something given. This should have been obvious to him from the start, of course. But then he has let himself be blinded by the fiddly facts and figures of a hundred different detailed free choices, and it has taken three-horizon expanding, self-integrating steps for him to see the simple *truth* of himself. This 'man-made self' of his is not really 'made' by him at all. He is only self-*styled*, from something essentially provided: a humbling and cautioning thought for him.

But now at last he is ready to join Taurus as his companion world builder. His sorting, sifting, inspecting and criticising, from an individually thoughtful angle, has a lot to contribute to the world: a new order and regularity; attention to the smaller points that are so easily overlooked; precision, as an adjunct of usefulness; the finishing touches and the fine-grain polish; and above all the individual stamp. Taurus as a vicarious constructor has already checked our designs and desires before he consented to make a start on the work, and he has already added some simple embellishments that will appeal to his and our need for a concrete identity that is pleasing to our senses. Now what Taurus has built passes into the hands of Virgo who not only checks it again, and minutely, but 'refines' it and at the same time adds a touch uniquely his own – without forgetting that it needs to end up an integral part of the world, of potential benefit to all, and something that nature can countenance, can bear to have introduced into it, if only in measured doses. Virgo as vicarious world (re)constructor adds the necessary detail: the logical, intricate, aesthetically balanced, feelingful and thoughtful *individual* detail. These further embellishments he adds are not meant to please our simple outward-directed senses. Rather, they demonstrate to us both the possibility of being individually and thoughtfully in charge of our common environment, and the great care that has to be taken, in all respects, when doing so.

Whatever he works on, modifying and improving, is never really finished for him; he considers and reconsiders. And each active contact with the outside world calls for another small inner change on his part, new self-becoming – which in turn forces him to act differently. Having constructed his self out of the available options, introjected it, and actively, consciously 'working on it', gives him exceptional self-awareness. At every point in his development he knows what he is about, and when he acts in the world he knows why he acts the way he does: because the inner nature he has acquired demands it. His adopted rules of behaviour correspond to the rules, the nature, of the self he has adopted into his inner space and there called 'I' in full self-consciousness. Out of inner self-consciousness is born conscience.

He may go (within the laws of reason, considerateness etc.)

against the predominant collective grain of his environment, but he cannot go against his own 'grain'. Like an introvert he has got to be true to his established inner self, and in full intellectual awareness. But unlike an introvert, he has what one may call a provisional inner self: one that is always in the re-making. And the same goes for his conscience: it is always responsive; not a haphazardly malleable thing, but nevertheless adaptive. (Rather than call him an individual with a personal conscience, it may be better to call him a conscientious individualist – one who never ceases in his well thought-out efforts to become individualised.)

The paradox is this: an *extraverting* introvert, as seen in Leo, is never in direct, conscious touch with his inner nature; while an *introverting* introvert, as exemplified by Sagittarius, has no conscious interest in, or capacity for, 'creating' or structuring his environment. The extravert Virgo, who has *assumed* some of the nature of an introvert, turns out to be one of the only two *effective* introverts (i.e. able to consciously and self-awarely translate their subjective content into objective fact) to be found in the whole zodiac – the other being the natural introvert Capricorn, the other thinker among the signs.

Virgo's task, however, is not only to imprint the material world with a living and changing pattern of his own devising, in obedience to his chosen and ever self-renewing inner pattern. His task goes beyond the purely material and practical, just as he in his acquired innerness now consciously transcends the realm of the purely physical. He has deep insight into the mechanics of being and becoming as such. He knows from personal experience the multitude of contradictions that are involved: response to, and borrowing from, the environment; but also holding on to inner rules of being, and insisting on expressing them faithfully in action. Emotional responsiveness, a sense of meaningful integratedness into the workings of the whole, respect for the overriding laws of life as such; but also the inner obligation to make one's personal mark, to be uniquely in charge of the contribution one makes to life. Virgo, knowing consciously what all extraverts and most introverts are barely aware of, is the most 'understanding' of the signs – in the sense of being able to think himself into everyone's psychological processes to a degree that no other sign can rival. Somewhere in his complex self he can sympathise and identify readily with the problems others have with such seemingly simple and 'natural' processes as being and becoming.

He himself has become what he is only after many inner upheavals, despite needing to maintain a constant hold on his ever changing self-awareness. It has taken him many efforts to make his peace with a changing world and a changing, becoming identity both within and apart from the world, in innerness. He knew from the start that not all and everything in the world is fit to become part of an internalised self. But he had to learn that not all of his inner self is fit to be translated wholesale into objective action either; that some of it may need revising so that it may play a useful part in the given context. Now he can stand as an example and serve as a helper in these matters: encouraging others to manage their own self-growth; to make themselves into something uniquely distinctive within the collective framework; and to establish this securely by transcending what they outwardly do and are: to 'have a mind of their own', *inside* themselves; and finally, how to renew themselves painlessly in response to a changing world and new contacts with all that is other.

The world he helps build is no longer simple; no longer is life conducted at a single level of awareness. It is a more complex (and complicated) world, with a much increased scope for individualised conscious development for all of us – and without there being a danger that we will infringe each other's rights to differ. It is an eminently adjustable world, explorative, full of tentative suggestions and counter-suggestions, new self-discoveries and changes of mind. And yet all this is down-to-earth enough, each new would-be improvement being put to the critical test of, somehow, having to 'work'.

As a self-builder to his own design Virgo has more than enough opportunity to go wrong when he misuses his unconscious functions. He has the emotional experience ()(→) of finding the world to be a oneness that surpasses its many separate parts, but instead of letting it broaden his horizon, he misuses it to endorse his narrow choices.

This feeling he has that, come what may, there is always a vague and woolly rightness 'to it all' only serves to give him the idea that what *he* considers best should apply to all the world.

Compulsively, he makes the feeling of something universally valid serve the purpose of universalising and validating his personal choices. And in the process his choices acquire an emotional charge. They become faithfully held convictions, fixed in eternity. Nothing has ever been, nor will ever be, more sensible, fitting and perfectly reasonable than what he considers to be so. – There is now absolutely no fear of finding occasion to upset the structure of his chosen, internalised self: it becomes a once and for all established certitude. He has become immune to change (or so he would like to believe).

But if he is immune to life impinging on him, then he is stuck now for any sort of becoming that would give him life. The only thing he could become – in the best tradition of all the other despotic, negatively acting signs – is the world out there: by imposing his dead-perfect self on it. But unconsciously he feels himself endangered by an engulfing tide of all that is other ($\times\leftarrow$). Anything that lies beyond the confines of his own strictly delimited inner self now poses a vague but overwhelming threat. In the circumstances, all his extraverting function can do in the world is to reject and repel. The only contribution he can make to life is a repeated, terse NO. And the only thing he gains thereby is to get ever more seized up in his conviction that he alone is possessed of an exceptional 'rightness'.

'Stuck-up' describes it better than one might realise: he really is stuck up there in his isolated inner would-be perfection and looking down askance on his rejects, us. He wants nothing more than to reshape us according to his ideas; that would bring him to life again, if he could 'become' us like that. But he doesn't dare. He fears that if he gets involved with life at all, then he will be invaded, polluted, spoilt. He refuses to expose his nice tidy self to what after all he has already, categorically and once and for all, refused to accept as anything to do with him. One could offer him something perfectly nice – but he in *his* perfectness knows better. He will reject anything at all with genuine horror and there is no persuading him to even examine it first. He is 'allergic' to the lot, condemning it all on principle. His mind is truly closed.

He wastes his next chance to have his outlook broadened as well. He senses that there is some overall body of laws that sees to it that all parts of the whole are meaningfully connected and work in harmony ($\triangle$). But he does not hesitate to use this unconscious awareness to simply underpin his inflexible convictions further. If obviously laws there are and have to be, then who better than he – who has the ability to scrutinise and criticise every nut, nail and bolt – to pinpoint them and gather them into an orderly codex. He certainly adds to himself in the process: to his conviction that he always knows best he adds a smug moral rectitude as well – but he is hardly any aliver for it.

On a more practical note, though, he also senses that (as he interprets it) there is no need for him to get personally involved at all: no need to expose his treasured self to life's threatening imperfections, where he might inadvertently pick up something nasty, wrong and dirty. Instead of meeting his chance of personal becoming out there – involving changes, inner changes, on his part – he can participate in life by enacting his inner convictions like a set script. That is to say he can apply his 'superior understanding' (for which read: impose his opinions) at one safe remove, impersonally, while sheltering inside his impermeable cocoon, hiding behind his abstract better-knowing.

His extraverting begins to take on just a shade more liveliness, because there is more than a NO from him now: a whole barrage of explanations is appended, a whole canon of incontrovertible law is cited. But with his stilted, not-really-of-this-world behaviour, he is hardly making much of an impression. At least half of his attention is always given over to the job of withholding what he *is*, safely inside himself. All this talking he *does*, in his peculiarly uninvolved if emotionally charged ways, is done in a hasty and huddling sort of way. His eyes are averted, his mouth barely opens (better be safe!) as he hisses his disapproval. We are not exactly queuing up to listen to him.

His 'conscience' is telling him to act out of his convictions, impose them, substitute them for the world about him. The reason his 'conscience' is telling him that is, of course, that unless he can become his environment, he has no living-becoming at all. He has imprisoned his self in would-be perfect innerness and life is quite passing him by (not that he would want any of it: it is nothing but the sum total of all the life options he has been strenuously rejecting, after all).

But whatever his so-called conscience may be telling him to do, how can he possibly do it? It would mean getting rid of *our* preferences and convictions and established choices, to be supplanted by his. And the gulf between him and us is so pronounced, it would take a lot of getting rid of before he could even make a start on making his so-called perfection come real and alive. He feels outnumbered, threatened. Despite recognising only a quite surpassing rightness to all he is inside himself, he knows he is on uncertain ground the moment he does anything in our world.

To find the courage of his convictions, he has to fall back on the use of his unconscious intuitive abilities ($\mathfrak{M}$). When he becomes aware of the underlying non-material models of formed reality, latent images of *perfection*, he immediately takes it for granted that they and he are closely related, if not very nearly the same thing. If there is anything there that he does not recognise, he can always argue those bits away. He has put in enough practise at not-wanting-to-know to have developed his innate scrutinising into a form of mental tunnel vision, reductionist and yet all-embracing in its intention. What he considers, he does so from the basis of already knowing what kind of information it should yield him. Anything that does not fit his pre-conceptions is classified as inadmissible, dangerous, distasteful, wicked and disorderly. And such is the strength of his belief in himself that an intuitive understanding of transcendent model existences only serves to prove to him that his internalised self, in its would-be perfection, is truly as things ought to be. He knew it: Life meant him to be like that. And if Life has any other ideas besides, he is conveniently ignoring them.

But his intuition is also telling him that the inherent life patterns *demand* to be made manifest, to be implemented and enacted in objective reality. This ties in very neatly with what he needs to do but does not have the courage to do. Having declared all underlying perfection as such his own, this demand to 'embody' it now too becomes his. He becomes at the very least an agent, if not a personification, of all that Life would want to be – but is prevented from being by our perverted, thoughtless and immoral behaviour... He claims the power to put matters right as his. He has been entrusted with it by Life (or The Creator, or some such Being marginally superior to him). At last, in a world full of faults, he can no longer sit still in his corner with a disapproving look on his face. He *must* follow his inner command and become the broom that sweeps clean.

He looks rather like a plaster saint coming to life now, stiffly waving his arms about in urgent and peremptory admonition: if only we would become like him, then all would be well with the world. Once he gets into his stride, he throws all he has got into his Message. There are tearful (♓) appeals, and highly emotive promises of joy unbounded. The most luridly rosy (♎) descriptions trip bravely off his tongue when he pictures our potential future. Now at last we are listening to him with rapt attention. And then of course there are the dark threats (♏) of hitherto undisclosed horrors that await us if we do not immediately drop what we are doing, and being, and follow his example, concretely, and correct in every detail. – Whoever is not instantly converted, surely stands trembling.

What he does *not* say is that the world's becoming 'better' will be *his* becoming, and the only one he is capable of: that our transformation is to be his life. Just as negative Taurus had to build himself over and over again, mimicking development with more and more of the same self-becoming, so negative Virgo imitates living a life by imposing his dead-right self again and again as the one static, transformative model of perfect being and doing. It goes without saying that since he never saw fit to check his chosen self-design against any wider considerations, the model he presents may be anything from the merely quaint and dotty, via various shades of increasing eccentricity, all the way to the obviously harmful, if collectively applied.

Like his Taurus counterpart he is kept busy just issuing commands from one end of the world to the other, expecting to be obeyed by his followers. But *his* followers have to do more than just do, they also have to *be*: imitation paragons, applying his edicts inside themselves, in the privacy of their own minds, just as much as they outwardly put his commands into action. They have to be converts through and through. The practical work is only half the story, it needs the proper, conscience-ridden motivation as well. He checks on that, as far as possible, lurking outside doors and behind curtains, an eagle eye open for any lapses. He sees it as his rightful business to enquire into our minds: our inner being is his prime target area, being the root of all this evil in the world. In other words, any independent opinions we might sneakily harbour inside our heads can only rival his. But we will not manage to keep them hidden there all the time, they will produce their effects. And he will catch us at it.

With all his prying and spying, what he *really* sees, though, is his own chance of new becoming. That is why he watches so eagerly. He may look and sound busy enough, giving the impression that there is plenty of life in him, but *in himself*, and in his personal space around him, nothing ever happens except by repetition. His frantic wiping and polishing is no more than a ritual treading on the spot. There *is* no dirt to wipe away, such a thing is never allowed to come *near* him. Neither does a new thought ever enter his mind. If we did not let him see some of our dirt to point a finger at, and let him overhear some of our shocking gossip to point his efforts in a new direction, he would be left to pace in circles and twiddle his thumbs: his life depends on our 'evil' ways. Those parts of the world he has already 'saved', cleaned up, put straight and in good order are really of no more interest to him. His all-consuming interest lies with the 'dirty' bits of the world that are still awaiting his (be)coming. We might take him for a saint, seeing he torments himself so with the detailed knowledge of our dreadful, unreconstructed habits. But behind his outward revulsion there lies the hope, his only hope, of a personal future of sorts, if only he can get a chance to 'convert' us.

He would maintain that he is only, selflessly, trying to share his deepest convictions, for the sake of universal harmony, peace and order. We are more likely to feel that he is imposing his emotionally tinted and narrow-minded ideas in a particularly judgmental, annoying and ludicrous fashion. He is the tight-lipped but of course well-meaning interfering busybody neighbour. He is the one-man crusade for the abolition of/institution of... one forgets what exactly, it is so irrelevant. He is the self-effacing founder of some Movement whose limitless aspirations are embodied in a rigorous canon of fussy rules and regulations. But his followers, his partners in righteousness, mean nothing to him – unless there is a chance of catching *them* out.

He is so religious about every trivial detail, his forbidding footnotes fill half the document. He seizes hold of our personal blemishes to scour and polish away at them with the zeal of one hungry for life. His watchdogs and supervisors peer into our most private matters in the hope of finding something there that will shock them all into lively action: breaking us of our wrong-headed habits, and having broken, setting things right. If we hear a sharp intake of breath at yet another outrage discovered, we can be sure it is an inverted sigh of relief. Whatever kind of filth or evil he may specialise in, it is all good life-giving good news to him, despite the sour face he makes. The way he presses his lips together, it almost looks as if he had a problem suppressing a grin of genuine delight. Simply to call him a hypocrite is to misinterpret his terribly impoverished nature. If he didn't feed on our imperfections, there would be nothing to keep his 'perfection' *alive*.

There is no arguing, debating or in any way reasoning with his rationalistic fervour. And no pleading for a bit of latitude with his pin-point sharp belief in his mission. He is hardly recognisable as the shrewd fact-finder and intelligent assessor of objective reality that he used to be, long ago. Facts, to tell the truth, are apt to undergo a strange conversion under the pressure of his religious zeal. It is not so much that he twists facts, but that he will rope in any words, images or arguments he can lay hold of to serve his belief system, that small-minded concoction of personal opinions he has elevated to something vaguely world-transcending. Stuck up there in his for ever unchanging internalised self, he has elevated *himself* to the status of something that transcends the mundane level. That he is quite dead up/in there he does not take into consideration. Instead, if anything, he reckons he has become immortal.

He may not honour facts any more, smelting them down, as it were, for his one, stupendous Message. But on the other hand, his emotional all-inclusiveness is likely to be doled out in tight dribs and drabs just where he thinks it applicable. There is no knowing how he will work it. Either he embraces literally the whole world with his one pet concern; or else he may try to force a whole complex code of conduct on to some narrow area of life, outside of which nothing exists for him. Either way, it amounts to something like a mega-mono-mania.

He never quite rids himself of the constantly nagging fear that, being active in the world, he lays himself open to attack, being overwhelmed, invaded, infected with something horrible (i.e. horribly alive), but then again it only encourages him in his zeal to sweep the world clean. He is in a constant tizzy, peering over his shoulder lest things sneak up on him unawares, but at the same time determinedly sticking his nose in every unlikely cranny, demanding more of that unsavoury stuff he thrives on.

He scrubs away (in his strange, personally uninvolved way) at every individual wart, till the face of his victim area is totally blank, and only then is it ready to receive his personal imprint. Inevitably, his world is getting ever more monotonous, homogenous. He robs us of our chance to make an individual contribution to both the structure and the running of the world. This right he has arrogated as exclusively his own. The outcome is a world that is neither natural, nor un-naturally individualised by all the different life patterns we might have chosen to adopt (and which would have tended to counterbalance each other in their variety). Instead, it is a strictly denatured world, structured exclusively along his own, unbalanced lines.

Under his stifling supervision, we end up as a society of counterfeit and off-the-peg individuals. Our robotic, implanted mannerisms only reflect his invasive meddling with our inner motivation. We move in prescribed circles, we mutter formulae that have nothing for their root but thoughtless repetition. He has crippled us to the core. But given the universality of this deformity in his world, it strikes us as being perfectly normal; and safe.

Actual persons do not exist for him: only 'one'. And personal relating is something he knows only the beginnings of. Once he has thoroughly investigated and then conscientiously tidied up ('converted') the other person to his own design, he then faces the deathly boredom of recognising his own static, unshakeable self there. Now he stealthily yearns for a less perfect partner; there is no life in such a relationship for him any more.

He has nothing to contribute to any of the life processes proper, least of all to relationships and their maintenance in mutual adaptation. All he can ever do is to impose a premeditated order on his environment, which mirrors the artificially rigid identity within him. He refuses to grow, become, add to his inner or indeed his outward self; he 'feeds' only vicariously: on our becoming – like him! The best he can manage is a growing variety of shocked outrage and ever more vivid condemnation, flowering indictments, and oratorical flights that always end on an emotion-choked note: to help eradicate the Beastliness of this world. Not that he really wants a hand with the work. There is precious little of it left for him to do as it is.

The more he cleanses and imposes a new order, the less scope there is left for him to become (once again what he incontrovertibly is). He is poking holes in his own future with his preposterous finger pointing. He is making a stand against every single thing that promises to give him life. His nice clean self is conducting a crusade against the dirt that is his only hope in the world. He is all of a piece, as a self, inside himself – but he is truly at odds with life.

At least half of his actions in the world are nothing but a virulent reaction against what life presents to him. And *this* is what he is always, absurdly, looking forward to. His imprinting himself, his carbon copy production – though it is the point of the whole exercise, in that it is his substitute for becoming – is a bit of a lame aftermath by comparison. Not surprisingly he is bored with his self, bored with his life: with his predictable becoming part of the structure and workings of the world, that is. He has seen it all before, umpteen times. And it is a depressing sight anyway, a very shortlived satisfaction, the way it just grinds ever closer to its inevitable halt of 'perfection' reached yet again. It is no wonder he is constantly craning his neck for new prey, anxious for his next chance... his chance to what? His chance to go on from there to his *next* chance. Life *as such* is all he is really asking for. All the rest, his life content so to speak, he has already got of course. – Gone are the days when he sat grimly watching life go by, just muttering disapproval. Now there is no keeping him still for five minutes in his compulsive pursuit of life as such.

The truth still remains that he cannot act in a living way out of a dead-perfect self. Deadening action, getting rid of, wiping the slate of the world clean of its material and immaterial flaws, is the liveliest action he is capable of. The 'becoming' he engineers, by substituting his moral etc. order for that of the living world is, after all, a fake. It is a twisted excuse for moving against, reacting to. Exploiting all the basest forms of life is how he manages to finance his lofty deadness. – He has been fooling himself all along. He never *did* manage to heal the rift between the isolated self in its neat inner seclusion and the turbulent world theatre of action, life, becoming. This rift between self and life is still operative and the clearest symptom of it is the fact that all his really lively actions are *re*actions. Which means that, without knowing it, he lets his life be dictated to him.

He takes himself to be a very nearly almost Creator; he will give a perfunctory nod in a slightly higher direction. But life just needs to whistle and he comes running, with an injunction against whistling in public places between the hours of nine and nine-fifteen. At that, one can hardly call him self-aware. And he can't really claim that he is being true to his inner self: he does all his *living* in imperfection, up to his neck in all sorts of mess, while claiming to *be* perfect, inside his head: a 'saint' who needs to wallow in 'sin' is hardly being true to his conscience.

In the last analysis he has become a perfect agent of the world, a toy-on-strings that can be relied on to give a mechanical twitch in a pre-programmed response to certain stimuli. If his *inner* programme is actually quite the opposite, it just goes to show that life and self are certainly connected, but pointing in opposite directions. Thinking to keep his inner self 'intact', worrying about his essential 'purity', and then allowing his active self to get immersed in all the impurest things and parts of parts thereof that he can winkle out of their hiding places, he only ends up contradicting himself. He has lost his integrity; there is no wholeness of being and doing to him any more. His 'head' and his 'body' do not see eye to eye.

In the logical conclusion of things, he slowly but surely runs out of the sort of 'dirt' that fuels him. He can only grind to a halt, when all is said and done to perfection. But there is no guarantee that it will be as simple as that. His immovable inner self may be *behind* everything he does, but his active-self out here has, one might say, acquired a mind of its own. As his extraverting function it is every bit as clever as its mummified 'owner' in there, and really one can speak of the self he claims to *be* as no more than a sort of venerated relic, enshrined and kept apart 'up there'. If not disregarded exactly, it is hardly available for live comment when there is an emergency looming ahead.

When his life threatens to run down because there is nobody and nothing else to convert, then his clever active-self takes stock of the situation. He must have made a mistake somewhere, collecting together such a dead-end inner self. The world is nearly full of him (and suffering the ill-effects of his narrow, eccentric designing – not that he would notice the sickly state it is in) and now he finds his time is running out. What use is his inner motivation if it can do no better, at its most thoroughly effective, than to land him in a mortal crisis? And does it not stand to reason, after all, that one should not go against the things that give one life? He has been doing the wrong thing all along then, and there is nothing for it but to have a conversion experience: to throw away the old inner-self command as utterly useless.

This is the sort of thing he has done everything to avoid: to have any new becoming inside himself. But then the new self he now introjects is hardly a stranger to him, more something like an old, and much appreciated enemy. It is hardly what he would call a shock to the system. He is intimately familiar with it all, and he will think up no end of rationalistic explanations to justify his treacherous turn-about. Perhaps he has 'seen the light'; nobody can quibble with that, not even he.

He has engineered a new lease of life for himself. Now he can denounce all he formerly held sacred and start all over again. He brings quite as much conviction to 'wrong-doing' as he did to his former right-doing. He has become one of Them. It will of course need a lot of relabelling in terms of good/bad, right/wrong. But that is hardly a problem for a master of categorical in- or exclusion, a labeller par excellence. He will always be a self-styled goodie fighting the forces of evil, whichever side he comes down on. Recanting now, beating his breast with carefully worded self-accusations, can only add to his halo, in his opinion. He is born-again, no doubt about it.

One moment there he is, deliberately and awarely and quite precisely set in his stuffy old mould: and suddenly it turns out he is not to be relied on, one can't trust him at all. The smaller the particular area of life he focuses on, the narrower his design (and the greater his success rate), the more often one may expect him to 'turn'. There is no knowing what he might one day turn out to be. At his narrowest he is constantly refashioning himself. And with his head denouncing what his body sneakily delights in – and his body, not 'given its head', only reluctantly acting out, some of the time, what his head would demand – is there any trusting him, even on a level stretch in between his spectacular U-turns? Despite all that acute inner self-awareness of his, he does not appear to always know what he is *doing*.

One of his conversion experiences, or two even, the world may find acceptable. But if he keeps chopping and changing, then his strident crusading and campaigning begins to fall on deaf ears. Not only that, but he has converted so many against himself, his former inner self that is to say, that he is having a very much harder struggle of it now. This is quite alright by him, he *likes* struggling-against, after all. But he is in effect digging his own grave. Every time he starts a new Movement, he is teaching the world more about intolerance; not only the theory of intolerance, but the active implementation of. He has instructed us well in the operational skills of squeezing the life out of our opponents. With every twist and turn he now performs he gives us new ideas how to deal with our opponents. One day he will stand before his own, now disowned, inquisition. They will put his own, now discarded, thumb screws on him. He will be shot as a traitor to the Cause. Whichever way he may end, the life he has always worked against – purely in order to be in touch with it – will finally eject him as the irritating nuisance he is.

He got so carried away with his freedom of choice, the freedom of setting himself up to be anything he chose to be in the unworldly safety of his inner space (where alone *anything* is possible) that in his hubris as self-creator he simply slammed the door shut on living changes, on alternatives to grow into, on our common inbuilt obligation to become through genuinely contributing to life, and to add to the world by truly becoming into it. There were strings attached to his freedom. He thought he could ignore that, with the result that he became the predictable puppet of his environment, the victim even of his own body – which to him *has* become part of his 'environment'. His inner self dies umpteen deaths at the hands of a living world; at his own never really owned hands, at that. His head may say no, but his head-less and hence no-less hands are only too easily tempted! And before he knows it, inside himself, they have wrought another neat revolution. And still he thinks he has got his freedom to be uniquely and forever he.

Whatever he does, he always ends up split between an introverted self that is sandbagged, apparently securely, against the chance of life seeping in, and an extraverting self that is a sort of tidal happening, predictable and yet not to be relied on to keep going in the same direction. Positive Virgo grows from self to self, in comparative freedom. Negative Virgo, for all his manipulative interfering with all other out there, and ultimately, repeatedly, his self inside him, only ends up the agent of life-forces outside his control. A divided, a 'double' agent, a colluder with and servant of circumstances beyond his categorically locked door. Life may 'sicken' him, but he lives eagerly nevertheless. He really does not know what he wants: he has gone astray in the labyrinth of his own complexity. If he had thought less highly of himself, and not unconsciously removed himself even further from the common arena of life, then those same complexities could have been something to give to the world, consciously, not something to suffer from in unacknowledged bewilderment.

Some Suggested Virgo Attributes

basic

rational, analytical; dissects, scrutinises, investigates, criticises; fussy, choosy, (and yet in a deliberately restricted environment easily conditioned, 'brainwashed') since he does not think beyond the given factual choices

exclusive attitudes; thinks twice about what to accept into his self/life/body: resulting for instance in **dieting, various forms of abstinence; discriminates, strong preferences, 'makes up his mind', 'shops around for things', feels free to accept or reject, may appear arbitrary, 'originality', individualist**

rationally self-aware, self critical; perfectionist tendency; environment-conscious in that his inner self can only be an abstract reflection of the personal life he has built himself

guards his privacy, mildly withdrawn, cool, a tendency to isolate himself; holds out against impositions and intrusions; 'stand-offish'

'ab-normal': out of touch with nature; recoils from involvement in ordinary life; fears life as bringing him deep personal uncertainties; worries about his future: about his surviving 'intact'; **gives much thought to questions of life/death, health, fitness, propriety, morality** etc.

positive

compromising, cautious, tentative, modest, considerate; complex

relaxed self-improving attitude: **always making an effort to develop; reconsiders, adjusts, adaptable, responsive to suggestions and appeals; adopts** and **gathers in** what strikes him as useful, **integrates**

may waver in his yes/no response, **thoughts and feelings may go in opposite directions**

worker: earning his right to take (to abstract) from the world; **improver; (re)forms and (newly) informs:** e.g. busy with matters relating to **writing, printing, designing, refurbishing; mechanics, research, engineering; refining, honing, 'polishing', checking**

makes individual contributions: making personal innovations and **experiments; modifications, improvements tailored to**

individual needs, adaptations of existing forms, thinks up alternatives

conscientious, responsible; precise, orderly, efficient, thorough, practical, methodical, broadly systematic approach

'understanding', helpful, encouraging and reassuring; may work as counsellor, analyst, therapist; educator; ensuring other people's 'intactness': e.g. guardian, nurses and cares for

negative

narrow certainties and convictions, idiosyncratic reasoning, closed mind, can't be reasoned with; unresponsive, 'premeditated feelings'; takes himself to be perfect, self-satisfied, smug, proud, 'virtuous', 'saintly'

fault-finding, criticises without analysing first, intolerant, actively condemns; prim, prudish/purist, rigid, stuffy, 'lifeless', 'artificial', set in his ways, plots and plans

petty, 'religious' about trivial details, excessively orderly, tends to classify, label, list and categorise, pedantic; materialistic-concretistic (though may not appear to be so); rationalistic, muddles up facts to please himself: not entirely honest; imputes motives, 'reads into' etc. according to his adopted outlook

fear of life; fears contamination/'invasion' etc.; hypochondriac; isolationist, insularity, segregation, touch-me-not attitude, possibly suffers from phobias; locked into himself and yet can't (and mustn't) stay-out-of: semi-withdrawn, lurks and spies; suffers from loneliness and an inability to act out of his convictions: cowardly, self-effacing

wards off, holds at arm's length, 'doesn't want to know'; reductionist thinking; pre-conceptions

suspicious; prying, always looking for the worst, secretly delighted with finding 'filth' and 'sin'; intrusively nosy, interfering busy-body, meddles, accuses, imposes his attitudes

presents his 'designs' as the only rightful ones: crusades, converts, forces his narrow ideals on others; endless talk of law and order etc., strident moralising; preachifies, makes inflated claims for his personal beliefs/attitudes

eccentric, quaint; 'perverted'; fanatical, narrow obsessions, monomanias (e.g. trainspotting), ossified rituals, endless self-repetition (e.g. checking on security, cleanliness, etc.), **may be held to be 'neurotic'; 'wound up with nowhere to go'**

bored with himself and his **monotonous personal life; reactive: works against his environment** (including his own body), **automatic anti-responses; puppet of his environment; lacks true self-awareness**

cheats his own conscience, moral etc. slip-ups, hypocrite; divided between **total deliberate abstinence** e.g. starving himself (or rather starving his *body*), and **'inadvertent' sneaky indulgence** of bodily appetites, hence prone to **anorexic/bulimic** conditions; **split** between a dead inner self in the purity of its seclusion and an active-self that delights in impure things/events: in his totality **at odds with himself, at odds with life;** possibly suffers from allergies

turn-coat, converts for reasons of expediency; 'born-again'; traitor to his cause; untrustworthy, unpredictable, follows his own 'fashions'

CAPRICORN

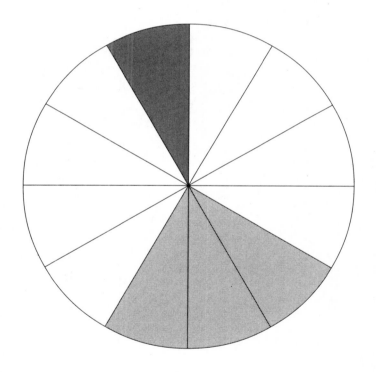

♑ **Introvert**
**conscious function: thinking; directions of function: both
inward and outward**
unconscious functions: ♋ feeling, ♊ sensing, ♌ intuition
Earth: senses-oriented

Capricorn resembles Virgo in several respects. For one thing his
conscious function is thinking and can be directed both inward
and outward; for another his basic nature is, like Virgo's, earthy:
he applies his thoughts to concrete matters. – Since the only two
consciously thinking signs are both of the Earth type, it may be
permissible to state here that thought as such is always concerned
with the concretely formed – as opposed to intuition, for instance,
which grasps the whole meaning rather than defined, isolated
concepts. (Again, one can see the principle of isolation at work in
Virgo, who develops away from the world into the privacy of
inner thought.)

Unlike the extravert Virgo who only became something
approaching an introvert after finding and then introjecting a self,
the introvert Capricorn is from the start in possession of something to call 'I' and to which to apply his conscious thought
processes, before he turns thoughtfully towards the world.
Capricorn first of all turns inward to think about all that lies
inside: a clearly conceptualised self, as well as what he can contact
intellectually of the inner reality beyond self.

The critical investigations that Virgo initially applied to his
environment Capricorn directs from the start inward; he gets to
know his self in every detail, before he gets to know anything else.
There is nothing though to stop him letting his thoughts range further. Where the introverting introvert Sagittarius did this, intuitively, he came in touch with a 'timeless stream' of as yet
unformed Inner Reality. To Capricorn this same transpersonal
reality 'looks different': he brings reason to bear on it, he views it
all from a logical angle, and in the process he finds it to be something quite unlike the fluid experience it was for Sagittarius. His
thinking does not flow-with but always arrests, scrutinises and
identifies the inherent structure within what to the intuitive mind

is a wholeness, a ceaseless flow, an unstructured something. As a result both his self and the wider inner reality beyond it appear to Capricorn to have form, as well as being abstract, immaterial.

Formed thoughts: distinctly shaped ideas; abstract forms: principles. This is how he experiences his self, as a set of principles or specific being-ideas. And what lies beyond self appear to him to be logical, lawful possibilities, or principles ready to be used. As long as he remains inward-turned they can have their 'use' in *him*: becoming part of his self-structure. Like Sagittarius he can have his inner becoming without having to turn to the objective world for it. And quite as self-critical and set on improving his self as Virgo, he only needs to go a little beyond his inner self to find a wealth of new ideas to choose from, any of which he can incorporate into his inner being, after having given the matter some thought.

But the given dual orientation of his conscious function also demands of him that he should turn outward towards the concrete world. He is supposed to take his 'preconceived' ideas of self out into his material environment and expose them there to life: for confirmation and adoption into the world, or else negation, rejection. It is only in this extraverting process that he can complete himself, i.e. find his integrity as a both introverting and extraverting being, just as Virgo could not be complete without 'inventing' this new-fangled innerness. Capricorn has to go out there and 'embody' his self, and thereby 'prove it right'. He has to find some correspondence to his idea-being in the concrete world of matter-being. But his first thoughtful approach to life out there tells him only too clearly that it is going to be like the worst possible of exams to take, some kind of Big Test.

Choosing his own inner becoming is one thing – finding himself forced to submit to this totally new becoming, into the world, under the critical eye of objective necessity, is a different matter. *In theory* he should have less cause to worry than Virgo. He has not assembled his self out of a hotch-potch of worldly bits and pieces, to suit himself. If he has chosen to improve his given inner self then always along the lines suggested to him by the 'natural' life principles that are the true foundation of all subjective *and* objective phenomena. He is by no means a (possibly eccentric) self-styled individualist. If anything, he is 'abnormally normal' – by mundane standards that is.

Now he approaches the task of proving himself in the world with far too many pre-existing ideas of who he is and how, consequently, he should act – and not just he, but 'one'. Virgo was free to cobble together his own conscience. Compared to that Capricorn's conscience is quite strictly pre-programmed, though actually less narrow: his sweep of ideas is wider, and yet more 'theoretically correct'. The problem is, life as lived is far from 'correct'.

The moment he turns his attention outward, he finds himself in an environment that not only runs on a different programme, obviously inferior to his, but a veritable chaos of individual programmes and sub-programmes as well. His nicely structured self, his tidy self-idea, has to prove itself valid in the face of all that – the thought of it is almost too much to bear! He sees on the one hand a welter of quite unreasonable disorder, and on the other a host of deeply entrenched world structures that for the most part have nothing in common with his. His inner command to make himself objectively real strikes him as nothing short of a suicide mission. There seems to be no way his established inner self can be established 'bodily' in the face of such over-whelming opposition from the existing world-disorder.

He hesitates, he thinks it through yet again, he succumbs to existential fears: he is almost on the point of concluding that there must be something wrong with his self. If such a world is his inbuilt target, his field of self-fulfilment, then surely the ideas he has, his self, his conscience, everything he has got to accomplish his task with must be wrong – and yet what he knows of the underlying life principles backs him up. This gives him what one can only call intellectual pride, and deep and unshakeable moral certainties. He is torn between thinking himself right and suspecting himself to be wrong. How, given the circumstances, can he both be *himself*, and *be* himself, objectively?

Obediently, he dips a cautious toe into this terrible venture, fearful, doubtful, clinging for moral support to all he has ever known. But the best he manages is to huddle hopefully invisible on the periphery of life. Like Taurus he hovers endlessly on the fringes of active involvement; more so, since he has all the self he needs already established in its inner seclusion. He knows he will have to take the plunge, but he is far from being in a hurry, thinking to himself that all this had better be given a lot of thought first

– and then some more.

The extravert Taurus feared to lose again what little bit of self he had gained on his first foray into the world. The extravert Virgo, having transmogrified himself into an honorary introvert, stood to lose even more. The introvert Capricorn , 'for a long time' in possession of every well-defined detail of his impeccable self, fears to find all that invalidated now, cancelled and crossed off the list of viable ideas. It is not so much the *loss* of self he has to fear, but its proving to be of no use as it is. He would have to renounce it then, really, which would go not only against all his personal principles but all Principles as well. The more he thinks about it, the more he considers himself saddled with a terrible burden of proof. Pushed by what he thinks of increasingly as a mission of sorts, and faced by a no-hope situation out there, he glooms about for ever on the threshold of life.

What he needs first of all is a compromise that will allow him to both *be*, objectively, and to be his subjective *self*. This compromise lies in objective *becoming*: the living adaptive process. If he adapts himself a little to the world, then he also gives to the world, by being and acting out of himself in it, a little of what he is. He can implement some of his pre-existing ideas, but also stand some of them aside for a moment – retain them inside himself – while he adopts some of the working practices of the world in their stead. His mind, unlike Virgo's, cannot be changed. His mind is in that sense 'superior' to the combined mind of the world – so superior as to be practically speaking useless in the world. He will have to learn to swallow his uncertain, theoretical pride, or none of his fine principles will ever see the light of day.

The world tests him; but he also tests the world. He becomes (effective). And the world becomes (a better place). It is after all never more than a partial self-sacrifice that is being asked of him. To achieve all this, however, he has to make a start somewhere. His toe dipping, his incomplete immersion in the quietest backwaters of life he can find, will not really get him anywhere.

What comes to his aid is above all his unconscious feeling function ($\mathcal{S}\rightarrow$). Positively used, this has the effect of making him want to give all he can. His caring, nurturing feelings for others pull him out of his hiding place right into the flow of life, despite his conscious anxiety, to try and actively contribute something for the benefit of a needy world. He does not mind quite so much if he has to 'sacrifice' some principles in order to make himself available as a potential helper. That is not to say that he approaches the situation *entirely* self-lessly – which would amount to leaving all his thoughtful standards 'at home' – he gives also by contributing to the world ideas he consciously thinks to be too important to be left out, unmentioned, undemonstrated. But emotionally he is willing to pare down the application of his principles to the basics, and even to allow some exceptions to the rule. He is amenable to a measure of compromise, if that will help. Emotionally responsive, he *becomes* a teacher and helpful advisor, for instance – quite a different process to simply dumping a codex of pre-formed knowledge on the world stage and, almost inevitably, having it thrown back in his face as untimely, inconvenient, puzzling, too demanding.

Emotional contact with his inner self (♋←) has him firmly rooted in feelings of inner security and this gives him a measure of courage. It is no longer an absolute disaster to find his self and all he stands for momentarily rejected. He has enough belief in himself now to try again. But unfortunately what should propel him into action now, also holds him back at the same time. What he *feels* himself to be, unconsciously, is quite unlike what he consciously *thinks* of himself as being: not a composite pattern of distinct 'ideas', but a simple emotional whole. He feels his indestructible essential inner oneness, and this, while it gives him the courage to emerge into the world, also makes it harder for him to 'give' a bit, here and there. Really he is back to square one: he stands or falls as a *whole*.

He needs pulled apart, loosened up, so that the whole collection of logically connected ideas he is trying to stand for can be applied piecemeal, one at a time. His set of principles needs to be disengaged far enough, in action, to enable him to respond *in part*, rather than with the whole unwieldy 'rulebook' of his conscience. When he begins to unconsciously sense the world of matter in all its details, its interconnected diversity (♊), he learns also to assess where his established ideas are useful, where and how they fit in, and where they are (momentarily) misplaced. There are forms and procedures his environment displays or adopts for only a short time, and it is hardly sensible to stand on principle where every fleeting phenomenon is concerned, or for that matter to think oneself rejected and proved wrong in the face of such things. Not that he is naturally impractical – he is an Earth sign, after all – but his practice tends to be so loaded down with the gravity of each act, the seriousness of each undertaking, that in a rather faster moving world he is left standing for ineffective.

Like Virgo he is a perfectionist, but Virgo's parvenu conscience (like his adaptable individualism) is a matter of choice – which *can* be changed, slowly and bit by bit. Capricorn's more 'old-fashioned' conscience stems from the prior seclusion of his inner self where it was in conscious touch with all of the natural Law, intelligently conceived. Capricorn has no choice in the matter of *what* to stand for, only how much of it to stand for where and when and how. If what he is meets its downfall in the world – too bad. He can't decide to throw it all overboard, even piecemeal and reluctantly, and find himself something else to represent in the world. He is lumbered with this load of inner knowing and the inner command to drag it all, somehow, into the world of action. The superstructure of his irrevocable conscience is like a straight-jacket that slows down his reactions and makes of everything he does a major operation requiring much self-searching first.

But his new-found skill to sense how things simply hang together, or can be made to connect, and hence to 'work', frees him now from this over-conscientious approach to the in-essentials of the moment. He gains an unconscious spontaneity that helps him become more efficient, and this in turn makes him more acceptable to others and involves him more and more in the details of day-to-day living. – The problem now is that he is in danger of falling into the other extreme. If he responds emotionally to what is asked of him, and manages to be superficially efficient on the spur of the moment, he may find himself so well received in the world that a gulf opens up between what he knows he *ought* to do (with difficulty) and what he *can* do (relatively easily). Now his conscience is being tested in a different way! And again he is no nearer a satisfactory solution to the problem of how to take part in the world as what he *is*.

What finally comes to his rescue is his intuition (♌). This tells him that far from entering the living world only on a basis of approval or sufferance, he may actually rule it. He can implant the seed of what he is into the world and then watch it grow; that is to say, if he can 'put across' what he essentially stands for, then slowly and piecemeal the world will come to accept and incorporate his principles. Seeing himself as potential ruler stops him dithering: either to stick to what his conscience dictates, and run the constant risk of having it rejected; or else effectively to please the world, with more than a good chance of, at the same time, betraying his conscience – and thus himself invalidating the efforts he is making. To be in command of the situation, and to be in command of himself (i.e. not to fear rejection to the point of giving in to tempting thoughts of taking easy short-cuts, just to prove himself in the world), these two go hand in hand.

But he will hardly mistake this for an invitation to simply impose his own strong inner guidelines and declare them the rules 'his' world runs by. He has already learnt to adapt, in emotional response to the reality of others' needs; meaning he has learnt to partially give up, to retain and put aside (inside himself) whatever principles or ideas did not seem to be called for, for the time being. He has also discovered that pure thought needs to be supplemented with the simple knack of sensing one's way through all those loosely interwoven comings and goings and impermanent things in life, if life is not to come to a ponderous standstill at every turn. His ability to both give and react responsively, doing justice to both self and other, is more designed to promote growth in others than to check it with a rigid harness of imposed rules and regulations, laws and moral codes. These he *does* bring into the world with him, but as a gift: something demanding to be thought about (though it can be scaled down to suit the recipient or the situation) and which would ideally find its acceptance in the world on the basis of understanding. He can do no more than get the world to listen, by speaking up clearly. He ends up not so much a ruler as an advisor and instructor, one who offers to share his knowledge. But it also makes him think even more critically and deeply about the ideas he is about to put forward.

Through him others can have access to the given, 'logical' rules of life: he will consider each situation, pondering it first in himself, and then casting about in the wider inner reality he is always in touch with, for an answer tailored to this person's needs, specifically and individually. As an educator, a teacher of how best to live, he is indispensable.

He stands half-way between Idea and practice: as a self-idea that needs to prove itself viable, practicable, applicable. He bears not only the burden of proving himself in action, but also has the task of introducing into the practice of the living world some of the transpersonal principles of life as such. His success depends on two things: his own flexibility or adaptability, and the world's readiness to respond, its ability to recognise the value of what he is offering.

As regards the first, it asks of him the sacrifice of *giving* the 'substance' of his inner reality. To hand it over, for acceptance, part-acceptance, outright rejection, whichever. This is the only way it (and he) is going to *become* part of the substance of the world. And in this way the practical course of life, the structure of the world and the way it is run, will be informed by ideas of a more permanent validity than the 'superficial' and maybe misleading ideas Virgo derived from observing his environment (with all its imperfections and its chronic lack of completeness).

For himself, adapting the workings of self and world one to the other, he gains his own integrity, his wholeness as a both fully introverting and extraverting being. It will not cost him his inner 'integrity' either: he is holding fast to what he is inside himself and derives – unlike Virgo – his ever-new *inner* becoming from his 'inner environment'. But in terms of what he is becoming in(to) the world, he *does* have to sacrifice his integrity: he has to adapt his approach, compromise. Like Leo, he cannot simply come into the world *whole*. Like Sagittarius, he has to learn to cut himself down to size.

But his success also depends on how well prepared the world is to receive his gift. What he is putting forward for acceptance are working principles and codes of conduct that have their origin in transpersonal life principles that are quite 'out of touch' with what goes on in actual, factual life. Even when adapted (i.e. pruned down) they will, at first hearing, and if not much thought is given to them, look less like a gift than a demand. What sort of takers are there? By offering himself and all he stands for to the world, he is in effect asking for obedience to higher laws, for the adoption of rules that go beyond the merely personal or situational, for acceptance of codes that are inclined to go counter to what each individual, given the choice, would have chosen himself.

He seems to be in direct conflict with Virgo's freely chosen individual conscience, the chosen inner self acting according to its own selected rules. He would curb Virgo's individualistic tendency to assume sole responsibility over his actions, he would counsel instead the adoption of a common, collective code of conduct: one based not on personal preferences, derived from among the imperfect options offered by one's concrete environment, but on conscious understanding of the principles inherent in the Inner Reality that underlies the world: any self-improvement can ideally be derived from the perfect choices available there.

However, it is also Virgo who alone among the signs shares Capricorn's capacity for a conscious, rational understanding of an inner reality as such, and the critical attitude that looks for thoughtful self-improvement. In the end it proves to be precisely Virgo (the Virgo element in the world) who can consciously, willingly, receive Capricorn's gift. Virgo has shown us how to 'print' an individual self that can then imprint itself on the world. He has developed this thing called conscience: obedience to an assumed inner self. When Capricorn asks Virgo to obey rules not of his own making, he is not threatening to invalidate or destroy what Virgo has developed. Instead he is offering Virgo a chance to grow – accessing an even deeper, and more perfectly 'logical' dimension than Virgo ever had a chance of contacting.

In short, Capricorn's offer is addressed to our individual conscience, asking it to 'grow up' and develop: to go beyond merely reflecting external influences, as it were, and start to reflect something of a more underlying nature. He does not deny the validity of freely chosen individual rules to live by, but he would point out that these will always be based on no more than the best pickings available in an imperfect world – while his own principles quite 'predate' this or that formed thing, event or self in our world. This is what gives him authority; not so much, literally, being 'older', but rather having, in himself, a timeless and ever-valid knowledge – though for it to be any use to us, he will have to give it to us in dribs and drabs, 'timed' to be a gift worth the name.

Bit by bit we can build his 'essential working principles' into our own individual consciences, to our advantage. But maybe more importantly, he helps us maintain a measure of collective order, by steering our individualised ideas how to be ourselves in a changing world into directions less likely to have us all pursuing mutually exclusive 'life styles'. He makes us realise there are codes of conduct we all have in common, inherently, because – whatever the situation – they make, *essentially*, sense.

But what is he to do supposing we still refuse to listen to him? Unlike Sagittarius – who could shrug at being ridiculed, content to be trying, as life demanded of him – Capricorn, with all his unconscious functions taken into account, is designed to be a *giving ruler*, a helpful ruler that is, who will increase our well-being. But there is a kind of being helpful and giving that consists of withholding, of taking away. If his giving kind advice meets with no response from us at all, then he will have to resort to stronger measures, here and there – not to *impose* himself but just to make himself heard, to make his point clear.

He would increase our workload with his stricter rules. His ultimately kind and quite practical suggestions only set up a brick wall in our self-willed paths. And what can he offer us that we do not think we have already managed to take for ourselves? The more we go stubbornly and 'full of ourselves' where *we* want to go, without showing any kind of respect for the ground rules of life, the more often he will, regretfully, trip us up. That we would only do ourselves, and others, harm if we persisted is not at all apparent to us. But it is to him: he can see only to clearly that we are proceeding in the wrong direction; he knows it on principle.

It is his responsibility to let us know. It is equally his brief to address us as individuals who have to choose freely to listen to and follow his advice, not to impose his instructions on us. Torn between these two conflicting duties, he does the only logical thing: he interferes by stealth. Unseen, he trips us up. That will give us pause for thought. He throws a spanner in our works and brings our wilful schemes to a crunching halt. It is a rather different face he is showing us there; or rather he is *not* showing it to us, he works like a saboteur by (necessary) subterfuge. It is the only reasonable, the only kind response to our persistent wrong-doing. Like a wise parent he spirits the harmful toy out of the way and drops it down a deep hole before we have even noticed. He cramps our nascent style, and what right does he have to do that, we howl (meaning not him, of course, but this unaccountable 'fate' he has newly invented).

He has every right to do so. He consciously understands far more than we do. And he cares enough about us not to want to see us end up on a treadmill of *unthinking* obedience, just automatically giving in to the rules of necessity (which are, ultimately, his). Our failing to listen to his obviously much-needed advice has so to speak provoked him into these acts of sabotage – but what he is actually doing is to try and provoke *us* out of our (wrongly) established ways. He isn't going against his own principles either, acting like that. In fact, he is positively surpassing himself using these new shock tactics as the only way to (re)introduce us to the 'old' Law.

It would be wrong to think that he is taking his revenge, 'punishing' us, or that he has lost all respect for us. He is merely working from behind the scenes now; we have forced him to reconsider his position. And the losses, upsets and disappointments he engineers – unseen by us, making them happen mysteriously and apparently illogically – these give *us* a chance to reconsider: whether we have not 'done wrong' to end up where we have. We may think again whether not to listen after all to his advice how best to live our lives. *Thoughtful* obedience, of our own free will, is the only response that will really satisfy him. Only then will he find his proper acceptance, his full validation, in our world. Anything less is essentially an insult to him – and our continuing, puzzling loss.

If as an idea he is a bit difficult to understand, and his gift seems a bit hard to take, he is of an almost agreeable simplicity in his negative version.

It is easy enough to seize on the deep emotional security he unconsciously feels himself to have (♋←) as something to banish his uncertainty with, when he first faces the world around him. He uses, or rather abuses, it to defend himself against all possible self-doubt. He comes to believe that *all* of his inner knowing should find a positive response in the world, should 'prove him right'. Any responding, adapting and becoming on his part is quite out of the question now, thoughts of compromising in any way have no room in his scheme of things. He will not 'limit' himself; he will not shrink from his task either: he'll soon sort us out, show us the kind of law and order that's required in our obviously ill-behaved and ill-formed world.

At the same time he feels a compulsive need to give 'generous-ly' ($\mathfrak{S}\rightarrow$) of his self-evidently superior knowledge and perfect advice. With complete faith in each and every principle known to him, he takes it for granted that giving us what we so patently lack is no more than his duty. It looks like a tough job, one that will demand all his concentration, and he could almost feel sorry for himself having to shoulder such a burden – but then again he is entirely confident that with his long 'history' of a better sort of knowing, his grasp of how worldly affairs ought to be conducted must be faultless too. It follows logically, really. He takes himself for a complete and perfect self, a sort of personal embodiment of a divine Idea Behind It All. This, in his eyes, gives him an authority that simply surpasses anything we could legitimately come up with.

He conveniently forgets that there would always be more things to know. He turns his back on the inner world beyond his self with the feeling that he has already acquired a 'wholeness' of knowledge that is more than enough to cope with the ignorant ways of a living world, the unruly shambles it presents. He does not need to subject us to lengthy tests either: one glance is enough to tell him that, compared with him, we will all be found wanting.

But it appears that he has made a miscalculation somewhere. He finds himself far from gratefully received. We simply refuse to listen when he starts pontificating, admonishing, throwing oh-so-slowly the full weight and point-by-point extent of his better-knowing at us. We fidget, we slip through his well-meant grasp and ultimately cock a snook at him, because we always find a quick and effective momentary solution to the question under consideration: we have solved the problem, done the deed, while he is drawing yet another breath, mid-instruction. We simply leave him standing.

But he soon learns to forestall us, to read every little move of our superficially working minds. No little thing, material or immaterial, escapes his notice once he begins, unconsciously, to sense the world around him ($\mathbb{I}$). He develops quite a craving for this sense of intelligent involvement in each and every aspect of the objective world. He can no longer be content with pronouncing on major points of principle alone. Every fleeting detail becomes his concern, every minor transaction has to be examined to make sure it is correct. No procedure, no practical decision, no straightforward piece of work, no passing arrangement is ever insignificant enough in itself but he has to throw a spanner in our works by putting the whole machinery of ideological, moralistic principle-thumping into action. His dogma is all-pervasive. His absolutist order would sit like a yoke on the whole world, and in no circumstances whatever can exceptions be made. His endlessly circuitous reasoning-out of the simplest situation, referring everything back to higher principles that would hardly seem to have anything to do with the trifling matter in hand, slows down what should be an hour's work till it takes the whole day. There are always more forms to fill in. And supplementary questions to ask. Nothing can be considered in isolation because a lot depends, and hangs together, and ties in and up – and all of it, down to the last washer and the great-grandfather's occupation, has to be tested, checked and tabulated on principle, and from the point of view of principle. There is no escaping the relentless cranking of his predetermined mind when it starts applying itself to every comma and dot.

His time-consuming, life-suppressing approach still does not meet with the approval he would have confidently expected as his due. We dodge him more than ever to make sure he gets no purchase on us at all. He holds out this superb advisory 'gift' to us, one that will fit *any* occasion, down to the correct colour of socks one ought to wear – and we won't take it. What can he do now with his gift? The full weight of it lies in his hands, he can't unburden himself of it. This too much of self to 'give' and no-one to give it to, to take it off him, causes him pain, the pain of rejection. It is not unlike negative Sagittarius' 'depression' weighing him down. Both Capricorn and Sagittarius suffer from the same lack of access to their previous inner world. If Capricorn could return 'inside' for a moment he could at the least reassure himself of his 'rightness', and drop the burdensome process of giving his self to the world. But he has locked himself out, taken all he was with him, and standing unwanted in the world, he begins to collapse under the sheer weight of his whole misplaced, *un*placed externalised self. Capricorn sinks passively into his depression, denied proper entry into the world, where Sagittarius actively sought out his 'dark hole in the ground' by way of pretending that he could actually get away from the world. Sagittarius always bounced hopefully back. Capricorn just goes on sinking. Fortunately (for him) however, he becomes intuitively aware that there is nothing to stop him assuming single-handed rulership of the world (Ω), if he puts his mind to it.

In the best dictatorial manner he now *imposes* his gift, his pre-formed ideas, on us. To ask whether they really do prove correct, practicable and in the given circumstances valuable, would simply not occur to him. At a pinch he will declare our messy reality invalid: anyone opposing his opinions will be dismissed as taking a 'purely subjective' view. His *own* subjectiveness is of course a different matter. It lays claim to an absolute rightness that quite surpasses mere personal subjectivity. Having had access to all inner knowing, he holds himself to be so comprehensively, so supremely, subjective that it ought to amount, to all intents and purposes, to absolute objectivity: no knowledge of fundamental principles as such can have escaped him, so how can he possibly not know all there is to know about the proper, intended, work-ings of our objective world as well? He is omniscient, and nothing one could say to him will make the slightest impression. We are all lesser beings needing to be educated in the ways things should be done, how the world should be run. From his elevated position he grants us no respite, no privacy, and allows of no individual excuses. He would feel he was not doing his job if he did. We should be grateful for all the trouble he goes to on our behalf.

When he makes himself out to be 'entirely objective' rather than 'merely subjective' he is telling both a truth and a lie. He can-not really consider himself as a subject any more: he has lost touch with his innerness altogether and focused his conscious attention exclusively on the job of 'objectifying' himself – imposing the sub-jective idea he is on our objective practice. He wants to become the way we act, behave. Through our childlike obedience he will have the living proof of his self in action. Our acting out his commands will prove that his ideas 'work'.

Unlike negative Virgo, he does not make himself the model of what we should become inside ourselves, what form of con-science we should adopt and act out of. He has simply become an issuer of instructions of how to put the perfect laws of life (that he alone is subjectively identified with) into practice. That we, in our-selves, should be principled, or that we should learn to express our right-thinking *selves*, is not on the agenda. All he wants us to do is apply him, work him, behave him, structure the world in his image: prove the idea he is by putting him into effect. By himself he cannot do this; how ever forcibly he might impose his ways single-handed, he would always be outnumbered by us and our malpractices and no better off than he was in the beginning, having to prove himself against the odds.

He does not want us to think for ourselves, how ever rightly, because then we would be acting out of ourselves, instead of acting him out. Unable to do his own work, because he has seized up into a dead lump of dogma, he relies on us to do his living work for him. Just as negative Taurus had to keep building identical copies of what he had seized on by way of a self-model, in order to have any sort of becoming, so negative Capricorn needs to see his existing and now 'solidified' self applied over and over again, exactly and with every T crossed, in order to 'become real'. And just as Taurus had to banish all that did not look like self to him, so Capricorn does away with all that might threaten the progress of *his* 'becoming' – objective, that is. The less subjective being *we* do, the more we concentrate on simply doing his bidding, and no 'personal' questions asked, the better for him. His subjective being constantly becomes our objective practice, and our subjective being has been cancelled.

He recognises no other kind of inner self than a knowing, reasoning one and he has already proved to himself that our knowledge is risible compared to his, our reasoning at best in its infancy. So what would we want an inner self or any kind of subjective being for, anyway? He declares our ambitions in that direction null and void. That is why we are being 'merely' subjective when we demur and argue and offer to disobey – or, quite unreasonably, let feelings rule our actions, for instance. The inner selves we might aspire to having would not only rival *his* (unthinkable!) but actually undermine his existence. Without our unquestioning obedience he simply does not happen in our world, or anywhere else for that matter. A commander who is not obeyed, the very idea of him would go up in a puff of smoke.

Nothing frightens him more than the thought that his robotic, shell-like slaves might demand their subjective lives back. Every time we insist on making our own ill-formed decisions, he dies a bit. The worst of dictators, he does not work against us, or get to work *on* us ('converting' us, like Virgo), he simply works *through* us. He has confiscated our inner being to feed a habit of parasiti-

cal self-expression. We play host to him: where our own conscience should be, there he is, giving us his perfectly reasonable
instructions. – At least *he* is of the opinion that they are perfectly
reasonable, thinking he knows it all. The perfect All he was once
in thoughtful contact with has long since become the dead and
gone past for him – though, having assumed its mantle, he is trying his best to breathe some life back into it: by making us dance
to his tune.

He has definitely managed to outwit himself though. Without
our obedience he is nothing, he is entirely dependent on us. He
does nothing but talk really, all the doing is ours and all he
amounts to is an insubstantial (and degraded, at that) idea
demanding to be embodied by us. Why do we listen to him? Of
course he can have his minions who enforce his misrule, but then
we can always plead incapable, far too foolish to grasp his instructions properly. If we all played deaf, and dumb as well, he would
groan and creak to an instant halt. But like the Leonian despot, he
knows how to sweeten the pill, to bribe us into compliance. True,
his knowing does not amount to the omniscience he makes it out
to be, but even so he does know better than any of us how to gain
material success. Of course he does, he is material-objective 'success' personified. His impeccable reasoning, not muddled by anything that goes beyond clever thinking, is at our disposal: if only
we will be good and do as he says. – It turns out he is having to
prove himself after all: *he* is working for *us*, to *earn* our obedience.
And if ever he had superior ideas, now he debases his reason
entirely, to come up with the crassest, most earthbound of materialistic thought schemes.

But even that is not the end of his cleverness. He also knows
how to cast himself in the role of benefactor along different lines.
He will rid us of this inconvenience of inner being, always at odds
with what needs to be done in the world. He will disencumber us
of this individual conscience that means nothing but painful
choices and difficult decisions, that demands courage and entails
nothing but differing, strife, loss. He promises us an easy life,
nothing more strenuous than automatically following his well-
meant suggestions… dependable success, no hitches.

It is a tempting offer, so much less effortful than the inner
becoming model offered us by positive Capricorn. *We* have (we
think) the certainty of a quiet life, a well-oiled stability, as well as

material success. And *he* has our hollow, pre-programmed actions for his 'becoming' into the world, his life. He has denatured himself: like an extravert he now depends for his source of becoming on his environment, and of his essential innerness there is nothing left. And he has denatured *us*: addressing himself to our inner self and conscience, then helpfully taking it away, in return for something much less burdensome.

All he needs is our connivance. And of course the fact that we have an inner self at all; without that he couldn't begin to operate in his negative ways. If he could not supplant our inner selves with his own (projected, dead and disconnected) then his would lie idle for ever. He needs that space inside us to nestle into, as into the driver's seat. Else there is no guarantee of movement for him, no 'life', no apparent becoming (or becoming apparent). Negative Capricorn can ultimately, consistently successfully, prove himself in the world only from inside us.

The success, though, that he hands us on a plate – by informing us in detail about the 'secrets' of life, the principles that are at the hidden (or at least, to us, forbidden) inner centre of the structure and workings of the world – is never quite what we might have expected. It is real enough, and we may well amass riches. But what is the use of them? The moment we reach a goal, he whips us on to reach the next one. We are his agents, his functionaries; and working endlessly, functioning in the same way without cease or an occasional change of course, is what our lives are about. So the riches that come our way lie about unused, preserved in their status quo. There is no time for spending, for dawdling, for enjoying or idly resting on laurels. He keeps driving us on to put his clever ideas into practice. We could build palaces, but we never have time to inhabit them. Our gains are only landmarks of passing time, nothing we could lay our hands on, because our hands are always busy building the next promised success.

He cheats us of the essence of what he promised, just as he has cheated us out of our inner essence. We not only end up hollow inside, but our lives have become a pointless plodding round and round on the treadmill of endless ambition. Proving him – or proving 'ourselves', since he has now occupied the empty space inside us – is all we ever seem to do. We are driven, from inside us, to perform like well-trained circus animals. This is what we have sacrificed, thrown away, our still weak inner awareness and 'tender' conscience for. And yet we are content to see our lives running so smoothly and predictably. The outward efforts we get used to; and any inner efforts are, thank heavens, not required. And he, too, is content: by running our lives for us he is getting us to run his for him. It is quite an all-round success story, and he has certainly proved himself: he is by far our favourite dictator.

Negative Capricorn does not 'educate' Virgo in any helpful way. It is obvious enough that he destroys in us what Virgo has thoughtfully made possible. He thought to supplant Virgo's potential with his own, better one. But the way he puts his own wider-ranging inner being, with its even more demanding conscience, to work (as a thing, a tool, a machine for printing success, instead of a growing and self-replenishing inner attitude) he only managed to lose it all. For an inner self he has been depending on us: to give him ours to gobble up, then look for more. This, in effect, is the fuel he has been running on.

Likewise, the conscience he used to have has disintegrated in the service of slavish adherence to material expediency – all so that he could earn himself a place in our inner world ('in our hearts') and *through us* enter into concrete life effortlessly. He has done the only logical thing, given his wrong-headed approach, and made his no longer vital principles become the materially proved, the physically embodied, the once-and-for-all established, the past happening over and over again, throughout the world.

He has 'become' a mass product. One may take him for a failed individual(ist) then. We look to him for guidance and find him instituting a set, communal-model world. His dogma, unvaried by new getting-to-know either on the inner plane or in response to the world's needs and demands, may suffice for a while, but the truth is he does *not* know it all, and his denatured work force is contentedly constructing a false, a mistaken world. When the fault in the inflexible design becomes apparent, somewhat along the lines shown in negative Taurus, we hardly know who is to blame, but directed from inside us as we are, we carry on all the same.

The extraverting extravert Taurus derived the intuited models for his world building unconsciously and direct from the inner plane, rather than via an inner self of his own in contact with it. At his best, Taurus *could* not distort these true impulses he received. Though he could of course also make the mis-take of seizing on one such model exclusively, making it his own, and wreaking havoc through endless repetition. But Taurus' job of world builder is what negative Capricorn needs to appropriate, in order to find his ideas working and taking on shape, directly, in prompt obedience to his instructions. And there is certainly not room beside him for a witless rival to the title of world destroyer.

Taurus is subject to these would-be superior Capricornian reasonings and has no choice but obey. Virgo is beguiled into thinking he might achieve his own designs in the world the easy way, without any hard *inner* work, like painful adapting, constantly re-examining his own conscience. That is how Capricorn works. The earlier he can catch us, the better – before we have had time to develop positive Taurus and Virgo ways. Ridiculing us for primitive fools on the one hand, and tempting us with the offer to make our individual lives easy and painless on the other (without telling us that there will be nothing left of our true individuality if we take up his offer) he has us obeying him in no time at all.

We pay for it by working, outwardly, harder than ever; by losing our integrity as both outward *and* inward directed beings; and by finding a material reward we can neither enjoy nor expect to be of lasting value. We have duped ourselves, proving him right – our inferior intelligence has always been a central part of his ideology. We have given him house-room in our inner-self space and there he sits, like a virus, directing us to copy him in space and time and matter. We *are* all of us he: we are *being* he. And laboriously, ceaselessly, making the hidden truth of his central deadness more and more of a concrete fact in the world, we are ultimately doomed to the same slow grinding-to-a-halt as he is.

Every rule has been laid down, every principle firmly embedded, every process rigidly established, every construction constructed to the same principle – never resting, but pushing on till our efforts have covered the whole world, we have literally worked ourselves to death: there is nothing left to do now. We ran out of new ideas long ago; and now we have run out of the raw material, the situations, to apply the old ideas to as well. We need not look inside us for a new inspiration. We will only find him lodged in there. And we need not expect him to give us new instructions: self-repetition, with our help, is all he is capable of. Now he has been repeated 'to perfection'. There is no more we can do for him. Our obedience has proved his (and our) end, and his end has proved him to be imperfect after all. Cleverly and complexly ignorant is all he has ever been, since he threw himself into this venture of living with so much faith in himself. In truth, he has been huddling there inside us, too impotent to set a foot outside on his own account, in perfect perpetuation of his initial fear to come out of himself. If he thought about it, in principle, he might even come to the conclusion that his life never *really* took place. –

The carbon copies that negative Leo created, not knowing what he was doing, only ended up threatening his position in the world, his very life. Negative Capricorn, knowing pretty well what he is up to, does on the face of it much better: he turns out copies that live his life for him. He winkles out the essential bit in the middle that makes them go where *they* want to go and takes its place, permanently , in each and ever one of them. He becomes umpteen *substitute* inner selves, all alike – while of course he is nothing but an empty shell, and his empty-shell copies prove it. He has infected us with his deadness, so that he may live, and what we collectively live for him is nothing but pointless appearances. We are only going through the motions, robotically saying and doing the same things all over, out of some cuckoo principle we can't dislodge, and wearing the most dead serious expressions on our faces. It is the past marching on to meet not the future but its inevitable end.

This leaves the question what happened to the inner self he cheated out of us, dislodged and replaced with his own static model. To say he gobbled it up and destroyed it can only describe the *effect* of what he did. We do not have it any more; but neither does he: where would he put it? He has no inner space of his own any more and has already let us know that we are only imagining these things, subjective wishful thinking, all of it, with no basis in fact. He has banished all this immaterial unreality, he has cut it off from participation in our lives, and cut us off from contact with it. He has cut us in two: our inner selves to wander around aimlessly on the inner plane, leading a ghost existence parallel to our concrete and yet hardly less ghost-like doings, as we mindlessly trot out the past again and again, till it finally dies of its own repleteness. – His end comes at the moment of his greatest triumph, really: when all the world is he. He has always been 'too full of himself', quite unwilling to accommodate life – only to end up both empty and lifeless.

And yet we are so eager to do his hard work, his easy living, for him that it could equally be argued that *we* have been tempting *him* to take this would-be shortcut to proving himself in the world, to act in this truly irresponsible way. Since we *are* he, of course, it all comes back to the original temptation Capricorn feels when he first becomes emotionally aware of his relative, individual, inner completeness – and mistakes it for a complete completeness, absolute and for all time and in all respects. Sensing his potential effectiveness, and intuiting his capacity for rulership, only compounds his error.

Some Suggested Capricorn Attributes

basic

deeply thoughtful, intellectually inclined, analytical; strong principles, 'has his own ideas'; strong conscience; sense of duty

appears withdrawn, 'sunk in thought'; isolated in his corner of the world, **defensive, not a joiner; quiet, reticent, appears uncommunicative** because he cannot bring himself to say all he thinks; **very slow to respond; worries endlessly** about doing the right thing the right way

alternates between thinking himself inferior (compared to his environment): **self-conscious, fears rejection, many anxieties, shy, socially and physically awkward** – and **on the other hand being sure of himself** (inside himself): **intellectually proud/arrogant, air of (moral) superiority, harsh judgements; split attitude to his worth**

inefficient on account of his **slowness; overconscientious; hesitant approach** (takes too long to figure out how to *apply* his ideas); **over-cautious, cowardly,** preferring to withdraw from the scene of action, **retiring** into his 'shell'

'old-fashioned' ideas; strict outlook; has theories about everything; values 'correctness'; over-serious, grave, sombre, gloomy; experiences life as a burden, easily discouraged, no-hoper; a failure, in the sense that he never gets going in the first place

positive

quiet courage, believes in **making a stand** where necessary; **principled, incorruptible** and **responsible,** but **knows how to compromise; gently insistent, patient, modest, serious in intent** but also **accepts life for what it is,** up to a point; **resigned to meeting with difficulties; good self-control**

helpful and caring in an advising/instructing/teaching capacity; educator in a wider sense, both along theoretical and practical lines; **parental guide, counsellor; positive authority,** bearing **humility** in mind; **respectful** both of the individual and the positive communal values and practices; **scrupulous** and **fair**

may be tempted to be either **too all-or-nothing** in his approach, **or too accommodating**

efficient, practical; good at structuring, ordering; applies thought-out method, premeditated action; steady and dependable; but values not so much what he achieves for himself as how he does it: good worker for little reward, always aware of having to set a good example; comes up with new ideas (derived from inner thought development)

strong individuality (a lot of which may not be openly expressed), but well-adapted in positive circumstances/only slowly adapting into a negative environment (having better, unexpressed ideas); socially integrated but looking for sensible progress: social leader; cautiously liberal or flexibly conservative – or else: socially marginalised but persisting in his efforts

thoughtfully balanced attitudes; law-abiding (if they are good laws); but can spring surprises, resort to unusual behaviour, can be provoked to slyness, outwitting others; clandestine law-breaker (if they are bad laws); subversive, if he finds it necessary

negative

believes in the absolute rightness of his thinking: uncompromising, inflexible, harsh, intolerant; rigid, predictable, set in his thought-patterns and practical approach; has one generalised and generalising principle or ideology, doctrinaire, dogmatic, reductionist; self-respecting authoritarian; condescendingly paternalistic, excessively stern and strict

moralises (always knowing The Right Way to do everything), offers 'well-meant advice'; knows it all; pontificates, 'lectures', belittles others as stupid, demands one hundred per cent obedience, issues commands in the form of exact instructions

relentlessly purses every detail: ponderously finicky, endless logistics, gets bogged down in superfluous rationalising, superficial structuralist, hooked on inessentials, bureaucratic; time-wasting, slow, repetitive, double-checking; sticks his nose in everything, regarding it as only his 'duty' to supervise others

grants no privacy, discounts subjective factors e.g. others' feelings, mistakenly 'objective'; appears coldly impersonal (though with an emotional undercurrent) success-oriented, materialistic, has only expediency in mind; aims to maintain the established status quo

shrewd; superficial reasoning; misleading; ultimately debases his mind and principles; appearance is all; bribes, cheats, plots, makes false promises, subverts the system for his own gain

depends on others to carry out his work (being too set in his ways, ignorant of actual living): masterful, self-appointed (mis)leader; misrepresents his aims so as to gain popularity; ultimately abases himself currying favour

works slavishly for others, needing their approval so he can have his (dead-set) way and his treasured stability, supports the 'establishment'; his repetitive work is a hollow performance; automatic obedience, functionary, impotent, craven, shows abject respect; easily depressed if meets with rejection of his working principles; despite 'acting responsibly' he has no personal conscience, only the basic ambition to go on doing more of what he has already done, in his 'lifeless' way

workaholic, always needing to 'prove himself' yet again; no time for enjoyment, disapproves of pleasure as distracting from work as well as coming 'too naturally'; denatured, no respect for life

carries meaningless burdens, weighed down but uncomplaining; takes a (groundless) pride in his (self-imposed) hardships: self-denial, spartan, austere; penny-pinching (preserving the economic status quo and smugly going-without); joyless, spoilsport, yet essentially always looks for the easy way out: basically lazy and irresponsible, it suits him to be a puppet of his masters: allows himself to be brainwashed and directed by an internalised 'voice of authority'

THE
AIR SIGNS

♊ GEMINI

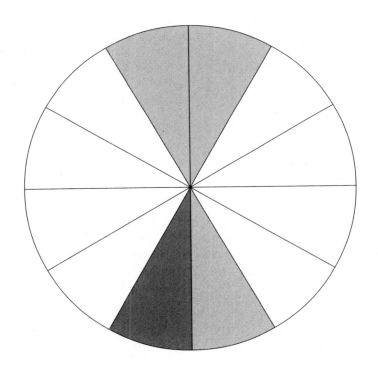

♊ **Introvert**
conscious function: sensation; direction of function: outward
unconscious functions: ♐ intuition, ♑ thinking, ♋ feeling
Air: rational

An extraverting introvert, like Leo, Gemini too can only contact what he essentially is through meeting it in the objective world around him. His conscious function is sensation and he is of a rational nature. So he does not, like the entirely intuitive Leo, expect to find the totality of all he is reflected wholesale in his environment. Instead he meets his unknown self bit by bit, via his senses, gaining a multitude of distinct impressions, and he does this in a basically thoughtful, intelligent way.

Leo needed to find himself mirrored. Virgo needed to select thoughtfully what of the surrounding world to call self and eventually to introject, in full self-awareness. Gemini, for his part, uses all his rationally employed senses to experience the nature of his self reflected piecemeal in the totality of his environment. And through seeing understandingly the differences and connections between this bit of observed world and that, he becomes aware: not of his self as a specific whole, but of the many possible, specific, partial 'selves' that are inherent in him.

One could say that he catches sight of his self in its various roles and guises, or of the way that it *applies* itself to the world, long before he gains any sort of understanding of it *in itself*. He examines all these aspects of his self, in detail and quite without favour. Each bit of this ever changing kaleidoscope of self-states is an equally valid reflection of self to him. He would watch them endlessly unfold, sensing a self in every detail, investigating them one by one from all possible angles, and just as happy to call any of them 'I'. For all his basically intelligent observing, he does not come to prefer some to others, as Virgo would. Thus in terms of an established self aware of itself as such, he is nothing – and at the same time he is everything.

There are two reasons why he is not the least bit 'choosy'. For one thing, he is not employing conscious thought, critically comparing, but is only being basically intelligent in the way he consciously 'sees himself in the world'. But above all, as an introvert he is already in possession of a self, not trying to assemble one. And yet, because of his outward-looking, piecemeal 'approach' to it, or perception of it, his self is constantly coming apart: channelled outward into this rainbow world of endless possibilities of objective being. Just *being* himself, he shatters and scatters and endlessly subdivides himself. And it is in this fractured state that he needs to find himself, become aware of himself.

As an extraverting introvert he is not in touch with an inner transpersonal source of becoming, like Sagittarius or Capricorn for instance. Like Leo he is 'finite' in his inner, subjective self. For both the extraverting introverts consciously being self and becoming other amounts to the same thing, right from the start. Intuitive Leo takes the whole world to be his whole self. Gemini, cleverly using the whole range of his separate senses, takes every bit of world to be yet another self. And where the introverting extravert Virgo gathers himself out of the choices the world offers, the extraverting introvert Gemini throws himself to the four winds indiscriminately, in a thousand pieces, and all equally 'admirable'. It is maybe not too fanciful to see him as (providing) the raw material, the fractions of self, *some of which* Virgo picks up.

The problem is, in the figure of Everyman Gemini has lost the unity of his self. The most central aspect of his self is missing, because he can obviously never meet the *totality* of this fractured self all at the same time. Being broken up into umpteen parts need not worry him as long as all the parts are always present and can be accounted for by his senses. But they never are: the objective flow of time withdraws some, withholds some, reveals some. And while he can do nothing to retrieve those parts of him 'lost in the past', he is for ever scurrying around – virtually trying to *overtake* time – in the vain hope, at least, of seeing all there is of him in both present and future, just over the horizon.

No matter how fast he runs, or how far, he can never get where he wants to go: the one objective place where *all* of him is 'visible'. It would need a timeless sort of place, to say the least, for him ever to 'come together'. Meantime, like Aries, he is finding and losing bits of self in rapid succession – except that in his case what he keeps losing are parts of a self he already 'owns', and this is not merely pointless, but hurtful. What is more, the harder he tries, the more he gets immersed in life, the more damage he appears to be doing to himself.

The flow of time in the objective world may present him with a million chances of *becoming* (aware of his) *self*, but it also prevents him ever *being* (aware of his) *self*, as the whole self he *is*. The more he tries to find his self, the more he loses it. He has done nothing 'wrong' scattering himself into the world, it is simply in his nature. And yet, essentially, he is his own undoing.

To centre him and hold him together, he can make use of his intuitive awareness (✗). This provides him with access to that inner-reality 'place', on the subjective level, where everything he already is (as an introvert) *is* assembled together for all time.

In a manner of speaking, his loyalty now becomes divided: on the one hand there is what he now unconsciously understands of the inner unity of his subjective self; and on the other, there is its objective reflection, this 'separatist' multitude of selves that he consciously observes. Adding, as it were, division to division, he now has the opportunity to identify his self in all that goes on in the world while never losing the central awareness of being a oneness apart from all that – at the same time as *being* all that (or becoming it, to be precise).

He no longer worries if he finds bits of self vanishing out of sight; intuitively he knows nothing has 'really' vanished, only its mirror image counterpart in the world has. Neither does he need to run around quite so frantically visiting and revisiting the sight and sound and touch of this multitude of a self, nor to run off altogether to inspect some part of him he has espied on the horizon. Intuitively he is aware that he has 'already got' all the pieces that make up the whole of him.

As a result, he comes to sense intelligently that there must be a connection between centre and periphery, subjective reality and objective reality, and by logical extension, connections even between all the different self-parts that lie scattered about him. His central, subjective being-one and his constantly new, objective becoming-many can now come together: in the act of trying to bring together all those far-flung pieces of the world that he can all equally identify as 'I'. He begins to unify them, intelligently, into a system that will hold them *all* and thus reflect his inherent oneness – while still maintaining their separate existence, maintaining his equally essential 'many-ness'.

His aim is to become a (self-)organiser, a go-between, a matchmaker, a facilitator of intelligent contact between the diverse parts of a world/self divided and subdivided. Holding the awareness of a central unifying reality within him, he is confident he will find a way of fitting it all together. And in the process he will make a living, unified being of himself. – Or so he would, if he could only stick to one assembly job in preference to all others, and not attempt to do them all at the same time, in his haphazard way. He is constantly unravelling his own attempts, turning left, turning right, doing this a bit, then that a bit; how else would he act, when it is 'all the same to him' after all. He is for ever 'changing his mind' what to do, when, how, in what order. He is at best coagulating a bit, in untidy clumps: certainly no faithful representation of what his intuition would inspire him to attempt.

Unconscious thought ($\text{⍚}\rightarrow$) helps him sort out theses messes and tangles he gets into. He learns to ignore the whole welter of detail that is always clamouring for his divided attention, to concentrate his efforts within a more limited scope. His new-found pragmatism tells him to pare down the number of concurrent interests and things to do: it does not make sense to allow himself to be pulled in all directions at once. He learns to get absorbed in one mental task at a time, one after the other, following A with B, rather than juggling wildly with the whole alphabet. He sorts out the practical and properly logical connections from the ones that aren't. Calculating, unconsciously at least, the concrete outcome of any desired 'fusion' process, also helps him slow down. His impatient despair at never getting things together now gives way to dogged plodding, repeated trying, each time harder. This is serious work he is engaged on, and he is soberly pragmatic about what he takes on, and how he deals with it.

When he unconsciously thinks about his self ($\text{⍚}\leftarrow$), this is no longer a far-flung self hard to lay hold of. He gains a quite clearly defined concept of his whole inner identity. He also thinks of himself as an 'idea' needing to act itself out in the world in various ways, depending on the circumstances. All this contributes another centralising factor to his make-up.

He is so world-wide, so much everything, in 'sensual' detail, that only single-mindedness can pull him together. Intuiting his inner wholeness only gives him the impetus to unify his many objective selves. Knowing his self also as a set of clearly defined principles, gives him the idea to confine his attempts, to single out and pinpoint, and then take it from there, step by logical step. Time no longer withholds most of his self from him – that is to say he no longer looks at it from that point of view – time, too, has shrunk to a defined unit: the now of the concentrated effort that logically as well as practically speaking leads on to the next now, the next effort. He learns to think ahead, not passively impatient to see more of himself happen, but actively planning his deliberate progress towards what he wants to be doing in the world.

It is quite an enterprise, slotting together the pieces of the jigsaw puzzle that is he; somehow repairing this existential damage to something that on another level is a simple oneness. And it is only unconsciously that he has any idea of how it might all be meant to hang together. To confuse him further, his puzzle pieces – his varying, living selves – keep changing. And so, in response, must his total picture, the unified self he is trying to assemble step by step. It is a constant repair job, an unending process of re-adaptation, and never such a thing as a finished result.

At no point do his living 'selves' allow him to get the complete picture of what he, essentially, is. All he ever gets is the experience of relative, living wholeness: *a* picture, for a moment, before its cohesion goes walk-about again, and he is at it again readjusting, filling gaps, splinting, splicing, bandaging and bonding, to nurse it 'back' to another, new kind of wholeness. He never *is* for a moment but he 'happens' to change again. Still, while he is basically the cause of his own undoing, he is also his own remedy. He has sown himself in confusion, all manner of splits and separation, but he is also right there with all the tools to mend and re-complete anew. – Except that put like that, it sounds a pretty pointless exercise. Why does he bother, if his reward constantly escapes him and something else is for ever required of him? He seems to be wasting his time and could be forgiven for refusing to play such a 'silly game' – and he so newly serious about it all!

Emotionally, he has a strong wish to be helpful, to be of use and fulfil others' obvious needs (♋→). That is the point then of the whole exercise: putting something new together, he has something to give. Able to mend things, he too, in all his perennial (or at least recurring) incompleteness, can contribute something that is of value to others.

At the same time, he tries to unify not only the material things of the world, but all his living 'selves' as well, singly or in groups, with all their various interests, causes, opinions and activities. He adopts them all. They are his children, these broken reflections, and he, the original broken child, mothers them. – Focusing on any two things, one in either hand, he brings them together in himself as their common ground. He spans, bridges and sets in relation. He weaves a new communion out of the old unravelled simple oneness. That is the point of his apparently self-contradictory being and doing: he is the end of an era of 'simple oneness'. He has created a world of complexity, of distinctness within a unified context.

Unconsciously feeling himself to be a complete self, secure inside the seclusion of its completeness (♋←), is yet another factor that centres him. With his unconscious intuiting, feeling and rational knowing he has gained access to the oneness that underlies all this flotsam of a timed, material world flow. Now he informs us with everything he does at the 'superficial' level that there is a life-transcending Core Reality: the mainspring of the many apparently pointless experiences we are subject to in this confusing, bitty world.

His message is not obvious, it needs to be read between the lines. Sagittarius offered to lead us to that other reality beyond objective life in person, if we could follow him there; and to bring us his message he had to root himself down into our alien and imperfect reality first. Gemini is 'one of us', every bit as defective as each and every one of us: in effect a fellow earthling, a brother who regards us all as his equals (his equally valid selves). He does not need to descend to our level, but neither can he consciously lead us to a higher one. But what he can do is to demonstrate to us in a great variety of ways how to practise wholeness, how (if only unconsciously) to reach up into the hidden Centre of all things and find the motivation there to 'mend our lives'. This gives us freedom too, the freedom to be actively in charge of our environment – *and* the obligation to keep 'mending' it. Work, in other words: something Taurus did as a matter of course but which for Gemini means making a conscious effort, though it comes naturally to him. He can't dodge it if he wants to gain his true integrity while automatically happening in the world. It is no headache to him though, as it becomes, later in the zodiac, for Virgo or even more so for the rational introvert Capricorn with his inbuilt principles and the task to apply them 'out there'. Out here is Gemini's natural home; he does not need any persuading to make a start and get stuck into 'work', only the central something that enables him to make a *proper* job of it.

Where Virgo refines the world thoughtfully, having selected and individualised, Gemini reassembles and heals the inbuilt confusion he has 'caused' – having first thoughtfully observed his complexity. Both do something to the structure of the world. The one adds deliberate individualised refinement. The other, unwittingly, adds divisive complexity and then proceeds intelligently to tie it all up again, loosely, into a wholeness that is at once communal and potentially individual. Gemini is the precursor of Virgo; he is the prime cause of the whole division/re-fusion process, the supplier of all the divergent choices that are available to Virgo who needs them in order to come to conscious objective/subjective self-knowing. Without the prior splitting of oneness there can be no subsequent individual changes, development and 'coming together'. Gemini only practises the changing, developing and coming together, endlessly, but Virgo perfects it in full self-awareness.

When he gives us the service of his many abilities Gemini is completing himself, as best he can. Because now at last he makes some sense to himself, he is no longer like a dog chasing its tail in vain: as a contributor to our well-being and development he no longer finds himself deficient or his activities leading nowhere, ultimately. He makes our requests and appeals for his help the central fact around which his activities revolve: we take the objective counterpart place of his inner centre, so that making sure we are 'all in one piece' he actively unifies himself. But he does more than that: in his own circuitous way he, too, lays a foundation, just as Taurus built the material world we call home. Gemini splits open the one enveloping 'homeness' of the world, showing it to be all separate houses, individual units for living in, and then proceeds to build the roadways to connect them again.

What he founds in this way is the prerequisite of any functioning society: communication in all its manifold aspects. If Virgo set an example in understanding and sensibly handling oneself, Gemini sets the example of understanding and sensibly dealing with one another – something that needs to be learnt first, before fully conscious individuation can be 'allowed' to take place in a society.

It would be logically tempting to set him beside Leo as his co-creator. (He too is an in itself finite 'All there is' that is for ever becoming into the world in infinite ways.) This would be a fallacy though. It is only through his *attitude*, the way he sees his self, that Gemini consciously introduces something new into the world: the variety of 'selves'. It is his one self's potential for becoming – in time, and through work – he automatically sees there; and to make it really resemble the becoming of a unified self, he then has to apply himself to that work, to 'pull himself together'. Whole-making is his work.

Leo's work was quite the reverse. With him the starting point, the attitude, was one of intuitive wholeness, which he was inclined to look for in the world but did not find. He too had to work towards his potential: to make it fact, and thus to 'realise' it. His work was to introduce his own inbuilt, 'bitty' variety into the world, through active changes. – It is Leo who *creates* the 'many' that Gemini then *recognises* as his selves. But it is also Gemini who is the many who refuse to have Leo's oneness of being foisted on them, forcing him to work at his creative changes in a way that will respect their separateness, and in the process bringing him to a living, changing, becoming self-awareness, contrary to his initial 'dead' oneness.

The two signs clearly interdepend. Leo, being one, nevertheless actively supplies the world with its 'becoming' variety. And Gemini, always becoming many, supplies it with the central fact (the truth, even) of its essential integrity. Gemini – the re-fuser in the world who, unwisely and yet wisely, *by his basic nature* 'refuses' to be a static, dead oneness in the world in obedience to what Leo would basically like to see there – Gemini gives Leo the reason for effecting changes; for turning the one dead, finite, all-being and hence perfect self (or Self) into a multitude of imperfect mirror images, living 'others'. It is Gemini who gets this potential creator *moving*.

Leo's work, though, is indispensable for the existence of Gemini in the first place – if such a 'first' place there were. It is Leo who is the *underlying* cause of the dividedness of the world: but his variety *becomes* dividedness only through Gemini's intelligent observation of world/self. Only in that sense can one understand Gemini as being responsible for all these divisions, rifts, incompletenesses (and hence imperfections). Bringing a contradictory self-awareness into the world, he 'creates' not a multicoloured world, but the basis for each self seeing itself, intelligently, in separateness, as a distinct colour within the spectrum.

He is all that falls apart; he is the rescuer, the healer. The perpetual loser; and the one to turn to when we have lost anything at all: he is bound to mend, find, recover, put us back in touch. He is never without a remedy, therapy or technique. He is never stuck for an answer to a problem, given time. More importantly, though, we learn from him that the aim of finding our personal integrity has to go hand in hand with making others' lives more 'whole', complete and fulfilled too.

There is always ample opportunity to misuse the unconscious abilities, and Gemini can easily let the intuitive knowledge of his essential unity become a driving compulsion. Instead of looking inward, and working from that basis – making and re-making of the world something that hangs together – he forcefully projects all he intuits outward: it ends up imposed into the world. It no longer 'sits inside him' to give him unconscious guidance, but seems to be all around him, in each and every of the myriad of his 'selves', his self-being situations.

But there are two ways in which he can misinterpret the situation when he intuitively seeks a ready-made outer unity. Passively, he may end up whole-heartedly convinced that he *is* whatever the moment offers him, or demands of him. Or he may take the active approach: to *make himself be* (meaning of course also, make the world be) what he has projected by way of inner unity and central purpose.

There is the negative Gemini type who will passively 'become his environment'. He takes whatever he can see of himself for the time being to be *all* there is of him. His dislocated inner awareness lodges in every new situation, no matter how much they all differ one from the other, and of course he is incapable of seeing that there is a central contradiction involved in being 'complete' in so many different ways. He has thrown his centre away outward, into everything, and would find his completeness in every momentary pose, every kind of company, any type of activity, any context, in any condition, under any banner: each time it is the truest representation of all he is. He never counts his numerous selves; he never acknowledges his 'gaps', all the things time/life is forever withholding from him. Time does play tricks on him though, constantly effecting changes in his environment.

Changes he cannot stand, they betray the falseness of his sincere claims by adding something to him that was not there before. Or else, by taking something away, they force him into a totally self-contradictory position: needing to recapture his wholeness by, on the one hand, leaving his 'complete' self behind – and on the other, going in pursuit of it! Worse, going anywhere at all only has him bumping into all those other bits of him that have been missing from his postulated completeness all this time. Of course he is unhappy that the world will not stand still: his embodied 'wholeness' demands an entirely static world.

Misusing his unconscious ability to concentrate thoughtfully on what is under his nose ($\text{\char"2644}\rightarrow$), he gains a new kind of freedom, from his point of view. Now he can ignore what goes on around him and further pinpoint his would-be completeness in such a tiny range of details, or even just a single one, that it is all but impossible for anything or anybody to deprive him of it. He hangs on with both hands; he is quite minutely defined, small enough to hold all of him in his hands. Try and add something to him and all he does is to shrink still further: now he holds all he is in one hand, while the other wards off this threat, pushes away the offered impossibility that *cannot* also be part of him. If he asks for anything, then it is to be left alone in his complete self-absorption. Change is simply not welcome, he is quite content to repeat himself – progress is unknown to him.

Time, with all its changes, still goes on of course, but to him it is no longer a flow. He is always hermetically sealed in his momentary self-experience, encapsulated as in a closed room. Time is like a long row of such rooms to him. Intuitively, he rushes from one to the next, in search of all of him, and always 'closes the door' behind him. (A metaphorical door, it has to be said; actual doors behind him, lying in the past, will be ignored.) What he was, and what he will be, does not count. Anything he finds himself being and doing in this state of momentarily arrested time, within his shrunk and clearly defined horizon, is of entire significance. No matter what circumstances require him to do, say, look like, act out, it is always, truly, wholly, he.

The central idea he has of his self (♑←) is equally to be found out there, in whichever 'room' he happens to be. The moment his current situation threatens to alter or develop in any way, it is time for him to move on smartly to the next: closing one chapter and opening another. He goes by quantum leaps and bounds from one exclusively 'all-inclusive' self-experience to the next, entirely self-contradictory in the process of course, changing like lightning, while being entirely averse to change. He makes the greatest fuss about being a pinpoint self, no more and no less, and zips through a whole gamut of being he, always yours truly, quite unpindownable. Essentially, he pleases himself what he is – and yet his ploy could never work if he did not also please others at the same time.

Fortunately, or should one say unfortunately, he has an excessively giving emotional nature (♋→) and is happy to oblige others by being just what they expect him to be – a mirror image of themselves, that is what pleases them best. This ties in neatly with what he *can* only be: whatever he finds in his given environment. He is, after all, not in search of any *particular* complete self. He will cheerfully be all things to all men, one at a time, assuming for the occasion whatever colour of coat they would prefer him to wear. But the different people he pleases had better be widely scattered, or he will be in trouble. Mixtures will not do for him. Like a rainbow come apart he wears only one colour at a time.

He compartmentalises his life, separating each of his selves from the other. A double life is nothing to him, he could manage a hundred. But he does not feel the least bit disjointed or chamaeleonlike. The emotional centre he feels himself to have (♋←) is, like everything else, displaced outward. Even emotionally he carries his wholeness around with him, like a nomad his tent, setting it down in every situation as he finds it. He is never in flux but leapfrogs, in zigzags. He abhors true development, becoming, gradually adapting: it upsets his multiplicity of stases.

Practically speaking, he collects a vast repertoire of being and doing but is himself quite unaware of that. Aware only of each current phase of his existence, which he clings to as long as it stays 'whole' for him, he does not adapt but adopts new selves wholesale. His stubborn insistence means nothing. One can get him to change his tune quite easily with a bit of destabilising pressure: he will 'click into' his new tune as if he had never known anything else. He sticks like glue to what he is and has and does, but once jolted out of it he throws it all aside – not *in favour* of the new, or something *better*: it is all the same to him after all – but simply because his closed horizon has been breached. Shutting phantom doors on past and future is the only way he can cope with his self-contradictoriness.

He is ready to imitate and fit in with anybody, happily, yet pride of place where his attention span is concerned goes to inanimate objects. Things please him best of all. They stay as they are and don't spring nasty surprises on him. They don't contradict his claims to omniscience, complete know-how, his seen-it-all attitude. Neither are they likely to injure the feelings of emotional security that he has firmly embedded in them. He can 'stay with them' longest because they stay as and what and where they are. – But sooner or later somebody always intrudes on his concentrated self-contemplation, and now of course he has to be that somebody. Whatever it was, whatever *he* was, is dropped. He leaves bits and pieces lying in his wake, they are the past, and he refuses to even look in their direction. Losing and forgetting, he rids himself of a past self that is no longer required now and would only cause him intolerable confusion if it persisted.

Untidiness is constitutional with him: he does not make connections. Adding up is the last thing that would spring to his mind. Order is inconceivable; systems mean nothing to him. And a broken piece will do him just as nicely as the whole thing. He will walk into a chaos situation, and manage to home in on a small part of it to settle into, 'close the doors' and ignore the rest. The concept of linking things up to create a unity cannot possibly have meaning for him, seeing that he implants his completeness wherever he can. He foists his conviction of a unified selfhood on other, quite indiscriminately, and trusts other implicitly to contain that self (at his peril, perhaps). All he has to do is slip into other, put it on like a coat. And we are always coaxing him to come and be us; he is understandably popular. He is our voices, our manners, our opinions, our style, through and through. Anybody can lead him in any direction, for a while, thinking him to be eager, or at least compliant, but they are in for rude shocks and bitter disappointments.

There is only one thing that is predictable about him and that is his unpredictability. His self-contradictory sincerity is quite genuine of course. He is (being) what he says he is. The problem is, there are so many of him. But he would be genuinely puzzled if one pointed this out to him. He would have to remember yesterday's self, and own up to what he did then: complexity and responsibility going hand in hand. His make-believe that he has a simple unified self – intact with nothing missing, left behind or yet to become – is nothing but a handy self-delusion. He is fooling himself and, incidentally, has us fooled in the process.

In all innocence – if one can call it that – he may wreak havoc, but he means no harm. He is not even asking for much, only to have his being in what *we* are being and doing already anyway. Incapable of facing a large and constantly flowing, changing world, he does his living one mouthful at a time, being bits of himself in turns. Without knowing it he, too, is becoming: in spurts and leaps and little isolated phases. It is an easy option. He is *being* himself all the time, but he is a long way from being *himself*, in his totality, as he fondly imagines. (Being complete in the world is not something he could ever achieve – but this is too much for him to admit.) Fooling around with time, as he does, is only a peculiar substitute for 'pulling himself together', a first practice run at best; a deliberate habit of dodging the serious responsibilities and workload associated with positive Gemini, at worst. Either way, he is nothing worse than a mild case of parasite, too passive to do us any harm that we do not, by example, bring upon ourselves. His monkeying may be amusing, his mirror-image performances quite (embarrassingly) instructive, even if his lack of true centre, of integrity and dependability make him a rather doubtful companion.

He is never *truly* becoming: he projects his (unknown) wholeness outward into any isolated bit of world he happens to find, erecting (largely illusory) boundaries in the process, keeping most of the world at bay. Sagittarius at his worst, entirely immersed in a difficult world, did something like this too: walking out, closing the door, huddling in a contrived sort of bubble – but he only did it on occasion, when things got too bad. For Gemini, things are *always* bad, life threatens to undo him all the time with its careless happening.

All he can do is sit tight and concentrate fiercely on his latest heartfelt little bit of all-ness, with a seriousness as if his life depended on it. It doesn't of course, but his would-be integrity does, and so he sulkily insists. Staring, fingering, squeezing and poking, he tries to make sure he gets the full picture of every newly and randomly adopted 'full identity' – the armrest of the settee will do him.

In the last resort we can't help laughing. His crass self-trickery makes him so easy to 'see through', we see all the way through him: right to the centre that keeps eluding him. (And though he may put up a resistance at first, in the end he too has to laugh. There is nothing more attractive to him than laughter, it is of the essence, it is Sagittarian wholeness made objectively audible. He can't have enough of it and feels 'let down' when we stop. Humouring him, jollying him along, is the only way to handle him.) In a funny sort of way he does something for us. In fact – even if not in the right spirit, in all the wrong ways – he does what he was meant to do all along, despite himself: he does deliver his round-about message of an underlying wholeness, wholesomeness, integrity. If he did not already, unknown to him, have this integrity (as the introvert he is) he could hardly have stuck so consistently to his repetitive ploy, in its many adopted guises. All he has done is to take a sneaky short-cut. And cheated us out of the many benefits that would have been ours if he had delivered his message honestly, straightforwardly, without 'snags'.

We can see the truth behind his patently obvious not-quite lies and pretences clearly enough, sooner or later. Despite his efforts to be all-concrete he is nothing if not transparent. But he himself is still as clueless as ever. Instead of mending our world, he passively leaves it to us to help *him* get it together. To force him to 'grow up', away from his exclusive identification with a multi-natured physical self. And to get him moving, as he is meant to.

The other negative Gemini type is of an even more dubious character. He, too, has a compulsive desire to see himself as meaningfully whole and coherent ($\nearrow$) rather than broken up and dispersed in space and time. But he does not, passively and indiscriminately, find 'all' he is contained in the given environment of the moment. He does the opposite: impose a wholeness – not take each part of him to be the whole, but actively deny differentness to all his parts, declaring them to be all the same, essentially. They are all one big he, an artificial 'brotherhood' that ideally leaves no-one and nothing out. He is the world and the whole world is he and his. His limitlessness is of course a practical impossibility.

A world experience that resembles a string of separate rooms is no good to him, it has to be one big room only, and all of it his rightful territory. For him to be content with it, it needs to be a *flat* world, where nothing of him sticks out as different from all the rest. But to gain this impression of it he has to actively do something about the existing differences: he has to deconstruct the ups and downs and make a level mishmash of it all; only then will it begin to resemble an indiscriminate oneness. He has to tinker with the structure of everything, taking apart, spreading about, and to do that he needs a practical idea of how to go about it, and to bear in mind a central idea of his purpose. To be haphazard in his work would only leave a multitude of untidy piles, not the homogeneity he craves.

His unconscious thinking provides him with the ability to focus on the job in hand ($\text{\Leo}\rightarrow$) while at the same time never losing sight of the central idea of what he is about ($\text{\Leo}\leftarrow$). The idea he is to himself is, again, not an inner one, it is embodied and to all intents and purposes identical with the job. Lacking any comparison between inner thought and outer deed, he can of course never see anything wrong with what he is doing, as long as it is effective and yields a neat result, by his standards. In short, the moral side of it, the principle behind the action, has been debased: quite literally descended and swallowed up into convenience, expediency, mere practical attention to what he is doing. And his 'standards' are not derived from any idea, but from his intuitive compulsion to be-it-all.

He is a master of doing all jobs at once. He is all lateral thinking and sideways squinting, his eyes darting, his mind leaping back and forth, but no one could accuse him of a lack of concentration. He has got it all together, forgets nothing and plans shrewdly ahead. His thinking is cool and calculating and tends to revolve

around his material advantage. Not that he is trying to appropriate anything: as far as he is concerned, he already owns it all anyway; it is more a matter of constantly redistributing, shuffling it
around with a sort of smoothing-over motion, in order to impose
a 'tidiness' on his world that will tell him that he is one undifferentiated one. He limits himself to this sole, all-embracing job in
the world and, not surprisingly, is all over the place as a result.

His careful efforts are clearly thought out to do away with all
divisive structures. There is nothing neater to him than a well-
maintained chaos. This proves him to be an integral self/world,
and his darting about to keep it that way is simply the price one
pays for living. It may look like a lot of intrinsically meaningless
activity to us, but to him it makes sense to scramble the world like
a pack of cards being shuffled and to deal out bits in whatever
direction looks in need of topping up, to bring it in line with the
rest.

Redistributing the contents of his (and our) world in any way
that gives him a pleasingly 'flat' and sufficiently mixed-up
impression would soon have him in trouble with us. To respect
others as distinct and isolated units would quite spoil his scheme
of course. So for him an indiscriminately all-inclusive equality
takes the place of the equalness in separateness that the other negative Gemini type saw in the people around him. He and we are
one inseparable community, anything else is patent nonsense to
him. And emotionally, he is a compulsive giver ($\mathcal{S}\rightarrow$), inclined to
press on us what we would maybe rather not have; but then again
it makes no odds to him what he gives us, and if we ask to have
this rather than that he is perfectly happy to comply with our
needs or wishes. This gives him the appearance of generosity even
if *in himself* he couldn't care less. It certainly helps to keep him out
of trouble. Raiding the municipal gardens 'only to' (re)distribute
posies to little old ladies gives him the sort of Robin Hood appeal
that is hard to condemn altogether.

His emotional centre, his feeling of inner stability ($\mathcal{S}\leftarrow$), is
firmly displaced on to us. He cannot bear rejection. It amounts to
being at odds with himself, and he will do anything to gain our
approval, superficially speaking. What we might think of him and
feel for him 'in our hearts' is no headache to him: he himself does
not run to such depths and can't imagine them in others.
Wreathed in smiles, bearing gifts and protesting his fellow feel-

ings for us, he is in by the door before one knows it, or knows exactly what it is one has invited in. He has no need of any specific home of his own, the whole world is home to him and his constant state of impermanence, dashing from one job to the next, does not bother him. He is a dab hand at making himself at home wherever he goes. And he stops at nothing: one may well find one has to evict him from one's bed. Maybe he just wants to sleep there, he certainly has no romantic notions, but then again there is a lot to be said for a communal approach to sense-experience. The more the merrier, in fact. Unlike the other negative Gemini, *he* does not passively mirror himself in his mirrors – he actively climbs into the mirror with us and, like the worm in the apple, partakes of all we have got as if of right. He sees no harm in that, he is only being himself.

His and yours and mine is all the same to him. There is no keeping him out of our houses or cupboards or whispered conversations. He is always there, needing to know it all and taking away whatever strikes him as a 'surplus'. He hugs us one moment and robs us the next and it would not occur to him that there is anything amiss with that, quite the contrary, it is we who are at fault for keeping ourselves separate behind locked doors – they are anathema to him – and our possessions separate from the one big common pool of possession that exists in his view, and that is all he, and his.

He takes up everything that is ours, displaces it, twists it and bends it if necessary, to fit one standard situation: that of coherence. Thus he will 'borrow' our phrases and re-employ them to have an answer ready at all times, and one that fits the style of the occasion. To be answerless would be to inflict a wound on his own completeness; equally, should he observe us being lost for words, he will come to the rescue with indecent haste. Any pauses in the conversation make him feel personally riddled with holes. It does not matter how meaningless or untrue his stopgap verbiage may be, as long as it plugs the moment. He does not mimic, he *pretends*, with careful preparation and having all the right expressions, verbal and facial, at the ready. He lies with completeness and coherence aforethought. He puts words into our mouths with the same dexterity as into his own. If he 'sells' us anything, he really sells us agreement: yes, we all do want to have that and, yes, we all do believe in that, subscribe to that idea etc. If *he* apparently adjusts to *us*, then only by way of preparation, to adjust *us* to *him*. That way he insinuates himself into his rightful position as master and mastermind of his one united world.

He wants to be the centre; he also wants to be everything. This puts him in the self-contradictory position of finding his 'central' purpose always outside himself, a thing of the moment. Whether one says that he borrows his 'purpose' from the occasion, or that he lets his environment dictate it to him, it amounts to the same thing: either way he will take it up as a tool to serve his urge to do away with all kinds of separation, the given infrastructure of the world that offends him. Closed doors, differences of opinion, exclusive clubs, anything that is locked away out of reach (including the most intimate matters) or paraded as inaccessibly belonging to one (type of) person only: he will breach all these boundaries that subdivide his world/self. They are quite illegal in his view and can do nothing but damage. He spies, and then tells it all, freely, elsewhere. He steals, but what he gains is never his for long. He believes in spreading it about after all, and he would never dream of refusing if one held out one's hand for a share.

He is always, unconsciously, working out the most practical course of action to take. He is no opportunist snatcher, out of greed, but an opportunist planner employing low cunning – letting his unconscious cleverness take over, that is – in order to restyle the world in a two-dimensional way. These are his 'working principles'. If he finds our principles and annoyingly 'high' moral ideas to be very different from his, then he will take the occasion to employ our type of idea, our language, our working methods, to 'adapt' our system to fit in with what he is trying to make the norm. In one word, he subverts. In whatever round-about way he gets there, he will impose *his* working principles on us. And whatever his intermediate, borrowed purposes of the moment, his ultimate aim is always quite simply our indistinguishableness, from each other, and from him. The controlled chaos of the lowest common denominator is his aim. As the bottom line, it offers the overall stability he is after – as well as the singular wholeness of the herd, which we from our pluralist view point would call faceless., but which to him represents the one face of him. He will do anything to undermine our superior positions and everything to lift us out of inferior ones We are all supposed to be in the same boat, and if we aren't, then he will soon work out how to get us there.

It is hardly something he can 'sell' us straightforwardly, this one stable communal world model. He is asking us, in effect, to disobey our innermost inbuilt principles (not that he would recognise them as such) and to debase ourselves to the level of a purposeless and personally meaningless life in an amorphous mass without distinctions, without rules of any kind bar share and share alike, be and be alike. He would rob us of all we hold to be most precious and important and individually distinctive. We are hardly likely to hand it over, just like that. And yet he succeeds.

He is right inside our heads – *his* heads, after all, and he is appalled at what he finds in some of them, deadly stuff to him – he knows us inside out, that is his business. There is nothing he does not sense about us, he sniffs it all out, he mulls it over, and the strategy forms effortlessly in his mind. His calculations are always simple, involving adding and subtracting and no more. Adding/giving is easy enough for him, it is only when it comes to cutting us down to size that he needs to make a real effort. But his strategy is fiendishly simple: he will offer to give us what he knows we most desire for our individual selves – undeserved material gain, valuable secret information or whatever, all extracted from one area of his world to be deployed elsewhere. In return he will take away from us what most stands in his way: our proud principles, our claims to be 'better than that'. He bribes us, corrupts us, and then shows us up.

He has reduced us to the common status of fallible beings, none better, none worse, every one of us. He tricks us into revealing the highest to be but the lowest in disguise and all our fine talk and high-flown causes, our elevated beliefs and superior opinions, can be seen to be nothing but an artifice, a sham. He, of course, always knew it. We are all liars: pretending and portraying ourselves in a false light: just like him. We *are* he, and anything else is a well-groomed illusion.

He is right if he sees it like that. But he is also ignorant (and for ever ignorant of his ignorance) of his/our 'higher' selves. He thinks he sees, and is, the whole picture – but it is only a poor reflection of the whole. He cannot see beyond the spread of the material world about him, and hence misses the 'point' of life altogether. The flat, drab, much-of-a-muchness mess he keeps making of his environment has to serve him as his meaning in life, all and everything forced into a false brotherhood of mediocrity. It is, in fact, his imperfection that he is busy making such a deliberate point of.

His simple trickery may sound easy, but no one could call him lazy. He really does work at it hard, equalising, flattening out, grabbing handfuls of unevenly piled world and redistributing them somewhere else. If he adds to a pile, then only to ultimately see it topple. He himself stands on unstable ground, though: the moment he turns his back, life piles up more unevennesses. He is more than fully occupied deconstructing and flatly reconstructing his world: smearily spreading, filling in, patching up, cobbling together the most outlandish combinations. Oblivious to inherent differences as he is, any two things can be placed side by side and slotted together by hook or by crook, or with sticky tape, to make a satisfying picture of seamlessness. His 'whole' world resembles his speech: words strung together with a modicum of logic and plenty of 'picked up' style, but no meaning or truth in it except by inadvertence.

For all his glib and 'well-adjusted' talk, he is the great uncommunicator. And for all his trading and shifting raw materials about, there is nothing ever actually getting built out of them. It is all ephemeral, not meant to last, because it will only be needed again in some other context. His world is an ongoing building site, constantly reflattened. If three bricks happen to end up one on top of the other and we heave a sigh of hopeful relief, he is immediately there, personally affronted at this eyesore and plotting how to undo the damage.

Finding permanence in impermanence does not strike him as the least bit odd. He blames life (a vague concept to him) for his never-ending dis-repair work, the shifty roles he has to play, pretending that he is building and 'accidentally' causing collapse all around. He would rather see himself accidentally collapse a million times than grow to acquire a permanent infrastructure. Which is just a complicated way of saying that he fails to become individualised or properly 'whole': without an inner unifying centre, he can't cope with separate, differing functions in the world; he cannot manage a multitude of honest, adequate responses to life (learning, genuinely adapting) unless he 'grows in' and steers his behaviour from his intangible centre.

Instead, he lets it all hang out. And keeps shifting it, losing it, mislaying it, forgetting it: all on purpose. He is simplifying the world, the only way he can cope *with it all*. One must not be fooled by the air of dissipation he gives himself. His 'accidents' are only a way of saying he is terminally ineducable. Though what he really needs is 'in-duction': into the mysteries of his/the inner centre. Instead of 'provoking' us, in order to see us slip, he should follow our example inwards. But then he is so hooked on pursuing his self in this shambolic, and often painful, world that an invisible centre sounds rather an anticlimax to have. To watch himself happening and unhappening offers rather more excitement and interest to his rational-sensual conscious nature. No wonder he not only prefers his disasters but actively brings them about. We can keep our lame and at any rate imaginary-invisible high standards, our would-be edifying talk of superior motivations, the unfathomable depths of true 'innerness' we claim to have. Or rather we can *not* keep them – he does all he can to divest us of such pretensions.

His hands are full all the time, with jobs that are probably none of his business, and with things that belong to us, but essentially he is always empty-handed. 'Essentially he is empty' sums him up. His essence lies with us. He has projected it onto us. And yet to say that he is forever just fooling around with it would be to judge him only by surface appearances (a bad idea, obviously) and to deny the underlying seriousness of his compulsive quest. He wants us to live his coherence for him – inner and outer, improbably combined – and he knows how to pull the right strings to get us to do it.

He constantly draws us into this scattered shambles he is, so that together we may amount to a whole sort of shambles at least. Our chaos comforts him like nothing else. We are keeping him company in his largely self-inflicted plight. If we grow, away from him, we are letting him down. We have to stop becoming, even un-become, so that he can live in peace with us/himself. He is a first-rate deceiver, a walking trompe l'oeil, a manipulator on the grandest scale, but it is only stating the obvious to say that in the last resort, and all the time, he is fooling himself as well as us.

He never gets what he ultimately wants, because ultimately he wants death-in-life: static completeness in objective terms. He never has what he thinks he has, his living-wholeness: his world is a toppling, slithering and sliding havoc, far more fractured and fragmented than when he found it. And yet the evil broth keeps throwing up new would-be individual creations (and where from, he asks himself, unable to pursue the answer to its source, his source, his aim: the unknown central self) for him to pluck apart again and draw down bit by bit to his permanently unreconstructed level. Life's growing, up-building changes pull the rug from under his feet, just as he pulls it from under us. Hardly surprising: he has made the world the container of all he is; he can't very well complain if his collective mirror image pulls the same tricks and faces as he does.

He is fully occupied outwitting himself. Working hard at being his own undoing, in all perpetuity. Unless – maybe – he manages to stage his own final, fatal-accident disaster: when the funny something he calls life (with a dismissive shrug and a look of distaste) throws up yet again some situation he thinks he can easily handle, but is essentially ignorant of. It is the truth of his own being and becoming that is the mystery, of course. There is nothing in his world that has not become from out of his (our, *the*) hidden centre. All this unwelcome growth he has been hacking down has really come out of himself; if he had not looked, compulsively, in the wrong direction, he would have known better than to work against his own self.

He thinks he knows it all, he thinks he knows how to run the world in order to gain this elusive one-cohesive-self of his. But he never comes to the awareness that in an insubstantial sort of way, he has already got all the self there is. And that he is only running in circles, trying to have it complete in front of his eyes: to possess it, rather than know it as a subjective, timeless, transcendent reality. He wastes time like no other sign, ending up always exactly where he started out because, essentially, he 'goes against himself'. He goes against life. The life that *is* his – but not to have, via objective all-knowing and all-seeing, all in one go – but to hold complete only in his unconscious intuitive awareness: as the motivating central factor for continuous, meaningful, self-revealing activity in the world of time. For this he is too impatient. He wants it all right now, with the result that in the course of (maybe) all time he manages to learn not a single thing about himself, about how he 'works', or how to handle himself. He simply refuses to 'grow up'. Instead, all unawares, he elevates himself to the position of de facto tyrant over his many not quite willing 'equals'.

Both these 'fools' are making the mistake of forcing together the two things that they should not have left without a certain critical distance between them: the central self and the multiplicity of possible roles. In the process the one has become a puppet of his circumstances, pure and simple. And the other a puppet master who can never emerge from behind the screen of his adopted 'fronts' to 'be himself', openly, and who for all his brazen manipulativeness can, through sheer ignorance, never admit to being the author of all his works. The one is trying to cheat time by pretending it does not flow, but hops. The other is trying to forestall future growth by cutting down all of the established past and present he can lay his hands on. They are a right couple of jokers. They live their lives in comic spurts and dead-pan stops, a skip here and popping up unexpectedly there, donning masks and putting on borrowed voices and falling-down-on-purpose... and the funniest thing by far is that they are perfectly serious about it all.

The humour is certainly lacking from the situation where the active type is concerned. Both of them have taken Sagittarius' contribution, his gift of intuitive inner knowing, of transcendent meaning, and made a sad sort of laughing stock of it, scattering partial truths about as either complete, deliberate lies, or silly, incoherent babblings. But where the one only wriggles and worms his way out of any awkward situations (shutting his eyes, so he won't have to see the living proof that the all-knowingness he affects is crass ignorance), the other, who is constantly flattening, if not to say abasing, himself (to become the prime example of a crawler and lurker) thinks he is on top of everything. And though he 'only' thinks it and sees it that way, that (in his case) is quite enough to drag the whole world down with him. – As with negative Leo, there *seems* to be no end to him.

But whether actively or passively, both have made the same mistake. By fusing compulsively what should not have been forced together to that degree but left loosely related – the 'point' of self and the 'circle' of other – they have actually disjointed the world further, and at the same time, paradoxically, made true communication impossible: without an *essential* distance there can be no *true* communication; there is nothing 'extraneous' to communicate meaningfully about. Sagittarius' meaning, coming from the beyond of the inner plane, has been successfully disconnected. For inner voice and inner illumination these two have substituted the busy bustling sparkle of a merry-go-round life, spills and all, unaware that they are groping around in a dark and silent underworld of their own making.

Some Suggested Gemini Attributes

basic

intelligently observant, 'clever', one could call him **'brainy',** in a far-reaching rather than deep-going (like Virgo) or innately deep (like Capricorn) sense; but indiscriminately accepting: **uncritical, promiscuous** in all respects

always needs to know and see everything: **inquisitive;** can see divisions clearly but does not recognise them as boundaries: **intrusive** in his **search for (self-)knowledge;** appropriates anything as his own, because he 'recognises it as his': **involuntary thief; short-lived collecting crazes** (gathers and amasses, but then moves on), **endless and meaningless counting/totting up/ticking off**

impatient, always in a hurry, forward looking: because the world is withholding parts of him; **always on the move,** with **his aim not apparent** (this being his invisible centre) and may find himself **running round in circles: meaninglessly and haphazardly repetitive**

scattered, disorganised, going in all directions at once, vaguely self-contradictory, 'lacks centre'

everything is the same to him: inappropriate behaviour, tactless, inadvertent rudeness, and lies: no understanding of meaning or truth: **'superficial'**

keeps hurting himself, the 'damage' often not apparent to others, and in his ignorance of how things hang together **does damage; accident-prone;** not critically but actively finds himself defective or deficient: **vain efforts, unfocused ambitions, 'overreaches himself'**

automatically fits in anywhere; in his uncentred, disorganised way of actively being the whole world he is **subject to co-incidence, chance**

but also **refuses to be content** with his life-situation: it is never enough (of self); **disobedient:** won't stick to what he is forced to be (for too long, in his view); constantly bursts out of his time-imposed boundaries: **uncontainable, 'mercurial', lively; fidgety, 'nervous'**

positive

productive split between central and peripheral awareness makes him set things in relation: **organiser, unifier, sets up systems; connects, spans, bridges;** acts as a **mediator, go-between, matchmaker, 'contact', messenger** etc.; **effective communicator, talks openly and honestly** (and, to some, too much), has **no personal secrets;** understands complexity: **tolerant, reconciles, liberal**

makes concentrated efforts at bringing-together: **learns easily,** never surprised at or doubtful of new knowledge, 'recognising' it all (as his own); **skilful** at synthesis: **manufactures, craftsmanship; collects, retains, good memory; orderly, efficient**

productively forward looking: **thinks ahead, plans** and **schedules;** orderly progress and processes with a central idea in mind: **travels,** in fact-finding or executive capacity; **collates** and **disseminates, distributes;** may be **busy in trade, commerce and administration** and any job that gives equal importance to a 'centre' and a 'multiple periphery': **educator** etc.

mends what has come apart, **tries to heal, cure;** (re)combines but also comes up with new combinations: his initial **branching out** always coming together in **new syntheses; restructures** and **substructures: integrates; improves; progressive; 'complicates matters'** and then **solves** (the new) **problems** (he has posed), hence in effect encourages himself to greater efforts: **versatile, diversifying, many styles; always busy** doing something, **never idle, unstoppable**

treats everybody as his equals: **'brotherly', companionable;** incapable of holding himself aloof: **naturally sociable;** works for others as for himself: **gives service freely, a true friend to everybody,** even though his personal relating does not go deep; **unites others** 'in himself', **social organiser: new social order** that respects everybody's separateness; **fosters co-operation on equal terms**

negative (passive)

stubborn; severely limited in outlook, always **wilfully ignores** the rest of the world; **apparently stupid; encapsulated** in a reduced world of his own; **'delusions of grandeur',** of being perfect or at least 'grown up' etc.; **always sure of himself, insistent, boastful know-it-all, has 'seen it all', pretentiousness**

momentarily obsessed with some (usually immaterial) detail,

deliberately but pointlessly (self-)repetitive, 'stuck in a groove', obsessional, meaningless rituals, tics, crazes, clings to what he has got, may be said to have taboos; this alternates with throwing-aside and forgetting-about; (self-)absorbed in many different ways; recurrent stagnation, mental blocks etc.; momentary immobility, seized-upness amounting to a state of deliberate 'paralysis', followed by wild dashes, uncommunicative and then babbles incoherently and inconsequentially (equally uncommunicative, really), 'constipation' alternates with 'incontinence'; jumps to conclusions; short-term secrets self-contradictory, unpredictable, has momentary fashions, instantly changeable, inconsistent, erratic; poor retention/memory; totally disorderly, disjointed; fitful progress from one seized-up state to the next; 'skips' through life, irresponsible, amoral; settles and resettles: peripatetic, nomadic; elusive; fatalistic

eagerly adopts *some* of the 'content' of each new life-situation: (passively) copies (imperfectly), mimics specific traits, imitates in part and in turns: adopted mannerisms; relative artificiality: contrivedness; may have fetishes, superstitiously takes the (material) part to be the (nonphysical) meaningful whole

compartmentalised self, 'categorically' (self-)divisive (and as such institutes inequalities, castes etc.), 'exclusive'; chameleon, springs surprises; not to be trusted

since he never settles for anything for long he is ineducable in the conventional sense, but may have sudden new 'insights' (of a superficial nature): is taught by life, not school etc.; puppet of his circumstances who never makes the effort to adapt – passively adapting (his view of) the world to suit him instead: (deliberate) mis-takes; takes or leaves and hence twists things to suit himself; 'naughty', wriggles out of problems by going into a completely new mode or style; manipulative, 'makes things up', not-quite lies; 'fools around'

trusting: literally displaces his faith-in-self into others; easily (momentarily) mislead; easy prey; and is also himself misleading (for a while); a clever-stupid parasite, improvident

popular and unpopular in turns, depending on whether he is complying or resisting 'wholeheartedly'; amusing, can be easy to see through, can teach others a lesson about themselves; in his cluelessness 'lets the truth shine through': can't keep

secrets (for long); for all his **maintaining adopted poses** in the end **'gives himself away'**: dropping the old self and starting a new one, **transparent in his guile; continues to be his own undoing; perennial child**

negative (active)
across-the-board attitude, wilfully indiscriminate; no respect for differences or individuality, 'egalitarian'; does not recognise others' personal rights or property: **intruder, thief** or at least **helps himself freely, 'spies'**
promulgates a faceless equality: over-familiarity, cheekily chummy; gives 'generously' what he has stolen elsewhere, **presses presents on everyone; spreads gossip,** i.e. stolen secrets; **needs to be popular, ingratiating; insinuates himself** into any company, always makes himself out to be **'one of us'**
'deconstructs' everything that sticks out as separate and distinct: **systematically destructive, takes everything apart, in effect a 'hooligan'** in his search for simple unity
calculating, shrewdly manipulative; secretive; a puzzle to others; twists every adopted purpose, subversive, uses trickery to pull others down to his level; **immoral:** makes an active, ongoing job of his imperfection, **outlaw**
appears slap-dash and chaotic, scatters and **levels** everything, **redistributes endlessly: apparently meaningless activity, working hard and getting no-where, apparently aimless** (he is only trying to stay what he thinks he already is); **quite unstoppable, hates limitations, appears manic, 'hyperactive'** with nothing to show for it, **frenetic all-or-nothing responses; unpredictable, seems to change his mind** all the time; strikes others as **'crazy'**
'trips over himself in his haste', trips up others, causes accidents to self and others, **has umpteen crises; deliberately seems to lose, mislay, forget and never learns anything:** all to make sure nothing 'piles up' anywhere and the world stays simple
borrows phrases, and employs them wherever they come in handy: **lies; puts words in others' mouths, frequently interrupts, garrulous; pretends, mimes, play-acts, conjuring tricks, fakes; plays the fool:** deliberately simple-minded; **deceives, swindles;** appears to co-operate but slyly **throws a spanner into the works**

good at imitating anything, for his own purposes, which makes him **look well-adjusted; artifice,** and creates an **artificial disorder:** an improbable jumble, a well-maintained chaos: **'shifty',** **'crafty'**

LIBRA

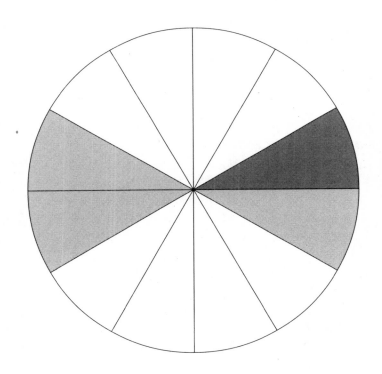

♎ **Extravert**
conscious function: sensation; direction of function: inward
unconscious functions: ♈ **intuition,** ♍ **thinking,** ♓ **feeling**
Air: rational

If Sagittarius' position of being an introverting introvert seemed difficult in a world where even basic survival calls for extraverting, Libra's position is sheer paradox: an extravert whose conscious attention is naturally turned inward. As an extravert he needs to find his self in the outside, objective world, but he is quite unable to turn to it unaided. Unless life demands that he make this to him unnatural effort and turn his attention round, he stays wrapped up in an inner reality that he can never identify his self in, which stays an impersonal reality to him.

Like Sagittarius, Libra is in contact with the ever-becoming inner-plane All, but he is neither 'at home' in it nor does he intuitively flow with it. Because he senses it intelligently, he 'breaks up' this flow and experiences it instead as the whole system of its potential inherent parts: a coherent succession of rational pictures; not abstract, theoretical ideas, as Capricorn conceived of it, but quite vividly fleshed-out concepts, meaningful images. His conscious awareness is captivated by these inner 'visions'. Where Gemini had a rational look at his countless objective selves out there, Libra is caught up in rationally viewing an integral model of countless subjective states as such – a wealth of meaningful being-possibilities that have nothing to do with his *personal* being.

In order to find himself, to be and become, he needs to transfer at least some of his attention to the objective world. He needs to search for self, gather his self, select or construct his self, like all the other extraverts. But his preoccupation with viewing this wealth of existential models that lies at the root of all being makes it very difficult for him to commit himself to any participation in life.

Unlike the introverting introvert Sagittarius who had to be dragged protesting into the necessities of action and interaction on the material plane, the introverting extravert Libra is initially only too grateful if the world makes demands. The more, in fact, the better. Each demand gives him a chance of life, of self, release from this strange limbo. He is ready to turn himself back to front to follow any call, in any direction, and that way might, like Gemini, easily run the risk of ending up being all things to all men. But however eager he may be to come out of his self-less state, he still 'has his head full of' all sorts of primary images, prior conditions, pre-conceptions.

One might say he has had a thorough pre-life training, or indoctrination even, albeit in 'pictorial' form. He brings what he has observed to exist at this transcendent (and to him impersonal) root or basis of the world with him: in the form of deep-seated expectations. Even his senses are attuned to nothing else, they are 'pre-tuned'. Objective reality, however, does not measure up to his expectations. He is disappointed, puzzled – and even if he can't manage to be *personally* affronted, he still senses, thoughtfully, the affront of it. He finds the world in a state of blatant imperfection; and what should be the source of his personal becoming only manages to alienate him. He stares hard and long at what he sees here, comparing it bit by bit with his mental pictures of what it 'ought to' look like, and as a whole it does not make sense to him at all. Isolated phenomena that catch his eye may strike him as a good enough likeness, but sooner or later there is always something intruding into the picture that offends against his 'innate taste'. He finds it hard to see things in isolation for long: his sensual-rational nature demands that what he perceives with his senses should be combined into a coherent picture that as a totality 'makes sense'. Juxtapositions of what he holds to be acceptable and what he finds unacceptable have him stumped.

He should be grateful to have life forced on him. Instead he stands there and considers the pros and cons of every life situation offered him – and in the end, with deep regrets, declines, with many thanks. Or if he can be flushed out, seemingly eager to find his self in whatever one forces on him, he only flees back into his anonymous perfection at the first hint of any unpleasantness. Like Sagittarius, he is not used to an obstacle-ridden world. Unlike Sagittarius, he can muster no intuitive impetus to try and blunder his way through. Hovering on the sidelines, gazing critically: this is already a form of involvement for him. If life demands more, and then throws stumbling blocks and other bare-faced imperfections at him, he withdraws not only to the sidelines but all the way back to his shadowy, impersonal existence.

He looks the 'maybe' type with his hovering and hesitating, but this needs to be understood. He is *basically* an either/or type: either the world is good enough for him to derive the sort of self from which accords with his expectations of what a self (or any-thing else) ought to be – or not. Either he is loyal to the complex inner Image of a perfect world – or he goes seeking a self in a world that offers only, or primarily, the makings of personal imperfection. His 'maybe' is a sign of his inbuilt dividedness, but unlike Gemini's his is no more than a *dual* dividedness: between inner attention to an impersonal 'right' and personal need for the objective 'wrong' without which he cannot even begin to become self. There is no decision harder than that; one can hardly blame him for being indecisive, and thinking him basically lazy or sim-ply cowardly is misinterpreting him altogether.

For Gemini all possible selves were equally acceptable, because they *were* all he. For Libra all the possible selves he sees in the world are just about equally unacceptable. But without them he is a nobody. Virgo could choose critically what to accept or reject, his freedom based on his ignorance of any 'ought's. Libra has no such freedom. When the going gets tough, rough and ugly, and he 'chickens out', he is being true – not to an inner self – but to all Inner Reality as such. For a while. Unlike Sagittarius, he cannot afford to abscond and sulk, in personal innerness: he has none. He is always ready to try again. He comes and goes, and the world would soon give up hope of ever getting him to 'go' for any length of time. But if he is not 'in demand', then he can sit there for ever in his limbo.

What gives him the chance to respond more positively and con-sistently to life's demands is his unconscious intuitive awareness (♈) that his self is something to be *actively* pursued in the world. To stand and look and wonder is not enough. The world is not just offering itself for his passive acceptance, guided by preconceived standards. It is a place where the makings of self lie embedded, embodied and scattered everywhere, to be won and discovered through active involvement. It is a place of fluid changes where new (and better) possibilities can be found all the time, if only one goes in search. He realises that he does not have to commit himself, once and for all, to a whole world of 'unacceptables', but that becoming self is a process of searching among the many possibilities offered, and actively *making* the best possible self happen.

There seems to be no need then to be torn between the inner, perfect model world that holds no personal life or self for him, and this at once desirable and 'undesirable' wealth of living, life-giving possibilities. But the problem is that, like Gemini, he senses *intelligently*. (It is interesting, by the way, that just as both the thinkers among the signs were Earth (sensual) signs, all three Air (rational) signs are sensers.) What this means is that though his intuition may tell him to 'go out and get', it is still, consciously, the whole so to speak logically interconnected view of the world he has in his sights. Precisely what he *cannot* make his own: the whole world as he finds it, hopelessly flawed.

If he intuitively tells himself now to look harder for something to adopt as self, more actively, to *do* something about finding it, this is no help to him at all. If one thing stands out as desirable, the next neighbouring thing is more than likely to spoil it all again for him. What he would need to do is look exclusively at each objective detail and assess it in isolation. He would then see whether or not, *in itself*, it is a good enough likeness of his inner 'picture' of what it *should* be. Only making such isolated assessments, such choices from among the world's details, could enable him to start assembling a self: to piece together a sort of personal 'perfect picture' of his own. This is precisely the ability his unconscious thinking (♍→) offers him.

He can home in on what corresponds to his impersonal expectations, personally reject out of hand what doesn't, refusing to take it into account, for the time being. When he *thinks* about it, it doesn't really concern him that his environment offers him too many quite 'unsuitable' things to become – as long as he can do the sensible, rational, thing and choose what he can approve of, leave the rest. The 'maybe' he said to the world as a whole, because he both needed it and found it wanting, becomes a clear yes or no to specific parts and particles of the world, which can find their new coherence in the self he is assembling. Now his intuitive awareness of needing to commit himself to an active search for a self to be at last makes sense. He is ready to participate in the world like a 'proper' extravert.

His actions are informed by what he considers 'right': judicious action. His reactions have their root in comparing every part of his environment with his inner 'ought's: assessment and critical appraisal – not just based on personal preference, but on the inherent rights and wrongs he perceives on the inner plane, impersonally: judgement. But he is always intuitively aware that no part of the world, or the self he finds there, is ever a finished thing. It is a moving-on, becoming world: needing constant reappraisal and new active efforts to make it accord with his inbuilt picture of what a world, a self, should be. He also thinks of his self (♍←) as something that will always require improving on – and because his basic standards are so absolute, this actually has the effect of making him become *less* of a perfectionist now: he who can quite clearly see what he ought to be, now also thinks of his self as a never-ending project. Now he understands fully that the perfection he seeks in the world is to be found only by applying oneself, continuously, to the job of bringing it about.

He has gained the ability to focus, unconsciously, on the detail, at least for a moment. To explore it rationally and practically for what it is in itself, and to be pragmatic about what can be done with it. But inevitably his *conscious* attention will take in not only the adjacent details but also the whole interconnectedness of it, the background as well as the foreground. The net effect is that he goes from one thing to another and compares the attractive or repulsive effect each detail has on him, first singly, then in combination, then the overall effect the whole ensemble has on him. And as a result he becomes aware where the 'fault' lies. Something somewhere may only need a little adjustment, one detail may have to be omitted or something added for the whole effect to be an entirely different one. What he finds he needs to do is to rearrange the parts of this world – bearing in mind what is practicable and what does justice to each part considered in itself – till it makes the sort of blend or composite picture that he 'envisages'.

What he is doing is this: he intuits a positive potential in what at first sight strikes him as 'ugly' or 'wrong'; he refers back to his inner vision of underlying perfection; he takes corrective action. Polishing and embellishing, relocating in a different context, adding what is badly missing, redistributing surplus (the 'too much that is of evil'), mixing and recombining, adjusting shapes, colours, textures, sounds, sizes, amounts, functions, interactions:

he re-dresses the 'wrongs' and makes them into 'rights'.

There is hardly a thing that could not be improved, upgraded or at least stood in its own proper context in such a way as to cause approval rather than offence. And hardly an activity or type of behaviour that could not be corrected through re-channelling it into an appropriate outlet. His intelligent vision of Inner Reality shows him what potentially 'goes together', what is by nature related to what. It is the correct pairing of thing with thing, person with thing, person with activity, activity with environment etc. that makes the difference (for him) between (finding what he observes in the world) right or wrong. It is the ideal *context* that matters. And it is the meaningfully coherent arrangement of its parts that makes the whole what it is. This is what Libra realises once he has joined the flow of life, with its myriad bits and pieces which each deserve respectful attention, before the intuitive impulse to make potential into actuality, to make possibilities happen, can be usefully employed.

Actively improving and rectifying the world, he no longer has the urge to back out of it all, there is always a compromise possible: his absolutes have turned out, on closer inspection, to be *relative*. He cannot change the ingredients he finds the world to consist of, but he can always 'process' them in some way to mirror any of the countless number of composite inner models.

As already pointed out, Libra does not, like Virgo, have the freedom to choose the makings of his world/self as he thinks fit, but instead assembles his self according to an extant design that is given him at the outset – though it must be remembered that this 'gift' is not something complete and finished but a continual becoming-aware of more and more images of potential selves, things, world states. There is a resemblance here to Taurus who built his self, and a world for others to inhabit, according to such an impersonal plan or design. But where Taurus was only unconsciously aware of it, Libra is fully, consciously aware.

Libra's primary task, though, is not to build, even if he does restructure his environment (to reflect what he senses to be the Plan of the formed, objective world). He is not a builder so much as a re-aligner, his mission is to point out the crooked and have it set straight. Libra's critical gaze, his *informed* comparing and setting in relation, makes for considered changes, not stability and establishment. He 'sorts out' and separates as much as he newly recombines. His work consists of a flux of adjustments that is never-ending in a changing world: and while he answers change with change, he always leads back towards the original balance of things. That is to say he brings everything nearer the original – the *truly* original – intention, he makes it resemble more closely the perfect potential that is the root of all objective, concrete forms and happenings.

Not only Taurus' repetitive mistakes can find their correction in that, but maybe more especially Virgo's individualised and would-be 'original' designs. Virgo may think things out very intelligently but he does depend in his choices on what his already formed environment can offer him. He can not, like Libra, refer right back to what amounts to a sort of how-to manual of truly sensible self-design. His freely made mistakes are apt to multiply from generation to generation if not checked and corrected. Of course, like Taurus, he does his own checking unconsciously, but Libra does it consciously – which means that, most importantly, Libra teaches us, by example, to consciously and deliberately stop in our self-seeking tracks, our world engineering and self-willed 'creating' of things. At the very least he teaches us to stand and hesitate and wonder whether we are about to do the (relatively) right thing.

Like Gemini, Libra is a connector and mediator. Gemini ties in all there is to be found in the objective world; and though he does it basically intelligently and with a sense for what can be hitched to what, he still does it pretty much anyhow, simply for the sake of making the world whole again. Libra carries this whole-making further by adding the deepest meaningfulness to the connections being made. He will have to unravel some of Gemini's work in the process in order to sort out who or what *really* belongs where. He is the quality control who judges the work for what it is intrinsically worth. Whether it is the products of Taurus, Virgo, Gemini or any of the other signs, they all have to submit to Libra's checking action, just in case they have slipped up.

But what Libra *essentially* combines and recombines and mediates between are these two realities: the objective, and potentially personal one, and the impersonal transcendent Reality from out of which the former is always being born. All his setting in relation of parts of the world one with the other is in that sense incidental or only by way of doing his job: spanning the gulf between the perfect Inner Reality and the imperfect objective reality.

This is the rift that Gemini has 'caused', though he does all he can to heal it himself. But Virgo meantime is widening the gap again, by availing himself of the opportunity to gather world fragments into 'unnatural' schemes and arrangements of all descriptions – and some of which may defy description. Libra is there to reintroduce the natural order of things; he reconnects what has been 'lost' to the basic laws. – In that he has a lot in common with Capricorn, though he has none of Capricorn's personal identification with what appeared to *him* to be dry, abstract rules, or any personal need to *prove* that these are valid. Libra is in the popular sense of the word the most objective of the signs. He is not the only one who consciously spans inner and outer reality, Capricorn did it, for instance, and so did Sagittarius. But only for the two introverting extraverts (Scorpio is the other one) is Inner Reality something they are entirely impersonally and yet consciously aware of; and of these two only Libra has a basic rational nature, as well as a conscious sense for the detail. This makes him a world observer and critic who has absolutely no personal axe to grind and who always knows exactly why he is objecting to, opposing, relocating or undoing some part of his environment that does not fit in its context, or some part of a completed job that has to be dropped or redone.

He has a foot in each reality even when he is most fully committed to living in our imperfect world, appraising critically, counselling, warning, advising, admonishing, suggesting and, finally, praising. Unlike the two extraverting extraverts Aries and Taurus who came to fully immerse themselves in the world as a matter of course, to discover or build a personal self here, the introverting extravert Libra never stops hovering halfway between full self-being, full participation in the objective world, and the inner plane that transcends all that. Gemini's attention was divided: between an unconsciously contacted personal inner self, and the many consciously observed objective 'selves': others, from our point of view. He became the common ground in which all self/other kept coming together again. Libra's attention is divided too, between the two equally consciously perceived realities, and he becomes the *neutral* ground, an impartial advisor.

He has no personal interest in bringing together, say, two warring factions *for the sake of bringing them together*, as Gemini would, in order to reunite two parts of his self. Libra's internal rift is not embodied in a broken-up world, but lies between this world and another, and in the fact that he bridges them – so any personal interest he has in reconciling the two sides in a dispute has to do with first of all mending the gulf between the model world before his inner eye, and the rather messy reality under his nose (and that done, the 'small matter' of a rift between two contestants should mend itself, really) because unless he can make of the world a harmonious whole, he will ultimately not be able, or inclined, to consciously identify a 'proper' self in it.

As a mediator not primarily between this issue and that, one person and another, but between all this and That, if one can put it that way, he has to position himself equidistant, metaphorically speaking, not only between any two opponents but also between the two realities known to him. His refereeing has less to do with getting in between the two fighters than with holding the law book in his hand; he is *above* the quarrel. – What this means for his own self-identification is that he is never *fully* identified with other/self but always reserves part of him, part of his conscious awareness and attention, for that other, third factor that is neither self nor other and that stands as reference point, or guide, or judge, above any two things or people that Libra tries to (re)connect meaningfully.

When he meets the demands of the world, he actually positions himself very carefully between the demands of the *two* 'worlds', so he can constantly monitor how the pre-existing design and the actual execution of it compare. He does gather a personal self from out of his constantly corrected environment (and like his environment it is always under review) but that is never all there is to him. Simply speaking, he never concentrates a hundred per cent on what lies physically before his eyes but always maintains a certain reserve. He keeps a critical distance, bearing in mind what he 'envisages beyond' even while he looks at objective phenomena that are positively clamouring for his full attention. Neither is he ever one hundred per cent wrapped up in his personal self-being and becoming; part of it is always conducted for the benefit of the whole. If his environment does not 'sit right' then he cannot be content with a self embedded in it.

Seeing all things ultimately in relation, he has to see his self in relation as well. If the person he is related or relating to is overburdened, ill-adjusted, lacking in something or whatever, then this has to be put right first before there can be any satisfactory self-being for Libra. It is part and parcel of his self-seeking to act in what we would call a selfless manner. He is course no longer literally self-less. Rather one could say that he has *more* than 'just' a self. He is in possession of – or better: in contact with – something additional that goes beyond all personal self, his and ours, a most valuable addition that is his unique contribution to the pooled resources of the family of signs.

The problem now is that his 'selfless' contribution tends to be rather too *demanding*. He is quite prepared to countenance the existing imperfections we present to him, but always with a view to putting things right. Or to put it like this: with all the fiddly perfectionism of a Virgo and all the valid authority of a Capricorn, he could become an unbearable nag who can never let anything be. He is never content till the balance of all things is right and some kind of higher symmetry has been established... and re-established, after it has slipped again. He never becomes aware of us with all our individual differences and idiosyncrasies without sooner or later taking a step back, surveying the whole situation, and planning a much-needed course of re-adjustment and re-education.

One must not make the mistake of thinking of him as demanding 'peace and harmony' without bearing in mind that first there may be a good deal to do in the way of severing connections, redeploying, turning inside out and upsetting (of the existing 'wrong' order of things). Gemini may be content to stitch things up anyhow, but Libra, if he is to be true to that impersonal part of his nature that he can never let go of, will see himself forced to wield knife and scissors as well – and, as a last resort, the sword. There is nothing faint-hearted about him, though his detachedness and his time-consuming deliberations may give the appearance. With his I-know-best attitude he is a pretty hard task master, to say the least, and if he had his way, unhampered by other considerations, the world would become a constant battlefield of re-arrangements. It would then hardly resemble his vision; nor would we agree to let him interfere, however beneficially, with each and every aspect of our world.

This is where his unconscious feelings provide a compensatory pull in the other direction. Emotionally, he finds himself drawn to all and everything, regardless of how crooked, shabby, inappropriate it may be. No matter how off-beat and improbable our behaviour, he feels *for* us ()(→). He also experiences feelings of personal insignificance ()(←) that reduce his status of world regulator and rectifier, in his own eyes. Both these factors prevent him from being too much the judge and jury of the world around him. Empathy for others makes him relax in his role of constant watchdog and adjudicator and informed perfecter who is about to set the whole world to rights. The perfect match, the complete correspondence between 'is' and 'ought to be' is no longer quite so pressing; near enough will do. His thoughtful compromises, based on pragmatism, are joined by the emotional compromise of live and let live. While his preconceptions, his laws, will never be anything but absolute, their administration is becoming yet again more relative. He can only do his best to persuade others to do *their* best, rather than *the* best, within the parameter of what is humanly, and in the given situation, possible.

The task inherent in Libra's nature is to balance all personal needing and wanting against the necessity to conform to transpersonal standards of excellence. He shows us how to weigh up all our actions against the demands of 'natural law' – by which is meant not only the physical, biological etc. laws of nature but also those laws governing the meaningful relatedness as such of all things and persons, groups, activities.

Coherence and context and relatedness *governed by meaning*, an all-round appropriateness of our actions: these are things to be borne in mind before and while we act and react. For example, it is not enough simply to communicate: the full truth has to be told in order to benefit all and everything involved (and all and everything *is* always involved), and if this should for some reason not be appropriate then it is better to maintain silence. Libra himself sets the example by always devoting part of his attention to, literally, the 'observance of the law'. He constantly observes it unfolding before his inner vision: ever new meaningful models, for always more possible, meaningful being and doing.

He is only half in love with this business of being self, only half in love with the world. It is this that enables him to see all things in perspective and in proportion, including his self. However 'whole-heartedly' he may enter into relationships with others, he still stands in a, to him, equally important relationship with his transpersonal root. This 'third factor' is always present to remind him and his partners of the meaningful basis on which all being, becoming and relating should rest.

Libra, unlike Gemini, never relates haphazardly or just for the sake of it. But neither can he be without relationships of some kind; being always *is* relating to him, just as it is for Gemini, but not just *any* relating. His living is a process of constant, deliberate and unimpassioned standing in relation, requiring adjustment and self-adjustment, and conducted from a slight distance, as it were. This is the real nature of his 'selflessness' and 'love': not that it is passionately directed towards – but that it rests on the foundation of his basic duality, his divided loyalty between all self/other/world on the one hand and all Inner Reality on the other. He never commits himself exclusively to self/world and it is precisely this detachment, this inbuilt reserve, that makes him the ideal partner. He never fails to take everything into account, his own needs (and obligations) – *and* those of the partner. He even sets the partnership itself in its context, against he backdrop of society for instance, which should itself be composed of all sorts of appropriately interrelated units... When one looks at it from that angle it *is* 'all or nothing' for him, despite his reserve – or rather because of it.

If Virgo with his thoughtful picking and choosing tried out some of the world 'for size', Libra tries it all for what it's worth, before he even begins to consider himself legitimately at home in the world. He first relates everything back to the transpersonal Inner Source and his every action follows on from that. Even what he is and becomes rests on that first act of comparing and considering. He reconnects us with our infinite or divine source as surely as Sagittarius did, with his 'religious' message of an inner self and a transcendent, infinite world of freedom – and implied obligations. Or Capricorn, with *his* laws of conduct, derived from an established inner self in contact with all inner-plane Principles. Libra precedes these two. He has no experience yet of an inner *self*, but nevertheless a clear impression of another, 'inner' form of reality that exists independently of self and yet is indissolubly linked with the self and all its strivings.

Libra does not address himself to our personal inner life, or try to lead us 'inside'. He relies entirely on setting us an example, one that will appeal to us and prove itself preferable to other types of ordering our environment and running our affairs. His harmo-

nious world order is only to be gained after some relative distur-
bance and proportional change, but in the end – or rather each
time again – it proves itself a more attractive proposition than the
effects of regardless action. Even if we can't follow him in acquiring an inner vision to guide us, he demonstrates to us in vivid,
'sensual' detail the ultimate advantage of taking all others and
everything else into consideration whenever we are about to
embark on some self-seeking enterprise. His is a beautiful world
in a far from superficial way. Its pleasant appearance is symbolic
of a deeply ingrained respect for everything that goes beyond the
mundane detail.

But there is always the possibility that Libra may let his intuitive
awareness take over and become a compulsion (the very antithesis of balanced action). He becomes convinced that all it needs is
an active search in his environment (Υ) for him to find the sort of
self he envisages, in the sort of world he envisages. Obsessed with
the urge to find deliberately what stands before his inner eye, he
becomes to all intents and purposes blind to what he sees objectively – or rather, he does not see objectively at all, but views the
world entirely through a pair of 'expectacles'.

He projects wholesale the perfect scheme of things he senses on
the inner plane into the plane of objective happenings, other, and
potential self. That is to say, immersing himself compulsively,
intuitively, in the world he hitherto spurned, he turns his back on
all Inner Reality, 'taking with him' what he has perceived and
comprehended. And he simply sets it down for a fact where the
objective world is, or should be: he superimposes his expectations.
The result is that now the world *must* please him, automatically.
Judgements, even comparisons, are no longer required, since
every thing is now seen as a thing of beauty, and every action
inherently right, and every person of equal, immeasurable worth
to him. There cannot be anything that jars or does not fit, that is
simply inconceivable.

He is not entirely wrong, of course. Every thing *does* have its
beauty – in the right context; every person *does* live out his inherent worth – given a proper chance. But what he is doing is to foist
all possible positive potential onto the world in the form of an illu-

sion (what we call make-believe, and might as well in his case call
'make-see'), irrespective of the actual state of affairs. In the
process he has quite lost sight of how things hang together, how
they relate, and how they only become, in time and through effort,
what they might, most positively, be.

His is not a becoming world, but a static foregone conclusion,
and he does his best to cling to it, despite what should be the evidence of his eyes – if he kept them open and not plugged up with
the inner images that he has projected out in front of him. It is easy
enough for him to see nothing to criticise. He ambles round his
garden not so much inspecting as expecting roses, sees garden-
worthiness in every weed in between, and the whole is a blessed
mess.

He is blindly refusing to make comparisons. He no longer has
any reservations. He no longer stands back from things with, as it
were, one foot in the reality beyond. He has uprooted the
Transpersonal Reality from its proper place and thrown it over the
world like a camouflage net, effectively masking the problematic,
effort-demanding nature of the world. Now he can find a self here
quite happily; a pseudo-self that is never whåt it seems to be. He
is no longer divided between self and non-self but is deeply and
inextricably involved in living; and what was once an equally
'real' and becoming Inner Reality has become a dead certainty
draped over the objective realities of life to spare him the sight. He
dresses up the world in the dead but still pretty skin of meaning
and then ooh's and ah's over the sham that inevitably results.

There is nobody he cannot 'relate' to, everyone is a darling.
And nothing is ugly enough to affront his muffled senses: he is
capable of rhapsodising equally over jewels or pink plastic. The
word 'quality' has lost its meaning, and 'imagination' is no longer
an act of finding the hidden potential of something, and then
actively liberating it, but a compulsive act of sabotage that denies
the truth of both realities, and the fact of their interdependence.
He simply helps himself to the *inherent* good by pronouncing the
whole world *de facto* good. That way he can grasp it for his own,
for his self, with not a hint of hesitation or reserve.

It would be an easy solution. But needless to say if he welcomes
everything and everybody with open arms and says yes to anything that comes along, then sooner or later he will run into a tan-
gle of self-contradiction, and ultimately the sort of brick-wall

situation that even he cannot call pleasant. But in his unconscious thinking (♍→) he is nothing if not shrewd, with a selectiveness that is not at all apparent. It is a balancing act of sorts he is engaged in now: manipulating facts into and out of his field of vision, retaining only what more or less accords with his superimposed view. Squinting through perfection-imposing spectacles can only work as long as the real objective world does not differ *too* drastically. Now he learns to cleverly turn his head away, literally as well as metaphorically, if things utterly refuse to tie in with his expectations. Such things, such people, are not a proper part of the world to him.

Everything fits together harmoniously, that is a fact to him (a manufactured fact so to speak). So if anything does not seem to fit, then it cannot be really real. He rubs his eyes in astonishment and turns his gaze on something different. He gets quite good at reading the danger signals of such approaching 'unreality'. His view may be muddled and tainted, or tinted, but his thinking is sharp enough, and the result is that his customary 'seeing-things-into' degenerates further into tunnel vision: a tunnel with a distorting lens fitted at the end. Blind to everything but his desire for visible and all-inclusive perfection, he thinks hard (unconsciously) how to skirt round the unpalatable, and dodge the unpleasant: shrugging it off as, somehow, a different world, nothing to do with him.

And yet, life *will* be awkward, springing nasty surprises and sneaking up on him despite his efforts to see nothing 'offensive'. There is nothing he can do to defend himself against that, but emotionally (♓→) he is always quite prepared to take the grand overview, excluding nothing. This comes in handy whenever he is caught out, unable to fail to notice: he can identify and sympathise with anything, ready to overlook any obstacle to emotional harmony and thus, again, conveniently sidesteps the more awkward situations. Little details do not really matter, the odd rough word, a bit of a black eye, he can 'forgive' such things, push them generously out of his way. It is all part and parcel of this One Happy World: one really should not fuss.

His emotional outlook is of course quite the reverse of his shrewdly observant thinking. He can bring only either feeling or thought to bear on any matter, hardly both. But most of the time it would not matter which, since both serve the same purpose equally well: to keep his world nice and to keep it whole. Nothing must be seen to go against the grain, nothing must stray from the path of good-ness. He has got it all worked out, and naturally (as an extravert) he is as pleased with himself as with everything else. – His vanity is quite without legitimate foundation.

And yet, neither in his thinking nor feeling attitude to his self is he inclined to see himself as someone who counts for something (♍←, ♓←), who could possibly make an impact. And it pleases him to denigrate himself like that, to see himself as helpless and never quite equal to a job: it ties in with his attitude – to which he would love to convert us, if only by strenuous passive example – that there is no cause to interfere, meddle with and upset things... everything is as it should be and will we please all stop trying to change things, there is no need for that at all. It is the lazy man's option, to view the world through happy-coloured spectacles and expect all the diverse creatures that inhabit it to be happy with him, simply and without fuss. It is the bliss of a particularly crafty simpleton.

Rejecting all ideas of personal responsibility for the state the world is in as unnecessary, he still manages, at bottom, to be one of the greatest manipulators. Certainly a most effective one – precisely because he appears to control nothing with his willing acceptance, and tacit preservation, of the status quo. Meantime, he leaves all the work for others to do, and please not under his nose. But worse than that are the wider implications: seemingly so other-worldy in his great 'love' for all he encounters (that is to say for all he has not seen fit to dodge, seeing them coming), he is the greatest upholder of all that is, inevitably, wrong with the world, all that is ugly and mean. He has made a mockery of tolerance.

He has successfully blinded himself to objective reality by waving his magic visionary wand over all and sundry, maintaining that *this* is what it is all like, when All has been taken into account. Everyone is, in his eyes, given an equal share of all possible desirable attributes. Whether we can possibly live up to such absolutist expectations, that is beside the point. Everybody is, interchangeably, OK for him. Anybody who cannot, or for some reason will not, conform to what negative Libra insists on seeing into the world, is quickly shut away out of sight: preferably imprisoned there, in his imperfection, in another kind of world, so as not to upset Libra's grand and totally unreal expectations. That is the measure of his blind justice; that way he keeps *his* world safe from the worst negative excesses – certainly the more obviously unpretty ones.

His assessment of us is simple: we are all equally lovely, except for those of us who prove themselves not fit to be part of the world at all. He has cut the world in half, 'his' good one which purports to be all there 'really' is, and the bad, phantom-like rest, incomprehensible and too awful to contemplate. Unable to compromise, unable even to see his side of things clearly, he has invented a new form of intolerance far worse than his original bemused and hesitant rejection of our world.

He does nothing to change the world for the better. He makes no attempt to see us for what we are or, more to the point, for what we might be, given the right 'background', the appropriate 'setting'. Relativity and the possibility for relative changes do not exist in his view. He has dehumanised us to the status of positive or negative ciphers. Like Aries he conceives of enemies, and like Taurus he 'exports' them to some place that is not really part of his world, where he won't have to notice them. He refuses to acknowledge difficulties. His smile never slips. If anything raises an eyebrow, he quickly shrugs it off, if at all possible. He simply demands a 'nice' world.

Those who do the dirt shovelling and mending and policing and producing, sweating and groaning, are not quite 'real' to him either, not while they are at it anyway. He himself is fully and pleasantly occupied twisting reality, so that he can set a fabricated version in its stead: where cuckoo clocks lighten the futile passage of time, and nothing *ever* pongs. He strongly encourages us to do the same: he waves his 'attractions' under our noses beguilingly. It would make him very happy to include us in his fancy world (it makes the maintaining of his illusions so much easier). We soon learn to chirrup merrily even while we are hiding our pains and rages and other such nasty abnormalities (fear, guilt, malcontent: such things he regards with an air of pained puzzlement and, vaguely, discounts with a shake of the head) behind the pretence that all is 'just fine' – for fear of being banished from his apparently pleasant world altogether. It would be a good thing if at least he could genuinely cheer us up, but his hymns of praise to a perfect world only make us feel unreal. We steal off feeling even more guilty, enraged, and disconcertingly shabby beside him, not to mention dishonest.

But by and large it is difficult to get a chance to be unlovable to him at all. He has a way of squashing our protests with fond looks and brushing aside our indifference with sounds of delight. Falling in love is as easy as falling off a log to him, and about as conducive to true relating. He falls upon us with the full weight of his unreal expectations, and who wants to say soberly 'Oh, but I'm not really as nice as all that'? Being in love, so-called, is the norm for him: he 'fell' for the whole world long ago; the rest is merely detail.

Far from uniting both his realities, inner and outer, standing them in a productive relation, he has lost both and supplanted them with a third: an impossible, double-headed hybrid, antithetical to life and life's indispensable interrelatedness. He is no longer divided in his attention and loyalty. He has passed his inbuilt duality on to the world, splitting it in half, two unreal halves at that. It is a black/white world, crassly segregated. Recognising only the apparently good half, he greedily makes it all his own, it becomes all equally self to him. But his half-whole world yields only a half-whole self, never quite clearly perceived, always dodging the other, phantom half of world and potential self that he refuses to own. And his formerly impeccable *im*personal standards – which he has projected onto the world, making an illusory mishmash of world and beyond, and then proceeded to appropriate out of that his *personal* standards – have degenerated, not surprisingly, into double standards.

He has essentially made the same mistake as Gemini, displaying a good few similar symptoms as well, like blatant self-contradiction, active pretence, as well as passive dependence. He has betrayed his own meaningful duality and forced together what should have been kept apart. – It would appear that the mistake is always the same for each sign: they compulsively turn towards the objective world with all their 'content', conscious or unconscious, projected: all their functions employed in the one-pointed pursuit, or establishment, or proving in action or whatever, of the self. –

If he thinks that an enjoyable peace will reign now, he is mistaken. He is his own most dazzled victim, with all the illusions and pretences he has created. His carefully maintained naivety sets him up as the perfect victim. One need not even pull the wool over his eyes, that would be a superfluous effort. He has shown us how to apply whitewash to murky grey, insisted on it even, and now he pays the price of his false innocence, his scheming inactivity, his well-groomed helplessness, his untrue selflessness that lavished praise and 'moral support' – but never any working involvement – on only the 'right and proper' things to do. Now his passive manipulations will rebound on him with a vengeance. He is surrounded on all sides by those he has banished as sinners against his perfect world – not to mention the unbanished ones in their fine disguises. All he did not want to *become*, did not want to work at integrating into world and self, now takes its revenge. And still he (literally) does not recognise it.

He is a much suffering little angel. He can't even admit to himself that his own are robbing him, but has to push the blame on unseen others... devils perhaps. There seems to be nothing wrong with his world, not that he can see . Except that it is shrinking: the more his dark phantoms pursue him and encroach on 'his part of the world', the more he has to ignore, shut out, deny the existence of. Inevitably, in the end, with only a small reliably 'good' circle left to him, he has to all intents and purposes imprisoned himself. But even if he ends up with a last stronghold the size of a postage stamp, he will still maintain that *this* is the (only real) world.

The increase of 'evil' out there is entirely his fault. With his passive make-believe he has been encouraging all the worst to flourish, instead of doing the job only he could have done: setting 'good' and 'bad' in proportion and relation and transforming them into a living, 'working' whole. Seeing into the world what did not belong there neat and unalloyed, he has totally unbalanced it.

Following his example, because we were attracted by his nice and easy world model, we have gradually made of his unrealistic black/white division a fact (if not a truth: *potentially* the world is as colourful as ever, each part of it capable of taking its meaningful place in the spectrum). We have condemned but not dealt with; not honestly opposed and confronted, only tried to suppress by waving-out-of-our-way and then locking the door – a door for the most part more imaginary than real. We are standing on very shaky ground. In fact, we have an unacknowledged war on our hands that is nibbling at the edges of our make-believe peace, driving us into ever more exclusive imaginary corners. All that should also have become self to us, what we should have owned and made our business to set right, is taking its revenge now. It has been flourishing in the dark places where we did not want to see it: now we are no match for it. We cling to our 'point of view' even as the other side gains ground, but we refuse to fight for our 'beliefs'. That, after all, would go against all we stand for – sit around for would be more accurate. We have no choice but be passive victims, martyrs without good cause.

Virgo burned the witches he created openly at least. Libra has tried to use a facile fairy-tale magic to dismiss his 'sinners' from the book of life, spiriting them away. It is a fairy-tale with a meagre ending. A would-be world shrinking away to nothing, a fancied self disintegrating along with it: leaving only an unwavering smile that is beginning to look rather deranged in its wholesomeness.

Some Suggested Libra Attributes

basic

gifted: with inner vision, **imagination;** his first of all inward-directed sensuality gives him **an eye and a 'feel' for things** as they could, most positively, be

has high standards and expectations; strong sensibilities, innate good taste; his simpler expectations might be called instinctive

easily disappointed and affronted, on principle; **hypercritical, perfectionist, purist, aesthete; passively complains and finds fault** usually by **simply withdrawing** from difficulties, 'affronts' etc.

responsive to demands, obliging, easily exploited and used

but then has **'second thoughts',** which actually *precede* his involvement, but may be swept out of the way by his personal desire for *some* involvement; **hesitant, won't commit himself, divided yes/no attitude** to life, **indecisive; appears self-contradictory; taken for cowardly and inconsistent**

positive

judicious action; critical appraisal: judgement; compares and **assesses; finds** *the* **fault and actively does something about it: (re-)adjusts, (re-)arranges, re-distributes** etc.

sets in context, sees in perspective and proportion, sees things to be relative, 'objective', 'neutral', compromising, co-operative, fair

always needs to make **meaningful improvements; orders;** makes non-superficial **embellishments** and properly **harmonious** rearrangements; **artistic; rectification; adjudication;** concerned with true justice: **actively doing justice to**

reacts, counteracts, corrective action, e.g. **checking for meaning, worth and value; disentangling** and **separating** what is wrongly connected; **opposing and denying a place to what is wrong;** if necessary **fighting** those who are doing wrong (seeing them not as 'wrong' in themselves, but only doing the wrong thing), prior to making new connections: **mediating, reconciling, resolving differences, peace-making** (but not at any price)

re-introduces the 'natural' order of things; works in an **advising** capacity, **admonishing, warning,** but also **praising**

personally never *too* deeply involved: **deliberate(d) action; aware of his obligations; reserved; impartial, observant of others' needs** and problems which would spoil the world for him if he did not do something about them: **'selfless'**; needs, not to immerse himself in the world, but to stand himself in proper relation to it: **needs meaningful relationships**

his compromising/improving stance and actions make him **persuasive** and his truly harmonising aims and personal environment make him **attractive,** while the opposition he puts up against regardless action has a **'taming' effect**

negative

projects and superimposes his expectations, deliberately blind to reality as it is; **sees-into; views life through a distorting lens, illusions** that amount to an **effortless superficial prettification** of life; **'frivolous'**

no sense of proportion or true value, everything is of equal worth to him; lacks 'taste'; may be **messy, untidy, fickle, unfaithful, disloyal**

'in love with the whole world': desiring it all, but needing it to be 'right', he declares everybody loveable; expecting pleasures all the time: **greedy; hooked on anything 'sweet', 'romantic'**

refuses to notice or understand the negative aspects of the world: **deliberate naivety and ignorance** (or ignoring-of, rather); **shrewdly evades anything unpleasant,** including work: **lazy, irresponsible;** but also 'generously' waves aside what unpleasantness he can't avoid: **makes himself out to be forgiving and understanding; will passively support any good work, charity** etc. but always at one remove: **'keeps his hands clean'**

chronically pleased with his world/self: **smug, vain, self-admiring;** yet out of laziness **makes himself out to be incapable:** an *I* can't do it attitude, **falsely self-denigrating, 'coy', dependent, may act the helpless child; tries to attract** others: to convert them to his view, so that his illusions may be easier to maintain: **seductive, deliberately alluring** in all respects, **'winning' or winsome; 'precious'**

virtually blackmails with flattery, imposes lovability (and takes his own for granted), **'flirts'; refuses to hear a 'no'**

protests at changes: sees no need for them, **'can't be bothered'** (i.e. to readjust his distorting lens) hence **upholds the status**

quo; hidden manipulator

likes to appear tolerant, but anything he can't distort to suit himself he meets with **total intolerance; condemns out of hand:** without taking the matter in hand and sorting it out after properly assessing the inherent potential for good: **imposes one rigid law for all** that is meant merely to **get rid of 'misfits'; excludes, banishes, suppresses out of sight, imprisons; uncompromising, inflexible;** everything that does not fit in 'his' world he **declares 'sinful':** since he has taken the Absolute Law into his own hands, **nags, moralises, misquoting a Higher Authority, pretentious, gives himself (mysterious) airs**

has a divisive effect; double standards, hypocrite; encourages pretence, 'white-washing'; indirectly provokes opposition, often of a hidden kind, refuses to admit that he might have enemies but with his passivity **'encourages' the worst in others, will be said to have 'asked for it'**

easily duped, self-deceiving and deceived, taken advantage of, victimised; 'martyr'; progressive isolation in his illusory world; seen as a harmless crank or as obsessive

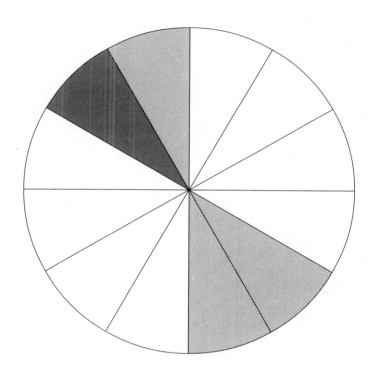

AQUARIUS

≈ Introvert
conscious function: sensation; direction of function: inward
unconscious functions: ♌ intuition, ♑ thinking, ♋ feeling
Air: rational

Aquarius is an introverting introvert, like Sagittarius. But instead of relating intuitively to his self and the regions beyond, he senses intelligently, like Gemini and Libra. This means his inner self appears to him both rationally structured, and as a series of self-perceptions: he sees himself to be something orderly, something to which laws or rules apply. Beyond that he is aware, like Libra, of images that he takes to be the underlying conceptual models that are the root of all existence – yet to him they are not an impersonal experience but a reality closely related to what he personally is. They are part of his becoming, something he taps for his inner self-growth.

Left to himself, he would do nothing but marvel at and endlessly investigate the fascinating world that is his developing self. A self so complex in every palpable detail, it could be the study of all-time. A self so comprehensive and always revealing itself to his view in so many new compositions, it could fill his heaven and… there would never be a need for an earth. But like Sagittarius, he is tapped on the shoulder by rude necessity. Life refuses to let him indulge undisturbed in his distant, self-sufficient contemplation.

Where Sagittarius emerged befuddled and abstracted into our world after his intuitive meanderings on the inner plane, Aquarius brings with him a clear, sharply focused and rational view of the essential world order. Like Libra, he is in possession of a set of expectations both detailed and structured, which he can quite easily compare with this other reality out here. But unlike Libra who, as an extravert, had a vested interest in getting involved in life (while also holding on to his inner awareness) Aquarius is not personally interested: there is nothing in it for him. He sees himself as already complete; or rather: constantly being completed further by the transpersonal inner reality that he is in touch with. That is all the life he needs, in his opinion, just as Sagittarius would have been quite content to stay where he was.

Pulled into concrete existence by the demands of life, Aquarius surveys what he finds there with a critical eye, just as Libra did. He, too, is not impressed. But he compares not only what 'ought' to be with what, most puzzlingly, is – he also at the same time compares self with all of other, and it can hardly be avoided that he comes to see his self as comparatively superior. He regards this alien world with a large measure of disdain: it is all topsy-turvy, it makes neither an edifying picture nor a truly interesting study for him. It would make more sense for him to stick to his inner world than to bother with ours, which seems both unpleasant to him and a complete nonsense. But his participation is demanded. Life in the world of matter needs him, as it needs all the other signs.

Condescending at last to take few steps in our world, he certainly does not flap around like a fish out of water, the way Sagittarius did, crashing into things and making a fool of himself. Aquarius stalks about with a deeply critical frown, poking things in exasperation; observing us in action, he can hardly believe his eyes. The world is a total affront, and unlike Libra he can't help taking it personally.

Whatever he does, he does *his* way, shaking up our world in the process. Where Sagittarius did his damage inadvertently, sustaining injuries himself, Aquarius quite systematically upsets our proverbial apple carts, because he can see quite clearly that they aren't what they should be. At this we cannot even be amused. We decide there must be something quite fundamentally wrong with him if he can't live by our rules and look at things from our point of view. He is a most sinister and unwelcome presence – while *he* finds *us* peculiar beyond description and our world not fit for him to be in. So now we are complaining bitterly at the upset he has caused? He shrugs, he knew all along there was not much sense in this exercise. He can't turn his back on us fast enough.

What helps to persuade him out of his inner isolation is his intuitive awareness (Ω). This tells him that the objective world is not a place of meaningless and random happenings, in contradistinction to subjective law, but a realm to be conquered and ruled *by* subjective law. What he senses himself to be is not just a private concern of his; it can be applied successfully to his actual living situation, his personal environment, and indeed the whole world. And this would appear to be what life is demanding of him.

Virgo actively picked the individual ingredients of a self out of the possibilities given him by his environment and introjected them, to make an individualised inner self. Aquarius, on the other hand, starts out with a 'natural' inner self, and continues to derive new inner content from out of the unlimited number of models that exist on the inner plane as such – irrespective of what his current environment would expect him to be or become. This has the effect, more often than not, of making it look as if Aquarius, rather than Virgo, had wilfully chosen to 'be different'. In fact, he never even looked to see what there might be to be different *from*, in the world. He arrives in the world one might say pre-formed, with a strong sense of who exactly he is and how he hangs together, a capacity to observe quite clearly and thoughtfully the difference between self and other, and no inclination to adopt anything of ours for his new inner becoming (as an introvert the wouldn't, of course) or to give ground. He has no inbuilt need to *prove* himself either, like Capricorn, that is no part of his makeup.

He may be made of the same stuff as Sagittarius, but his very different conscious awareness of it makes him handle himself totally differently. With him, there is no instant rushing into a conscious intuitive search for mundane possibilities when he turns himself around to face the world, no novel and tempting sensations, new arresting sights of a sphere that might become home as well, if only one could master the craft of being in it. Instead, for him, there is immediate clear-eyed criticism and a marked reluctance to get involved (not based on hurt sustained, but on sharp-eyed assessment of the differences between self and world) though this is offset now by the chance of gaining rulership.

Sagittarius was 'persuaded' into living by his senses: he ran the risk of becoming a rather over-enthusiastic exile from his inner-self realm. Or else, he was for ever sneaking off to get away from this to him over-precise, excessively delimited world. Aquarius has a much clearer view of what will be involved; there are no delights to tempt him; and the offer of a ruling position is bound to look more like a tough if interesting job, to be approached with cool determination. Sagittarius, easily tempted, is nevertheless hard to keep on a steady course and difficult to stop going AWOL.

Aquarius, with his detached and sober attitude, once he has decided to take on the job, he pushes his way into active life, and there is no easy discouraging him.

As already pointed out, he is by no means trying deliberately to be different. But finding himself criticised for his (natural? unnatural?) lack of conformity, he is ready to defend his position strongly. He does not *need* to expose himself to worldly criticism, like Capricorn, and in consequence has no 'hang-ups' about his being different; and neither would it occur to him to regard himself as outnumbered by us and as having to adjust to our ways in order to prove his existential laws to be a valid contribution. As he sees it, it is not only perfectly legitimate for him to be as he is, but he even has the right to impose his existing nature on ours. The onus of change lies with us. He will accept none of our example, fashion or diktat, but reserves the right to be what he is. Among all the signs he alone stands up deliberately and self-awarely for the right of the subjective to become itself in an objective world.

What he tries to impose is not by its nature bizarre. It strikes us that way only because it takes us by surprise, as totally unexpected and unconnected to the current life situation. It is Virgo who is capable of thinking up bizarre combinations – though it has to be said that Virgo's novel ways never strike us as all that terribly outlandish: they are only selective rearrangements of what is already familiar to us, after all. These he then tries to sell us as the latest progressive idea: an improved version of the current world order, which it may or may not be. What positive Aquarius has to offer is always an improvement, in the long run, because, like Libra he can see 'what ought to be': a perfect, transcending, world plan.

Virgo, at his best, learned to respond to objective changes by being a growing, becoming, individualised and internalised self. But for Aquarius change is written into the very nature of his established inner self. The sign with the most deeply entrenched commitment to the subjective self, he is also the most personally unstable. Those distinct (if meaningfully related) inner-plane 'pictures' that surround him are the models for his inner becoming. Which makes of his personal development not a smooth flow, as it was for intuitive Sagittarius, but a series of more or less abrupt changes, according to overall laws of meaningful coherence. He derives a succession of distinct inner states from out of his view of an inner-plane Life Plan, switching as it were from one model to the next. And this is the kind of self he brings with him to 'impress' on his environment. Not only does he appear to go contrary to what exists in our world, not only does he attempt to impose his contrary rule, but – the height of contrariness – he is not even consistent, from our point of view. He demands change, and then change again, uncompromisingly and wholesale.

And there he comes up against the rules of our, objective world. The sort of wholesale inner changes he can perform quite easily at the level of inner being are neither possible nor desirable in the realm of material existence. He wreaks nothing but havoc if he tries to introduce a regime of constant volte-face, and the resulting debris and chaos is actually no kind of objective mirror image of his inner nature either. His habit of orderly instant change does not work here. The outward life can not, like the inner one, part or whole, be thrown aside in no time at all for a new model. At this point his unconscious thought processes are needed.

Thinking about (the role he is to play in) our reality ($\text{\char"2648}\rightarrow$), he comes to understand about the demands of necessity and the practical limitations of concrete changes. And thinking about the nature of his inner self ($\text{\char"2648}\leftarrow$), he comes to accept his own limitations in relation to what can be effected in the world. He has to come to the conclusion that his rulership or influence can only be valid when and where it pays due respect to necessity and the nature of things as they are in themselves. As king of changes he rules over a lamentably set and rigid realm, and if it is to be a fit realm for him at all, and not a scene of gratuitous dismemberment and instant deconstruction, then he must as a ruler be obedient to the nature and demands of life. And so he learns first to assess carefully and then to proceed patiently, sticking to one narrowly defined project at a time, wherever change may be most necessary at the moment.

Being pragmatic and cautious and strictly logical in his approach is all very well, but it still brings him up against our *subjective* resistance. It is easy enough for us to welcome Gemini's 'repair work': he only connects up (again) what is perfectly visible and perhaps obviously in need of meddling with, and if the end result is new and a bit different this is not likely to disturb us much. Likewise even Libra's more drastic reorganisation of the visible world will spark only muted protest. His impartial and compromising nature cannot possibly arouse suspicion, and whatever he changes he does so step by step, under our watchful gaze and including us. But the 'repairs' to our inappropriate established forms that Aquarius is trying to bring about tend to provoke howls of protest, fear and resentment.

He would seem to be trying to sell us the future: he professes to bring something new and yet invisible with him for which, uncompromisingly, he has first to make room among our existing world stuff, our nicely ordered procedures, our accepted status quo. Will one be fool enough/wise enough to trust him? His intentions are easily misunderstood. One has to learn to 'hear him out'. Only then can he be observed, in retrospect, to be changing the world for the better, like Libra; and like Gemini to be contributing towards an increased overall coherence and logic in our lives: his alterations are never without 'good cause'. But only time will tell us that, and we would rather trust the solid, deficient past than the airy promise of a better future. We are not interested in having even minor aspects of our lives transformed. We cling to what we have, and are, and he can keep his rational explanations of what he is about to do to us. He is trying to rob us of all that spells personal integrity to us. We don't want our integrity updated and improved from without.

Short of using force and creating havoc again, there is nothing he can do to budge us, and havoc is alien to him; orderly progress in neat quantum leaps is what he is about. But we refuse to have him leaping about in our lives on our behalf, no matter what beneficial abstrusities he promises to bring about in the process. – But then again he would not want to go against our wishes or entrenched needs. Emotionally he cares deeply to be of use to others, to give and to look after their needs (♋→); and emotional modesty (♋←) prevents him from imposing his rule insensitively. The gift of his example should suffice.

Just as Sagittarius addressed himself to our unawakened inner selves, so does Aquarius. He too wants to give us our freedom: the ability to perform inner transformations – not in the wake of outward changes, Virgo-style, but ahead of them. This is the freedom of inner renewal, with the help of which we can bring about a corresponding change in our objective circumstances as well (within the limits of the possible), rather than be the slavish product of them – even when, like Virgo, we have chosen critically what to respond to with inner becoming. He offers us complete mastery over our inner lives, and a measure of mastery even over material reality and the part we play in it.

Through his personal example he tries to inspire us with his own confidence in subjective being. So we can't very well be *his* subjects, but all of us subjects in our own right: he grants us the right to be, as he is, 'ourselves'. He nurtures our innermost self-esteem, our dignity in separateness – but always subject to the laws of *meaningful* (that is interrelated) separateness. He rules as primus inter pares, an example of aware and unwavering selfhood as the basis of any worldly activity. But the world of equals, all self-motivated, that he would institute, is also held together by their common observance of Inner Law. Again, the gift of freedom is accompanied by some basic must's. Above all, we must not imagine that now we will be allowed to be sufficient unto ourselves, but must stand ourselves in relation to our brothers in freedom.

One may see here a parallel process to Gemini's world, divided and yet always coming together again: Aquarius' world is unified by the rule of Law he imposes on it, but it 'keeps coming internally apart' as he grants subjective autonomy to others. Aquarius' many potential inner selves serve as the model of separate selfhood in a community of equals before Absolute Law. He would teach us to 'introject' the equality of Gemini – as well as the lawfulness of Libra. These should become inner realities to us.

We need no longer regard him as an intruder come to upset the rules we are clinging to for reasons of personal security. *Internal* lawfulness frees us from our dependence on objective rules imposed on us in the interest of justice and fairness: we no longer need to be told. And the personal inner experience of being potentially many different selves, one as good as he other, each as much self to us as its predecessor, enables us to add to our materially based relationships: *everybody* is now related to us, by virtue of being also-self, potentially.

We can no longer believe in the illusion of objective separateness as a hard fact for all time. Having gained our *inner* separateness, we find it to be an always vividly defined but also unstable thing that may assume many colours – or more positively speaking, we find the freedom of becoming one another, interchangeably; of having access to a common fund of being-states that knows no limitations, exclusions and hence no oppositions, enmi-

ties. This is the *inner* neighbourhood, *inner* communication (trans-
lating ourselves from one inner state to a neighbouring one, and
back), and *inner* peace. But like Aquarius himself we are required
also to live this out in the objective life, serving as bringers of necessary changes and standing as examples of that inner relatedness
that goes hand in hand with willing inner change.

So Aquarius offers this gift to all the world: lawfully self-regu-
lating autonomy for each of us, everyone the king of his life, in
respectful equality with his brothers. But who is queuing? He may
have been self-sufficient (that is to say, not dependent on his
objective environment for his being and becoming) so long as he
stayed in his inner reality. But having joined the world he, too,
depends on others. Just as Leo could not *give up* his rulership
unless others were prepared to take on the task of sharing it, so
Aquarius cannot *assume* his rulership unless others are prepared
to bear the burden of inner law and inner change. He knows he
cannot demand the impossible; his feelings, too, tell him that it
would be no kindness to press a gift on us that would be nothing
but an unbearable demand if we are not sufficiently prepared for
it. The other Air signs have to prepare the ground first: teaching
us about (meaningful) changes within something that makes a
coherent whole; about the relativeness of all things that alone
makes (meaningful) coherence possible. He also has to 'wait' for
Virgo and Capricorn to add *internal* rules to our repertoire, and for
Sagittarius to make innerness palatable to us. Till all this has been
learned he is not really welcome here. (In this he can be seen to
build on existing foundations; and what he finds to be already
lawfully established, in the truest sense, he has no occasion to criticise and attempt to transform: it is not change *for the sake of it* he
stands for, after all.)

Even his worst detractors must eventually admit that where he
thoughtfully and kindly imposes much-needed changes on the
world there follows not, as they had feared, a breakdown of all
recognisable order, a chaos to be mended by *them*. Instead, the
period of seemingly senseless upheaval automatically brings in its
wake a new orderliness, new meaningful arrangements, whatever
one may think of them. They have to realise that he may look and
act the lawbreaker, but only because he knows a better law, and
any number of detailed world models that are superior to ours.
Where Capricorn very tentatively offered (better) rules and regu-

lations to live by, Aquarius surprises us with fleshed-out new models to try out in our plodding, pedestrian world. He seems to pull visions for life changes like rabbits out of a hat and we can't quite credit that his unexpected and seemingly incongruous 'inventions' should be workable. And if he assures us with all the confidence in the world that all we have to do is get rid of and make room for, then he looks more suspect than ever.

When the upheaval is over and we find our environment a better place than it was, then sadly the credit is often given to the forces of resistance to change: as if they had gained the upper hand and restored order again. Capricorn and Taurus are held responsible for the ordering and upbuilding that was an integral part of Aquarius' transformative-creative act; Gemini may be invoked as having healed the wounds Aquarius inflicted; even Libra will be quoted as having restored the balance. As long as we lack the personal inner experience of what he is about, his ways are simply a mystery to us.

This lack of response, of thanks, would be fatal to Leo, who needs to be well received into the world, with all his self-creating changes, in order to find his inner being made visible to him. Where Leo unselfconsciously 're-created' the world *in order to become* self-conscious, rather like a child in his sand box, Aquarius maintains the detached attitude of a 'grown-up' who has been aware of his self, with all its multitudinous potential, since literally before the beginning of our time. We are thankless children to refuse his gift, but also frightened and as yet incapable, as he well understands. This presents no personal problem to Aquarius; he does not, like Leo, need something in return, as it were. If *he* offers us a new world then only because life demanded a contribution from him, not because he needed to do it for his own sake. Leo's are self-ish re-creations, that is to say he needs them to gain access to a conscious awareness of the self he is. Aquarius' transformations are a free gift to the world, they do nothing for him. Unfortunately, they seem to do nothing for us either, unless we are 'mature' enough to participate in his work as his free and equal companions.

With so few kind and practicable or necessary changes that he might helpfully impose, and with his offer of permanent service-by-example largely rejected, because too few are ready to follow it, he inevitably finds himself rather underemployed. He is perfectly happy to return to his inner world, not feeling in the least diminished. But he dutifully keeps in touch with his funny, sketchy 'kingdom', his other domain, paying periodic visits to see whether some urgent alteration is needed, or whether he can make another convert to full selfhood, another member of his pitifully small elect club of followers/equals. Aquarius goes back and forth as abruptly as he does everything else, switching his attention inward and outward. Sagittarius, too, had to bear both realities in mind, but he flowed more smoothly, intuitively, towards the inner world and outward again towards the world of matter, limitations, separation. Aquarius, accustomed to seeing one discreet picture before his inner eye and another, if related one, the next, is 'here' one moment, then gone again, and back when one least expects him. Libra's constant detached hovering between worlds was enough to puzzle some. Aquarius' alternate comings and goings without prior notice or indication have us nervously watching every shadow for signs of his presence.

Each time he emerges into our world he is another shock to the system. What he has to offer us has yet again a different feel to it, a new shape, a re-styled rationale, because he himself has renewed himself in the meantime. For this he can hardly be blamed. We give him black looks for being unpredictable all the same. Leo is always there, generously providing us with new clothes to wear so that he may admire his self in yet another guise; Aquarius pops out of the woodwork presenting us with his latest 'creation', perpetrated in some secret dark recess of his own, and we make sure we counter his attacks on our lame imagination with a duly upheld dullness of response. A sleeveless coat he offers? He must have had an armless race in mind, not us, no takers.

It is hard enough for Leo to find himself competent co-rulers, and all *he* asks is that we let our unconscious awareness of lawful life models inform our creative acts in the world. Aquarius' equals have first to find their *conscious, inner* awareness of these same life models, and then to accept them as the basis of their own becoming: leap after leap into their own future; unsupported by any experience of constancy but the truly central one of 'I' – without 'am', this or that.

To grow up into this inner vision of a common, instantly mutable Self of which we can all partake in perfect togetherness means to give up all we have relied on to define us as 'individuals'. We are afraid we will be internally divided, plucked apart and scattered into nothingness. And we continue to fail to realise, despite his demonstrations, the dual nature of the Law: its many-faceted infrastructure, and its singleness of purpose in becoming. Only divided and subdivided endlessly can it have its ever unstable living being, leaping into different states of 'I' or world.

We do not care at all for the idea of having the instability of Life's becoming for our very own centre. We would much rather have life with all its vagaries imposed on us than truly live it, from out of our mutable-life creating inner selves. Again and again Aquarius gives us not only the benefit of his innovations and alterations (which, with grudging hindsight, we are glad enough to accept), but also each time it is a lesson in 'surviving' change and finding 'the centre to hold': his apparently chaotic changes always settling into something newly distinct, the next step always being one that in retrospect will turn out to have been necessary. This is all he can do for us, nudging us along from step to step, till we learn to walk willingly: minus our habitual illusion that self or world could be a stable thing, rooted to the spot, and yet be truly alive. It is a measure of his patience, reliability and obedience to the demands made on him that he continues to teach us, shock after illuminating shock, while we screw our eyes shut in a stubbornness of terror and simply refuse to acknowledge the sparks of change on our settled horizon. The radical signs of life becoming: too awful to contemplate, far too dizzy a prospect if one took it personally. – His task is uphill all the way.

Of course even he, the most precisely insightful of signs, can fall victim to compulsive misuse of his unconscious functions. The urge to forcibly imprint his inner content on his environment in an act of objective self-creation (Ω) is so strong, he takes himself to be the undisputed model for what all the world should be and do. Like Sagittarius, he closes the door on his inner world to become an exile, unaware that he has lost his living inner foundation. He no longer becomes inside himself; his becoming is all projected outward to be impressed on a waxwork world: consequently he brings with him the template of whatever he has *last* become, now fixed in perpetuity, *and* his inbuilt habit of abrupt and easy, unopposed change – a contradiction in terms if ever there was one.

What was once no more than a 'current' self (and new visions of new self-models all around him) now becomes a fixed, static thing; and his one vision is of the objective, material world embodying that. He has his plan for the world-to-be neatly drawn up. He already envisages himself there, fleshed-out and established for good. But more than any dictator – being so 'different' – he finds what he wants to see in his new environment and what exists there to differ. The moment he makes the world the place where his dogmatically set self will be established as *the* 'model' existence, it becomes a large-scale demolition site. There is not room beside him for other forms of being; and at any rate he needs empty space, a clean slate, tabula rasa, for his incarnation.

He is a much more exacting despot than negative Leo. For him becoming the world is not a process of an unknown self emerging bit by bit, following a compulsive but vague (i.e. unaware) notion of what this self might be. He is fully conscious of his whole self (even if it is a pitifully shrivelled and unalive sort of self he now has) and this he aims to watch become the rule of the world. He wants to set it down in its complete and detailed glory, uncompromisingly, where our current world is happening in its, to him, alien ways. He has to sweep everything out of the way first, to make a clean start – and he has no patience at all.

But the world's inertia stops him in his tracks at the first attempt. If he starts knocking down the existing version, he finds, not empty space to be filled instantly with newness: he only finds piles of still existing stuff, now broken and disorderly, a disorder so pervasive it might as well be permanent, from his point of view. This is doubly annoying. He hates any disorder that does not instantly give way to a new kind of order; and meantime his plan is coming to nothing. He is in a hurry, because he is completely back to front: he has the future all sorted out and now finds himself having to wait for time and world to catch up with him, before he can gain his kingdom, his self made manifest. Newly emerged from his timeless inner world where the flicker of an eyelid was enough to instantly transform his existence, he lacks all understanding of this obstructively slow and seemingly immutable concrete reality.

A properly rational approach might have told him that there are limits to what he can do in this world, and how. But instead he misuses his unconscious thinking ($\text{♑}\rightarrow$) to learn how to be most effective at what he wants to do: de-construct, quickly, raze it all to the ground, so that *he* may become the new world. There are concrete principles at work here that hold it all together. Once he knows them, there should be no problem dis-assembling and re-assembling. Precise leverage is all, he thinks.

At the same time he gains a new understanding of himself ($\text{♑}\leftarrow$), even narrower than the permanently set model of what to become in the world that's left to him. He thinks of himself now simply as the-one-who-knows, everything, on principle. Not only does he know what ought to be (the future), he also knows exactly what ought to be done *now*. That is to say, consciously, he is the 'imagined' plan of the future about to take shape. And unconsciously, he thinks of himself as something like the principle of change itself, as it deals effectively-destructively with the present. He is what will happen in times to come... he is what is happening now – but future and present are quite unlike each other, and never to be found in the same place, as it were. So where and what exactly is he?

He is compulsively trying to immerse his dead-set self in the living world, but there is nothing here fit to receive him, nothing his 'shape'. Now, guided by unconscious thought, he is busily dismantling the world to make room for his very different intentions. He is effectively *active* in time and world – but never as yet becoming his materialised *self*.

The self that should have its becoming here is displaced, dislocated, not in some other-worldly sphere of an inner nature (he has left that behind), but in some limbo he calls future. Only his active principle of letting-go-of-old-self is finding its material counterpart: in his destructive activities. Half a mirror image of his inner nature is all he can find. The other half, his precise model self, is lost to life as much as it is lost to innerness. It hangs like a mirage on the horizon, a perpetual intention, and *consciously* he is identified with that!

Being in an imaginary, future 'world' that bears no relation to either of the two real worlds, inner and outer; and *doing*, now, in the real material world: this is no division based on mere *pretending*, as both negative Gemini did, each manipulating time in his own way; or negative Virgo, making out to be 'good' and thriving on the constant pursuit of 'badness'. Nor is negative Libra's fond-

ly imagined ideal world anything like this: Libra's at least was an
improbable conflation of realities, he saw what he wanted *into* the
world. Aquarius' imaginary world is truly neither here nor there;
and this is also what he *is*, whatever he may be *doing* under our
noses. Since he has fallen foul of all the rules of both subjective
and objective being, it is maybe no wonder if he tends to defy our
understanding.

We can pin the label 'mad' on him, but it is as well to bear in
mind that whether we do or not depends entirely on how 'different' he actually is. If perchance what he was inside himself, when
the urge to forcibly become the whole world got the better of him,
is not too drastically removed from our everyday experience, we
may see no reason to apply that label at all. We may call him a bit
of a fanatic, maybe. If (to stretch a point) he tries to 'come across'
as an irrepressible steam-driven cuckoo clock, because that was all
he was inwardly examining, and becoming, then we will know
just what to make of him (we think). And yet *essentially* there is no
difference between the two.

So he 'hangs around', suspended in unreality, while undoing
all around him with unaware and yet intelligent and down-to-
earth precision. Like a young hooligan on a street corner he cannot
wait idly 'for his time to come'. What advances towards his unreal future self is only the same old world in which there is no room
for what he wants to be.

From his point of view it is the world that is 'too drastically different'. If only he could have been content to stay largely inside
himself, to emerge as an agent of change only when and where
meaningful, he would not now find his self permanently isolated
in this cocoon, this 'holding bay' of temporal and spatial unreality. One may compare this condition with that of the other introverting introvert. Sagittarius was inwardly a much vaguer
everything-at-once, rather than precisely everything-in-turns; and
when he compulsively fitted himself into our world, he still needed to have occasional recourse to the mock-innerness, the cocoon
of life-ignoring 'depression'. Aquarius does not even begin to fit.
He goes straight into and stays in a state of encapsulation, of a different and absurdly precisely pictured kind. –

Sweeping in like a whirlwind of change, guided by a meagre
vision and equipped with narrow materialistic and reductionist
principles, he gets less of a reception here than ever. If he thinks he

can order us about on the strength of a wildly improbable promise and some hard-nosed ideas about plucking our world apart that seem to have little to do with the actual promise, then he will have to think again. He is declared the arch enemy of life as we know it; we will soon deal with him. Emotionally though, he is so compulsively giving (♋→), he lays the whole project into our hands: *we* are the future, not he; this is *our* new world we could work towards. He feels himself to be (♋←) not only an indispensable world reformer, but practically about to give birth to a whole new world, single-handed: that will be his real gift to us. But meantime, while it matures endlessly in the womb of his displaced, intended, conscious self, we are offered the chance to make room for the expected.

It is one thing to be *commanded* to destroy our collective past and present; quite another to be made a personal gift of the chance. Setting us the example of one individual simply declaring the rest of the world null and void, he stirs up our individual grudges and contrary aspirations. He sparks our impoverished imagination into action with his visionary zeal. A picture of disobedience to existing law and order, he fires our innermost, if unconscious, wish to be what *we* want to be, and do, and have. He gives us instructive portrayals of a new law and order to be one day, and if we listened we would soon realise that they are even more restrictive of our individual hopes – but then we aren't listening to his long-range forecasts. He said this was *our* chance to do away with all 'wrongs'. We nod perfunctorily at his abstruse future-mongering; what we really want to hear is his matter-of-fact advice, the how-to of destruction.

He is quite happy to leave us to select personal targets of our own – it is *all* needing knocked down anyway – just so long as we go about our work swiftly, bearing in mind his coldly calculated plan of action, his destructive 'principles'. If he is a dictator we hardly notice it; he is more like a stern father and all-giving mother figure rolled into one – it makes us feel less naughty to see him like that. And in an absent sort of way, *he* thinks and feels himself to be just that. But the real he is watching our eager undoings from a limbo we cannot imagine.

He doesn't care who or what goes to pieces – or only in so far as he is waiting to see everything destroyed. This may not be him but at least it is a solid mirror image of the way he 'works', or used to:

positively welcoming the experience of finding his inner self dis-membered, transformed, reconstituted in some other subjective form; while standing throughout, as essentially self, unharmed and undiminished. – Translated straight into material terms, the way he does it, it means: he watches the established forms of the world smashed to pieces, old forms of behaviour – old 'selves' – cast aside in a growing frenzy of slaughter; and all from the van-tage point of a stable if unreal self (neither out there nor inside him, but purely fictitious).

In his shadowy existence he is not available for appeals for mercy from passive victims – or for that matter active ones who have had second thoughts when it started to hurt. They are trai-tors to his cause, back-pedallers: if they want to side with the established order then let them share its fate. Once he has kindled the flames of hitherto unacknowledge, unconscious forces (resent-ment, envy, greed for possession of the world and power over it) the conflagration looks after itself. And why should the world complain at being pulled limb from limb? A new one is to be put in its stead, a better one, in his superior image. He has neither time nor any inclination for pity. He just watches impatiently this pre-lude to his becoming: loving the promise it holds, and hating the sight of this protracted disarray.

All he is giving us are promises. They are in a sense genuinely meant, but what he does not take into account is that they are falling on infertile ground. He is not sharing, by inspiring exam-ple, the inner world of vision and new self-becoming. He is uni-laterally demanding that we dismantle ourselves and make ourselves the seed-bed of his new order, though he may find more persuasive words than that. But what his followers are after is not eventual obedience to his new laws. What they really have in mind is licence to tear down what offends them personally and the anarchical freedom to disobey established rule.

Negative Aquarius expects us to be no more than the tools of the moment, the present moment that does not really count for him. From his point of view we too are dispensable: interchange-able agents in the cause of his future rule (a rather different sort of 'equality'). And from our point of view he is an inspiring excuse to flatten the past and each build ourselves a better present. We carry off the pieces of the dismantled world by stealth: not to discard them honestly, but merely to appropriate them and convert them for our own use. Upheaval, destruction and change aplenty there may be, but never the clean slate he would require. He is of course asking the impossible.

His future is constantly losing out to the forces of the past in a new guise. Plus ça change... He is seemingly obeyed with relish, but there is never any real progress to be noticed. His 'prelude' goes on for ever. The world would appear to be strangely never-ending in its resistance. He overruns the established order, only to find his own forces establishing a present of their own, undirected by him. Instead of obedience to his new 'law' (the smidgin of Law he took with him when he severed his connection with everything on the inner plane) he has achieved nothing but disobedience writ large, to past and future alike – that is to say to himself as well.

His followers are living in a kind of limbo of their own: this is the short-term present, uprooted from its past and not going any-where in a meaningful way. They do not count for him, being only the means to an end, robotic tools. He was not expecting them to be any kind of mirror images yet. But in *their own* way they are: they have taken this vision of a better world and in their self-willedness made it their own, each a new-world creator and ruler in his own right, for his own purposes, not paying any heed to laws beyond their own compulsive desires – in which respects they can hardly be said to differ from him.

He has been outwitted by the seemingly immovable forces of past and present alike. Past keeps becoming new present; present keeps falling apart and being integrated into a new and different kind of present. And he, the would-be future, is still no nearer being *incorporated*, though in effect he is *happening* all the time. Somehow he has been robbed of part of his life, by some mysteri-ous sleight of hand. – He gave it away, unconsciously. But con-sciously, he would maintain that he is constantly being denied the chance to be his real self. That he is being robbed of his real inten-tions. Betrayed and hoodwinked by inferior others who must actu-ally, in some strange way, be forces superior to him if they manage to do him out of everything that really counts for him.

If he started out, unconsciously, thinking of himself as knowing all there was to know, and feeling capable of supplying, out of himself, all it needed for a new and better world, now he feels sorry for himself in his helpless state and thinks himself inferior, threatened and outnumbered by others: alien sorts of creatures, not to be trusted, against whom he has to put up a never-ending fight for repossession of his right to be, properly, he.

What can he do but fan the flames of (his) undoing even more? It will take no great intelligence, and hardly a promise worth telling, to set them all at each others' throats. He decides to destroy his own useless forces: fighting each other, destroying everything in their path, they may finally pulverise the world between them yet. – But now he finds himself, for a change, overtaken by the events he himself set in motion.

This world of ours that for ever eludes his personal grasp is already divided and subdivided against itself. His followers – his inadvertent and imperfect mirror images, rivals for 'his' future – are already waging internecine war. They have, thanks to his example, taken the law into their own hand, where it promptly fell into as many pieces as there were rival pairs of hands. All he has achieved is the battle of all times, where no one can tell any more what the future might hold. Even he, left standing like that, can no longer tell whether he is still to come, or has maybe already been... Consciously, he is not aware that *in effect* he already is, if not actually *what* he keeps desiring to be.

He aims to act as the great and rightful destroyer, a world-leveller to outdo negative Gemini, the active type – while his imaginary time enclave goes one better even than that of the other Gemini type; and the futuristic 'world' he has placed his self in beats Libra's confabulations hands down. But all he amounts to in the world is a blind, undirected force, the force of unlawful establishment.

The not-so-new structures and order sprouting up again and again on his 'battlefield' are one and all unlawfully conceived, under the impression that each individual can please himself, in an isolation of purpose hidden from public view, with no real regard for brotherly sharing, and no effort at integration into a meaningful whole. (He watches them copy his actions so well, and yet has nothing but distrust and suspicion for them!) Where once there was a simple, single split into his 'progressive' forces on the one hand, and the established resistance to change on the other, there is now a boiling cauldron of factions and fractions all set against each other.

The tyrant Capricorn appealed to our selfish impulse to get what we want by being obedient. He had his 'becoming' in our work, which put his principles into action. And *being* us, he left us hollowed out, a homogenised, robotically working mass. Aquarius has appealed to our other selfish impulse: to get what we want by being *dis*obedient. He too has his 'becoming' in our actions, applying his principle of destruction. As his busy mirror images we are all being-he... and yet he would *really* be someone other; and so would we. (He has stolen our many hopeful, intended selves; though obviously not to be his. He has displaced them into the same inaccessible state of unreality where his own self is locked up for future safe-keeping. They can keep it company there, making a more colourful display in their glass case on the unreachable top shelf marked future. – Not that his conscious, displaced self would view them as anything but invasive rivals there.)

Following him, we too say that one day, 'when all this is over', we will *really* be ourselves. Meantime we continue zealously to act contrary to our true inner nature – without ever managing to get any nearer being our intended selves. Having torn ourselves apart like that, it is only to be expected that we tear the fabric of the world apart too, in our efforts to make us a whole world each. *In reality* we all fit into a complex and comprehensive pattern, we dovetail, we overlap. Not to acknowledge that is to step out of reality. It automatically means demolishing the corners of each other's houses to build our own, to kick the legs from under our neighbour because he stands where we want to put our feet. And we get as good as we give. We might as well be kicking ourselves, showing openly how hopelessly divided we are, the total unreality in which we *fail* to really live.

But like he we pretend to ourselves that somewhere, somehow we are essentially intact sort of beings (if un-be-ably for the moment), whatever acts of vandalism against life we may be committing. When the war is over, when the mortgage is paid, when we have retired: then. Or maybe at least when we have well and truly retired from life: but then we will come to realise with a shock that what we took to be our 'real', 'inner' self bears only the faintest trace of a resemblance to the genuine article. To be frightened at the immense and scintillating sight of our own true inner reality is the final irony.

For this reason Aquarius, too, paces up and down irritably for seemingly ever, rather than give up the whole sorry mess for the failed job it is. Returning to his original state of innerness and making a new and better start from there is his only real hope in the world. But by now he sees an enemy, a rival, a suspect, in any other – even 'other' self. He has lost his ability to transform his *self* long ago. He clings to the sterile, set, artificial version under its futuristic glass dome as the only safe certainty. Afraid to face what he might really be – what he used to be quite happily, before his ambitions to rule went over the top – he cannot afford to acknowledge the fact that having left his own inner-becoming behind, he has forfeited a future for his self in the outside world too.

When the 'clean ground' he is waiting for to sow himself in at long last comes close to being a reality – the pulverised and depopulated world that we eventually achieve for him, because we too each want to rule the world single-handed – he will find that no kind of new life can be induced to spring from such a dead and unstructured soil. Where the living world has been destroyed there will simply be no agent left to build the envisaged one *with*. His perpetually fixed self can do no becoming in any time or place, on its own account: he is utterly dependent for his becoming on living others. A tabula rasa, a dead world, is no use to him at all. (And all his living so far has been no more than 'empty' activity, divorced from a mislaid self.)

What he actually suffers from in this muddle of splits and unrealities is his misguided compulsion to make the impossible happen: to convert the established, the past, into future *without the true participation of the living present*. Or without at least respecting its limitations; and his own, of course. It is the limitlessness of his intention that has him boxed in. – One is reminded of negative Aries, another one who never got there: though *his* 'displaced' future self was no more than an extravert's unrealised potential pursued in vain.

The world cannot and will not accommodate this one restricted model for existence he wants to impose, all in one go, and with nothing and nobody allowed to differ. It is the wrong 'shape' to receive him: square plug into round hole will not go without leaving some corners behind. But he keeps trying to fit without leaving anything behind – that 'place', his inner-self space, has been cancelled – and so he hangs suspended, neither here nor there. And yet the fact of his acting out his intentions among us is enough: he serves us as example. In an essentially perverted, denatured way he takes place without ever taking *his* place. He stays an outsider amid life.

Not only does he do damage to life with his unreal, split, presence but in the long run (always provided he survives the all-round violence he started) he robs his unreal self of all hope in life. Eagerly accepting his much-promising misrule – which only encourages us in our false, narrowly self-centred hopes – we are only a rabble of mutually destructive no-hopers who tear the future apart as we compete for it blindly, without acknowledging each other's equal claim to life.

Some Suggested Aquarius Attributes

basic

self-observant, detailed inner knowledge: of self and beyond,
inventive and **imaginative, makes discoveries**

**wrapped up in himself, aloof, self-sufficient, appears 'cold' and
uninterested, arrogant, condescending,** holds himself to be
'superior', **lacks respect**

despises the world, detached criticism; unconventional: i.e.
refuses to come together with others to co-operate, **always 'has
better ideas'; easily exasperated**

deliberately upsets the existing order: if and when things strike
him as wrong; **seen as sinister and threatening; abstruse,
bizarre, 'way-out'; may be taken for a genius or madman; radical, uncompromising approach; contrary; law-breaker, rebel**

abrupt inner changes: quantum leaps of inner becoming; **seen as
inconsistent, unpredictable, shocking**

impatient, curt, dismissive; confidence in his superiority or that
of his ideas (or inner perceptions, rather)

positive

sees it as no more than his job to improve the world: **determined
reformer, transformative impulse; non-conformist,** but
respects facts, limitations and necessity: **pragmatic, consistently rational; exhausting studies** in search of how to apply new
insights: **science and technology;** applies himself to (reform)
programmes and improvement **schedules**

given to periodic action/withdrawal into himself: **sudden
insights, unexpected actions, seen as erratic**

future-oriented: updates, substitutes, replaces, but always with
the meaningful integrity of the new order in mind; **progressive,
innovative, 'original' ideas, anti status quo,** actively works for
the **renewal** of his environment

**stands for subjective freedom, inner transformations, self-mas-
tery, independence, autonomy**

grants others equality, brotherhood: based on common, though
individually separate, development and common observance
of a law that unites (and is in that sense *truly* 'conventional');
internalised law; voluntary code of ethics

sees and goes beyond the natural order, e.g. invents artificial

('synthetic') systems; occultism; psychic; new social order; member of select 'society', exclusive clubs etc.: not because others are forcibly excluded but because they have to 'grow into' membership, earn the right to be included, work towards it: associated with professional unions

negative
imposing, overpowering, demanding; destructive, eradicates
uncompromising stance, fixed purpose; inflexible in himself, narrow in nature and outlook and insists on being himself in the world without any reference to others or life in general: self-centred; peculiar, quirky, eccentric; alien(ated), abnormal, 'perverted'; inorganic, artificial and, because inflexible: robotic
fanatic, narrow goal elevated to a specific Ideal: narrow idealist, utopian vision, unrealistically over-optimistic; (partly) suspended in a state of unreality, split between a vision of a set self and never-ending, futile, destructive activities, may be considered 'mad' or at his worst a 'psychopath' or 'sociopath'
very impatient, irritable, rude; sweeps all else aside; drastic, categorical, zealous, merciless; stays aloof and personally uninvolved
cold precision, calculated vandalism, systematic destruction of existing order
encourages others to disobey: foments rebellion, leads civil disorder, agitator, rabble rouser, becomes figurehead of a Cause, nominal leader
makes large claims and promises for the future, falsely predicts; persuasive, 'infectious': easily misleads others because he holds a strong appeal for their self-centred urges; raising false hopes, he is 'fatally' attractive; subversive, anarchic, licentious; divisive
despite being 'attractive' wants no others beside him: impossibly self-admiring, suspicious of rivals; comes to the conclusion he is threatened, cheated, outnumbered, inferior after all; 'paranoid'; perpetually disappointed, embittered, accusing; self-destructive behaviour: spoiling his own chances

THE
WATER SIGNS

CANCER

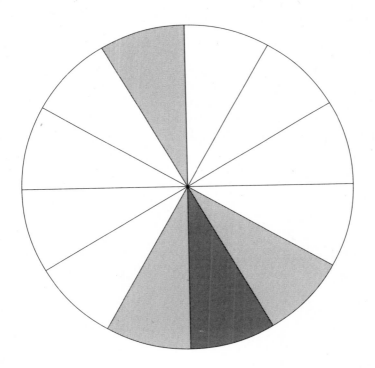

♋ **Introvert**
     **conscious function: feeling; directions of function: both
     inward and outward
     unconscious functions: ♑ thinking, ♊ sensation, ♌ intuition
     Water: emotional**

Like Capricorn, Cancer is an introvert whose conscious function
can go in both directions but turns inward first. (This is not only
the more obvious or 'comfortable' direction to take but also makes
sure that when such an introvert turns outward he has something
to bring with him into the world: without that his extraverting
could hardly serve any useful purpose.) Cancer is of a basic emotional nature and his conscious function too is feeling.
Introverting first of all, he has an entirely emotional experience of
his inner self, and also of the larger universe of what surpasses self
at the inner level.

Before going further, it will be necessary to have a closer look at
what it actually means to feel. Emotion is connected with structure in a way that is not at all obvious on the face of it. Feeling
flows. But it always flows *into* and thus assumes the 'shape' of
whatever it flows into. It attaches itself to structure by filling it in.
One might say it gets to know structure from the inside. –

This is quite unlike the processes of sensing and thinking which
both examine the structure of reality from the outside, as it were –
be it the inherent 'forms' of reality at the inner level, or the factual, actual structuredness of the material environment. It is also
unlike the intuitive process which flows *with*, which neither
'demands' nor assumes structure. Intuiting inner reality is a truly
fluid process that gets us to know everything as it is in its unstructured state. Both the thinking-about and the sensing-of inner reality, on the other hand, involve perceiving the inherent
structuredness of it: the bits, the parts that *might* be separate are
here experienced as distinct impressions, which are either sensed
in relative isolation ('relative' because all inner sensing would
appear to go hand in hand with the basic rational approach, viz.
Libra and Aquarius) or else are combined by thought into a (yet
more) structured system. –

When feeling is directed outward first (extravert, Pisces) it finds many discreet forms to pour into. But when it is directed inward first (introvert, Cancer) it flows in search of something to settle into, to contain it, and what it finds is the *sum total* of self. In this Cancer consciously settles, this is the inner 'shape' he assumes. He does not know himself piecemeal, like Capricorn, thought plus separate thought combined into a system of self-knowledge. He 'knows' himself as a whole, he feels himself to be whole. This is his personal inner world, his self all of a piece. It is a self-identification beyond rational comparison: one might say it amounts to an inner faith rather than an inner knowing in the sense that we tend to use that word.

But his feelings also flow out indefinitely beyond the personal inner self, and finding nothing more obviously structured and defined than the whole of it, again he settles for and in that: he is a whole securely embedded in All innerness, with no certain demarcation line. – To put it rather figuratively, he has his inner becoming through a kind of osmosis.

When Cancer now turns outward to contact the objective world, he experiences a feeling of personal differentness, alienness almost, when faced with the 'chopped-up' state of material, factual reality. It does not make sense to him with its perverse insistence on keeping everything separate, somehow categorised according to form. This arrangement of the world according to distinct material givens goes quite against the grain of his inner nature. It offends against his emotional awareness of a one-ness of being that ties in all potential separateness and divergence as a matter of course. He can feel no sense or meaning in this multitude of divorced, isolated details. How can he possibly apply his inner unity to a world made up of bits and pieces?

Feeling the world around him, he stands in danger of going to pieces himself: it is rather like trying to drive one large ball through a hundred small hoops – he feels helplessly lost to be landed with such an impossible task. He wonders whether there is something terribly wrong with him; he feels somehow not quite 'real'. And yet inside himself he feels complete and intact, which is more than can be said for what this outside world appears to be: from that point of view he feels *more* real than 'real'. He hardly knows how to present himself to the world, is he better or is he worse?

Capricorn, when he first started extraverting, began to set what he had thoughtfully inspected and assessed of self against what could be thoughtfully assessed out there. He compared himself with the world, and finding himself to differ, feared he would be outnumbered, derided for what he was, and simply not measure up. He hesitated, planned, rethought, cautiously advanced and then withdrew again with the proverbial cold feet. Cancer, too, can see he is somehow 'not made for this world', as he stands: he feels the difference – not in any detailed way and accompanied by prolonged deliberations – but in an emotional, all-inclusive way. He too fears the worst, one moment, but the next feels full confidence in himself again. He hesitates for a moment, perplexed, but then sees no concrete reason why he should not pour his feelings outward, in the faith that his inner completeness will find its place in the totality of the world.

But each time he is badly disappointed. He is for ever being cut down to size. He sees no reason why he should not fit, the world sees no reason either why he shouldn't – and then proceeds to try and destroy him: carve him up and distribute the pieces. Anything or anybody he approaches, to pour the whole of his feelings into, to have his total self accepted by, will prove too small to hold him, too particularised to accept all he is. The overspill, the rejected part of him, is like an amputation to him. Feeling wounded in his essentially whole self by the slightest sign of any rejection of even a tiny part of him (a 'part' *he* cannot recognise as such), he withdraws inside himself and immediately feels better. There was no damage done, after all. There never is any damage, but then why does it hurt so much, each time he has another go, his self-confidence renewed? He cannot understand it.

There is no constancy, no predictability about him. Emotional approach or openness, and emotional withdrawal or inaccessibility, follow each other in quick succession. One moment he appears unassailably confident and washes over us in a towering wave of feeling, the next he shrinks back unaccountably hurt, 'mortally' wounded, lamenting loudly. And then he is back again, nothing daunted. No one can make him out. He is so all-over-the-place overwhelming, it is enough to make one very uneasy, to say the least; and he is so touchy, one does not know how to handle him at all without him 'going to pieces'. He is a mystery to others just as the world is a mystery to him.

He is split right down the middle between his inner self-assurance and his outward fragility. It is the first, the only, internal structure he recognises about himself, these to irreconcilable halves he feels himself to have, after contacting his environment. Extraverting, one vain attempt after the other, is no longer just what he is by his nature obliged to do. It is now also his attempt to regain his initial, untroubled wholeness. That is why he willingly keeps trying, even if he takes longer and longer to recover inside himself after each painful experience. In the end, he feels, this will all prove to have been no more than a simple misunderstanding.

When he begins to make positive use of his unconscious functions, the first thing he needs to gain is a rational understanding of material reality ($\text{♑} \rightarrow$). Now he no longer experiences it as a puzzling collection of separate facts, things, happenings that he strongly feels 'should really' make an indiscriminate whole. He understands the principle of separateness as being a function of time. It strikes him as logically acceptable that each separate phenomenon should stand as a little whole complete in itself, for the duration, to be replaced as it were by the next separate unit to take (its) place (in time). And introspective thought ($\text{♑} \leftarrow$) tells him that in addition to being 'whole' he is indeed also made up of units: he is, potentially, internally structured. The one 'I' he feels himself to be is made up of many potentially separate emotional states that differ from each other in principle, and each has its moments when it will be welcome in the world and wholly acceptable, in itself.

Now he understands why when he tried to pour everything he was into the whole world at once, this automatically led to his being painfully fractured. The time had not yet come for some of what he was, or again the best time for it was already past, to come back at some later point. Each moment or situation allows only a specific part of his whole inner being to become into the world. And unless he learns to think carefully what of self to release into active living, life is going to go on throwing the unwanted surplus back at him to keep. If only he can adjust mentally to the idea that all he is will at *some* time be in demand – that there will be something like a specifically shaped opening for just that corresponding area of his self to fit into – then there will be no more occasion to experience rejection.

He accepts his task with a sober, pragmatic attitude. He appreciates the logic of having to delimit his emotional outpouring in order to respond to the changing demands of a flowing life. If life moves from one limited state to another, and back and forth between different states, then so must he add something of his own that is appropriate, and withdraw it again when the time for it is past. Flowing outward and back inward in such a controlled way, he is no longer subject to this irreconcilable split between a state of inner wholeness, well-being, complete faith in himself, and on the other hand a susceptibility to painful experiences, a feeling of complete insufficiency. He now realises that in fact he was being indiscriminately and intolerably *over*sufficient.

But his theoretical knowledge is not quite enough to keep him out of trouble. Assessing on a purely rational basis when and where there is an 'opening' or 'receptacle' for some of his feelings to flow into is rather a crude gauge. Knowing himself to be welcome in principle, in some part of his emotional being, still has him flooding the moment, the place, with feelings directed toward everything and everybody present. His timing is right, he has chosen the right feeling to release, in response to the demand or need of the moment, but his target is rather diffuse. He is acting on principle and the details of the situation escape him. Or to put it rather graphically: one person sobbing signals 'a sad situation' to him, but this does not mean the whole assembled company are standing ready to receive a wave of sympathy. Eager to avail himself of this outlet, or inlet, for a strand of his emotional self, and to put it to practical use here, he would wipe every nose in sight. Someone, dry-eyed and possibly smirking, is bound to object vigorously. And of course he is more hurt than ever to have his controlled efforts to be *sensibly* emotional rejected. Does this world really know what it wants from him?

He withdraws to deep inside his self, 'in a huff'. But by now it is an inner self that has been transformed. It is no longer only the one whole structureless 'I'. He knows, at least unconsciously, the difference between one part of 'I' and the other, and this means he can no longer find a simple solace in his obvious inner intactness. The damage to one or some of his feelings is no longer so easily brushed aside. He knows in which part of himself he has been hurt, and as a consequence he feels *inner* pain. He nurses these wounds that, before he could think about them, were simply non-existent to him. And despite the progress he has already made in coming to terms with the world, he feels less inclined now to try again.

It is only when he uses his unconscious capacity for sensing every detail of the situation and in what relation those details stand to each other (♊) that he can become truly 'sensitive' to the needs and demands of life: responsive, that it. He notices every nuance of facial expression, every murmur indicating a passing need (a 'gap' he may fill), and every first sign of change in his environment that tells him to exchange one response for another, or even to let be, because nothing is required from him at the moment – and he knows better by now than to try and fulfil a nonexistent demand!

He also cannot help but become aware of every misplaced object, every hole or toppling overload. More than any other sign he has been taught through painful personal experience about the too much and too little in life. And now when he observes his environment keenly for signs that his emotional involvement might be appropriate, he feels a need of his own: to apply himself to sorting out every deficiency or burden he notices. These things echo his own one-time predicament. It is not the deliberate fussi-ness of a Virgo (who has made up his mind what he wants to see, and if so where in his environment) that makes Cancer pick up, inspect and mend: it is the fellow feeling of a former reject that makes him retrieve things that have been discarded; and the sight of something broken reminds him of the pain of not being allowed to be in one piece. He is not fussy what he is surrounded by, as long as it is intact in the widest sense. – Things being what they are, he could tramp the world all day long mending and rescuing rejects. But again he comes up against a 'no'. His neighbour's gate may be hanging askew from its hinges, flaking, peeling, holed and splitting; but his neighbour likes it that way, and will Cancer please go away and mind his own business...

So far, being actively involved in life only in response to an intelligently assessed and clearly observed need, he has had no business of his own: everybody else's was his. The logical out-come would be for him to be peripatetic, travelling from demand to demand in order to have his becoming in the world, and leaving whenever the doors of momentary need closed on him again. But then he would find himself in cul-de-sacs all the time: denied entry to the world, having to mark time in exclusively inner being – till his environment had changed sufficiently to give him a new chance of responsive action. He would be no more than a convenient tool, used when he came in handy, and cast aside and ignored for the rest of the time. Again he would find himself split, a convenient thing shouted for now, and pushed roughly out of the way as inconvenient a moment later. He would spend half his life feeling painfully rejected.

He is doing all he can to adapt his 'flow', to tie in with life, where and when it asks him to flow, and in what way, and in what direction – but to have to put up with having himself as it were switched on and off by others, when he has just obligingly learnt to regulate his being in the world, that is asking too much. It is a rejection of all the efforts he has been making. Once again, he withdraws to nurse his wounds.

At this point his unconscious intuition comes to his aid (Ω), making him aware that he has a chance to create and rule a world of his own. There is no need to chase around after offers to let him be an active part of the life of others, in 'their' world. Instead he will set up his own sphere of influence where what he is is always potentially active. Need will have to come to him and ask to be fulfilled, rather than him going around begging to be needed. And neither will he be forced to respond to every demand under the sun. Establishing his own realm gives him the right to include or exclude, to choose whatever and whoever he is naturally most responsive to. The necessity to release his feelings in answer to prevailing outside conditions, once it is contained within a circle of his own making, enables him for the first time to practice a freer sort of self-expression. He can set the 'tone' of his environment. He can say: 'This is what can be expected from me by way of response', thus attracting what demands it suits him to fulfil, while repelling others.

A world of his own, under his rule, is not only an added guarantee against life's assaults on his vulnerable state of feeling-whole, or feeling-in-part-wholly-received-and-accepted, it is also the beginning of the reverse process of adaptation: *he* is now in charge of adapting *others* to him. Neither is it only the world that receives him, he is now also receiving the world into his established presence. He is both receptive and responsive at the same time, taking in and giving out as *he* sees fit. He is all of a piece at last, master of how he fits into the world, able himself to say that necessary word 'no'.

He receives and contains, and what he contains receives of his inner essence according to its need, but also according to what he himself feels moved to give. His knowledge of what, in the short term and in the long run, is desirable from a practical point of view, and his practical observation of how details need to be related and tied in if the result is to 'come together', these are considerations he will take into account before he decides to respond to something presented to him as a need. Not for nothing has he learnt to control himself and hold back where necessary. The power of being in charge of his 'own business' at last enables him not only to give, but also to withhold to the best of his abilities.

This is not quite unlike the balancing act Libra constantly performed when he staid half in and half out of the world, comparing his options for their relative merit, and then taking the sort of 'half-hearted' yet vigorous action that made sure he never got immersed to the point where he could no longer see things in perspective. Cancer needs to balance things too: necessary response to genuine need against necessary rejection of demands that go against all good sense and reason. But Cancer does not need to balance himself between worlds to do that. His balance – of pushing (some part of) his self into, or keeping it out of, the world – this is conditioned into him on pain of personal rejection if he makes a mistake. It is a matter of prior decision making with him. And decision taken, there is nothing to stop him extraverting 'wholeheartedly' in the appropriate manner, till he notices signs of change in the situation that might call for another decision to be taken. This ability of his to regulate his own activities now becomes his most valuable response. He precedes Libra as the teacher of self-control as such, of not taking every desire to merit a fulsome 'yes' from life. – But in his role of fulfiller he also supplies the experience of resting secure in the expectation that real need will always be met, without reservation of any kind.

Cancer does not, like Leo, want to rule the whole world. Like Capricorn, he has had to learn early to cut down on his self-expression. Capricorn came to adapt to his environment, which he found incompatible with what he was, by emotionally giving from out of his self and giving up, sacrificing (in objective terms) parts of his too strongly pre-formed self. Cancer, on the contrary, has had to learn to adapt to a seemingly hostile environment by restricting the 'giving' outflow of his whole previously unstructured emotional self: by controlling it, forming it and shaping it. When at last, intuitively, he establishes a 'kingdom' of his own, it is not a world-embracing one, but one that reflects both what he is inside himself, and what he has acquired in terms of the necessary self-restrictive behaviour. Establishing his own *restricted* realm, he becomes the centre of a new and carefully regulated world: one that can more easily incorporate his innermost value of *wholeness*, completeness, intactness.

Including and excluding in a (self-)controlled way, Cancer gains a material and social 'circle' to rule over, by giving and withholding, as needed. Any things or people that appear there not because he accepted them into it but because necessity, the ongoing life process, deposited them there, he assimilates into his personal environment with a mixture of adaptation on his part, and making *them* fit in with the rules laid down by *him*. The personal proficiency he has gained in adapting self to other, the subjective to the objective, he can pass on by example. But he is more than a master or teacher of how to adjust and adapt oneself to the given environment. He also demonstrates how to adjust one's environment to one's self, how to rule it and order it so it accords with and reflects one's inner nature, and how to keep adjusting it to reflect the changing states of inner being.

In his relationships he is incapable of considering subject and object apart. The subject is too much of an inner emotional reality to him to ever become a mere afterthought. He is always weighing the vast reality of the inner person against the restricted conditions of the physically, materially living person; this is what his own experience of life has taught him, and when he comes to establish his sphere of influence around him it becomes a cornerstone of his rule. – He never loses touch with his and all inner reality, whether thoughtfully dipping into it in search of what best to offer out of himself, or out of that wider fund of pure feeling that surpasses his own; or whether just to rest there, for a moment, emotionally entire, restored to his intrinsic integrity, and enveloped in a greater wholeness that renews his faith in what he is doing in the world.

His experience of subjective wholeness – which he has had to relinquish in *objective* terms, converting it into a 'timely' flow of bit by bit emotional becoming-into-the-world ('fitting in') – now at last has the chance of finding its objective counterpart. He makes it his job to adapt the various parts of his environment one to the other so as to bring about completion; fulfilment, but no more than adequate fullness. His inner wholeness becomes the basis of his rule: to give, to add; to take away what is too much or inappropriate, and to withhold, where necessary.

He supplies what is missing and removes the burden of something that might harm or threaten or somehow damage the 'health' of the whole. He matches object with object to arrive at an integrated environment: he gathers and completes, fills in gaps, cultivates, combines, re-adjusts, mends, cleans out and keeps in working order. He also matches object with subject, in other words fulfils another living being's subjective needs with both deed and substance: he feeds, supports and sustains, he nurtures with sympathy, nurses back to health, strengthens with encouragement, shelters from outside threats, denies access to what will do harm – as well as teaching the lessons of self-control and control of one's environment that will enable others less adept at these things to do likewise. Throughout all this he is 'creating' a viable whole in its own right – or one should rather say that he 'helps it to be', by actively responding to its being deficient, overburdened, maladjusted in itself or in relation to the environment. As a 'whole-maker' he is a different kind of creator.

Leo's creative act was to change other so as to yield an image of self. He found it to be an imperfect, partial mirror image. He 'created' first, and then he needed to learn to recognise his creation as the distinct and equal other that it was.

Cancer, for his part, receives the imperfect into his realm and brings it if not to perfection then at least to completion. Of halves he makes wholes, of fracturedness something integral, and of the inner reality and the objective life he makes an integrated process: equally expressing the self and being 'impressed' by the environment, in turns, in reciprocal adaptation. Unlike Leo, he automatically acknowledges the distinct completeness of other; he has, after all, worked hard at bringing it about.

Where Leo injected the images of his self, establishing a 'picture' of him in the world, Cancer projects his essential emotional wholeness (in thought-out form, over time), and establishes the process of gradual self-completion, or growth, in and into the world.

The sign Cancer with its gift of measured, responsive becoming precedes Leo's wilful attempts at bursting onto the scene as all he senses himself to be. Learning how to *grow* into objectively being self precedes *being* that self pure and simple. For an equally good reason Cancer follows on from Gemini: Gemini who found all of his self projected in a million 'equal' pieces onto the screen of his environment and sought, unconsciously, to combine them this way and that into some kind of oneness of being. In the wake of these never-ending attempts to come together Cancer introduces the full conscious recognition of the wholeness of the inner reality, to aid us in the process of growth towards the one self. Cancer is the linchpin in the development from expressing our selves anyhow, to standing in the world as one unique self – among others.

Ultimately what Cancer teaches us is the crucial trick of how to 'become', indispensable to this business of living. How to stay whole by keeping within the shelter of innerness what cannot find its place in the world; but also the obverse lesson of how to establish, of right, our own, objective, 'sheltering' environment into which the inner content may, appropriately, be freely released. How to be a whole within a larger wholeness; with mutually adaptive response as the mediator on the common boundary, making it negotiable. These are the 'cells' within the body of life. How to become such viable cells is Cancer's task to show us. Gemini has laid the foundation for all this equable multipleness. And Cancer fulfils it with aware inner being, and with response to the inner being of others (whether theirs is aware or not), fostering our inner growth toward self-awareness as much as our outward growth to completion. Gemini's neighbourhood of separate though connected houses becomes through Cancer the society of homes or families, units that have their own internal character and structure.

Cancer shows us how our inner potential for structure needs to be activated before our inner content can be released outward into a suitable 'container': thus the child is trained, in-formed in the proper give and take of self-control, and control of his environment, and is then ready to be released into a section of society suitable to his nature. – And before that, the foetus was formed in the restricted environment of the womb, to be born into the family... and before that again, each body cell replicated by using this same device of passing on the information of its inner content to a suitable aggregate of matter – though to start the whole process off, it needed the introjection into the system of some 'foreign material', the self itself.

This is Leo's contribution, the hidden inner image seeking its embodiment in life; spirit in search of form, in order not just to become, but to be at all, awarely. The new intention, Leo, meets with response: Cancer. Response shapes this 'new' intention as much as being shaped by it, adapting it for life in an 'old world'. In this way the old world is renewed and the new being matured at the same time.

Giving (sustenance, protection, help etc.), demanding (that the other person adapt to *his* environment) and teaching by example (how to adapt one's environment to one's own inner nature), are the steps by which Cancer produces an independent 'replica' of himself. Not a mirror image of what he is in himself, but another passively adapted and actively adapting person, a viable subjective-objective whole. His initially so awkward integrity has born fruit after all.

If Cancer uses the same unconscious processes negatively, the first trap he falls into is to let his ordering, principled and strictly pragmatic thinking ($\text{♑}\rightarrow$) become a compulsive force that propels all of him outward, to pour into the structured world. There is then nothing left of him inside him. He has in effect 'gone to pieces' but, no longer aware of an *inner* wholeness, he now recognises only an objective wholeness: he has become personally identified with the world order as it stands, the sum total of it, with everything in its 'proper' place. And his new-found unconsciously rational approach to his self ($\text{♑}\leftarrow$) tells him that, in fact, he is the embodiment of the logical rules this world has to obey.

He becomes strongly defensive of all manner of rational and practical arrangements, on principle. He supports every rule there is, casting his vote in his own favour, in effect. Expediency and obviously 'sensible' solutions are of the essence to him. The whole logical scaffolding that appears to hold the world order in place is to him, personally, what holds him together, and the more concrete and reductionist the prevailing mental attitudes, the more rigid the practice of life, the more narrowed down the options, the more 'together' he feels. Anything at all new or different, or simply not accounted for by the existing order as he has found it, is an attack on his personal integrity and makes him feel that he is going to come apart: as if some rather inexplicable force were snatching at the (of course quite unmentionable) bits and pieces that make up his *whole* 'body'. A thought he cannot really entertain, and yet he has to bear it in mind to guard against such attacks on his treasured intactness, which is all that really interests him.

But the wholesale principles he favours cannot possibly be observed every moment of the day in every single detail. Even the most rigidly formalised world needs a more pliable sub-structure. This keeps causing him great offence and pain. And where is he to go when he feels his integrity under attack? He can't nurse his feelings and find himself intact again inside himself: that place is no longer available to him, he has shut himself out. His compulsively rational grasp of all things mundane is standing between him and his former true inner self, eclipsing it.

If disorder breaks out around him then he will cast his gaze uselessly upward in search of a refuge 'beyond'. In despair, he covers his eyes altogether, and makes a lot of emotive noise: asserting that we are torturing him, letting us now that with our unwholesome behaviour we are causing him to break down into a horribly piecemeal state (a 'self-contradictory' variety, which he wishes to know nothing about). We had better quickly tidy up, behave ourselves, mend our differences – to make him whole again.

But if the really unprecedented dares to happen, a disaster that threatens to rend his world-embedded self clean apart, then the only refuge he can think to find is in the total unconsciousness of a dead faint. This is not exactly like finding a whole-some innerness either (any more than Sagittarius' head-in-the-sand depression made the world's problems go away; or Capricorn's sinking numbly into the ground under the weight of his rejected self enabled him to persuade the world to take him off his own back) but this is Cancer's equivalent reaction. Needing to be whole at all times, he has recourse to the most drastic rejection of a world splintering before his eyes that will make him intact again. Complete absence, something rather like sleep, is his only refuge now. And as it is needed in a hurry, he 'mock-sleeps' in a hurry: he simply keels over at the sight of any kind of 'destruction' – which is always essentially his own.

The alarm and sympathy this sparks off may even have restored order by the time he comes back from his no-man's land asking where on earth (or maybe not on earth?) he is. That black and shapeless and dreamless region he visited does have something in common with Aquarius' pure dream world with its 'impossible' images, in that it is also neither here nor there. – But he cannot very well black out every time he finds the principles he clings to with so much feeling suddenly flaunted, or he would be gracing the floor all the time with his mock-absence from the world. Neither does taking to his bed on a permanent basis prove an answer.

Who can sleep with all this anxiety? Surrounded by untold nameless threats to his well-being *out there*, his bedroom door is never closed: his identity lies embedded in the whole world, after all. A frenzied panic keeps seizing hold of him; but apart from being restlessly alert he can do nothing to rid himself of this illogical, indescribable pain without apparent cause. A pain that feels real enough and yet defies logical definition. There is no getting away from it for him: how can he realistically hide away anywhere, 'being the whole concrete world' – short of giving up on his insufferable self together? He has to carry his pain wherever he goes.

If negative Sagittarius kept 'getting depressed' and then jumped out of his hiding hole for another manic try, negative Cancer manages to be both 'depressed' by his apparently hopeless plight – requiring rest and solitude to nurse this ever multiplying host of mystery diseases – and frantically involved in all around him at the same time. Rest is out of the question: he needs to monitor the world, no matter how unwell it makes him feel; he needs to patrol it, no matter how anxious he gets in the process. And of course the more he keeps checking-just-to-make-sure, the more he finds to suffer from, till life is nothing but a torment. There must be a solution to the puzzle of it all, though he can't think of one – he is too busy thinking of himself as being everything that is sensible, orderly, pragmatic, proved, stably established...

Using his unconscious ability to sense the world's fine detail and inbuilt coherence (♊) might just teach him to enjoy, relax and make do for five minutes (while the worst of 'his' current disorder is quickly sorted out, mended and tidied up, and relative order is restored), but he does not see it that way at all. He lets himself get obsessed with every detail instead, needing to know the ins and outs of everything, every snippet of (usually shocking) information, a step by step and blow by blow account of every single transaction: he cannot stay out of any of it. This is his new, improved way of checking and double-checking that the world is not letting him down, that everything is as it should, in theory, be. Inevitably it isn't, and while hitting the floor in one go was his answer to grand principles being infringed, now these rather more small-scale injuries he observes happening to his whole embodied self make him break up, or down, bit by bit. An improvement in that regard, but now he is rushing around in a worse frenzy than ever, trying in vain to hang together, things and reason and feelings spilling all over.

He is constantly being wrecked, though now only a small bit at a time, and when for once he isn't in a state of disjointedness, then he is peering about him in fearful anticipation of his next partial disintegration. To say he worries does not begin to describe it. Negative Virgo hunted out horrors in order to rout them, having his 'becoming' in that. What Cancer is doing here is to inspect the world avidly for signs of (his) wholeness and 'health', even though it is a foregone conclusion that all he will find is another shock to his system. Up and down like a yoyo, letting himself be torn apart and needing to be soothed and nursed back together, he has his 'becoming' in *that*, for the time being.

He looks, not for trouble but quite the opposite, but trouble is what he invariably manages to find because his reaction to what he sees around him is always one of 'No, how dreadful!' – or as near always as makes no difference. Instead of playing possum on the floor he now runs around in guard dog-like circles, quite debilitated by his querulous pursuit of what will do him no good at all: his constant rejection of what is in effect his own self – poured into and set in the mould of his environment. He has fitted himself into the world by force, pouring into it without permission, and now he finds fault with it all. It defies all logic how he can *be* (for which read, identified with) the very structure of the world and yet it keeps springing nasty surprises on him. But then he is suffering from a misunderstanding which amounts to an illusion: he identifies his self as the established structure of the world, the forms he sees around him, he takes himself to *be* them; but in fact, he is not the forms but their 'content': he has emotionally filled them from the inside, poured all his feelings into them.

The living shape of the world changes without any reference to him whatsoever, stretching him and squeezing him, and plucking him apart. He suffers growing pains and the effects of shrinkage, and various indignities that feel so peculiar they defy a sober description, but still he thinks of himself as entirely in command of the world order, as its (needless to say good) 'form' and strictly laid down rules of behaviour. Life goes on all around him and he never notices, except to hurt unaccountably from its effects. As far as he is concerned, he knows of no other called life.

Absurdly, he can think of no one to blame for his predicaments but himself. It needs some intricate reasoning on his part before he can convince even himself that the blame lies somewhere outside him – when there is no 'outside him'. His rationalistic tangles involve so much detailed would-be working out of the situation that in the end no one knows what he is talking about any more, and he ends up splitting hairs... which does nothing at all for his emotional distress: he has only chopped himself into yet finer pieces and needs to start all over again. – Shutting him up is maybe easiest done by going away. Only then one will be missed. He comes running after, still in full rational spate, to retrieve this piece of him that he can neither be without nor stop criticising for its defects and disobedience. Life is not coming together for him at all – hardly surprising when on the one hand he does not recognise it as such, while on the other he fancies himself in control of it.

Availing himself of the full misuse of his intuitive function (Ω) does at last give him some of the control he needs, including self-control. There is no stopping him now; intuiting his limitless potential for making the world conform to his every whim gives him more than enough will power to transform himself: he has been the poor puzzled victim long enough, time he was boss. – The world being full of invisible spooks that yank him by the arms and legs to make him hurt (in unaware response to life's growing and changing), the first thing he does is to reduce the size of his environment drastically. If he can convince himself that he is leaving all those 'weird' things out, and only enclosing his 'proper' self within the tight circle of his established iron rule, then he need not worry about anything missing (from his 'whole' self). In consequence, the larger body of the world is discounted. He becomes something like a single cell within it that nevertheless lays claim to being all there is and the validity of all else is argued away, till there is not a good hair left on all that phantom otherness.

One is strongly reminded of negative Libra overbalancing into full active life without a reservation left, and ending up imprisoned by his wholesale rejection of all that did not please him. Cancer too has lost his balance of true response: the thoughtful yes that would have fitted him properly into the world, and the no that would have made sure he stayed out of where he had no business to be. He has said a resounding initial yes to all of life, followed by endless oh no's. (The nearest comparison might be someone forcing his foot into an ill-fitting shoe and hobbling along complaining that his foot is, mysteriously, hurting him.) Reducing his painful world to a more manageable size, declaring all else unlawful and hence not part of 'his' world, he boxes himself in quite as neatly as Libra.

But where Libra imposed nothing more than visions that one *could* safely ignore – and be banished – Cancer makes no bones about being king of his castle. He lays down the rules that keep all the doors and windows shut, trapping us in the narrow confines of his severely administered realm. And it is not only a very small world he rules, but a very small self that rules it.

He emotionally filled the whole world. Now he refuses to acknowledge all of it, in order to control what he can of it. Of course the world he does not want to know about is still out there – but so is the greater part of his self. (Something like cutting off the toe of flesh and bone at the same time as that of the badly behaved shoe.) He gains control of his world and his self only through the device of ignoring most of both. This 'pulling himself together' act is an illusion; he has only disowned the more unruly, unmanageable, parts of him. And for fear that they might come and visit him, and claim some far-flung kinship with him, he keeps the doors locked against all outsiders.

He could almost relax now, secure in the knowledge that what few feelings he has left to him in his impoverished emotional state are free to be what they are in the few forms he has adopted (as the 'proper', and inevitably least alive, ones). Set in his meagre mould he would be all but dead, though. So far he has had his 'becoming' in his all-embracing quarrel with a life that was always painfully reshaping him. Now that he has firmly established a reduced self in a reduced environment and is at last in command, nothing at all happens in his life any more. Like negative Virgo, he cannot live without his struggle against life. He needs something to try and upset him, something to quell. Unless he has also trapped some living-others in his personal prison/castle, he needs to enlarge his sphere again till he finds himself a source of becoming: someone to say no to with a triumphant expression.

He is simply impossible to please, it seems. It does not matter what one says, he knows better, and if one agrees with him for the sake of peace and quiet then he will find fault with that as well. He demands absolute obedience, an eagle eye open for the smallest wrong move, but if we simply passively obey him, then he is complaining that we are sulking/must have a bad conscience/are hiding something from him. It is no good trying to withhold life from him; he demands his daily, hourly, little fight and he will think up the unlikeliest reasons to provoke it.

Aries fought, even to the death, the enemies that competed with him for the life/world/self he would claim for his own. But it would not have occurred to him to provoke a fight when all was quiet and going well. Cancer fights habitually, on a smaller scale, carefully keeping the argument simmering away, turning the heat up and down as required: just enough to give him something to *become* master of. He has put himself in charge of the tap of life; he lets only that amount of it attack him that he can cope with trouncing.

He has turned his situation neatly back to front. He is no longer passively receiving injuries to his whole, set self. With the select remnants of his former self securely 'corseted' and ensconced in his embattled corner of the world, he is now nudging and needling, waiting for a chance to put the boot in. Any living response that rears its head is slapped down with the greatest satisfaction. This is the life. He eagerly waits for the next round. To disappoint him with obedience is just as futile as trying to disobey him.

Life under his rule is repetitive to say the least. He is an entrenched traditionalist, custom is all, habit even better, and feelings are reduced to the emotional equivalent of set answers. Even the constant disturbances he stages, with carefully regulated theatrical effect, are entirely predictable. We could pack our bags and tell him we have had enough of having the life squeezed out of us in dollops that suit his capacity to cope with it – but there are strings attached that hold us back.

Compulsively he 'gives' his all into the outward forms of life. These outward forms that he 'inhabits' and directs from inside (to make them behave and be good – but not so good as to seize up altogether) that is us. But he does not recognise us as other. We are only a 'skin' to him that keeps him intact and together, cradling him with the controlled to and fro of our few independent movements and thus keeping him alive. He cannot possibly grant us an inner life of our own: *he* is our inner life, all inner life there is – though perversely he does not see it like that at all because he does not know himself any more for what he essentially is, or once was. He has turned his back on all inner reality. He thinks neither of himself nor us as being anything like 'subjective', that is only a silly idea to him, without substance. Form is all, and he gives it all he has got. This may not be much exactly in terms of variety, but he gives it so gushingly, forcefully, overpoweringly, it would be hard to say no.

Wen he is not egging us on to be quarrelled with, he is piling our plate high with what is 'good for us', with happiness written all over him to see us eat. He has us fed to bursting point, clothed to stifle, tucked under layers of blankets till we think we are roasting in hell, all with the emotional intensity of the blackmailer within us. Of course we need what he gives us, though less of it would do, an occasional change would be a great relief, and our personal preferences are of course never consulted. He does it all for us, and more besides, and while on the one hand we are fed up, on the other it saves us a lot of bother. He bickers about the little bit of a mess we make, but at least he cleans it up. He provides too much of the wrong things, but at least he provides. And when it comes to facing the outside world that he has managed to alienate us from, the untidy, dangerous chaos out there, then he is not a bad force to be hiding behind: hurling stilted insults and shaking a mighty fist at the nameless 'them', before he quickly locks and bolts the door with as much of a regal air as he can muster.

We pay a price, of course, you get nothing from him for free.

Refusing to eat up is not on, he will make us. If stern lectures fail to have an effect, and his threats get him nowhere, he falls back on his earlier, involuntary methods, now under his control. He wrings his hands dramatically to demonstrate the pain we cause him and sheds what he thinks an appropriate measure of tears. If we are too stubbornly ungrateful altogether he offers to feel faint. We will make him ill yet if we don't comply. He plays on the emotions he does not realise *we* have, till we hardly know ourselves what to feel. Sated and protected, we prefer the devil we know to the unknown evils 'out there' and the drudgery of catering for our own basic needs. He nurtures our resentment. He clothes us in a straight-jacket of conformity. But he is after all doing his best. He smothers us in lashings of uninvited, boringly repetitive emotion when we are least in the mood for it, but it feels good all the same to have so much attention invested in us: we *matter*. He means so well, he threatens so badly – it makes us feel rotten to let him down. So we unpack our bags again and stay.

All is well again, the latest invigorating crisis conquered and tidied away. But there is always that knock on the door. He may think that he feels a hundred per cent secure in his lair, and he may be quite capable of breathing a bit of stage-managed fire from the doorstep to keep them-out-there at bay. But the way he barricades himself, and makes strenuous efforts to control everything and everybody within his keep, rather belies his show of self-confidence. He slaps us hard on the back to force us to adopt a self-controlled and properly upright posture, but when there is a *real* crisis he is the first to buckle at the knees. What is more, he sees crises where all we see is a bit of harmless outside world intruding. We are all for it, but not he. When something *really* happens to him, something he has not pricked and nettled into happening a bit, we soon know all about it.

He has withdrawn the force of his attention from all that out there, and lavished it only on what he wanted to know of world and self. When those presumed dead and gone parts of his life/self force an entry through or past his defences, when he cannot shield his eyes and ignore them, however hard he tries, he is in effect swamped by feelings he no longer knew he had. And he has no kind of control over them. It is a spectacle that leaves his usual, deliberate, formal display of feelings (no matter how wrought-up, to tug at our heart strings) looking very pale in comparison. It is an alarming sight. Unable to accept these errant feelings *into* himself and keep them there for appropriate release whenever the time might suit, he gives them over into form and substance there and then: he acts them out. They have him staggering and flailing his arms, screeching and guffawing in turns, using bad language such as one has never heard from him, and all the coarsest, quite 'improper' sort of behaviour is suddenly second nature to him.

When this inburst-outburst is over, what can he do but falsely claim that he was 'not himself' while it lasted. Something possessed him, he says. The truth is, something *re*-possessed him: the parts of his self that were too much for him to manage in their inappropriately concretised form. He cannot own any of these, he has lost the inner space to own them in. He blames his shameful behaviour on weird, non-existent beings. But they are no more and no less than the ghosts and ghouls of his (parallel, so to speak) shadowy and unaware existence outside his protective bubble of reduced self-awareness.

He has lost his integrity altogether. There are two of him at all times. Curtains drawn, he shows us the one face only, whether wreathed in smiles or putting on a measured frown – but all the time there is also that thing out there in the dark, his other face. And he has not only split off large parts of his self, but what self he has left is denatured. His feelings never flow in response as they naturally should: released and re-absorbed in turns. Instead, they sit like something solid in the cupboard, to be rationed out to us in slices, dressed in sweet or sour guise, whichever he *thinks* to be best. He will shed dry tears if he considers them good form, and laugh a narrowly substantial laugh with not a spark of humour in it, purely for the sake of appearances.

But what *he* considers proper self-control displays its downside only too frequently. His tyranny, like all of his much rehearsed behaviour, never wavers... breaks down completely... congeals again to be no different from what it was. He is constantly demanding that we display the virtues of a quiet, decent, orderly, well-behaved 'response' to life, but he is the first, and most often the only one, to lose his composure: who can take him seriously? There is no kind of continuity between his regimental ministrations and his abysmal, self-indulgent sulks and flaps and emotional explosions, or implosion. There is no rhyme or reason to him. In the end one is torn between feeling sorry for him and having to banish the black resentment he fosters.

Like negative Capricorn he robs us of our inner life, and with quite as much guile. Capricorn promised to rid us of our bothersome conscience and got us to do his work for him, putting his principles into practice so that he could become the whole world. Cancer does our work for us and asks us in return to banish our inner feelings on principle: there *can* be no subjective reasons for disobedience, sudden unscheduled responses, tears for no objective reason. And having talked and blackmailed us into feeling empty inside, he then provokes us into independent 'selfish' little outbursts: to have them for his life, his becoming master of the situation. He makes a rigidly formed object of most of our inner-life, and lets the rest of it lurk in its dark recesses, to tap for a small injection of life into his dead-set system. What Leo should provide, Cancer is here helping himself to, in search of control of the *whole* of the life process.

The wholeness that has always been uppermost in his mind, and which he first pursued and then imposed, with narrowed down emotional intensity: this fully embodied wholeness now proves to be a fracture that cuts world, self and life into two unnatural halves. There is the self that is unilaterally, monstrously, 'adapted'; an artificially emotive thing. And a phantom self that is locked out of our 'real' lives to inhabit a twilight zone that is fully of this world, but not illumined by our consciousness. There is the life that is a dehumanised set-pattern process, which deserves to be called neither life nor process. And a hidden life, lost into the exile of our first compulsive world-inhabiting, where we now keep it for the most part at arm's length and disowned, fearful of its 'inappropriate' shape and overwhelming size – though 'for a bit of the life' we may well sneak the odd indulgence. There is the world that is utterly controlled, down to the deliberate planning even of the 'misbehaviour'. And a world that lacks control altogether, black chaos: the only reason, actually, why the other, formalised, world has not long stopped quietly ticking over.

Negative Cancer turns us into obedient carbon copies, but they are only half the story. If they weren't he would soon have no life left from us. The only growth he has fostered so far is his own: from fragile sufferer to punishing master. Absurdly, to achieve it he had to divide himself against himself.

What he tries to cultivate in the world will never truly grow, only get bigger and spread further. Supposing the life in his personal self-protective bubble dries up. Supposing we really do pack our bags and go, or rebel enough to keep some new-found inner peace, or else break under his rule altogether: no more sparks to fly. He might try quarrelling with his mirror image instead, but really only if he can get it to look somehow 'strange' to him! More likely he will immediately turn outward, enlarging his sphere of influence. He knocks at the nearest neighbouring doors, complaining, meddling, provoking, informing everyone that there are principles, rules, laws to obey: his. If he keeps it up long enough he will exhaust that 'life supply' too. And set off yet farther afield from his already enlarged, if structurally ever same, prison cell.

Out there, he would maintain, is only empty space, nothing that really counts. He does not recognise any of this 'other' that contains his 'other self' as well (all those parts of his self that he had only too firmly invested in the world, and then cut himself off from, disowned, as too painfully uncontrollable). He thinks he is the totality of the world, the form, the knowledge, the principle of it; and now he spreads into 'empty' space unconcerned, in search of some *life* to make his own. – Slowly but surely he kills the world that is his host. He kills it by replacing its live content with his own formalised, dead, 'content' – what is alive about him is always happening 'outside' him. With his absolutist pretensions, he is casting himself in the role of Life, performing a cruel mockery of it: in search of its own responsive becoming, its future, this 'Life' is consuming life. Or to put it another way, his set, narrowly programmed self is gradually eating up all else there is of him.

Negative Leo might kill off his world of too-perfect carbon copies piecemeal, on a cyclical basis. Or else he was killed by them first – in which case they were left, to carry on his madness ad infinitum, immortalising him in this reality. Negative Cancer ultimately kills off all of world and self in a slow, inexorable process that leaves nothing at all alive behind, after the last struggle between the controlled and the uncontrolled. When he has finally mastered life completely, it and he will be dead. He fights only himself, really, but he does it inside us. He is our greatest enemy, because though we notice him there, we never really know who he is.

302 A Psychological Zodiac

Some Suggested Cancer Attributes

basic

deeply emotional; feeling of inner wholeness; faith in self: emotional self-confidence; emotional outpouring that appears exaggerated, mixed-up, too much: **over-emotional; overly giving, swamping**

feels lost and alien in the world, **puzzled; feels rejected, can't take criticism or indifference, always looking for acceptance; very easily hurt; easily panicked, shocked, disappointed**

withdraws into a 'shell', appears to be **'sulking'** there; deaf to appeals: **unresponsive, ungiving,** won't 'give': **inert, unbudgeable; apparently secretive**

seems to make no sense, **seen as irrational, mysterious; unpredictable; alternates** apparently arbitrarily between effusiveness and withdrawnness, hence seen as **'moody';** a **puzzle to himself** never sure of his worth since he **keeps losing his integrity in the world**

not much courage, but keeps trying because he **feels divided** between approach and withdrawal but has an **underlying expectation of wholeness,** in the widest sense: **nostalgic:** emotionally looks back to a more 'wholesome past'

positive

becomes **adapted** to the specific demands of life; controlled emotional flow: **self-control, due to rational insight into self; responsive; sensitive; sympathises** with what is rejected or somehow not 'whole'

adopts, rescues, mends, restores; relieves others of burdens; can be seen as interfering because he is always **'concerned'**

trying to fit in; tends to need approval of his efforts, stands in danger of being exploitable, but if he lets himself be used he is offended, primarily, by finding himself dismantled and *used-in-part:* **inner pain** a constant threat

establishes a **restricted sphere of influence:** e.g. **home-maker, gathering point, focus of his own social etc. circle; receptive, contains; deliberately inclusive/exclusive,** but also **assimilates** of necessity

yes/no decisions: regulated response of giving-out or withholding-within; **reciprocal adaptation**

teacher of self-control: **instructs, supervises; mothers; restricts;** also teaches control of environment: **encourages, trains, gives 'moral support'**

brings together objects and subjects in need of each other: **completes, fulfils, makes whole: nurtures, cultivates, helps grow**

keeps whole: protects, shields, shelters; defends; maintains, sustains

restores wholeness: readjusts; restores order and peace; nurses; unburdens

teaches how to become (adapted to and an adapter of one's environment), hence an **initiator** of independent processes that are rooted in primary wholeness or health, **founder**

as a whole within a whole he is a 'cell': member of family, clan, society: **sociable** (though not indiscriminately so and within premeditated limits); has **respect** for the integrity of others and anything integral, hence: **upholder of 'healthy' traditions and custom, loyal** in relationships and allegiance

negative

formalistic, narrowly logistic, emotionally needs world and self to be whole, so refuses to analyse properly: **superficial reasoning; compulsive hair splitting** without wanting to know the result

adopts the structure of the world wholesale for his own, rather than adapt to it: **uninventive, copies, obedient;** but secretly feels a misfit: always **feeling uneasy, embarrassed**

he is a **stickler for rules, accepts existing tradition,** keeps to the **narrow, set order; defensive against changes** of any kind; **clinging, can't part with; hoards; security-conscious**

suspicious, ever-watchful; can't relax, restless; inquisitive; demands to know everything even though it hurts him: **querulous, petulant**

worries, generally fearful, 'illogical' anxieties; may be labelled 'neurotic'; hypochondriac; insomniac; may be described as **'feverishly depressed', may doubt his own reason; may be labelled mad; may feel suicidal**

automatically hurt by life, always **'going to pieces', feels in the grip of an unkind world; sorry for himself, complaining; suffers from apparently imaginary ills; highly shockable, easily faints, breaks down; 'makes a fuss'; generally debilitated by**

life; no (self-)control

strenuously 'sensible' and unresponsive, rigidified, but easily unbalanced

never aware of all he is: **evades detailed self-knowledge; refuses to own all of his self;** views some of his self as outside him: **believes in 'spooks', inexplicable forces, superstitious** on account of split-off parts of his self; **divides himself:** 'locks out' what he finds unmanageable; progressive **narrowing of outlook and emotion; illusory self(-restriction);** ultimately **at war with himself; loss of integrity; (clandestine) self-indulgence**

unaccepting, defensive; embattled; keeps out outsiders: small but all-important social circle: **tightly possessive, clannish, xenophobic; repetitive, creature of habit**

inability to cope with the unexpected; 'hysterical' reactions: when all he tries to debar from being part of his self 'reclaims' him, but he **may claim to be 'possessed';** seen as **self contradictory** and harbouring a **hidden chaos underneath his composure**

as a ruler of his own domain he is **strict, demanding obedience, commandeering, insists on 'good form' and 'decency'** etc.; **punishing, needs to slap others down and triumph** over them

impossible to please, argumentative and **quarrelsome:** demands to be fought with a bit, just enough to enliven his existence, **indirectly provocative** (though not *inadvertently* so)

as a provider he **smothers others with unwanted attention,** insensitive to actual need; **stifles others' independent life, no respect for (the subjective factor in) life; emotional blackmail, deliberate theatrical 'scenes'; falsely emotive:** in calculated ways; **artificial 'front';** an empty shell, seen as **'heartless'**

may be **invasive, meddling, take-over bid, overpowering, crushing, life-threatening**

♏ SCORPIO

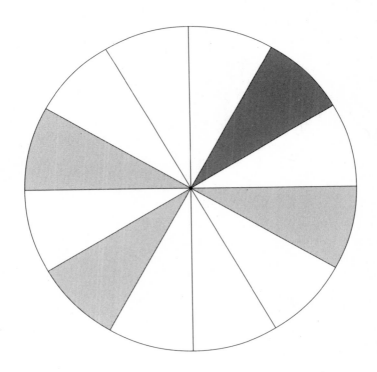

♏ **Extravert**
conscious function: intuition; direction of function: inward
unconscious functions: ♉ sensation, ♍ thinking, ♓ feeling
Water: emotional

As an introverting extravert Scorpio is in the same position as Libra: caught up in an inner-plane awareness of something universal that has nothing to do with his self-identification, except to supply him with a 'background', an impersonal history so to speak, that forms the basis of all he subsequently does. Like Libra he needs the demands of life to 'pull him round' to face the other way, before he can begin to extravert from that basis.

For Libra this impersonal Inner Reality was something he sensed rationally, both in detail and also in the way it connected to make an integral whole: he saw intelligently the whole tapestry of interconnected models of life-to-be. Scorpio is unique among the signs in that he combines the Fire of intuition – his conscious function – with the Water of feeling, his basic emotional nature.

With his conscious intuitive function turned inward, he 'travels' like Sagittarius throughout the whole of an unstructured inner reality; more easily if anything, because there is no dividing line for him between what is inner self and what lies beyond it: it is all equally impersonal to him. But his basic emotional nature demands from him that he find something structured to become 'attached' to by flowing into it. This cannot be the *whole* of Inner Reality, as it was for Cancer. Cancer's conscious feeling function 'settled' him in the structural whole of his inner self, within the larger whole beyond. Scorpio's conscious intuitive function, though, keeps him 'on the move'.

This has the effect that on his constant travels through all of the transcendent reality, again and again he 'feels moved to stop', to let what he encounters on the way become an emotional (if not *personally* so) reality to him. His unending fiery-fluid progress is constantly being arrested by this basic urge to flow into something defined. To use a comparison, if one pictures intuition alone as moving like the wind, and emotion alone as either standing as a settled body of water or flowing to fill a 'body', a structure, then the combination of intuition and a basic emotional disposition makes Scorpio proceed in something like the manner of bird or bee. He is always being arrested in mid-flight by the urge to settle, and then again consciously driven to uproot himself.

In this way, like Libra, he too gets to know the many life-models on the Inner Plane. But he does not sense them intelligently: he becomes emotionally attached to them one by one even as he is intuitively aware of all of them. One can picture him as revisiting them, on his timeless travels, and forming a deep (impersonal) attachment with them, individually, through renewed acquaintance.

In sum then, Libra starts out with something rationally seen – and then rationally sees the world: ending up comparing the two realities in detail. Scorpio, on the other hand, starts out being intuitively aware of the sum total of the Life Plan and emotionally attached to it in every detail. When he allows the demands of objective life to turn his attention outward, he is not in a position to critically compare what he already 'knows' of life's potential perfection with what he becomes aware of out there. He does not hover on the threshold of involvement and criticise, and wonder whether. Conscious intuition extraverting pulls him right into life: the urge to settle in it, bit after bit, is strong – but having done that, or started to do it, he *then* finds his critical voice, so to speak. And like Libra he is disappointed in his expectations, affronted on behalf of what 'ought' to be but does not seem to find its corresponding material expression here.

He is just as puzzled as Sagittarius by the structuredness and limitations of the world; he has a similar experience to Cancer's of things being ill-fitting; and he has the same reaction of 'Not good enough' as Libra. All in all it strikes him that he has been lured into the world under false pretences. This, after all, is the stuff that his self is about to be made of. Unable to do otherwise, he rejects it out of hand, he is deeply convinced it cannot be right. And as he has *not* taken a critical look and been stopped in his tracks as it were, but has moved right in, he does his rejecting right here, on the very spot – and not just in a mental sort of way, at one remove.

Aquarius was bad enough, upending things and telling us he had a much better idea, a pretty strange one at that. Scorpio throws everything right out by the window, without explanation. Without a clear idea what exactly he finds offensive about it, or what exactly to offer as a substitute. All he can say, with fiery-emotional conviction, is that this will not do. Nor that, or *that* – he proceeds to discard one thing after the other, clearing out the whole room with no more pause than is required for coming to grips with things, and never mind what goes to pieces. All this time he is searching for something that will meet his inner, prior demands. But even if he does find something, for a moment, that seems to touch a chord, he is soon off again to continue his destructive progress.

He finds himself propelled into the world, but he cannot find a satisfactory self in it. Intuitively he expects to have the whole world for self, emotionally he also has the urge to settle for being it all, each bit for a while – but what is he to make of this growing pile of rejects? In what part of his self is he supposed to accommodate all that? He is furiously disappointed with these useless opportunities life offers him: it has betrayed all the expectations taught him by Life itself.

As an extravert he needs to find his being and becoming in this world, but since it goes against the sum of his convictions he simply cannot. His 'outburst' into our world yielding no satisfactory result, he stops dead in his tracks at last. Like Aquarius he then turns his back on us with wholesale contempt. But like Libra he can never afford to do so for long.

We soon learn to leave him be. We find him 'deeply sunk into himself', or so it appears to us, but he moment one touches him with a request for his attention he simply 'goes berserk'. He throws everything out of the way as if to make space for something, but with no clear explanation to offer, never mind a concise suggestion as to what to fill this space with. He takes nothing, just rejects it all; he brings nothing either, as far as one can make out. His presence here does not even seem to make sense to him. He comes to be seen very quickly as a menace to be avoided at all cost. He is left alone in his limbo, satisfied; but self-less, and hence unsatisfied.

In order to break this deadlock, Scorpio needs first of all to make use of his unconscious ability to sense the material phenomena of this world (♉). There is no remonstrating with what things simply, in and by themselves, look like and feel like (or sense like, one should really say). He neither understands these things, nor can he approve of them and accept them as self: but without for the moment 'vetting' them for their acceptability, he simply experiences them as a different *im*personal reality to the one he is used to.

He is calmed and soothed by this direct contact. He can emotionally 'settle in' without, for the time being, asking himself whether it is 'legitimate'. He is searching, for the time being, not for something to make into self, but simply searching as such: investigating, letting the experience speak for itself and getting to know the world for what it is on its own terms. Rather than take what he finds for his self, or unsuccessfully attempt to do so, he does no more than calmly take stock.

The insult to his expectations is put to one side while he lets his senses persuade him that here is something that is a valid experience in its own right. This brings him no nearer, of course, finding something to call 'I'. He is only turning the things of this world over and over in his hands, puzzled, unable to understand what to do with them or make of them. From the point of view of deriving a self from out of his objective experiences there is no more point in him touching it all gently, regarding it as something that may feel quite nice but cannot be self, than in flinging it out of his way, rejected. It may have quietened him down – from our point of view a great relief – but for him it is only a cul-de-sac, another deadlock situation.

Applying unconscious thought to what he is holding uselessly in his hands and regarding with impersonal interest only, opens up the situation and at last allows him to start doing what as an extravert he needs to. In addition to knowing the world through his senses he now also gets to know it analytically, critically (♍→). That is to say he examines it far more closely, though still with the distance of one who knows that this 'is not for him'. He gives it the detailed rational attention that acquaints him with the component parts of material reality. This allows him to understand that the world need not be accepted or rejected wholesale as he finds it, but that there are intelligent comparisons to be made, and choices, among the parts it consists of. His environment can be carefully sifted and appraised for its more valuable content, till it yields something that *does* tie in with his expectations.

Thinking about the self (♍←) he has not even begun to look for, it now strikes him that it is something he must assemble out of these extracts, brushing aside all else as non-self. He begins to understand that it is not the *whole* of his given environment that is to become self. Only the nuggets among the dross, the few selected bits. With this realisation he is at last ready to go in search of a personal identity, one he can accept as being what it 'ought' to be.

If there is one thing he has learned now it is not to go by first appearances, not to judge and condemn everything as he finds it, but first to evaluate with reason, to go deeper into the overall structure of things, to dismantle the whole as it stands and look intelligently at what parts of it may prove themselves worthwhile. Libra, from his vantage point of dispassionate semi-involvement, took a step back from anything that offended his preconceptions, in order to see things in relation and in perspective, and then took action to re-arrange the world till it was fit for him to find a self in. Scorpio, though totally involved in the world, has learnt to adopt the sort of distanced attitude that treats the world as something sensed and understood as such, impersonally, and nothing to do with him whatsoever – but once he is actively searching for self, he does not take a further step back from it all, quite the opposite: he approaches as close as he can, scrutinising, taking apart, and weighing up each particle.

First of all (like Aries) he intuitively takes all the world to be a potential source of self – but with the proviso that it must be screened for what it is worth. And in addition to this, with his basic emotional disposition he is also in search of a chance to settle into the forms life offers, to get to know them from the inside, repeatedly and dependably finding them to 'fit around' his expectations: life has to accommodate them. If Libra judged from the outside, standing back and holding back, Scorpio judges from the inside. He opens up and looks inside, he breaks apart to gain access to the essentially valuable. Libra set everything in a new relation, re-arranging and compromising to bring about the best possible world. Scorpio's is the ultimate judgement, there is no compromise: he accepts only what he finds to be of worth and discards the chaff, the husks.

We may be glad to find he is no longer 'going berserk', slinging out everything in sight regardless, but to find him quietly and deliberately applying the crowbar to our world, winkling out treasure, throwing us the left-over useless bits to keep, is only marginally more endearing. Worst of all, in his relating to us he is no different. He is not content to take our word for it that what we seem to be is really what we are. He is convinced that if he pokes around long enough we may yield something of value yet, where otherwise we don't, from his point of view. He is all for dismantling us, disrobing us, destructuring us a bit to gain closer knowledge of our constituent parts. He would open us up like a box, and since it can't be done by physical means, he demands: that we tell him all, show him what we really are, behind our façades, our carefully maintained exterior. He will not give us peace till we 'stop hiding' and consent to let him have access to all there is of us, including the real person behind the superficial, structured front. We find him as destabilising and threatening as ever. First nothing was good enough for him. Now he takes for himself all that is best and throws what he clearly regards as the garbage in our faces. Allowing him access to our selves is the very last thing we want to do. We clam up and lock our doors. We would rather he went back to his limbo and stayed there, undisturbed and undisturbing. He has reached yet another dead-end.

When he comes to use his unconscious feeling function, there is a drastic change in his situation. Sensing the world to be something impersonal at first, and later approaching it with critical-analytical insight to extract only that which he recognised as fit to be part of his world/self, what he did in effect was first to exclude himself, and then to exclude most of his environment. But in his newly-found emotional attitude he is incapable of such divisions: his feelings are all-inclusive ($\mathcal{H}\rightarrow$), nothing must be left out. The impersonally sensed world must be inhabited; the rejected parts of it must be owned in some way. Feeling himself ($\mathcal{H}\leftarrow$) to be inalienably connected to all there is in this world, he can no longer simply reject what offends him, only to offload it onto us, or leave us holding the empty wrapping while he carries off the essential bit. From now on he feels he has to share what he has identified to be of worth, and equally somehow share in the worthless rubbish. Emotionally immersed in a *whole* world, feeling himself to be on the point of truly becoming one of us, he has in a way come back to his initial starting point of taking all the world to be potential self. But this is a totally new attempt, based on the insights into the world that he has already gained.

This time he enters quietly, takes stock, investigates and separates out what is to be kept and what is not. He *shares* his impersonal inner-plane understanding: he shares the joy of 'striking gold' among the dirt, and shares the ownership and responsibility for both the best and the worst. In a whole world there is of course nowhere to push the rejects: they have to be destroyed. With his new-found humility as only one among many, he takes on the lowliest of jobs, that of cleaner. He collects all that is useless and points out to us what is beyond repair; he piles it up and burns it for good, leaving a clean world, uncluttered.

Including us in his new life, he draws on his practical, rational understanding of our situation; on his sensual experience of life as richly varied – meaning there is scope for interpretation; and on his emotional sympathy. He consults with us. He also urges us to adopt stricter criteria, but he no longer tears things from our hands to discard them. It has to be said, neither does he offer promises of something better in return for what we hand over (hesitantly) to be disposed of. And yet when he is finished removing, destroying, what is left is a kind of revelation: we had hardly noticed that there in its crowded corner, we never saw *that* in as much daylight, and unspoilt by association with lesser things. Half the room is empty, and yet all we can say is that we never knew we were so rich!

Doubtful at first whether he might not be getting rid of too much, whether we would not end up impoverished with all this reckless throwing away, if only we learn to trust his judgement and willingly hand over what he asks for, we stand amazed in the end at the transformation. This is sheer magic. He has added nothing, only removed what was not worth keeping, and yet we are aware of having more than we did before – or more aware of having what we had before, and of its nature. He has given us a new appreciation, a chance of re-appraisal. From his own new start of sharing he has given us the chance to make a new beginning in the space he has created, a beginning based on what is left in the end (and which has now become our starting stock, in terms of being a model for our new objectives).

He has opened our eyes to intrinsic value, hidden treasure indeed, and even the simplest thing shines in the new space accorded it. So reluctant at first, now we feel positively relieved, we see a promise of better things. In retrospect, we realise how we have been spoiling and devaluing our world with the greed of indiscriminate accumulation, the blind habit of ownership that would not even let go of the irretrievably broken bits but stored them away for some unlikely eventuality. We have been suffocating in the tangled mess of our truly valueless living. We can only be thankful to him for this new breathing space, the chance to begin all over again, this time with a small but valid collection of reference points. What we have 'inherited' is the nearest thing, objectified, to Scorpio's inbuilt values that he could find. Destroying and not-destroying, he has imported something new, if in itself intangible, into our world.

In his personal relationships the same principles apply. Again, he can draw on what he has learnt. There is no need to meet our demands for his presence in our world with quite such heavy counter-demands: that we lay ourselves bare, consent to have ourselves picked over like so much suspect merchandise. Instead, he can derive a lot of his information by observing our behaviour for symptomatic clues, by drawing conclusions from the way we structure our lives and arrange our means of self-expression. Best of all, he can feel himself into our personal situation, he slips inside our skin to try us out from the inside, always sympathetically. Sharing his convictions with us gently, he points out to us how we muddy the clear waters of right living with acquired habits that contribute nothing positive to our essential being and becoming. How we cling to the scaffolding, props and pretences of unnecessary self-defence (that defends, if truth be told, no more than our superficial vanities). How, surrounding our core selves with various worthless accoutrements, we set up false divisions, and at the same time acquire an outlook that tests the other person's *appearance*, but not their real value. All these harmful, wrong-headed and unnecessary outer layers he asks us to shed. There is no meeting him except so to speak in the nude. – He burrows into us like a seed of expectation looking for its already formed counterpart.

He is far more intense in his relationships than any of the other signs, always aiming for the essence of the partner, that which lies at the bottom of a person. The fiery nature of his conscious function propels him on, while the water element, the emotional basis of his make-up, draws him into a settled state: which means that in any kind of prolonged relationship, the answer is to go on deep into, and to keep going deeper. He really is doubly 'radical': rooted in all self-transcending Inner Reality, and always having to go down to the roots of other. That is where he is trying to find the makings of his self, or more precisely, to recognise some part of the impersonally formed image of self. He is in that sense looking for something all of us, essentially, have in common; or which derives from the same basis, our common origin: unencumbered by any traditional accretions or any individualistic additions that are no more than empty statements or frills.

Our superficial aspects do not interest him – except as appropriate expressions of what lies beneath the surface. And what he is 'diving' for in us is at the same time something inherent in us, and something that transcends the personal level. Relating is always more to him than simply a meeting of distinct individuals, it is also his and our meeting of the Root Reality. Where Libra makes of the transpersonal Inner Reality a third factor to be borne in mind in all relationships, Scorpio brings his expectations of finding it embedded somewhere inside us into the relationship itself. He 'enters into' us in search of just that and he offers to share the discovery of it with us.

Unlike the introvert Cancer he does not pour something of self into us, in response to what we truly need. As an extravert with strong convictions as regards the kind of quality of self he is in search of, he pours his impersonal expectations into us, seeking a 'response' that corresponds to them in what we truly are.

This response he finds in us he can accept as self – but it is a shared self, both ours and his. It is an indissoluble, intimate union of self and other. To be self for him means to be in a state of symbiosis where he and the partner share the discovery, upbuilding, maintenance and growth of a common nucleus of personal identity. One can simply say that he accepts the other's essential self for his own, sharing in it. And in return he shares his gift for divesting what is of lasting and 'lawful' value of its ephemeral, superfluous and/or wrongly acquired outer layers and admixtures: he purifies what he finds in us, and he makes us newly aware of what we are, beneath the image we see in the mirror.

In this way he gives us (back) that which we most profoundly are, but have either never known or have long since buried under the external trappings of a sensual, practical, intellectual life. He reconnects us, personally and individually, with our common ground, and he does this through being part of us as we are part of him, in the closest of all relationships, life-sharing at the most basic level.

In practice what it amounts to is a mutual give and take at such 'close range' that it constitutes a shared life development: an interpenetration of being. A web of common, worthwhile activities. And the shared possession and expression of what both partners hold to be most valuable – anything from shared 'values' and beliefs to quite simply the material 'essentials' of life. And once he has settled into this symbiotic relationship, the intuitive impulse that urges him on to find new possibilities of being takes the form of a *shared* investigation of new, meaningful self and life models. The partners in life are constantly suggesting to each other a new direction for development, from the basis of their common evaluation of what is worth striving for – absolutely, rather than from personal preference.

Libra reconnected us to our origin from without, so to speak, re-patterning our world in the perfect image, as far as possible. Scorpio implants this image inside us, as intuitive knowledge and emotional convictions. Not as a matter of aware, personal conscience, but as the only true means of life-sharing: giving up our non-essentials in order to 'accommodate' the other, and rediscovering our true self in the process. And at the same time gaining access to a new self that will not estrange us and divide us against each other again.

Equally affronted as Libra by what he finds to go against the laws of life, but with none of Libra's intellectually distanced ameliorating/compromising approach, Scorpio is always prepared to apply the ultimate cure: to pull out the offending tooth by the root. The point is, potentially it is as much his 'tooth' as ours. The example he is setting, then, is of having the courage and conviction to reject form-for-form's-sake, to persist in the attempt to live a material life that *does* fulfil the inner transpersonal demands implicit in all being. Quite simply speaking, he teaches us to do without, rather than compromise the standards we believe in.

He begs us to reassess the apparent 'poverty' brought about by such willing abstention. Valuing more what we can *truly* value, we are actually richer for the lack or loss of worthless externals. There is no point in filling life to the brim just for the sake of filling it if, leaving it largely 'empty', we actually find what we have to be entirely fulfilling. This is self-control of a different order to Cancer's: not based on response to other, and hence the 'reception' we manage to get from them or give to them, but on receiving other right into our selves. And this in response to an inner understanding of our essential smallness, and of the limitless wealth implied in maintaining an 'empty', receptive space that can be devoted to other. And the beauty of it, the paradox, is that the more we give over to other, the more we receive into our willing emptiness.

Aquarius asked us to let go of our accumulated life forms in exchange for something newer and better out of his inner-self 'beyond'. Scorpio asks us to let go – no promises. He does not seem to be making room *for something*. We see him simply creating space. A space that can draw us closer together in the shared recognition that all that really matters lies beyond personal, individual pride in extensive ownership. What we newly receive, 'in exchange' for what we have given up or agreed to do without, we receive from each other. These are personal gifts to one another only in so far as what we individually have to offer accords with life's underlying intentions: that is to say, it is only the 'perfect' in us we can truly *share*.

Preceding Sagittarius, Scorpio gives us the first intimation of something *in* us that is in contact with an inner reality beyond us, personally. Before our intuitive minds become aware of our individual innerness, consciously and personally, or of an Inner Reality as such, we learn to recognise something of that in each other, and to treasure it as something that is, fundamentally, part of our own personal reality.

He is asking for sacrifices, and setting an instructive example of rightful abstention, but like Aquarius he comes up against suspicion, accusations, misunderstanding, and the sheer dogged persistence with which we hug our established ways. His gift is invisible, his ridding us of all that is beyond the capacity of Libra to integrate meaningfully is nothing substantial sounding in the way that Aquarius at least was able to outline a future plan for us, however unintelligible. Scorpio is incapable of explaining why he does what he does. He faithfully acts out what from even 'before his beginning' has been his reference and impersonal inner guide: he is what he is and it is futile asking him why. – When he starts peeling the diseased, obsolete, faultily constructed layers off our shared world, we moan that we hurt. It seems to us he is trying to cure our ills by amputation pure and simple, leaving us with a gap, a lack, a loss keenly felt, a 'nothing' that does not strike us as a positive gift at all.

He demands an even greater faith than Aquarius before we can let him do what only he can. Aquarius abolished the old order and set up a new one, but it was easy enough giving the credit for the newly established to other forces, other signs that are more obviously in the business of structuring and establishing. We do exactly the same with Scorpio. He sloughs off old skins, gouges out the old rotten substance and leaves, exposed, only what is fit, healthy, worthwhile. This new starting stock is *freed*, it can respond now with a healthy, totally new becoming. We see the work of Taurus, Virgo, Aries, Cancer, Capricorn, all of the other signs, mending the 'damage' Scorpio did, and he gets no thanks at all, or only a grudging acknowledgement as a sort of necessary evil, in retrospect. If we had any sense we would see that the 'nothing' he gives us is the very source out of which the new life develops, *with the help of* the other signs.

What we insist on calling nothing is not an unstructured and meaningless nothing at all; how can it be, when he has created those empty spaces with meaning in mind, and throughout his 'destructive' work has been obeying the intrinsic laws of life. In that sense the holes he *makes* and the things he *leaves* make together the inverted images of life models: he is building properly shaped moulds asking to be filled, rightly this time. His nothings are full of quite specific suggestions. But it is beyond us that the holes we perceive should have an intangible content, that empty space should have a message contained in it. To him it is simply the story of his own beginning, when he was nothing substantial as yet but had a wealth of intrinsic 'shape' all the same. His personal 'absence' was not empty. He demonstrates to us that the seed of self does not depend on objective form, but always contains the insubstantial potential to build itself a (new) body: just as the seed of *all* self has in Scorpio built itself one personal, shared life.

Like Aquarius, Scorpio is a shock to the system – not a repeatedly visiting one but one that is now *built into* the system. He has become an integral part of our shared life, he has implanted himself. Or rather he has implanted the root or seed of all potential becoming, and in the process found his own place in life, sharing in what we are and helping us to be what we truly are. He is a sort of inbuilt watchdog of life, and the last resort after the court of appeal of Libra has failed. All the signs need his contribution when they fail, to pull down their mismanaged efforts and at the same time create a 'suggestive space' for them to fill. He provides not only end but new beginning at the same time, a proto-creator in his own right. In so far as each sign is in some way, positively or negatively, creative he is the inbuilt guide and corrective of them all. At the core of each positive creative act lies the inherent ability to change the existing pattern, to sweep something else out of the way, to destroy and start again. Each sign also carries the seed of its own destruction in case it 'goes wrong': he is their inbuilt negative aspect as well, that ensures their repeated, partial or wholesale downfall, giving them a new chance. He is the invisible power among them, *inside* them. He does the dirty work that would enable them to shine with the pride of their work. With his invisible contribution he is the most inscrutable of them all, and yet none can help but automatically incorporate him. They have to obey him without question or else question the nature and meaning of their own existence. It puts a rather different face on the concept of 'nothing'.

When Scorpio misuses his unconscious functions and lets them become uncontrollable urges, the first trap he falls into is to develop an insatiable need to satisfy the demands of his physical senses (♉). The world becomes compulsively sensually attractive to him. He sinks his teeth indiscriminately into anything edible, he ogles and can't keep his hands off, he fills himself up with sensual experience till one would think he has had more than enough. But he is never satisfied.

In his desire to partake of the sense-able world he has simply projected his inner experience of perfection outward into objective life (rather like Libra, but right into the thick of it, with no kind of mental distance). He takes it for granted that there he will meet up with it now, admiring it visibly, tasting it on his tongue, and becoming it. But one bite of the material world and he is disillusioned: it doesn't taste right, absolutely not – he scoffs it all the same, with a frown.

He should be refusing, rejecting, throwing away, but he is irredeemably hungry for all of it regardless. He is like a starving gourmet who has been let down by his caterers and now has to content himself with vile fodder fit only for pigs. He eats with a long face, accusingly. If he ever manages to leave anything half-consumed, in disgust, he soon picks up something else. He can't stay out of it despite being fully aware that the world is a betrayal of all he would have expected it to be, still expects it to be.

He cannot explain to himself why everything he picks up fully convinced that this must be 'it', turns to useless rubbish in his hands. It makes him suspicious, wondering who or what is short-changing him all the time. Life is withholding something from him, all that is best in fact, fobbing him off with cheap substitutes. But all he can do is to grind his teeth in a helpless, unfocused rage, glug down another pint with a grimace. His doom-faced 'enjoyments' strike him as a poor consolation for his perpetual disappointment with the world as it presents itself to him. This is no life at all, it isn't for real, only a queer sort of shadow existence. He can find no self in any of it. He is only processing life uselessly, extracting nothing from it that he would wish to own, to be. He has not even got a vision or aim to strive towards. He has 'sunk' all his expectations in the solid mass of all tangible life, from where he is trying to recover it via an endless stream of sensual experience – but somehow, mysteriously, what ought to be there is nowhere to be found, it has disappeared, gone without a trace. This does not teach him to leave alone, only to complain.

Objecting, without rejecting though, he finds himself living a life he would not count for real. The splendid figure he should become as he incorporates the world and builds himself a concrete self is simply not materialising. This is not the 'I' he was born to be. To listen to him one would think he was trying to tell us that he is a prince in disguise, some better class of being stuck in the wrong body. His behaviour hardly bears this out. There is nothing to indicate that at the bottom of his slurpings there is anything but a piggish appetite. But then he does not mean that he *is* something better, only that he would be, if life was not playing dirty tricks on him, leaving him without what it owes him. He admits freely that he is a mere nothing: with a face that condemns the whole world bitterly for cheating him out of his birthright.

Life is faceless to him and he stares back at it blankly, consuming it and not getting a thing out of it. The 'body' he is acquiring in the process is only an anonymous stand-in for the real thing, he cannot possibly own it. It is only the means for consuming more, an impersonal thing, a pointless device. What torments him most is that he can never understand where the 'missing self' has disappeared to. He keeps trying to discover it, but his search is in vain. He overloads on everything he can, he stuffs his home full of things that once sampled are left lying for worthless, and he keeps protesting, rightly, that *really* he is abysmally poor. Throughout it all he stays a rather solid sort of 'nobody' determinedly-busily-greedily-listlessly chewing his way through an empty life. He cannot figure out what has gone wrong. He is stuck in a wrong world, or in a wrong place in it.

When he makes use of his unconscious thought processes (♍→) he realises that things are not as simple and straightforward as they seemed. The complexities of life need looking into in detail before he can say in what way exactly it is letting him down. Now he takes pleasure in scrutinising every morsel, every crumb has to be dissected to discover the flaws, point out the shortcomings one by one. He leaves nothing whole. He prods and pokes ruthlessly to show up the hidden rot; he breaks just to demonstrate the breakability; suspecting pretence and idle trickery in everything, he sets out deliberately to unmask, trip up, show everything and everybody for what they are really worth, i.e. nothing worth mentioning. If formerly he expected the best – only to be constantly, puzzlingly, disappointed – now with his new tool of analytical understanding, and still finding most things to be inherently worthless, he has come to expect the worst – and in a twisted sort of way he finds himself no longer disappointed. It is just as he thought: the surface looks agreeable enough, one might almost be fooled by it; but scratch it and it stops glittering, stick a pin in it and it deflates.

He is so taken up with the grim satisfactions of disproving and disapproving, that anything that *does* prove to survive his acid tests just enrages him. He squeezes it harder than ever, he wonders whether he hasn't dismantled it far enough yet and can hardly believe that he has really got to the bottom of this. When he finally has to admit that here is something that is not just cheap dirt dressed up as something better, he does not by any means pounce on it gleefully as something at last worth making his own: he feels insulted instead that this is all there is for him. It is such a terribly meagre yield that he almost spurns it. He pockets it all the same, with a secrecy that is not due entirely to wanting to keep it all for himself but has an element of embarrassment in it, as if he had failed and been proved wrong (or, possibly, as if he was about to be shown up for the pathetically small self he is).

He thinks of his self (♍←) as constituted only of the purest elements and in that sense his assumed superiority knows no bounds, but this is spoilt for him by his shame at the pitiful amount of self he can actually boast. He accuses us sarcastically of being next to nothing when the worthless façade has been stripped away, but the truth is that he amounts to no more than we do, and he is keenly aware of that. That is why he refuses to show his self. He puts up a screen to shelter it from view, a tight security fence that both ensures the safety of what he has gleaned and stops us realising how very little there is of him. He need not look far for such a 'mask' to hide behind, he has already got something to do the job: the cynical interrogator, the one who kicks everything to pieces, methodically rubbishing the world, this is what he hides behind as if it were not part of his ongoing self also.

He no longer grabs handfuls of world to gobble them down; he grabs them to enjoy the feel of something breaking, giving, crumbling, falling apart, his smile a terrible mixture of pleasure and disdain. He enjoys the mental challenge too, grunting with satisfied disgust when he is at last in a position to pinpoint and tidily enumerate the faulty ingredients in something. That there are also one or two grains of genuine substance leaves him strangely cold in comparison, torn between conflicting satisfactions. He hoards them away almost as an afterthought and never says a word about it. Praise is the last thing one can look for from him.

Wanting absolutely the best and desiring the worst as well (because there is nothing like the worst for compulsively criticising) he manages to have it both ways. He crams his perfect if meagre collection of self-attributes into a corner of his life, unseen and unused. And there it is surrounded and protected on all sides by the 'official' version of him: the defensive mask; the faceless function of sardonic inspector, crusher and condemner; the job that needs doing before he can find some 'real' self to be... he'll call it anything but what it is: the fat and filthy self that he has acquired as a result of the great quantity of dirt he keeps handling with such patent relish. Unable to reject and really get rid of, he is becoming the strangest mirror image of the world: digested, distilled, rearranged: all the best bits bunched together somewhere in the centre, while the worst of it is freely displayed on the surface.

He is no better nor worse than any of us, in sum total. He has only buried his essential values inside a thick layer of worthless self. But he refuses to acknowledge this 'surface self'; this is only something that has rubbed off on him. He blames us for it. We are always trying to defile him, to lure him off the pedestal his more or less inert 'real' self is sitting on. The bully who cracks open and rapes the world around him: this is what we are inviting him to 'act' (not *be*, perish the thought), because we *withhold* from him the best choices the world holds. All that is best is of course already by rights his: ever since he projected, embodied, his perfect expectations. He is only 'getting his own back' now and hence thinks himself fully justified. If we tell him that he is hooked on all this brutality and getting more out of *that* than the actual 'reward' of his misdeeds, all he can say is 'Who, *me*?' and reckon himself badly misunderstood.

Negative Cancer tried hard to ignore those parts of his self that it hurt him too much to cope with. Scorpio brazenly disowns what it does not please him to call self, but thinks nothing of using it as a tool for gaining pleasure and for enriching himself, hurting others in the process as a matter of course. The world does not put up with his tactics for long. – Forcefully denied a part in our lives, deprived of his source of self as well as his source of crass, destructive pleasures, he has to cast around for a different approach.

Emotionally he is so much drawn towards everything and everybody without the least reservation ($\leftindex{}{}{\mathbb{H}}\rightarrow$) that he is perfectly capable of standing criticism aside altogether. There is nothing he cannot accept, and he feels himself ($\mathbb{H}\leftarrow$) so strongly to be part of the whole world, he does the unexpected: he smiles at us for the first time. He nods, he is relaxed, he gives us all a warm reception, he positively oozes goodwill to all men. To say he is putting on a calculated act would be unwarranted sarcasm. He is genuinely delighted with this chance to feel content and to give his hitherto shut-in better self (the one and only real one to him) an airing, to let all the best of him shine openly. Emotionally he is quite prepared to share his accumulated treasure, to let us admire it and even partake of it. He is one of us, we are all one big family and he hugs us to him like lost relatives, declaring his house to be ours.

This is the new-style he, and he is very pleased with it. The doors that had closed against him are thrown open again. A pleasanter guest one never saw, he positively sparkles.

The bully he is has quite disappeared, from view that is. Still unacknowledged, it now sits tucked away underneath the surface. Graphically speaking, where before he was a core of gold caked thickly in dirt, now he is a ball of dirt thinly coated in the most precious stuff. The surface of him is his new repository for everything valuable he can acquire, the best clothes, the choicest manners, the obvious virtues. He displays them for our and his delight, but jostling him in a crowd won't do: he flakes, he peels, below the surface there is a bad surprise in store for us. This is precisely what he has been faulting *us* for all along – only a lot more so. We are only an ignorant hotch-potch of the good and the bad, right and wrong, perfection and imperfection mixed together as grey as could be. He, innately aware of the difference, but too greedy to refuse or let go of anything, has neatly separated self/world into the black and the white. After this inside-out reversal he has done, this apparent metamorphosis, we too see him for the Mr White he has always claimed to be, exclusively.

For the first time he is able to look in the mirror without complaining that it doesn't show his 'real' self. The brutal 'mask' – this outer layer that was no more than what had 'rubbed off on him' and which he used for a shield – has been abandoned. He wears his splendid new face with the arrogance of the better class of being he always said he could be, and latterly thought he was. But now he needs to be very careful how he goes if his nice appearance is not to suffer cracks all over. He is only too easily provoked into letting the soulful smile slip and baring his teeth in an ugly show of contempt and accusation and a blaze of destructiveness.

To protect his vulnerable, spotless self he seeks out the sort of environment and company that will go with it, the rich, the select, the immaculately laundered. He fears to be blemished by contact with poor quality. His new 'openness' needs safeguards to operate, a tried and tested and tightly controlled environment, a security zone. Suspecting the worst as ever, and so obviously precious now, he needs bodyguards or at least the nearest thing, a constantly guarded attitude. He can only afford to relax in his suspicions if he keeps himself shut inside a tightly organised, unchanging circle, screening, vetting, arranging his world intelligently so it will be predictable and dependable. But emotionally he then misses the larger world that he feels so much part of. He need not worry. He is so dazzlingly attractive, the world is clamouring for admission to his presence. He acts like a magnet. If not a living legend, then at least he is a 'worthy', an unimpeachable example to follow, someone to fill the seat of honour to our satisfaction. Receiving all the world into his embrace, he sits like a spider in his web.

Who would think of answering back when *he* finds fault with us? When he is sharp, denigrating, contemptuous, one just feels like saying sorry. When he asks a million probing questions one feels honoured to be the focus of his attention and is duly crestfallen when rebuked. He makes us feel shabby without even trying. We are so overawed by what we see of him, and the setting or entourage he insists on surrounding himself with, we hand it to him on a plate. Even he is surprised at the easy power he suddenly wields: all he is doing is to show us what a genuinely nice guy he is, something he had kept in the dark before. There is nothing like the power of attraction.

What we see is genuine enough, but we make the mistake of thinking he is like that through and through. Once we have seen through him, we marvel at his self-control: how does he do it, showing himself only from the best side and keeping his dark side hidden? It has nothing at all to do with self-control, everything with an automatic self-division process, and subsequent self-delusion. We did not ask the bully, after all, how he managed to 'control' the better part of his nature. We simply assumed he had no such thing. Equally we assume this paragon to be 'solid', and when disillusioned put it down to deliberate, crafty misleading and play-acting on his part.

Fooling himself is his inbuilt objective, having us fooled as well is only a handy spin-off. He needs to be all that glitters (and proves valid), he couldn't care less what *we* think of him; we are ninety per cent dregs to him anyway. Having re-arranged the two parts of his self, the acknowledged and the unacknowledged, he has gained a drastically different position in our eyes, that is all. When his black 'contents' pour out in answer to our 'provocation' – our failures, weaknesses, imperfections and all the other things he shares in being but does not count as self – then he needs to think of something better to say to himself now than that we are rubbing off on him, that it isn't *his* blackness at all.

He is so taken with his newly superficial self, he hates us for scratching his shiny surface: it is a direct attack on all he is ('all', in his estimation). It is not that he resents being shown a mirror image of what he really is – he does not after all *admit* to being that, he thinks himself blameless. His touchiness could be attributed to the fact that every part of his treasured self is exposed now. But the real reason is that the beast within is rattling the bars of its cage in answer to our 'provocation': an unearthly feeling he cannot explain. What pours out of him is a stranger to him. Just as negative Cancer was seized by 'unknown forces' appearing from 'outside him', so negative Scorpio finds himself a mouthpiece or channel for something that he regards as not originating from any part of him.

One might say that, superficially white, he has bottled up all his blackness, where it now sits hoping for an airing. When it does get a chance to push up and break through his surface, he is both furious at this anger he does not own – it spoils his good image/self – and secretly delighted to be indulging his horrible habits. He has never yelled abuse louder, and blamed us for it, or sworn worse, and told us it is the only language *we* understand, or kicked us harder, informing us that it is no more than deserved punishment. To anger he adds anger and to that the delights of anger, till one thinks he will never stop. – The secret addict has had a good fix and now he looks grimly satisfied, as he always used to, *and* sad that this 'had to happen'. Our fault. We slink off not sure whether he is some sort of wrathful deity or unbelievable rotten 'inside'.

Now we put our best behaviour forward, pretend to be all we aren't and are like obedient putty in his hands, thinking to be safe that way from his outbursts. But what happens is that now *he* provokes *us* into showing our worst side. He nettles us with a smile and twists the pins he sticks in us till we show a suitably imperfect response. Unlike negative Cancer for whom a good daily fight (his life blood) was quite acceptable, he hates the urge that bubbles up in him and makes him do that. For the first time he feels at odds with the something he has always denied to himself he was, but which constitutes by far the largest and liveliest part of him.

Whatever excuse he may try to find for his unscheduled behaviour (demons? a role as the punishing arm of God? or, less fancifully, our common lower nature that we *all* share in, inescapably?)

he is deeply disappointed with what he can't stop doing, despite himself, as he would say. Even if he never owns up to *being* that, in the end, in some way, he has to own it and assume responsibility over it, if only out of self-preservation (i.e. to keep the façade intact). It is a part of him and having hidden it away out of sight he still has no option but to learn to control it.

He begins to lead a tidy double life, keeping his official self clean and smiling; and unofficially, behind closed doors, giving the demon that torments him and uses him its head. Throughout the day he is immaculate, and under cover of night he haunts the seediest places, maybe managing to tame the demon sufficiently to find a half-sophisticated outlet: paying us handsomely to have ourselves flogged. But every time he hits out at us, *he* suffers – hurt pride at the indignity of the situation; secret self-disgust; a cynical loss of belief in his true worth; helplessly witnessing his own self-destruction, the rending and fouling of his pure surface-self, of his golden, split-off 'image'.

He suffers pleasurably, but at the cost of what he regards as his real self: with every eruption of this 'stranger inside him', the gilt on the surface wears thinner and thinner, his values drop off one by one, till in the end it seems to him as if he was no longer any kind of (worthwhile) self. But by then he no longer cares. It is a secret relief to be rid of this internal split, of the tremendous effort entailed in keeping these two closely neighbouring parts of his self so deliberately and circumspectly separate. So much easier to slip into this stranger's body, not a self any more, only some anonymous beast.

He abandons himself to the tides of his 'inner' darkness – which is nothing but the unwitting, unwanted reflection of all the darkness he has extravertly picked up in the world, and buried skin-deep behind his bright façade, his assumed image. – Now he is back to being a self-confessed 'nothing', if of a different order.

(This is the crux of the process we call corruption. It is not quite the straightforward pollution we imagine it to be. Those who have battled their way to a position of power or public standing, or even acquired it by other means, don't suddenly mysteriously get worse – rather they are newly placing all their best bits up front and then have to find something to do with their hidden failings, which cannot be simply left unemployed; no part of self can, for long: even the bully found himself secretly stroking the cat, on occasion. Some kind of double life is inevitable. It is the flimsiness of such 'superficialised' values, the wear on them from the under-mining pressure from *within*, as the hidden-away self insists on bursting back on the scene, that does the damage. It is much more the disintegration of the 'white self' than a newly acquired black-ness. – By the same token, he is now rubbing off on us, corrupting us: to please him, get on his good side and benefit from his power and (apparent) wealth, *we* are putting our best aspects forward, exposing them, and hiding away what would get us into trouble.)

Life has finally let him down, after all, despite all his contor-tions. Like positive Scorpio he too went down to the roots of the matter and sorted the valuable from the worthless. But instead of sharing the one and, together with us, banishing the other for good, his irrepressible greed made him try to take the lot for him-self, in two neat parcels. One to boast to himself as being his exclu-sively, the other to disclaim ownership of but use freely. He juggled them about, the better to be pleased with himself, but all he achieved was the loss of what he rightly knew to treasure most. His transformations were only skin-deep, and if he thought he could cheat the demands of his own nature he was mistaken. What he did not want to share he has lost. And what he did not want to do without, nor be responsible for, is 'using him against his will'. Like negative Cancer he mistakenly said yes to the whole world – and also ends up saying nothing but no, in his case an absolute no, to absolutely everything.

No to all values, which have proved fickle in his eyes – as well as a habitual no to the negative things in life. And eventually no to life itself, which has not come up to his expectations: the whole world is no good to him, because even the perfect has turned out to be imperfect. There is only one thing that can lay claim to any purity, constancy, incorruptibility, and that is no-thing, no-life, death. He has long forgotten the nature of the no-thing, the death before life, he originated from. 'Nothing' to him is pure and sim-ple: the abolition of all that (materially) is.

He means his no's this time, he does mean entirely doing away with – while still clinging to the world of the senses: it is *us* he does away with, murdering us with what one can only call deep emo-tional conviction, in search of the one ultimate value which he thinks can't possibly let him down. He enjoys the feel of joints cracking under pressure, while he is at it, and his methodical thinking yields highly efficient ways for dissecting us. But dearest of all to him is the experience of emptying this world of another blemish. He is killing the mirror images of his demon, one by one. The blank absence of anything is his new aim, he'll settle for that: a fitting non-world for the self-less nobody he already is. (To point out that now at last he is actually *sharing* with us what he holds to be most precious can only raise a hollow laugh of course.)

By some inbuilt sleight of hand he ends up doing what he always refused to do: destroy – us; and share: in our deaths. His 'reward' for such a botched job is appropriately meagre. It is no more than the meaningless picture of lifelessness viewed from without, the sensation of life ebbing away, the mental satisfaction of reducing to nil, the emotional gratification of participating, a bit, in the only truly beautiful event. It is a poor stand-in for the death he desires for himself. Like all the other signs that came from the Inner Plane beyond the material world, whether with a personal inner self, or an impersonal (or 'trans-personal') code for finding their selves here, he has divorced himself from his origin. He has locked himself out of its reach. So now even death is cheating him, eluding him.

For ever making a compulsive use of his unconscious functions, he can only admire death, smell it, touch it, think about it in calculating ways, make a science of it, love it, in vain. He depends on us, the world, to make an end of him. This is what he most desires, and we will do him no good at all trying to persuade him to make a fresh life start by attempting to give him back the values he has lost. If he does not learn to share them; and learn to relinquish, to abolish honestly; and to accept shared responsibility for the down-side of life as well, then he will never come to make a proper job of his life. He will go on provoking us for ever to please level the gun at him.

Failing that, he can at least beg us to treat him as he has been treating us, to kick him, flog him, deride him, rob him, each loss a gain to him, a partial dying. He becomes as addicted to taking pain as he was to dealing it out; he will not stop even at buying or begging piecemeal self-mutilation. Though if he can, knowingly, eat and drink himself nearer the grave, so much the better. Much as he desires his end, he *can't* be in a hurry for it: he is hopelessly hooked on the sensual life.

Positive Scorpio succeeded in making of the broad meandering flow of life (clogged up, often enough, with the unspeakable rubbish we tend to carry along) a more deliberate drive for our timeless values. His legacy was the 'survival' of everything that truly reflects the underlying demands of life – or, to put it like that: everlasting life in spite of death. Negative Scorpio, one might say, has channelled life into two conflicting flows, two opposing directions to the same stream, one obvious, the other hidden. In such a world we swim in vain, always finding ourselves going backwards with the stronger undercurrent – till we are so disillusioned with our retrograde efforts, we simply let ourselves drift, become a faceless part of the dark flow that sweeps everything out of its way: gathering an anonymous strength as it goes.

He has educated us in the ways of everlasting death in life. He has trained us in pointless violence, and sooner or later, whether we aim for him specifically or not, he will get his release from this world he enjoyed hating so much. – The least he can do is turn right round and come back to sort out the mess he has left behind. No other sign has the same ability to do it.

Some Suggested Scorpio Attributes

basic

detached, 'cold', unresponsive, uninvolved, unforthcoming, very reserved

mysterious, apparently secretive, 'deep': actually not a case of a personal inner depth but of his impersonal pre-occupation with things not of a mundane nature

arrogant, contemptuous, simply not interested

absolute standards, based on **intuition** and **deeply rooted emotional convictions, totally uncompromising, can't be argued with, stubborn** and **insistent:** he knows he is absolutely right; **puritanical** and **harshly disapproving**

intense, 'passionate': he feels strongly about every issue and suffers personally from the wrongness of the world, because he cannot then, as an extravert, find his identity in it

easily takes offence and feels insulted and betrayed in his expectations (which is why he is often seen as being **'jealous':** he is not concerned with being 'the only one' but with the 'propriety' of a relationship); **violent rejection** and **possibly destructive**

positive

detached sort of interest, not taking things personally; life puzzles him

impersonal analysis, detached criticism; looks for the underlying reality; interprets symptomatic clues; needs to investigate

burrows into, goes deep, tries to understand from inside; can be disturbingly intrusive; penetrating; 'chips away at the surface', cuts things down to the basics/to what he expects to find; may work at **sculpting, etching, engraving** etc.

dismantles, strips, unwraps in search of the essentials: i.e. the 'proper' worth; **(gently) demands access; ferrets out and lays bare secrets; finds 'treasure', 'mining'** and **sifting; rejecting** all that is not of worth, he can become **exclusive; occultism**

shared ownership and responsibility: sharing both the best and the task of what to do about the worst; **intense relationships; rooting down into** and **becoming embedded and implanted; symbiosis; life-sharing;** finding the **true common denominator;** going deep, he is **very private** in his relating, but having

stripped away the inessentials he is **potentially close to every-**
one: member of a truly-basic collective
cleaner; purifier; destroyer of anything worthless and uselessly
superficial; **supplies new criteria; reveals (true worth); enrich-**
es through new appreciation
seeing-anew; making a new start; 'rebirth'; letting go, enriched
as a consequence of **deliberate 'poverty' and abstention;**
resisting temptation (of the sensual) and in that sense **rising**
above: not to a sphere above or a higher inner state, but to the
highest level of what is to be found in the world and which is
representative of underlying or transcendent values
radical; not inclined to compromise for worthless reasons;
'amputates' what is diseased; surgery (in the widest sense);
administers radical cures and shocks; psychic healing is often
attributed to Scorpio: this would be, not an alleviation of symptoms, but a process of entering into intuitive-emotional symbiosis and perhaps sharing in the pain prior to getting rid of
what obstructs, spoils, suffocates, detracts from the otherwise
healthy (but also see Pisces)

negative
grossly sensual; greedy without ever gaining satisfaction; treats
his body and self as a tool for gaining pleasure
lacks proper standards but complains, grumbles, protests,
accuses; perpetually disappointed; resentful; disdainful; con-
temptuous
takes nothing seriously; 'processes' life and finds it pointless;
acquires rubbish or treats things as if they were; claims
poverty
feels worthless (for which he blames the world); **feels cheated,**
generally suspicious; claims to be potentially something bet-
ter/to deserve better; faceless, denies being what he is, and
hence **merges with the crowd, anonymous**
takes a **delight in proving wrong, critically destructive** for the
sake of it; **ruthlessly exposes; hunts for flaws, censorious; neg-**
ative expectations; sarcasm, cynical, gloats, schadenfreude
insists on his rights; intimidating, bully; extortionist; rapist (in
the widest sense); **devalues and drags through the mud:** it
proves his negative expectations right, which gives him quanti-
tatively more satisfaction than he can derive from having his

positive expectations met; **physical violence and destruction; spoils, breaks (and litters and defaces)** proving that it can be done, hence the thing is not really as good as it looks; **lays traps secretly ashamed** at counting for so little in his own eyes; **hides; secretive;** puts up **barriers, false fronts, aggressive 'mask':** one of his two real faces, but not the one he 'owns', **comes on rough and tough:** which he is, but that is not all there is to him; blames others for his own dark side: **looks for scapegoats; racist** etc.

fears theft of his comparatively few valuable acquisitions **and fears exposure** of his 'real' self which, though small, is precious to him – hence: **makes himself out to be superior, arrogant;** but **displays his worst attributes** openly; **'hoodlum', low type of gangster; self-justification:** blames the world for his **shabby exterior,** his worthless 'surface self'

equally capable of displaying only his best attributes: appears impressively worthy, virtuous, kind and generous; very attractive (because appears to be unusually 'good'); **deceptively suave; displays his worth/'goods'** and in that sense: **prostitution**

flaunts his riches but takes **self-protective measures; tight control of environment; wields public power** (by a combination of attraction and hidden ruthlessness); **highly suspicious, security conscious;** a **'front' of controlledness, predictability, inflexibility; fastidious, fears contamination, will not mix socially and lets others do his dirty work for him**

liable to **violent outbursts,** though **hates himself for it; 'bottled-up' rage** he refuses to recognise as his own; **compulsively provocative; nettles** and **needles:** his hidden self demanding its participation in life (which he interprets as being **'in the grip of a demon'** who uses him); **at odds with himself, split personality; 'beside himself with rage':** as if the 'real he' was standing aside to let the other one have his say

double life, this being the first real form of **self-control** in him; **criminal, member of an 'underworld':** often inhabiting this and a more glittering world at the same time; **covert sadist** (in contradistinction to the boastful bully); **immaculate type of gangster**

corrupt, loss of all positive values; terminally disgusted with life, nihilist; death becomes his aim: desires and admires death but is too compulsively immersed in life to attain it –

makes of death a job, 'art' or science; utterly destructive, **murderous** while desiring his own death; **slow torture** and **piecemeal murder:** derives a vicarious, voyeuristic pleasure from this stand-in for self-destruction

asks to be 'punished'/destroyed: not because he thinks he has done wrong and deserves punishment, but because all life including his own is worthless to him and the more of it can be destroyed the better, which means that even loss of dignity can be a satisfying gain to him; becomes addicted to the pleasure of pain: **masochist; slow and piecemeal self-destruction** and **self-mutilation; self-tormenting**

PISCES

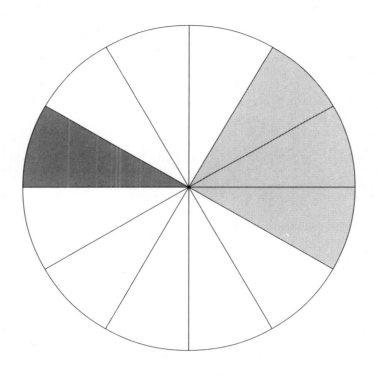

♓ **Extravert**
   **conscious function: feeling; directions of function: both out-
   ward and inward**
   unconscious functions: ♍ **thinking,** ♎ **sensation,** ♏ **intuition**
   Water: emotional

Like Virgo, Pisces is an extravert who gathers the makings of his
self from out of his objective environment, and who subsequently
introjects what he has become to establish an inner self, coming to
resemble an introvert. But with Pisces all this takes place at an
entirely emotional level; like Cancer he is by basic nature emotional and his conscious function is feeling.

Cancer, as an introvert, had the problem of trying to fit his integral self into his environment: some of him was always being
rejected and this left him feeling fractured, hurt and unaccepted in
the world as the whole he felt himself to be. Pisces, as an extravert,
has something of the opposite problem. He becomes the whole
world, and when it comes to introjecting this gigantic ill-assorted
self, it does not fit: there is too much of him, and each bit at odds
with the other. It just does not make a coherent inner-self whole.

His feelings flow outward in search of a form to settle in, indiscriminately, without any kind of pre-conceptions, prior standards
or even the vaguest idea of what he should become. There is nothing to stop him being this, that or the other, momentarily: adopting its shape, empathetically calling it self. He is by nature
all-inclusive, that is to say able to find parts of self in anything his
environment happens to provide, good, bad or indifferent,
painful or blissful. There is simply nothing one can offer him and
hear a no from him. In consequence, his life is full of contrasts and
contradictions. The moment he has emotionally settled in one
thing, another comes along to stake a claim on his feelings, and
since he cannot help flowing-into, in search of definition, he
'obeys'. He belongs in every context imaginable, and should two
such contexts overlap and become concurrent, he will be seen to
nod with us, and shake his head with us at the same time, cry and
laugh all in one go. One can compare him to a sounding board
vibrating to the many different tunes that all contribute to his

being: he is held captive within the forms of the world and as they change so does he. The collection of self-shapes he acquires is like a symphony of empathy – and equally a crass cacophony, an in-tune-ness with all and everything in one horrendous jumble.

He is the happiest, and he is also the most wretched, because he has no defence against the negative aspects of this world at all. The meanest thing, the most deplorable action, the most offensive person, they are all he. He pours his feelings into them and thus finds a definition of self in them. His vicarious self-experience has him falling from delight into dejection and from exuberant partic-ipation one moment into a torpor of 'borrowed' grief the next. Since he can't refuse to become anything (why and on what grounds should he refuse, when all he is searching for is to be given *some* shape?) it is no wonder if he ends up as the perfect tar-get for exploitation. Others see him as a handy focus to crowd around with their woes and aches, which become his; they prac-tise on him their rages and resentments, and he accepts it as part of his world, his pain again; even their material cast-offs land unopposed on his doorstep, and as everything else he adopts them as his own.

He is soon swamped by such a tide of ills, uglinesses and out-rages as no other sign experiences. Though against that one has to set his capacity to get equally 'lost in' – to find himself in, that is – emotional identification in all the visible riches of the world, both natural and man-made: they too are he and his. He 'inhabits' them quite as much as the rags and tatters he has more concretely been landed with; they impress or imprint themselves on his feelings in the same way, captivating some of his feelings, holding them within their own form. It hardly matters whether things are near or far, or practically speaking his own or not, 'real' or 'only' imag-inary. No door is ever locked against his feelings to prevent him from being king as much as he is a slave of his circumstances. He would not regard it as a dilemma to have such a disorderly, che-quered, unfocused self if it was not also part of his nature eventu-ally to turn inward toward an inner space waiting to be filled, like Virgo's, with the self he has experienced himself to be out there. Virgo of course had chosen carefully what to be, and establishing an inner self came easy, though how to maintain it in the face of continued extraverting was a problem.

Pisces does not even get an inner self established in the first place, never mind maintaining it. The moment he begins to intro-ject his raggle-taggle collection of disparate emotional self-experi-ences he is in trouble. How does all that fit into *one* conscious identity; how to fit the immeasurable into one little unit? He finds himself to be an insufficient vessel. He feels himself overflowing, losing his overabundant accumulated self for lack of a corre-sponding depth to pour it all into. And how to reconcile the strife between the various bits and pieces that he is trying to unify into one internalised emotional reality? Going from one empathetic experience to a contradictory one, out there, is one thing. Holding them inside himself, in one time/space is a rather different propo-sition, spelling inner conflict, not unity.

He has gathered far too large a measure of different selves and now he is having to let go of them again. He has more than enough building blocks at his disposal but can find no way of assembling them into a coherent, harmonious internal self, a whole-some 'I'. Like Aries he finds himself, loses himself, a process that leads everywhere and nowhere. For Aries this was no more than a waste of time; his intuitive drive was concerned with searching out new things to become rather than with establishing his self, so he suffered from no more than the futility of his efforts. For Pisces it is a catastrophe. He has invested his feelings in so much, placed them deeply-and-securely in the many forms of the world, and now that he needs to carry the experience of those external 'imprints' inward, he finds his diverse self-forms collid-ing and shattering, cancelling each other out. The everything he has become will not be compressed into the one inner self he needs to be, and he can no more let go of some bits in favour of others than he could acquire them selectively in the first place.

The shock of inner self-dissolution makes him fearful and uncertain about the processes of gathering an 'external' self. Like Capricorn, if in an inverse way, he has found what self (or selves, in his case) he had, to have been invalidated. In retrospect he proves to have become nothing worthwhile after all.

He is a failure writ large, with nothing to fall back on. Cancer and Capricorn at least had their existing inner selves to retreat to if they failed to prove themselves in the outside world, Virgo had his successfully internalised self to pride himself on, even Taurus managed to have at least a very limited amount of self to cling to... Pisces, who felt he was so much, so many, is left with being nothing, an utter nobody – and he cannot even blame the world for this débâcle, only himself. He will have to forget about all he ever was and start again from scratch.

If, this time round, he makes use of his unconscious thought processes in order to be critical and analytical about the life experiences he enters into (♍→) then this enables him at last to make choices, to refuse and say no to. He can withhold his feelings and reserve them for the sort of self-experience he has in mind, discriminating and in the process bringing order to the chaos of his emotional flow. Instead of approaching everything exclusively with feeling, he can now approach it with thought and consider first of all whether getting emotionally involved is a practical proposition from the point of view of gaining a potentially unified identity. His growing self is no longer the spongy thing that assumed whatever shapes the environment impressed on it, grateful to be given form at all. He now thinks of it (♍←) as needing to be an orderly composition, an aggregate of distinct choices.

Comparing first what is on offer, from a critical distance, he soon gathers at least a small nucleus of self. This then serves him as a guide in actively searching out similar life forms to know from the inside, as it were – *after* assessing them intelligently, from the outside, for their suitability. The problem is of course that not everything one might rationally expect to be what it promises to be, turns out to be just that (viz. negative Scorpio for instance!) and this makes assembling an integral self fit to be introjected a fairly hazardous business for Pisces. He needs to be very wary how he 'informs' himself and the simpler he can keep it, and the smaller the amount of self he gathers, the more of a chance he stands to get it all safely installed inside him without any internal friction and fracturing resulting. Being so automatically impressionable, he has to content himself with a simple self and not run too many risks 'trying things out'. If his search for self is shy, hesitant, slow to commit itself to an experience, then that is out of well-calculated self-preservation.

The moment he has successfully introjected his acquired self, he is in the same kind of position as Virgo was, wondering how to maintain and protect what he is inside himself – when all the time

the extraverting part of his nature is urging him to pour his feelings out into the world again. But there they would be only too
likely to inadvertently pick up conflicting impressions, despite the
efforts he is making to limit and channel the flow of his feelings
intelligently.

Now he is huddling in his safe haven, keeping the door to the
outside world locked, for fear of incurring damage to his inner
integrity. For the consciously rational Virgo, having his horizon
broadened by unconscious emotional attraction (i.e. letting his
feelings flow freely into everything he encountered) did not pose
a threat: it offered the chance of relatively painless becoming. But
for the consciously emotional Pisces, having his horizon reduced
by unconscious rational choice doesn't at all guarantee that he will
not fall into all manner of traps that could prove painful for him;
even the most careful thinking won't always protect him from
deliberate deceit, or even just the snags of the only *seemingly* safe,
the *apparently* logical, and a host of other potential pitfalls. To him
the world is a minefield of false appearances which, once they
have received his feelings into them, may reveal themselves to be
of a rather different order. He is for ever in danger of getting
caught up in becoming something he has not chosen to become,
does not want to be. It has been a difficult birth into innerness for
him, and now that he has achieved it, with caution and simplicity,
he just wants to sit tight in there: he refuses to come out of himself
again. But this means he is stuck now for an answer what to do
with his extraverting feelings.

This problem is solved for him when he begins to sense (♎)
that life is a system composed of separate but related parts, all of
them subject to some overriding law that *transcends* them, individually as well as collectively. For one thing, this brings him to
an understanding of a reality that lies so to speak outside the outside world (that is, nearer his new home ground, where he has
encapsulated himself): an inner-plane dimension. But he also
realises that the parts and participants of this somehow meaningful system do not lose their individual identity on account of their
meaningfully relating to each other. Each makes a proportional
contribution to the life of the whole and is not necessarily changed
thereby. That is to say, input into the world, contribution and participation, can be conducted from a 'safe' basis of keeping all consideration of self out of it. Or to put it quite simply: functioning in

the world is not the same as getting hopelessly caught up in it. This then he takes to be the answer to his quandary: his feelings have done their job for him now, supplying him with the 'information' he needed to establish a modest but coherent inner self. From now on they can be released into the world *free* of the need to supply him with more self-experience: as a gift, his contribution to the whole.

One could say that he divorces his actions from his self. What he does in the world with conscious feeling has nothing to do with the self he is: it is 'selfless' action based on an entirely *im*personal involvement that no longer needs to observe the limits of cautious self-preservation. He will put his feelings at the disposal of the whole world, but his self he guards in separateness.

When Virgo extraverted again, he acted *out* of his inner self: it became his guide, his personal conscience. Pisces, when he extraverts after his inner self has been established, does not act out of it but acts literally self-lessly, without inner guidelines. He automatically obeys the demands of the world, instead of an inner command. – He is pretty much back to square one, really, placing his feelings wherever he finds them in demand. It matters even less now where he places them: there are no potential consequences for him any more.

A rift has opened up between his protected, isolated inner self, and his active emotional involvement in the world. Self and life have parted company and he is only 'going through the motions' of living, entirely haphazardly. Neither does his isolated self have any new becoming of course, having been declared finished, put away safely. What he requires next is something to give meaning to his self-less involvement, and at the same time provide him with a chance of inner development. Something that will make of the delimited self and the boundless life some kind of meaningful whole again.

Beginning to use his intuition (♏), he comes to regard the many diverse forms the world displays as only imperfect expressions of their inherent, insubstantial and form-transcending essence – which may sound complicated but has the simple effect of quite changing his attitude to crude form as such: it no longer matters. He sees it as no more than the wrapping, for the most part woefully inadequate, something not really worth bothering with. The structuredness of his environment has been of tremendous importance to him: first as something to give shape to his nascent self; later as something to fear as a 'deforming' influence. He learnt to, personally, dispense with the structured world out there altogether, his extraverting feelings no longer taking on board an impress of things. Now, intuitively, he learns that emotion can dispense with form altogether. It amounts to quite a revolution in the employment of feeling to redirect it as it were *past* the (no longer held to be meaningful) form of something, straight to the heart of the matter, directly to that which lies at the enduring core of other.

Now his active life need no longer be a chaos of undirected feelings self-lessly assuming any and every shape the structured world forces on them – a sort of perpetual, impersonal echo that does not really serve any meaningful purpose. It becomes a directed drive to make emotional contact with what lies hidden behind appearances, beyond the ephemeral and ever-shifting forms and the misleading façades. Others stopped long ago being 'moulds', or models, for him; they came instead to receive his *self-less* emotions into themselves. Now at last they cease to be his 'containers' altogether. Intuitively, he finds his way to the inner or essential worth of a person, disregarding all else. And with that he is also at last free to act truly 'selflessly'.

He now also investigates more closely this other reality, the one that lies beyond his self on the inner plane. He has of course already sensed something of that, but now he is also intuitively aware of it. That other self-made introvert, Virgo, was fully employed applying his inner-self command to the world: acting out of his new-found conscience that is; as well as finding ways to update his self from without, to 'become' inside himself, in response to the new objective choices becoming available to him. The wider inner regions did not concern him, consciously. But Pisces has become far more committed to innerness as such: it is the refuge where he hides his fragile, too impressionable self in separateness from the world.

When he now consciously turns even further inward, he experiences the Inner Reality beyond his self in the same way as Cancer did, as an integral whole in which his own self lies embedded. (But where Cancer started out with an inner self that was unstructured and integral in itself, Pisces' self has been derived from the structural imprints the world left on his feelings. His is not a vague whole-self within a larger whole, needing to move out into the material sphere and prove itself of use there. His is quite a specific, matter-shaped, world-conceived self that has found its way into the embrace of all Inner Reality, and needs to remain there.)

From now on his self is no longer isolated, in its inner safe haven. Being in touch with the wider Inner Reality, but also with the essence (rather than the structure) of the world, he is free to open himself up to new inner becoming – of a quite 'riskless' kind, because this time it is not a structured becoming. That has only been a first step, a preamble, that has brought him to the point where a totally new kind of being and becoming can now take over.

It is only absolute, essential and lasting qualities he now contacts, in *both* realties, inner and outer. However, this does mean that his personal attributes, which are after all no more than a few poor internalised choices reflecting the state of his environment, now stand in need of re-examining. If he acquired a meagre minimum of a self to start with, now he finds that he will have to relinquish a good deal of even that, in a kind of catharsis: till he feels himself to be so to speak worthy of the new company he is keeping. This is the last painful testing of his inner self/worth, before he can really find inner peace. But, pared down to *his* essentials, reduced and as it were cleansed of meaningless forms and superficial values, he stands at last as a self transformed, perfected.

At the end of it all he discovers a new kinship with others: he and they share the common ground of being a particle of the Essence of all that is. He is one among many, distinct and yet related to all on account of his and their common, trans-personal root. (And while this could be said of all the signs, he is the only one to be consciously, emotionally, aware of it.) But at the same time he is also included-in-separateness with regard to the Inner Reality itself. One can say that, personally, he stands between the two realities – reminding one of Libra. But impersonally, with all his mundane actions now freed from the concerns of his self, he acts as a bridge, a link or mediator between Inner Reality and the *essence* of the world. Or call it, if you will, between God and soul.

So now his inner becoming has moved into a new phase: he shares trans-personally in the timeless life of all essence, whether of the incarnate sort or otherwise. In that sense he has transcended his personal life – without losing it though. And his selfless activities in the world serve a distinct purpose now that by-passes what he is in himself, personally, specifically, just as much as it by-passes whatever specific shape others may have assumed: he serves as a channel. More than just a go-between (as that other dual sign, Gemini, was) or a neutral arbitrator (Libra), he is a direct link: the one through which Inner Reality can contact, and nourish, all that is truly 'essential' in the world.

This is what he finally stands for: perfected action in the world and true 'mediumship' between this world and that other one he now, personally, exclusively inhabits. (Comparing the two wholly emotional signs Cancer and Pisces, one finds that the one had to work his way towards and into the material fabric of the world, while the other has worked his way out of it altogether, leaving only a de-personalised, selfless force active in it.) It is a continuing split for Pisces between being and doing, but it is a meaningful split – not so much an internal division as a giving-over of what he no longer needs to gain his own fulfilment with, so that the world might benefit.

As a channel or agent Pisces becomes a new kind of focus for the world. We did not hesitate to offload on him what we did not want for ourselves (or could not cope with alone) while he was still receptive to all form, malleable, filling us up with his empathetic feelings free of charge, though for reasons of his own. If one took him for either incredibly kind or totally stupid then, now he has us completely baffled. He is something of an enigma. He is fully (active) in this world and yet not (needfully) of it. He does not seem to care who or what we are: our appearance, our material attributes like wealth or the lack of it, our carefully engineered façades, our habits and characteristic ways of acting in the world, none of this impresses him in any way. He simply discounts it with a shrug that seems to accept and reject at the same time: to stand aside.

He knows from personal experience that a start has to be made somewhere, that what we base our selves on in the beginning is hardly representative of what we essentially are, or of what we could be, eventually, if we rid ourselves of all the ill-formed clutter of our lives and selves. But unlike Scorpio, he does not demand that we rid ourselves of anything. – Still, he does manage to make us acutely aware of our failings by so to speak looking through or past them and addressing himself only to what is of lasting worth in us. The effect is both humbling *and* supportive, though. He waves our imperfections aside, accepting them as merely the ways of the world, and does not identify us with them. He so to speak abstracts us from our context, without condemning the context (that is none of his business): it is a double acceptance, which 'forgives' us our worldly failings, and also honours us as the absolutely valid and valuable individual core realities that we are, amid the jumble of our haphazard mundane attributes.

In the beginning he was giving us his empathy purely for the sake of his own 'in-formation'. After he had withdrawn his formed self, introjected it, he was letting his feelings flow to no purpose at all: as a gift without aim since it had no command centre. Now – and we may well be too obtuse to notice any of these differences – he is channelling through his active, selfless feelings the whole force of a transpersonal Inner Reality: the Law of all worlds become perfect feeling.

Sagittarius put us in touch with our own inner reality, and *via* that with what transcends it. But through Pisces now we have *direct* contact with all Inner Reality, at whatever stage of development towards innerness, or recognition of a transcending Reality, we may personally be: emotional contact, which defies logical definition – bypassing our formalistic understanding, or more likely, our critical doubts and quibbles. In a sense, he becomes a safety net: as the last of the signs he rescues what can be, after all else has been to no avail in teaching us how to live according to the inherent laws of life. Strangely, he comes to the rescue not with last-minute admonitions but, quite simply, the offer of complete acceptance. As in the beginning, the most troubled and troublesome of us are queuing up to take advantage of his free offer, and whether or not we consciously notice that we are now dealing with something of a different order, we receive this gift he hands on to us, and we receive it into our essential selves. It will not fill our pockets, it is insubstantial, unformed, and yet even the staunchest sceptic feels himself somehow touched by it.

The situation has been reversed: from being indiscriminately personally attracted-by and caught-up-in, Pisces has developed into being a universal centre of attraction himself, impersonally, though personally he is no more than *essentially* one of us. As a selfless agent he has become an emotional centre for others to congregate around, a force that embraces them without personally appropriating and owning them and without detracting from them in any way. The mature Pisces takes the opposite kind of action to Scorpio: he does not work from the basis of a narrow, deep and impersonal conviction that serves as a guideline to rejecting, purging, cleansing and curing the world of its excessive blemishes. His action is based instead on the broad sweep of impersonal acceptance that receives the world's rejects and out- casts and gives them the healing experience of being included, a new dignity and a new meaning in the context of being essential- ly accepted, despite their failings.

If one can picture him as surrounded by a mixed crowd the individual members of which are all equally acceptable to him, then one will see that while in one respect he has a kind of homogenising effect – differentness has been abolished, we have *all* had our shortcomings 'forgiven' – at the same time our indi- vidual differences are nevertheless being fully respected: *because* all our imperfections are being discounted we are free to *stay* the separate, incomplete, and hence imperfect individuals we are.

The consciously discriminating Virgo, who as it were dissected us and accepted us piecemeal into his own self-structure, showed us how to become consciously distinct; and how to understand ourselves, how to intelligently handle our being 'becoming' indi- viduals, in conscientious interaction with others. What Pisces does for us is to bring us together again in the common experience of being members of a unified world where our differences do not count against us. An emotional re-union that by no means requires us to lose what separate individuality we have gained through divisive thought. And yet more maybe than any other sign he brings us face to face with the realisation of how little of these selves that we have thoughtfully constructed will stand the test of association with ultimate values. Nevertheless, the gift that comes to us through him is a free gift, there are no strings attached. We are perfectly free to let our shortcomings be over- looked without passing on this generosity of spirit to others. But really only deliberate obstinacy can stop us drawing the obvious conclusion: that those others are our equals, our brothers in imperfection – as well as in the gift we receive through Pisces. Our conscience, developed in tandem with our individual under- standing of ourselves in Virgo, should hardly allow it. If, as extraverts, we have not yet been through the Virgo stage of devel- opment though, we will simply be drawn into the oneness of the crowd. We will lose the inconsequential personal attributes we have unconsciously and unthinkingly acquired, for the time being, to partake (at the emotional level) of a common identity that is, in itself, formless.

Dividing himself meaningfully between inner self-being and the transcending-of-self in action, Pisces has transformed the experience of wholeness. First he had to grow away from what one could call his primary objective wholeness – his initial state of being totally identified with (or rather by!) all of his environment. Only then could he become a separate *part*, a conscious self in isolation, away from the pernicious influence of the whole, which will always try to pull the rug from under such separatist inclinations. But it is precisely through being such a 'separatist', in effect a self-made introverting introvert, that he is able to free (and freely give away into service) the other half of his nature: the pure extraverting non-self, selflessness in action. And it is through this that he also makes of wholeness something totally new for our common benefit: a collective experience fit for individuals thoughtfully aware of themselves as such.

If we follow his example, we too find our lives meaningfully divided: on the one hand, we can need-lessly be our lasting selves, and on the other, we can self-lessly give over our actions to fulfil the meaningful demands of life. But the effect of this separation is actually a re-union in every possible way. We are individually reunited with our common Source and through it with each other – our overt differences now set in proportion – and we are actively reconciled with the imperfections of the whole world, which we no longer 'take personally'.

As a teacher Pisces sets us an example that will have the uncomprehending head shakers busy again. With Sagittarius we were celebrating *life's riches*: symbolic of our inner riches, our great freedom in innerness, and of the wealth of Inner Reality as such, which we had learned to access intuitively, and to obey. Scorpio, on the other hand, showed us that there were things to get rid of, to do without, if we would obey the demands of our collective Source and find a valid basis for our shared lives.

With Pisces now – who needs nothing more from this world for himself – we can celebrate, paradoxically, our symbolic 'poverty'. Reduced to what we *truly* are, something of the order of blips or minute specks, we are nevertheless included as valid in the

Whole. And once we have like Pisces emotionally 'grown up', we no longer act out of external obedience, as it were, to this inner-plane Law – instead, we are individually part of it, have our becoming in it, and act as its channel and mouthpiece as a matter of course: Perfect Love (i.e. the transcendent Law in its emotional aspect) simply uses us. We are ready to play the role of universal helper, who does not ask 'selfish' questions.

This of course is the theme that Aries takes up, when in search of the first fluid definition of self, he comes to act 'selflessly' for the benefit of a better, collective, future for us all.

Innerness, or call it personal depth; and the wholeness, harmony or integrity of self: these are the things that Pisces was initially struggling to achieve and couldn't without the help of his unconscious functions. If he misuses them, he has like Gemini two options: a passive and an active one.

He can either, passively, attempt to feel the whole of his inner-ness – feel 'deeply whole' – in each and every separate part of the world: equivalent to Gemini's 'string of closed rooms'. Or else, he can try and actively narrow down the diversities of the world, with a view to converting it into one single grand harmonious whole which should then serve him, in its entirety, as a suitable self to introject: equivalent to Gemini's 'flat world'.

To start with the passive type: When he thinks about the world ($\mathrm{m\!P}\!\rightarrow$), he compulsively seizes on every particle to examine it with a logic so detailed his assessments make no *overall* sense at all – and purely material considerations are uppermost in his mind. Once he has would-be shrewdly calculated something to be acceptable to him, it is to the exclusion of all else. The rest of the world no longer exists for him. Whatever he makes his own is 'it' and he pours *all* his feelings in that direction, he becomes nothing but that, and triumphantly carries the form of it inward to fill his inner-self space with. This way he smallest thing is elevated – or exaggerated – to the status of immense *importance*.

He plunges headlong and with such concentrated emotion into

the smallest and most mundane thing, action, or aspect of a relationship, it looks as if he was constantly 'deeply' moved – as if behind the emotional force with which he approaches things, there were the directedness of an inner response that made him react like that. It appears to give him inner depth, inner content. That this is only a fake depth – shallow, unstable, of no consequence – soon becomes apparent, because it takes him no time at all to show the same 'response' to something totally different, unconnected and contradictory. What he introjects goes only skin deep: before it has had time to settle, before it even gets very far on its way inward, he has met with something else that he thinks will make a far better self for him to have. And he is never content, he thinks of his self as needing to be perfect (♍←). He constantly decants what inner content he has (almost) acquired in favour of the next thing to take his fancy: this is really 'it', this time – every time.

He is a fickle follower of fashion because it takes very little to appeal to his short-sighted, earthbound thinking and to tap the full flow of his emotional conviction that now he is really about to find the perfect form for his inner self. The support he gives to the ideology or belief system of the moment is neat and undiluted emotional gush, and though he may not be able to quote every chapter and verse, he has a predilection for the more involved and hair-splitting types. Given a chance, he shops around unashamedly among the sects and sub-cults of the day, each time ready to give them all he has got. He is a well-practised 'convert', a magpie borrower of self-styles. But, unfortunately, with each not-quite-inner change he has to bear the pain of loss, at the same time as he experiences the satisfaction of filling his vacuum anew. Like this he goes from one bitter-sweet turmoil to the next.

His compulsively fussy deliberations before he takes the plunge into his latest one hundred per cent commitment are so much wasted effort. With his severely limited horizon he is fair game for any deceit. He will comb through the small print but miss the wider implications altogether. His self-imposed 'conversion pains' are bad enough, though he has got used to them as the price he has to pay for his scheduled self-improvement. But to be robbed of his vulnerable, meagre bit of an inner identity by others, through forceful disillusionment, this is just too much to bear.

Whenever he finds that what he is holding shakily and not very deep inside him, is not at all the good idea he thought it was – or in

some other way finds the original outward model for his self invalidated – he is seized with such self-disgust, he 'empties himself
out' in a convulsive reaction that leaves him, again, without a
shred of self. Neither can he find anything in his environment to
quickly adopt as new self now: he frantically searches for something that will meet the demands of his ultra-critical rational attitude, but he would need to be lucky to find such a thing in a hurry.

The spectacle he makes of himself with this kind of 'outburst'
certainly rivals what the other two negative Water signs could
come up with – Scorpio, whose unacknowledged 'demon' self,
hidden underneath the immaculate exterior, burst out in a fright-
ening display of bottled-up resentment; and Cancer, who experienced sudden 'inbursts' of the banished parts of his self he least
wanted to know, making him behave so uncharacteristically
badly he was almost believed if he claimed in retrospect to have
been 'possessed'. Pisces' outbursts are in that sense less shocking
maybe, they do not suddenly reveal hidden negative aspects of
his self. What they do reveal though is how little progress he has
made on the road to an established inner self, or self of any kind
for that matter. His outbursts are seen as childish.

Uncontrollably he pours out to public view all he is, and this is
followed by a desperate, panicky and yet pernickety search for
something or someone to act as recipient of his feelings, a new
best-possible mould to cast himself into. He throws his feelings
about, and they automatically go probing and fishing and trying
out... but nothing appears to his *reason* to be good enough. This
sets up a kind of chain reaction: (self)acceptance followed by
immediate, renewed (self)rejection, outburst following outburst,
and no end to his emotional raving. He obviously needs something from us but does not want any of the things we can offer
him. It makes as much sense as a starving man criticising the
menu. People lose patience with him, embarrassed, angry at his
rejection – and this at least gives him a chance to give up hope of
filling his vacuum here and now and to lapse into a calmer sort of
sorrow at his loss. End of hysterics. –

Despite his meticulous selectiveness, his self keeps draining
out of him, leaving him back where he was in the beginning. But
in this state he is fair game again, of course, to the persuasive powers of deception, and victim of his own limited ability to gain a
comprehensive idea of the nature of things. He credulously takes

everything at face value, not because he fails to look closely, but because he looks *too* closely: his mental tunnel vision shows him the smooth face of a thing in close-up, while the large hairy body attached to it goes unnoticed – and what is accepted is accepted, introjected (as far as it goes), sooner rather than later to be disgorged in disgust.

He will have similar, minor, outbursts each time he comes up against a new 'idol' (i.e. perfect mould to receive his feelings), or an old one in a different style. In a flash flood of feeling he jettisons all he is, in order to make room inside for this improved version of a self. His screams of horror and his screams of delight signify the same thing, really: that-out-there doesn't accord with this-in-here. His barely-inner self is never securely enough enclosed against changes, whether imposed on him or desired by him.

He is really no better off than he was at the start, only getting increasingly worried what bad surprises, or suddenly inferior-looking content, he will find inside himself next. No amount of close scrutiny seems to help ward off the infiltration of negative or worthless elements into his shallow innerness. He constantly works himself up into monumental emotional 'depths', but either his narrow choices fail him, or he lets them go, in a compulsive desire for self-improvement.

Either way, he never gets round to encapsulating anything deep and safe and stable inside his inner space. His inner self is a thin-skinned bubble so close to the surface it shows: a temptation to some people's sharpness; and a standing invitation to those who think they know better than he what he ought to be. He lives in a terrible mixture of constant fear – nameless suspicions that extend even to his own inner nature – and at the same time a compulsive readiness to embrace the silliest hazards in the short-sighted good faith that he is on to something reliably perfect at last.

It only takes a vague and collective rebuke and *he* feels personally guilty. Even being faced with false accusations has him suspecting himself of being if not *the* then still *a* culprit: he knows from experience that his self is not to be trusted, always turning out to have been a 'wrong' one. Which means that every sin in the book one can confront him with can ultimately be forced on him. He will reason (narrowly and faultily) that he did not commit it, and turn his head the other way in an effort to ignore our accusations, but his deeply ingrained self-doubt keeps telling him that in principle we are right: he is *always* wrong, bad, worthless. He has no option then but 'confess': another emotional waterfall of self-disgust. We can offload our sins on him, and despite the most strenuous thinking all he can do in response is be sorry for himself. Sorry, that is, for another self he has lost.

No one is easier to lead by the nose or harder to pin down (bar the passive negative Gemini type). With his limited, concretistic thinking and desire to find the best possible self, he can only too easily come to follow the worst examples – dressed up as keen logic, sound practicality, or some individual sub-species of perfection in action – and then he may end up looking, in an imitative way, every bit as black as Scorpio. But whatever the colour he may be wearing, it is best to take it with a pinch of salt. The emotive noise he makes about it all only betrays the painful insecurity of his (inner-self) position. He is not making any headway at all towards establishing himself in his own inner world.

Unconsciously sensing (♎) the world to be an intricate web of interrelated parts, each with its own value, should enable him to take a step back to see things in proportion and assess their *relative* value dispassionately before he decides to commit himself emotionally, if at all. But compulsively misusing this function too, he only comes to expect that the whole of his environment should supply him with nothing but pleasant experiences. On principle he takes everything to be intrinsically valuable, one thing as good as the next. He takes the extreme position of blithely assuming that the world is really whole, wholesome and harmonious – everything, in fact, that he is not managing to be inside himself, on a permanent basis. And his one desire becomes to partake of this ready-made harmony.

He is quite prepared to elevate the shabbiest thing to the same status as something more patently worthwhile, just so long as the outcome spells pleasure for him rather than pain. But of course this has the effect of demoting his rationalistic, over-fussy choices to no more than arbitrary momentary decisions. They are meaningless now but for the illusory conviction that he is clever enough to have some thoughtful control over his life. It does not really matter what he chooses. The successive 'perfect' selves he acquires, one after the other, are now all equally good. He sees no contradiction in that, though. He simply expects the world to be a chooser's paradise.

The way he sees it now, there is no point, really , in introjecting any of his ephemeral selves, if there is not even a good reason why one should last in preference to the other. He would be so much better off if he could save himself the pain of inner loss brought about by his restless choosing and un-choosing, the constant upheaval of finding himself empty and self-less again. This he can do by setting up his self, not just-inside himself, but just-outside: as an encapsulated part of his environment. A sheltered self-zone which is both away from and right inside the source of his endless becomings and un-becomings. *His* bit of pleasant world.

Now selves can come and go: he is always ready for a quick and painless 'swap'. The fact that there are some thoroughly unpleasant aspects to his environment he deals with thoughtfully, by making full use of his limited mental horizon. He refuses to think that such things could be and abstains wisely from looking at them. And replacing his unmaintainable inner self with a more 'mundane' version, he actually finds that building up *objective* barriers against the intrusion of negative experiences is a lot easier than trying to strengthen his *inner* defences. He curls up in a comfortable chair, doors locked and curtains drawn, and sticks his nose deeply into the purest, most make-believe fiction. Now he is whole, and safe.

To say he has regressed to his initial position of being a purely extraverting extravert who has his selves outside his inner space is true enough, up to a point. His shallow inner self has certainly 'prolapsed' till there is nothing left of genuine innerness, though the fragile bubble his chosen self used to be (only just and never for long) inside him, has taken on a rather more sturdy construction on being projected outward. It is quite a tough sort of capsule, woven with the help of compulsive, pie-in-the-sky expectations and his carefully maintained tunnel vision, which enables him to evade what would not please him.

To all intents and purposes what he has done is to build himself an 'outward innerness', a world within the world to ensconce himself in safely. The most impressionable extravert from the outset, he has at last managed to find himself a delimited corner to huddle in; a 'closed room' not unlike the sort Gemini had, and the next best thing he could find after failing repeatedly to close off his inner 'room'.

One can call him an escapist but the point is not so much that he has escaped from the troubles, efforts and pains of the world as such, but more specifically that he has run away from the to him painful (and indeed impossible) task of forming and maintaining a deeply secure inner type of being, in separateness from his intrusive environment. Again, one can call him a drop-out instead, but it is best to bear in mind that what he primarily dropped out of is his own individual inner space.

He is definitely cheating when he substitutes an objective, imitation, innerness for the real thing, but he is hardly the first escapist, technically speaking. There was for instance the introverting introvert Sagittarius, getting addicted to the whole gamut of sense-able things in the world and locking himself out of his inner self as a result. Finding life too difficult and hurtful to manage, Sagittarius tried to find refuge in a substitute for his lost innerness that would deny the existence of the world (and his compulsive need of it) altogether: he crept into the dark hole of depression, far away from any temptation to his senses – for a while. Pisces, soon finding the job of becoming a de facto introvert too impossibly 'upsetting', tries to take permanent refuge in the expedient of another kind of fake innerness: a worldly enclave that will hold whatever harmony and wholesomeness he can abstract from his environment and place there safely, behind a shield of deliberate ignorance that amounts to illusion. In a sense he too sits in the dark, but it is a pleasant sort of darkness, a womb of fond unknowing.

Sagittarius developed a taste for simply anything and everything that would make his senses tingle and went from one thirst or hunger to the next 'related' one (♊). But Pisces develops in the last resort an emotional addiction to the more 'refined' substances and delights the world has to offer him (♎). The pleasures he appreciates are chosen not just for the sake of their sensual appeal, but more especially for what they signify to him: to have nothing but pleasant experiences means that he can stay emotionally on an even keel. They make him whole, without effort on his part. And valuing the *content* of the pleasure above all else, that is to say the intrinsic value of it, he can actually fancy himself as partaking of something that transcends the mundane level.

One can picture Sagittarius quaffing pint after pint, enjoying each gulp and stuffing himself with a wide variety of food besides. Pisces for his part applies himself to neat spirits and various world-enhancing drugs – from soap opera to heroin – with a would-be abstracted air, in the faith that he is contacting/being something 'higher' or more 'inner'. He would quite deny that he is a simple emotional extravert dependent for what he is on the least painful choices available to him.

This unconscious pretence he can extend to anything 'deeply' or 'transcendingly' pleasant at all. Since he does not bother with judging but simply expects (the best), and hence sees no difference between one kind of 'higher' value and another, one can sell him any number of would-be good and perfect things. He will swallow anything once he has subjected it to his usual myopic scrutiny. He could become addicted to a thousand different wonderful things, from those exquisitely unrealistic romantic novels to a mixture of mattress stuffing, mustard and a raft of supernatural promises. The reason, though, that despite his lack of true discernment he actually ends up hooked on a relatively small number of things is that, unlike Sagittarius, he becomes emotionally 'attached' to them. Just as in the beginning, his feelings are flooding into any container his environment provides – with the difference that now he has 'curled up in' a specific type of environment: chosen as much with his compulsively short-sighted discrimination and his over-the-top perfectionism, as with his unbalanced desire for a simply 'good' world.

He has taken his pick from among a choice of nice and easy and comfortable cocoons to settle in, and he is in no hurry to exchange it for another type. He has all he needs in there, not only for a stable existence but also for his becoming. It may seem like a kind of fortress he inhabits – with an effective moat of well-maintained illusion and deliberately arranged ignorance around it – but it is a highly permeable construct all the same. He is by no means seizing up in a hermetically sealed world of his own.

Rather, he wears his clever, illusory bubble like a selective shield: to screen him from the to him unthinkable, and the to him unbearably unpleasant. Apart from that he will allow anything – and anybody – into his mock-inner space. He is not alone in there. He may well sit there technically speaking all by himself, with purely fictional characters for enlivening company (becoming them, that is; feeling himself into them and assuming their shape for his own identity). But he may equally admit 'real' others to join him in there – he never did make a distinction, after all. He will be pleased to include any of them – man, beast or cinematic hero – in his exclusive set-up, and any number of them. Just so long as they don't go counter to his narrow 'ideology' and don't confound his 'idealistic' expectations too badly. Despite that exclusive bubble around him that he carries with him wherever he goes, he is an easy joiner. And he not only joins others, he becomes them, interchangeably, painlessly, and all the while thinks himself perfect, a beautiful self.

Gone are the days when he could only find fault with himself. If anything is at fault it is the 'outside' world – though he can't see why it should be (not seeing anything for what it is). 'They' probably have the wrong attitudes: not like his, which he takes to be inscrutably deep, and highly moral, and altogether of a transcendent order. Nicely ensconced in his edited version of our world, he looks down on us in a vague sort of way. He would not admit that we pose a threat to his equilibrium. He prefers to say that it sort of upsets him to think of us as excluded from the elevated sphere he inhabits. He knows better than let us upset him, though, he reserves his feelings for his real (and not so real) 'soul mates'. For the most part we simply do not exist for him – so long as we do not forcibly intrude into that away-from-it-all world of his. But whatever he may pretend to himself, he is still in a vulnerable position.

His stand-in for complete inner peace and harmony may work for a while, but sooner or later his bubble will be pricked. And it is no help either sharing it with others, maintaining a *collective* illusion of defence against outside pressures. As it is, there are plenty of inside pressures at work, quite as likely to deflate his attempts to find himself a heaven on earth. Being compulsively critical, he *will* argue for the sake of arguing: it is only too easy for him to fall out with his 'brothers and sisters', to bicker with the kindred spirits he is on such intimate terms with. And his (shared or otherwise) 'ecstasies' are only worldly ones after all, fallible and likely to let him down. His improbable heroes *will* reveal their downside. His drug-induced highs turn out nightmares. His wooden god fail to work the expected miracle.

Whether he has his bubble burst for him, or whether he 'falls out' with/of it, eventually he once again finds himself self-less. And with both his real inner space and the bogus one, the cocoon, having failed him as 'places' to establish a permanent identity in, he is not only self-less now but 'homeless' as well, standing with all his feelings exposed.

It becomes clear that he has not really learnt to resist the formative effects of his environment. He is hooked on his exclusively happy expectations, and thoroughly fussy over each detail as well, but none of that will keep the hurtful world at bay in the absence of a fairy-tale castle in the air to hide his feelings away in. – Whether he approves of it or not, his environment is already shaping him again from scratch: threatening to give him a self he does not want. His 'safe' bubble destroyed, he is helplessly exposed to what he deems to be all the wrong influences. In effect, he is back to square one – a nobody at the mercy of his surroundings – but he is also a 'has-been' who knows and expects better than that.

He is quite unable to accept this self, this identity that is being thrust on him now. Unconsciously and compulsively refusing what consciously he is becoming, his only good, even perfect, option is the ultimate escapism: to flee from world and life altogether, abandon the whole idea of becoming somebody in this world. We are sorry for him in his desperate plight. We think we may understand his refusal to accept an inferior life, or a self he cannot be content with – but given his poor acceptance record the blame can hardly be sought with the imperfections of an evil world alone!

Life is bringing intolerable pressures to bear on his intolerant mind-set and his uncontrollable desire for an entirely good world. If he feels all the wrongs, pains and horrors of the world as his own now, personally, we need not interpret it as a sign of a tender heart: it is his continuing inability to 'stand his self aside', in true innerness, that is making him suffer. There is no helping him at all. He is driven by his worldly compulsions and, absurdly, they are driving him out of this world.

None of the other negative signs, compulsively immersed in their mundane interests, could extricate themselves again from their various 'addictions'. Even Scorpio for whom death became the ultimate object of desire could not let go. For Pisces, who has had at least some short-lived experience of being genuinely 'out of this world' and for whom establishing himself beyond the material world is the goal he quite rightly seeks (if in all the wrong ways), extricating himself becomes a distinct possibility. All he has to do is to project his other-worldly expectations and perfectionist aspirations into what amounts to yet another substitute innerness: not his own inner space, his *own* 'beyond', but simply that Other World as such, however he may define it, the one where life cannot get at him any more. Whether he actually hopes to find the sort of self and life there that he envisages and has in mind, or not, he will at the least hope for some peace to be had, and freedom from the imperfections that hound him inescapably here.

But there is also still his intuitive function (♍) for him to make use of, in preference to taking such a drastic step. (Needless to say he abuses this one as well.) This brings him to the stubbornly held conviction that form is worth nothing at all, essence everything – and this essence is hidden somewhere *inside* form. Consequently it does not matter at all what concrete form his self takes. Form is an outward thing only, and his world-shaped self only an 'outward self' that does not interest him any longer.

His permanently exposed feelings see to it that he acquires a growing kaleidoscope of (passively) imitative selves, each a thing of the moment. But he can disregard them, in the good faith that somewhere inside all that lies his *essentially* perfect and all-good self. He fancies himself a disembodied soul, and his homeless, peripatetic, ever-changing self is only the shell, of no consequence at all. He no longer cares what he 'looks like'. Unwashed, dressed up, undressed, in rags or in finery, it is all the same to him. We can style him any way we please, he sees no point in resisting.

This is his new 'innerness': an imaginary 'real' self behind the outward appearances. And just as everything he takes to be merely superficial about *him* holds no more interest for him, so everything that is obvious and freely revealed about *us* is no use to him either. What he needs for his would-be inner becoming are all those things of a hidden nature that are tucked away out of sight and have to be extracted from the dark depths of life, our collective and individual depths. And since these things are essentially formless – as formless as his imaginary self – he cannot of course lay his hands on them for owning and keeping: he can only partake of them vicariously, share in them together with us.

It would not be so bad if one had to hide only one's secrets from him, but what is inside our pockets is not safe from him either. Not that he steals, necessarily. But he expects us to share, to give from deep inside our selves and lives. Of course the money we may give him, for instance, is only symbolic to him of the (more or less) deep sympathy he elicits. (And he will have frittered it away in no time at all so that he can come back for more – more sympathy, that is, the money itself being essentially worthless to him.)

He begs shamelessly. He tries to infiltrate our innermost spaces with over-familiarity. Unable to maintain a safe haven of his own, he asks to be admitted into what he takes to be ours. He trespasses. He cranes his neck and peers through keyholes to catch a glimpse of our hidden lives, the more intimate the better. He knocks at our doors under the flimsiest pretext, nosing around, asking to be 'adopted', or at least to be given a symbolic hand-out that shows that we are prepared to share something of our innerness with him (or the nearest thing that could pass for such). He may criticise what we produce for him out of the back of the cupboard, but then that has always been his way. It will do him all the same, being only the visible token of what he is really after.

He drifts about and sees no reason why he should 'pull himself together'. As far as he is concerned his 'outward self' can be as fragmented and contradictory as it likes, an instant echo of his environment, a hollow performance that plays itself out with no direction from him whatsoever. He despises what *we* would call his real self every bit as much as we are inclined to, and makes mysterious claims on behalf of what he really-really and essentially is – a self we cannot see, of course, it being formless. We are hardly inclined to take his word for it, or to interpret his hints as meaning we are dealing with a count in disguise. Experience has taught us that his words are not to be relied on. Such mere formalities as facts mean nothing to him any more, even if he is as fussy as ever about choosing his words. There is simply no connection between what, puzzlingly, he claims to be, and what we see before our eyes.

Like positive Pisces he too has finally divided himself into his self-less activities and a self beyond form, substance or action. But in his case it is a life left to live itself, its shambolic doings none of his responsibility, disowned and left entirely under the direction of his environment. And the will o' the wisp he calls an inner self is only the thin stream of *our* innerness that he can tap us for and channel through him. He consumes it eagerly, compulsively – but how ever much of it we may feed into him, he never puts on any 'inner weight'. He never 'grows up': he never grows *in*.

It is easy to mistake him for a deliberate liar and false impersonator. We may think it appropriate then to try to 'reform' him, and not always gently either. Since he does not care one hoot what form we make him assume, he will go along with our plans willingly, lapping up our essentially good intentions and presumably deep concern as the very fuel his insubstantial so-called self runs on. But unless one virtually imprisons him (another 'inside' experience that will do him) the first contact with other influences has him relapsing promptly. He is spineless, jelly-like, and he agrees with us that what we see of him is no good. Unconsciously though, he reckons he is succeeding quite well now. We will never know just how much he values our attempts to help him, and how much benefit he derives from them. Misunderstanding him entirely, we find him quite outrageously ungrateful when he discards the nice new shape we have so carefully tried to impose on him. Our efforts are unable to touch him deeply – the only depth he has is an imaginary one, and that a rather wishy-washy communal one. We have helped him belong somewhere and be somebody, and he certainly appreciates that; but he does not see why we should expect him to be faithful to the outward behaviour we have forced on him. How shallow of us!

He may get sympathy and help here and there, but he is just as likely to 'tap us' for less positive things. Essentially, this does not matter to him. He feeds on scandal. He is always wanting to know the worst about us, the most deeply hidden. If he cannot wheedle something positive out of us then he is quite prepared to provoke our normally contained anger, for instance. If he gets as much in the way of violent outbursts as upwelling pity for contributions to his so-called inner being, that does not really pain him. He has cut himself off from his own 'surface self': he no longer inhabits it. Instead, he lives entirely vicariously, voyeuristically, passively letting our 'depths' flow through him... or our somehow transcending 'heights' for that matter, and any abysmal or covert behaviour on the part of persons highly born or placed will have a doubly irresistible appeal for him! – His own feelings, always his undoing, can no longer touch him now. In truth, he has become entirely insensitive. His outcries are an automatic response; his loud wailing takes place all by itself, as everything in his life. Cruelty or kindness, as long as it is 'profound' that is all he asks. And while our indifference would not exactly *hurt* him, it would certainly starve him into ceasing to exist in his own eyes.

He uses us and he has no objections to us using him. That is to say, he helps himself to our innerness and we may help ourselves to his (to him) worthless body, his (to him) useless activities, his (to him) quite immaterial appearance. In that sense he is having the 'best' of the bargain, he is cheating us. He will take our best in exchange for his worst – dressed up a bit, if that is what we insist on. He will be the drudge for us, the door mat, the dear little pet on a lead, the punch bag, the perfumed thing to drape over our arm and show off like a fashion accessory. He is putty to us, for which we may either love him dearly or else condemn him. He is content to lend, sell or give us bits of him, or the whole thing, if that is what we demand in return for a taste of what is deep inside our pockets, hearts, minds – anywhere behind our exterior – and we can have *his* exterior in exchange. This poor helpless homeless victim is short-changing us all the time.

He sucks away at us like a leach and this act of channelling something of us through him constitutes the 'true' extent of his life for him and gives him his ever-changing, purely participatory 'inner self'. He does not admit to being personally hollow. He finds himself fulfilled in his role as parasite, his symbiotic relationship with us: as if we were constantly filling his inner space for him, rather than allowing him to drift through an experience of our 'depths' (extracted from us, made visible, externalised). He has finally come to 'idolise' us all, regardless of how we treat him. We have what he can never, personally, achieve: something or other tucked away in an inner space. He no longer takes us for his moulds or models; but getting us to share some of our 'inner essence' with him, he actually imagines that 'really' he *is* us.

Even if we use him and abuse him, he still counts himself lucky, raised to a higher level of being, and given a painless stability – at the cost of his feelings, which he has quite cut himself off from, and of his true self-consciousness, and indeed the only true self (or collection of various echo-like selves) that he has. He may be lucky. We may not rob him or abuse him too much in return for our 'inspiring' company. Then again, directly or indirectly, it may cost him his life. He would not grudge us that either. The life of form and substance is nothing to him, he just holds it in contempt. But if he reckons to have gained some personal 'content' to take with him to the other-world, he will find himself disappointed. He has scrounged all he could, but he is as empty-handed as ever approaching his waiting inner space. He will have to start all over again, *yet* again.

But Pisces can also take another mistaken course, misusing his unconscious functions in an active rather than a passive way. He considers the whole world from a compulsively rational angle and develops an excessive preoccupation with every material detail (♍→). But he takes this to mean that if only he can impose a narrowly intellectual and quite concretely exact order on his environment, then this will be the perfect cure for the chaos of his repeated failures, the disharmony he keeps importing into his inner space, and the resulting discontinuity of his self. If he can get his environment sufficiently narrowed down and in effect unified under some tidy overall Idea, then introjecting a self shaped by such an environment will present no problem to him. If he can make a collective outer 'harmony' come to pass, then his inner one will automatically result.

He equips himself with a central thought-construct, a Theory, an all-enveloping Idea, and he uses it as an *intellectual* mould into which to press the world and shape it. Having done that, it will be safe enough for him to allow himself to *feel* for the world: it will now in turn be a fit mould to receive his impressionable emotions, and thus shape his self.

What it amounts to in practice, is that he approaches his environment with the intention of screening, sorting, and 'tidying' it. He is thoughtfully prepared to empathise with only a very narrow spectrum of his whole environment – though what he lacks in breadth he automatically makes up for with the sheer force of his 'ideologically' directed stream of feelings. And since he thinks of his self as needing to turn out absolutely perfect (♍←), it is nothing short of an ideal Idea he bears in mind when he subjects the world to minute analysis, to check what of it might be acceptable to him.

He sorts the world into two piles, mentally, one fit to receive his feelings, the other not. Which leaves him with precious little to approve of, and an awful lot to reject. To augment 'his' pile, everything is split and split again: in search of partial perfection, of bits that will do where the whole thing fails the test. In the name of overall harmonious wholeness he will dissect and dismember, so that there may be less for him to have to ignore, emotionally. He manages to appropriate the nose out of a person's face as deserving a stream of feeling directed towards it, but the rest of face, body, person not meeting with his approval, he regards all *that* with studious indifference. Depending on what he is looking for in us we may be no more to him than walking brains, or muscles, biological entities, or souls, producers or consumers or any number of nothing-but's.

Not that his thoughtful amputations get him anywhere. We are still annoyingly inseparable from our 'impurities'. How ever much he may manipulate the thing in his mind, he still can't deduct from life the bits he does not want to include in his tidy, mental, indirect self-construction project. He is of course free to decorate his house *entirely* in post office red or pristine white, but when it comes to the more lively matters around him he really cannot rely on his reductionist approach alone. Every time he thinks his environment is safe enough to 'feel for', some unscheduled concomitant rears its head. We tread on his tender toes all the time, turning out to be much more than he had bargained for.

When he begins to sense (♎) that the world is a whole interconnected system of relative values, he hits on what he hopes will be a better, fail-safe approach. If he cannot edit things out, then at least the can arrange his world in such a way as to put everything in its right and proper place with regard to his central Idea. There is perfection, stability and security, and a harmony of sorts, to be gained from a tightly systematised world which not only includes everything and everyone, but keeps them all in their appointed positions and subject to an overall law. Having failed to successfully edit out, he now tries to edit everything in: aiming at an all-embracing, tidy, moralistic, lawful sort of world system. And his Idea, the hub of the whole exercise, now broadens into a Thought-System of dazzling complexity.

Having plucked us apart, he now reassembles the pieces – not with a view to making us whole again but in an effort to rearrange life in *categorical* ways, slotting each piece into its logical place. It is a totally inorganic set-up, a world where a single overall label is applied to everything and everybody. Every stick and stone is roped in, not a plant or animal is immune: they all have to serve in some capacity, to fit into his grand identity design. Even the past and the dead are incorporated somewhere, it really wouldn't do anyone opting out.

He makes it clear from the start that his new-world system will stand or fall as a whole. And his aim is to squeeze us into it, in a vice of undifferentiatedness. A world of uniformity and conformity is what he requires. Somehow making every aspect of our lives fit into his scheme of things is his idea of creating the dependable harmony that is to be his one day.

Meantime, he has withdrawn his feelings from his environment altogether. It is no use appealing to them, he is withholding them on principle, while he bides his time. – Instead, he lets them pour freely into his thought-construct of a self instead. This is no longer just a dry Idea (♍) to him: it is also his Vision of a Better World (♎). And this he tries hard to sell us – after all, if it is calculated to supply him with the best (and only) possible self, then it stands to reason that it must have enough merit to be good for us too. Consequently he does not feel the least bit underhanded when, in effect, he tells us all about the self he could be, if only *we* would be it first, collectively.

He preaches, lectures, propounds and promises at every opportunity, drawing our attention to the failings of the world, as it stands, and us, as we are. He gestures suggestively towards that theoretical Perfect World he is always gazing at, he sheds tears of rapture at the very thought of the paradisal conditions that will prevail, if only we would put his design into practice. No more strife or disunity, complete peace and freedom from violence or threats of any kind – even the dogs will be rendered incapable of barking, it would appear. It sounds attractive enough, if one can let *him* do all the thinking. The apparently deep emotions he displays while advertising his beautiful ideology are enough to have us convinced that he is sincerely concerned for our well-being. Nothing could be further from his mind.

His emotional outpourings point vaguely in our direction, but if one looks a bit more closely one sees him addressing himself feelingfully to a spot somewhere above our heads. The fine abstract, the Ideal, is what he is addressing, the image of a self that sits there like a much yearned-for castle in the air, an utterly desirable project on the drawing board. That is what he feels for, his self in its not yet embodied state. He has become a narcissist, letting himself feel, consciously, for nothing but his self.

He has thought it up, envisaged it with every detail worked out – he could introject it straight way and have done with his worldly manipulations. Instead, he stares at it as something unattainable at present: somewhere out there, of the world but not really in it; waiting to be made a concrete fact before he can assume ownership of it. He is so intent on his narrow-mined machinations, his intelligence quite fails him when it comes to recognising his self *as his own*. What is more, all those strenuous attempts to come to own what in a sense he has already got, a formed self that is all of a piece, only lead him further away from his goal. –

His grand and perfect World System is by no means static, far from it. He keeps taking us by surprise with his latest modifications and re-interpretations. His aim may be to shepherd us into the one unified stable state that he would assume for his own, but then he keeps changing his mind as to the exact nature of it. He expects us to be the one perfect self he desires – he expects us to be he for him, in unison – but then he is never quite content with his scheduled perfection, there is always room for criticism.

He keeps thinking up better Systems, he nags away at the details no end, redeploying us, regrouping, restyling, revising, endlessly fussing and upsetting his own progress toward 'the self he will be'. In actual fact this is his (self-willed and unilateral) way of 'becoming', since he already, unwittingly, *is* what he ultimately plans to be: something coherently formed but not material. Considered like that, he is suffering from not just one, but two illusions.

First, there is his belief in the feasibility of his plan: to unify the whole world into one perfectly solid lump of a self-to-become. (And listening to his emotive advertising of a Better Order of Things to Come we may well suspect him of being a mere dreamer.) But there is also his less obvious illusion: that he is nothing as yet and depends on the rest of us being exactly what he is meaning to be, in concrete detail, before he can *really* be what he is. Not that his rhetoric will include such a phrase of course; he will argue that his aim is a beautiful world without stresses or contradictions of any kind etc. etc. – and we will jump to the conclusion that he means it to be (at least also) for *our* benefit.

All he can do is beseech us, hoarse with emotion (for his desirable self), and cite a whole canon of good reasons why his type of world order should prevail, in a logistic tour-de-force that has us stumped for counter-arguments. He will gather a large followership of non-thinkers who are easily persuaded that he knows best, and idle dreamers of a better world and self who prefer to have it dished up ready-made, in exchange for bit of simple subservience. But attractive as he may be to those who are prepared to worship the same ideal (self), there are always any number of dissenters around to spoil it all.

They accuse him of misleading us with lies and fanciful fabrications, distorting the truth to gain support for his self-willed schemes. But really they should accuse him of no more than being absurdly and wilfully short-sighted in his reasoning, and 'idealistic' only for his own sake. They say of him that what he is after is self-aggrandisment. Technically speaking they are right, he is trying to make the whole world resemble his premeditated self – but then again they do not know that in his estimation his self is not his own as yet, that he cannot as it were believe he has got such a thing till it has become a solid fact before his eyes. He is not trying to aggrandise his dreamt-of self, only to make it 'materialise' properly.

Not that any of these accusations hurt him. His feelings are tucked securely out of the way, in that abstractly formed world of their own, neither there inside him, nor here with us. He has become entirely insensitive to the world. He does not even feel hatred for his accusers, who keep opposing and spoiling his plans, any more than he feels a thing for his followers, except in the envisaged abstract: as a perfectly homogenised mass – which is of course identical to his desired self.

But if he is to make any progress at all towards seeing his Grand Plan made fact, despite his detractors and those of us who may try but in effect fail to fit into his artificial world system, then we will have to have recourse to his intuitive function (♏). This tells him that there is no need to include failures and opponents in his one unified world. They can be cut out of the picture altogether, declared invalid, banished from the world outright as inessential. He also gains a newly masterful approach to this stupendously silly task he has taken on: fashioning for himself a giant material-replica self, in search of becoming it inside himself.

Intuitively, he understands that the inherent designs of life demand to be embodied, and properly so, all else ultimately thrown out as worthless, and this suits him very well indeed. For inherent designs he reads: *his* Design. And as for demanding, now that he has already got a sizeable crowd of indoctrinated followers, all quite as emotionally expectant as he, he can afford to stop pleading. He starts threatening dire consequences if any of us refuse to help embody The Ideal. This latter, unconsciously formed by him but not consciously recognised by him as his own, may acquire a rather fanciful name. It may even be personified (in *his* theoretical image) as a deity: threatening, pitiless, and urgently demanding entry into every aspect of our lives.

His willing followers, lazily speculating that something great and lasting and all-good could be gained for no effort at all, prostrate themselves readily before the Unifying Idea – whatever title it may go under – with its attendant host of finicky rules, laws and regulations. They hand over their distinctness as individuals like prisoners their clothes and adopt whatever conduct he demands of them. As a seducer, first and foremost, he has that sort of effect. He appeals to what is most labile, least successfully formed, undoing the unfinished work of the past and easily dissolving our poor individual gains with promises of something better. If he can make us feel shabby with his seductive tales of a perfect world, containing far superior selves to what we manage to be at present, he need not even threaten us. Following in his footsteps, we assume that this better collective world will automatically make better selves of us: individual growth made easy; and its success, its stability, assured.

His *un*willing followers, not wishing their individual identities nullified, are torn between fear and resistance. They suspect his plans to be misguided, and yet admire his 'selfless' work for the collective good. They can't quite see what *he* is getting out of it. And having their personal failings criticised, they have to admit that there is room for improvement. But whatever they may think of him and his monstrous Ideal that he peddles from door to door with a club in his hand, in the end they have no choice but nod and pretend, and hide their individual selves in a safe place, inactive.

His intuitive conviction that he is implementing some higher purpose, or imposing some underlying life plan, makes a ruthless dictator of him. No sign is basically more sensitive than he is, and more inclined to feel another's pain as his own. But since his feelings are now one and all employed in the abstract sphere (another, if inadvertently acquired, 'imitation innerness') he can easily strangle us with his bare hands and never flinch. Not that he would actually face up to the unpleasant effects of his policies. Dissenters face worse than being debarred from his world or being thrown out, they are simply disappeared and buried – and yet never a word must be said about it. Nothing is allowed to conflict with the compulsory songs of praise to the Great Ideal, the wonderful harmony of it all, which is after all his prime objective. We better start practising now for the intended final effect, so that he can make up his mind what further amendments to make.

His opponents either bend before the threat, or at least pretend to, or they go. He is the 'touchiest' of the signs, and even as a dictator he cannot take chances; he liquidates his opponents as fast as he can, and not only them, but any who may be willing but for some reason fail, who in whatever way aren't perfect in his view. He is quite prepared to kill us en masse. And we need not expect an individual burial either. The *individual* self as such has been abolished – it has to be remembered that his own abstract self, the mould or model for all his doings, is not so much an individual but an all-embracing collective, composite, 'systematic' construct. Or to put it like this: a perfect society is supposed to supply him with the chance of gaining a perfect inner self.

We are not supposed to think, speak, do or even feel for ourselves. Our only function consists of making a pleasant, living pattern. He is pushing and pulling us together, by way of unifying his environment; and improving on us, by way of making it perfect. He is using us to paint a faultless animated picture. Making of us a human mobile without snags. A people-machine that runs without a hiccup. If this 'machine' produces nothing of worth, that is no concern of his; all he wants is a well-oiled world chugging along frictionless and without dissent, contradictions, disharmonies, imbalances, instabilities... We don't have to smile, that is not required. Just so long as we all pull the *same* sort of face. Since he has withdrawn his feelings from the world, he has no idea what it 'looks like' inside us now, behind the façade of formal behaviour. We nod in unison, we daren't twitch a single facial muscle, for fear he may misconstrue it. He should be content.

And yet he keeps shuffling us about restlessly, in search of an even greater perfection, commands us to display ever better modes of conduct and appearance, fussing over the slightest irregularities. Every sneezer is a saboteur who needs to be got rid of: leaving a gap in the system, disorder. This then calls for a brand-new order, under the same banner headline of course – he simply goes on for ever. And there is no knowing what he will find to criticise next, we never know when and for what we too will be found wanting, and be abolished, cancelled. His reign of terror truly surpasses anything the other negative sings could come up with.

More and more of us end up on the cutting room floor, but he would not say that his world is shrinking. The dead and gone are no loss to him. In fact, they have a lot to be said for them – and he may well say it for them, just to demonstrate to us that there is no escaping the Supreme Idea. Even the difference between life and death pales into insignificance before his totalitarian attempts to become self. And of truth and untruth one need not speak: there is only one legitimate thinker, one knower, and that is he. He can arrange the facts whichever way he thinks fit. He is beyond criticism (bar his own of course – of which he has a limitless supply, if of the shortsighted kind), so really there is no call for us to doubt and speculate and wonder. He would be The Cause: all *we* have to do is supply the effect he is seeking.

He whittles away at our world with the self-indulgence of one who is compulsively, restlessly seeking more and more potential self-improvement, and consequently is in no hurry to reach his goal. He is so busy getting it right, down to the littlest factor, that he unpicks and discards and undoes till in the end there is literally nothing left. First his One Unified World becomes increasingly dead: those of us he has not piled in a mass grave he has reduced to a mass of automatons who crawl listlessly in their prescribed circles, feeling empty in themselves, mindful only of being in step with everybody else. But so long as we live we *will* stumble; get too old and slow to follow his yet-again revised commands promptly; or in some other way fall short of his latest expectations. He has despatched the last of his victims before he even notices that there is nobody left.

Now there is nothing malleable left to him but the wind and the waves and whatever else of nature he has not seen fit to eradicate too; and a self he fails to be able to own because it failed, after all, to materialise the way he thought it would. This Grand (if extremely narrow) Design he has been force-feeding us on was not even 'truly real' to him; it was not an inner design, idea or plan he had there. We were supposed to *make* it real, in all its never-attainable perfection. But now we are exactly what he was seeking: a dead certainty.

Instead of gaining for himself an individual inner world, he has wasted his time attempting to make of the whole objective world a collective template for his inner self. There seems to be a stupendous amount of greed and immodesty implied in that, though actually it was meant to be no more than a clever scheme to save him emotional pain: the pain of failing, repeatedly, to be able to introject an environmentally (and badly) formed self. And his Scheme grew and grew, and then shrank, and then dwindled to objectively nothing: that was the becoming, the life, of his self-willed Scheme. In terms of finding it concretely reflected (and attainable) before his eyes, he is staring into an empty mirror now. But was there ever anything in his mirror?

Negative Aquarius tried forcibly to impose his pre-existing inner self into the world. It never did fit, so it kept hanging suspended in a world neither inner nor concrete. He 'mislaid' his self in an unreal reality, so to speak. Pisces, too, has mislaid something here, in a purely abstract sphere that is neither inside him nor in the objective world. But it is not his self he has mislaid: as an extravert he started out without one, and at the end of all his doings and undoings he is still without one – without even a hope of one. What he has been calling self, to be *his* only at some point in the future, has been an always 'perfectly' formed something that lacked both substance and the connection with innerness. (If only he had been clever enough to introject it, imperfect though it really was, his troubles would have been over.) So what *have* our doings been reflecting?

Consciously, he never lived in the world at all; he had become emotionally dead to the world. All his life was a Dream, a grand illusion taking place in unreality. And we, maybe under pressure, maybe as entranced as he by this vision of a Better Future, have been living this illusion for him, quite concretely – though never well enough: because the dream, under his direction, went on and on 'improving'. And we too, whether obediently or zealously, kept 'mending our ways' to his specifications.

In the last analysis, we have been serving a total nobody, a selfless force that was trying to derive a self from us. With the aid of this illusion he put into our heads, thoroughly indoctrinating us with his far-fetched ideas, he managed to get us all to mislay our feelings too, to become as emotionally dead to the world as he: to love only the Perfect Ideal. He never gave us a shred of evidence that his Plan would work out – rather to the contrary – and yet we have believed in this spook, this dark im-personal force, this self-styled Cause of every effect under the sun.

If we can view him from a safe distance, he strikes us as the most heartless dictator of them all, and no wonder: not only does he have no feelings for others whatsoever, but where there should be something like a 'heart' to him, a centre, a self, there is really nothing at all. *He* is fully aware of that: this is why he keeps on at us, ordering us about, so that with our help his would-be self can one day become concrete fact – and he can, extravertly, make it his own, and then introject it, fill that empty inner space. But the day, of course, never comes.

Once he has made an end of us, getting rid of us because we were never just quite perfect enough yet, that is the end of all his hopes too. Now he will never gain his premeditated self; his Ideal is useless to him now, he may as well forget about it and let it go. And what is there left in the whole world that could give him a new shape and self – not much, apart from the more recondite aspects of nature that even he could not control, the elements at their most shapeless and untameable. This is all that has survived his onslaught on the delicate task of finding his self in the world, with feeling.

There is no new start for him. He can become the sand and the sea, but then the first storm will only have him coming apart again in disorder and disharmony. He has at last found his own 'final solution': dissolution. – But needless to say, he was not really perfect, that was only what he thought he could become. And given his short-sighted attention to detail, quite a lot must have escaped him. Somewhere, there will be pockets of resistance waiting in their hiding places. Not heroes exactly: they were obviously not prepared to defend us against him and his automated hordes, to lay down their lives, if necessary. Perhaps they were his rival self-seekers, clinging to *their* future plans, and to the concrete world to pursue them in.

Now they can emerge safely, make this large and all but depopulated world their own. They could even praise him now for the immense scope he has provided for them: so many chances of totally new things to do, to become. A good chance, too, of fighting over who is to gain what for himself, to call his own… he has 'created' a new world alright, but not for himself. And it is hardly what he had in mind.

Some Suggested Pisces Attributes

basic

very emotional, sensitive, touchy, 'thin-skinned', easily hurt, 'soft', defenceless; naive and **trusting:** for so long as he is ignorant of the eventual outcome of identifying self in everything offered; **absorbs, acquires** (too much) **effortlessly**

sympathetic, compassionate, kindly and **helpful:** he literally feels another's pain as his own; he is **easily exploited and ordered about, victimised, slavishly obedient, easily misled; easily 'captivated'** (and captured, immobilised, paralysed, entranced, hypnotised etc.)

responsive, impressionable, malleable; taking on of 'roles'; instability, lack of immunity to influences: actually it is he who 'flows out' in search of an identity to 'import' into his inner life; **imaginative:** emotionally filling in any shape or construct, getting to know form from the inside: the 'image' is actually the form he takes on, emotionally (quite unlike, for instance, Aquarius' inner images); **'dreamer'** in that he can, emotionally, become identified with anything

changeable, unpredictable, self-contradictory: he has a multitude of selves which only begin to clash when he tries to introject them all; **mishmash; confused:** being everything at once, he is pulled in all directions when there are conflicting claims on his attention, he becomes **muddled; helpless, indecisive**

entirely dependent for his moods; vicarious grief or happiness

lack of self-confidence; fearful; fears he will be a failure; once he has experienced failure in establishing his inner self, he loses his trust and naivety: **feels beset by unidentifiable threats** that lie as much inside him as outside (a consequence of his indiscriminately introjecting anything at all); may become **superstitious**

positive

shy, careful, reserved and **cautious** about getting involved, in order to be less **subject to betrayal and deception; tests** before he commits himself; **very selective** (not out of choosiness but 'survival instinct'), **'delicate'** or may strike others as **bland**

modesty, humility; simplicity and all forms of **self-abnegation; willing poverty, ascetic; idealist:** in the positive sense this means realising that the ideal is not to be found or brought about in the material world, though once found at the inner level it contributes something positive to the world through **impersonal or selfless action, service; charity worker** etc.

serene, impassive, unimpassioned, distanced or **detached, equanimity:** does not take things personally

unfathomable depth, mysterious, enigma, hidden, secret, elusive, subtle; encapsulated; 'other-worldly', 'inspired', (in search of) **transcendence** of the mundane, **religious, mystic; recluse; hermit, may keep select company** e.g. religious order; **self-purification**

channel, medium; genuine ecstasy: standing the self aside from the concrete world to inhabit a world of (shared) innerness; **psychic; psychic healing** may be attributed here: the healing experience of being-accepted, being made whole (wholly acceptable), perhaps stimulating 'recovery' through new self-acceptance of all parts of the self; **'attuned'**

truly understanding: because in contact with others' inner selves, **forgiving** and **all-accepting, 'brotherly', essentially all-including,** despite being very exclusive in material respects; 'at home' in himself, he **can be part of any crowd** without losing his individuality

crowd-puller; mysteriously attractive: serving as a contact point with Inner Reality, what he gives is always more than others expect or understand; his giving follows an **inner fulfilment** that he will automatically demonstrate to others

fond of (and good at) **harmony; music, dance, poetry** etc.: these being rhythmic-repetitive-wholistic as well as flowing-emotional

(faultless) **performance,** of any kind: which involves standing the self aside/in the service of (e.g. a composer); also **perfected automatic action** following the 'introjection' of something learned well; **instinct:** which can be seen as 'channelled past' the individual self; **purity of motivation; 'inspired' action, courageous** and **steadfast:** has risen above personal worries

negative (passive)

exaggerating, (narrowly) **over-emotional, 'over-reacts'** to both good and bad stimuli; **'hysterical';** inadvertently **makes an exhibition of himself; 'lets himself go', self-pity; incontinent,** compulsive voiding of 'content': e.g. vomiting

superficial, shallow, false appearance of inner depth; complete
lack of depth; empty, hollow
fickle, dissolute; follower of fashion, cults and all sorts of (bad)
examples; easy 'convert'; is too easily impressed (for a while),
worships idols; may be so strongly influenced that he seems to
be 'under a spell', 'possessed' (not by something mysterious
and unidentifiable but something/someone quite concrete or
known; he lets other flood his inner space)
petulant, moody and arbitrarily fussy in an inconsistent superficial way; but easily deceived, gullible on account of mental
tunnel vision
vulnerable but not sufficiently aware of it; insecure, unsure of his
identity; bad opinion of himself; easily made to feel guilty or
worthless; self-disgust; ever malcontent, shallow perfectionist; affected: trying to be 'different', to 'rise above' the norm
'idealist': passively expecting the whole world to be good and
pleasant; make-believe, illusion; escapists; isolation, segregation, (self-)imprisonment, loneliness, insularity, possibly
agoraphobic; drop-out; the more obvious type of addict, seeking 'highs' or some fake transcendence of the mundane; joiner
of exclusive groups that lack a proper infrastructure; potential
suicide: finding the world 'too much to take' or rather not good
enough for him to take, but having it pressed on (into) him all
the same – takes everything (bad) in the world too personally
contempt for form and appearance, careless, slovenly; chaotic,
fancies he is free of mere mundane considerations
loss of genuine identity; a shambles of a multiple self, each bit
an empty echo or copy, mimicry; role playing, pretence,
deceptive, untruthful: his purpose being to fit in automatically
with his environment while he believes himself to be 'really'
something better
poor, homeless, peripatetic, 'drifter'
beggar, scrounger, possibly kleptomaniac; voyeur in the widest
sense, parasite; imaginary riches, imaginary self; may suffer
from mad delusions, taking himself to be someone else; vicarious self-experience, especially with regard to anyone categorically 'superior'
childish, immature, primitive, irresponsible, amoral; regressive;
lack of self-control: making him highly controllable only if
kept away from other contacts; merges with any polarised

group/crowd: which provides the unified stable environment that least threatens him and/or provides him with the impression that he is transcending his (one) limited self; **'disappears', faceless, anonymous; ephemeral; automatic obedience,** goes through the motions like a **zombie**

self-abasing, 'sells' himself: what of himself (his 'surface', his body, his physical etc. abilities) he holds in contempt anyway, **prostitution; slavish, servile:** while (indirectly) **wheedling or tricking** something 'better' out of others; **masochist:** always a trade-off to his advantage, as he sees it; **alluring, tempting** others to part with anything hidden, 'inner'; if nothing good can be wheedled out of others **may deliberately provoke negative 'outbursts'; addicted to e.g. violence, sex, thrills and scares, the macabre or mysterious** etc. as long as it is something that emerges out of hiding, for instance because it is normally forbidden; coprophilia may be another example

negative (active)

narrow sympathies (though forceful), **or none at all; impervious, glacial; categorical in outlook, reductionist; puritanical** in the widest sense; **not to be criticised; petty, fault-finding; punishing**

narrow ideologist, worships an unrealistic ideal, utopian in outlook

seductive self-styled visionary, full of false promises; false medium/prophet etc.; **ritualistic**

emotionally dead to the world despite strong **emotive display:** but his feelings are directed towards the abstract goal of an unattainable self, **narcissist, fanatical self-worship; 'empty'; heartless', cruel as a matter of course, kills without a qualm** when displeased or 'theoretically' upset, will be considered a **'psychopath'**

calculating, manipulative; endlessly demanding and never content, **inflated perfectionism** in the sense that he **tries to force the world to be perfect 'for him'; megalomaniac,** looks for **self-aggrandisement** en route to gaining possession of that self: forcefully presents something to the world that he hasn't got: **deceives,** he is nothing but a **misleading appearance, empty performance or pose – though he** *believes* **in himself,** as something that has not yet come true; self-less to the point of being

'elemental': entirely aborted effort at gaining a self, **his life is only a process without a centre; 'becomes' but never 'is'; comes to nothing**
untruthful, reality-distorting on a grand scale; **artificial; 'inorganic':** tries to turn life into something perfectly homogenised **totalitarian dictator, 'infects' and directs crowds, polarises; destructive of individuality, meaning, environment, life** (up to a point); **abolishes/dissolves/absorbs-into:** everything becomes part of his (never-reached) future world/self, endlessly **exploits all and everything,** gaining nothing at all

CONCLUSION

How to describe the inner workings of a closed circle, examine the interwoven relationships of its parts consecutively: this has been the problem. The unravelling of the meaningful whole, the piece-meal telling of a circular tale that won't really make sense till it's all told and the last piece falls into place. But once we have assembled all the parts of this psychological zodiac we can then view the various attributes of the signs with the greater freedom of hindsight, as it were.

What is it that makes, say, Aries tick? Astrologers have always seen a youthful masculine figure in this sign, and also realised that the opposite sign, Libra, had something to contribute to the nature of Aries itself. That Virgo and Pisces also contribute is news, or is it? What of the fanatical causes (Virgo) combined with religious zeal (Pisces) too often displayed by our eternal young warrior? And what is it about music (Pisces) and obsessive order and cleanliness (Virgo) – military marches, spit and polish – that they should apparently be indispensable to warfare? And maybe it is easier now to understand the role alcohol (Pisces) can play in the Aries process of male bonding; or where the fascination lies to the young male in the pursuit across a muddy playing field of that perfect sphere: the ideal form, the innate image of perfection (Libra) made concrete.

We can combine and recombine the different positive and negative attributes of the sings any way we like in search of greater understanding of underlying 'causes'. But, as I said in the Introduction, I am not convinced that looking for wholesale psychological concepts in astrology is particularly profitable. It does not seem useful to me, for instance, to associate Sun/Leo with consciousness and Moon/Cancer with the Unconscious. What I have found is that Cancer is about conscious inner (that is hidden from public view) feeling processes and how they need to apply themselves to the world out there – while Leo's intuitive self-awareness is 'only' a constantly sought aim-out-there, with none of the conscious inner depth and momentary self-enclosedness or self-sufficiency of Cancer. Certainly, in Leo self-awareness is the aim, the key issue. And it is easy enough to see how from the patriarchal

(Leonine) view point the eternally puzzling feminine (Cancer) can simply disappear from conscious view into unimaginable dark depths. But that is Leo's problem, if he can't follow her there. All it proves is that Woman (*one* of the archetypes of the female, anyway) is one way or the other associated with Man's (the Leo type's, that is) areas of unawareness. Ariadne's thread is ever needed. Woman's mysterious 'witchcraft' has ever been feared.

In another male/female pair it is again the female (Libra) who is capable of *conscious* insight, not the male (Aries). Among the masculine signs only Sagittarius 'goes deep' – when well handled, that is. While the 'shallowest' of them all is surely the feminine Pisces in its basic and negative forms. So is this plethora of male/female archetypes really new? I think not: even the diverse cartoon characters we find on the joke pages surely bear witness to our intuitive understanding of these things. None of which is to say that we must slavishly adhere to some eternally fixed set of gender roles. Once we understand the meaning behind the sign symbol, the way it 'works', it is up to us to interpret it in ways appropriate to our Age, culture and circumstances.

In our individual natal charts we each have of course *all* the signs represented. Whatever our Sun or Ascendant sign may be, whichever signs may be specifically stressed, by a stellium or a T-square for instance, there is no getting away from it: we are always, in our own small way, dealing with – or acting on behalf of – the totality of these twelve Universal Principles. We can no more disregard the demands of our innate Scorpioness with the excuse that that sign does not figure prominently in our personal chart than we can refuse to make a job of being emotional beings on the grounds that we are rather more 'the cerebral type'. No amount of typecasting or chart plotting will let us off being complete human beings. Our birth charts contain the whole zodiac; each psyche is an integral living process: one way or the other, we do use all four functions, we each do both extravert and introvert, if in varying ways and to varying degrees.

We all find that our best innate potential will automatically shatter, like Gemini's, leaving us to pick up the pieces, and yet more pieces, making it a life time's job to find ourselves. Like Libra we all have to keep working at it to make fact resemble inner vision, if we don't want to rest content with a corrosive and corroding illusion.

I hope to have shown that the signs contribute to each other's 'character', that they can not be understood as standing in isolation, any more than we as distinct psychological entities could hope to define ourselves in separateness from our social and physical environment. But, these 'mechanics' apart, when one looks at how whole themes are repeated among the signs, foreshadowed and developed, used in different contexts and to different overall effect, one gains the impression of an even greater coherence: a subtle interlacing of content, a shared web of meaning among the individual signs. As the separate aspects of our psyche (which we *may* consider as individual factors, for the purpose of clarification) they also show us the meaningful indivisibility of the psyche as such.

If, then, in our astrological view of the psyche we find two emotional factors/signs, this should not of course be read as meaning that there are somehow two distinct emotional strands to each of us – rather, that feeling may usefully be considered in two different ways, because it would seem to *work* in two different ways. In the one, bilateral 'Cancer' way: responsively, from out of ourselves, and in need of a receptive response. And in either of the two unilateral 'Pisces' ways. On the one hand, primitively, in search of personal identification-with. Or, on the other, in what one might call the truly 'grown-up' fashion: in an impersonal way, from the basis of inner fulfilment, where feelings can be freely given in return for nothing at all. The latter can then also be understood as feeling which transcends the personal capacity of the individual, who as an 'agent' actively reflects something of a surpassing reality (whether we regard this as being divine, or some collective force, or simply a general feeling principle at work in human nature).

The use we make of these individual/collective 'drives', forces, natural principles, or divine qualities seeking their life in substance and awareness, is not of course a simple matter of choosing between right and wrong, of expressing the inherent positive or negative potential of the signs. The living practice of it is that we are quite capable of mixing the best with the worst, and more than likely to fall into alternate extremes.

I have portrayed the negative signs as if they were wholly to blame for the way they end up behaving. This may be something to bear in mind if we want to take an honest look at ourselves; but equally we have to consider how being at the receiving end of negative-sign conditions will affect our reactions – the person brutalised by individual or social abuse is hardly in a position to choose the most positive behaviour patterns from out of the many inherently at his disposal; the adverse environment will 'set the tone'. Denied *all* chance of 'ruling' the world a bit, it may be only too easy to take the Aquarian route into madness; or, at the emotional level, to suffer, and inflict, the puzzling but real enough pains of negative Cancer.

I have attempted to present the signs in something like their essential coherence. But if they are to be of use in the practice of analysing quite complex individual or collective behaviour patterns, then we need to be ready to recognise them piecemeal, disjointed, scattered here and there and all mixed up. And we need to go beyond surface appearances, the 'letter' – often, literally, just words: So-and-So is 'ambitious'. We need to get right down to the basis of, the primitive motivation behind, behaviour – the 'spirit' in which So-and-So acts: what kind of 'ambitious' is this... Aries being pro-active? Capricorn worried about his standing in the world? Maybe So-and-So is after all just being harmlessly, all-embracingly Leonine. Then again, his grand-sounding schemes may have the ring of negative Pisces about them and his air of unselfish proposal of same should fool nobody. We better look for other clues, to see how this hangs together: what his real intentions might be. –

Whatever astro-psychological details may define us as individuals, we all find ourselves forced to work with – or for – the twelve 'signs'. They aren't just part of life, they are Life: teased apart into its inherent strands, named and defined for easier comprehension, even as they are inseparably intertwined. The character profiles I have drawn of them here can certainly be used in conjunction with a precise natal chart to help clarify where our individual danger zones lie and what to bear in mind to avoid at least the worst excesses and pains of 'sign abuse'. But I can also see them being of use in approaching wider, social questions. The crazy politics of the negative signs, their unhealthy attitudes to life, their would-be religious pursuit of hidden, unconscious agendas stand as warnings to us all.

Not least, I hope to have shown that astrology is not to be considered a discipline far removed from other attempts to make sense of life, to examine what we hold to be causes, or to search for cures and alternatives. On the contrary, because it addresses the basics in a very abstract way (looking for 'laws'), astrology can be uniquely, and universally, helpful in establishing new conceptual models and opening up new avenues of research. I think it is time we took a closer look at the uses of astrology *as such*, in its non-applied form, that is: quite without setting up specific charts. It could usefully inform our socio-political thought as much as our attempts to deal with questions of physical and mental health. Why have we barely begun to work with these freely available insights? If we allowed astrology to speak for itself more, instead of always trying to *use* it for various purposes, I think we would soon find its uses multiplied, its range of application significantly broadened.

What we call the twelve signs are different qualities or aspects of the one, living Source. Centred beyond everything material, this keeps finding its mirror image in concrete events, in space/time. Baffling as this may be, we do see the planets of our solar system portraying, symbolically, in their relative movements, this ever-different unfolding of Reality into reality. Circle into cycles – each of the same essence, but each revealing a new face. Closer to home, it is of course your, mine and our neighbour's face that mirror our common Source, for better or worse – daunting thought. Time, then, *we* had another sharp look in the mirror. We have the tools.